ADVANCES IN RESEARCH ON TEACHING

A Research Annual

Editor: JERE BROPHY
College of Education
Michigan State University

VOLUME 1 • 1989

 JAI PRESS INC.

Greenwich, Connecticut   *London, England*

ADVANCES IN
RESEARCH ON TEACHING

Volume 1 • 1989

CONTENTS

LIST OF CONTRIBUTORS

Charles W. Anderson

College of Education
Michigan State University

Linda M. Anderson

College of Education
Michigan State University

Jere Brophy

College of Education
Michigan State University

Ann L. Brown

College of Education
University of Illinois

Thomas P. Carpenter

College of Education
University of Wisconsin

Gerald G. Duffy

College of Education
Michigan State University

Carol Sue Englert

College of Education
Michigan State University

Elizabeth Fennema

College of Education
University of Wisconsin

Susan Florio-Ruane

College of Education
Michigan State University

Timothy Lensmire

College of Education
Michigan State University

Annemarie Sullivan Palincsar

College of Education
University of Michigan

Penelope L. Peterson   College of Education
                                    Michigan State University

Taffy E. Raphael   College of Education
                                    Michigan State University

Cheryl Rosaen   College of Education
                                    Michigan State University

Laura R. Roehler   College of Education
                                    Michigan State University

Kathleen J. Roth   College of Education
                                    Michigan State University

INTRODUCTION TO
ADVANCES IN RESEARCH ON TEACHING

Although teaching is a well established profession that includes over two million practitioners in the United States alone, and despite the vital roles that teachers play in promoting the self-actualization of individuals and the human resources of nations, there exists only a limited and for the most part recently developed knowledge base to inform teacher education and teaching practice. Research on teaching is still in its infancy as a scientific endeavor, so most of the important advances that have occurred so far have taken the form of (a) fundamental definitions and taxonomic distinctions that help us to develop and differentiate our conceptualization of teaching or (b) the invention of tools to use in studying it (e.g., systematic methods for collecting and analyzing data). A few primitive paradigms have been developed and have led to increased understanding of particular aspects of teaching, but we are still a long way from the kind of systematic knowledge development couched within sweeping but unified paradigms that occurs in more mature sciences.

On the other hand, important progress has been made compared to what was available even 30 years ago. Where there once was a heavy research focus on learning but practically none on teaching, there now is a great deal of emphasis on conceptualizing and studying teaching, particularly as it occurs under natural classroom conditions. Where most research in classrooms was done by individuals who identified themselves primarily as psychologists, sociologists, or anthropologists and whose work emphasized the questions, concepts, and data collection methods stressed in their respective social science disciplines, contemporary classroom research is increasingly being conducted by individuals who identify themselves as educational researchers seeking to further our understanding of classroom teaching. The emphasis has shifted from using the classroom as a site for doing research on social science questions to attempts to understand education as it occurs in classrooms and to address issues of educational practice. Research on teaching has finally developed some coherence as a field of scientific study and established a knowledge base from which to build.

Advances in Research on Teaching has been established in the hope that it will make important contributions to the further development of this knowledge base, both by documenting advances in our understanding of particular topics and by stimulating further work on those topics. Toward that end, each volume in the series will be planned with an eye toward pulling together and providing visibility to emerging trends in research on classroom teaching that appear to be spawning important contributions likely to have lasting value. Scholars who have made programmatic contributions to the emerging literature on the selected topic will be invited to prepare chapters in which they not only describe their work but synthesize it, place it into the context of the larger body of research and scholarship on the topic, and give their current views of its meanings and implications. Topic selection for the volumes will emphasize conceptualization and analysis of the processes of teaching (including not only the behaviors that can be observed in the classroom, but also the planning, thinking, and decision making that occur before, during, and after interaction with students). Especially likely to be selected are topics that involve linking information about teaching processes with information about presage variables (especially teacher knowledge and beliefs), context variables, or student outcome variables.

To further enhance the cohesiveness of each volume, authors will be invited to raise questions or make comments on one another's work, and to reply to these questions or comments in crosstalk sections that follow their chapters. The first two volumes in the series focus on aspects of the teaching of academic content. The first volume is on teaching for meaningful understanding and self-regulated learning, and the second volume will be on teachers' pedagogical knowledge of content and their planning and teaching of lessons based on that content.

Jere Brophy
Editor

INTRODUCTION TO VOLUME 1

When I began contemplating the *Advances in Research on Teaching* series, the title *Teaching for meaningful understanding and self-regulated learning* came to mind immediately as the topic for the first volume. The phrase was coined by Linda Anderson in response to discussions held at the Institute for Research on Teaching concerning common elements in what different investigators were discovering about outstanding teaching in various academic content areas. I borrowed it as the title for this first volume because it aptly captures in a few words several of the most important emerging trends in research on teaching. These trends have developed in response to widely expressed concerns that current school curricula are characterized by too much breadth addressed at insufficient depth, using methods that place too much emphasis on rote learning of ill-organized facts and practice of isolated skills. The deliberately redundant first part of the title (teaching for meaningful understanding) underscores the notion that schooling should be designed not merely to cause students to memorize factual information and reproduce it on cue in response to test or assignment questions, but should expose the students to coherent bodies of information organized around key concepts and generalizations that are related to one another and to the students' prior knowledge and experience, so that the students find the learning meaningful and are able to apply it in relevant situations in and out of school. The second part of the title (teaching for self-regulated learning) expresses the idea that good teaching will not only enable students to understand and apply particular content, but also develop in them the dispositions and strategies needed to enable them to begin to regulate and take increasing responsibility for their own learning. To appreciate these and related implications of the title more fully, it is useful to place the research reported in the present volume within the context of the history of research on teaching.

RESEARCH ON TEACHING AS A RECENT PHENOMENON

Although social science research, including some work that could be called educational research, has been conducted for the last 100 years, systematic research on classroom teaching is a relatively recent phenomenon. Educators focused much more on issues of curriculum (what to teach) and school organization (grade levels, tracking arrangements, and so on) than on teaching methods and classroom processes, and they addressed these issues primarily through philosophical debate rather than empirical data collection. Many methods-comparison studies were done in the 1930s and 1940s, but these never produced coherent findings because of a variety of research design and data analysis weaknesses and because the differences between the methods being compared were usually too small to produce significant differences in student outcomes (Medley, 1979). Otherwise, remarkably little scientific research of any kind was conducted in classrooms, and only a small portion of this research was designed to analyze classroom processes and link them to student outcomes. Lacking a knowledge base developed from classroom research, educators seeking to formulate guidelines for good classroom teaching had to borrow ideas from elsewhere (most notably Piagetian research on cognitive development achieved through experience in natural settings and behavioristic research on learning under laboratory conditions) and hope that these ideas would apply in the classroom. Some of them did apply reasonably well, but many were irrelevant or counterproductive.

In the 1950s and 1960s, Ausubel, Bruner, Gagne, and other learning theorists who supplemented or replaced behaviorism with cognitive psychology concepts began to contribute ideas that have proven more applicable to the design of classroom teaching. Even so, the sixties' educational applications of these ideas focused more on development of curriculum packages than on the role of teachers in helping students to understand and respond to curriculum content. At the time, many curriculum developers viewed teachers more as nuisances than as resources and, therefore, attempted to make their curricula "teacher proof" by writing text presumably so clear and complete as to guarantee student mastery of the material without teacher interpretation or assistance. In these programs, the teacher's role was downgraded from that of an instructor to that of a materials manager and test administrator.

Others viewed teachers not as potentially harmful to student learning but simply as ineffectual. Those who held this view emphasized that it is students, not teachers, who do the learning, and that students bring with them into the classroom a great range of individual differences in aptitudes and motivation that are likely to be much more powerful than anything the teacher does in determining how much they learn. The highly publicized Coleman Report (Coleman et al., 1966), with its finding that socioeconomic status and other home background factors were more powerful predictors of academic achievement progress than measures of school characteristics were, seemed to reinforce these ideas.

PROCESS-OUTCOME RESEARCH IN THE 1970s

It was within this gloomy atmosphere, and partly as a reaction against it, that several groups of investigators began work designed to identify reliable relationships between teacher behavior and student outcomes. This work, reviewed in detail by Brophy and Good (1986), became known as process-product or process-outcome research because it was designed to link classroom processes (primarily teacher behaviors) with their products or outcomes (primarily student achievement gain). Initially limited to correlational studies and concentrated on basic skills instruction in the early grades, process-outcome research eventually was broadened to include a wider range of grade levels and subject matter areas and to include experimental verification of some of the causal hypotheses suggested by correlational findings. Along with a great many more specific elaborations, process-outcome research firmly established the following three major conclusions about teacher effects on student achievement.

1. *Teachers make a difference.* Some teachers reliably elicit greater gains in student achievement than others do, and these differences in student achievement gains are related to systematic differences in teacher behavior. The Coleman et al. (1966) findings were misleading because they were based on data aggregated at the level of schools rather than classrooms within schools, so that they masked the differential effects of individual teachers.

2. *Classroom differences in student achievement gains occur in part because of classroom differences in exposure to academic content and opportunity to learn.* Compared to teachers who elicit lesser achievement gains, teachers who elicit greater achievement gains: (a) place more emphasis on developing student mastery of the curriculum in establishing expectations for students and defining their own roles as teachers; (b) allocate most of the available classroom time for activities designed to foster such curriculum mastery; and (c) are effective organizers and managers who establish their classrooms as efficient learning environments, minimize the time spent getting organized or making transitions, and maximize the degree to which they keep their students engaged in ongoing academic activities. These teachers set out to maximize student learning and run their classrooms accordingly.

3. *Teachers who elicit greater achievement gains do not merely maximize "time on task" in their classrooms; in addition, they spend a great deal of time actively instructing their students.* Compared to other classrooms, their classrooms feature relatively more time spent in interactive lessons featuring teacher-student discourse and less time spent in independent seatwork. Rather

than depend solely on curriculum materials to carry the content to the students, these teachers interpret and elaborate lthe content for the students, stimulate them to react to it through questions asked in recitation and discussion activities, and circulate during seatwork times to monitor progress and provide assistance when needed. They are active instructors, not just materials managers and evaluators, although most of their instruction occurs during interactive discourse with students rather than during extended lecture-presentations.

These process-outcome findings were successful in reaffirming the teacher's vital role in stimulating student learning. The findings and the research paradigms that spawned them were limited in several important respects, however, so that even as replications continued to accumulate, it became clear that new research questions and paradigms would be needed. It would remain important to analyze classroom processes and relate them to student outcomes, but to do so using methods that were more sophisticated in several respects.

THE RESEARCH OF THE 1980s

One obvious need was development from more global toward more fine-grained and context-bound analyses. The typical procedure in 1970s process-outcome studies was to first calculate mean scores from classroom process measures that had been aggregated across a variety of teaching situations occurring over several weeks or even months and then correlate them with measures of adjusted achievement gain developed from scores on standardized achievement tests administered at the end of the school year. This method proved to be effecive for establishing that some teachers elicited greater achievement gain than others and for documenting the role of basic quantitative variables such as time on task and time spent in active teaching. However, it was not well-suited to the study of more subtle and qualitative aspects of teaching. It could not be used, for example, to develop detailed information about how truly outstanding teachers differ from competent but less outstanding teachers whose classrooms yield similar scores on variables such as time on task or time spent in active teaching. To accomplish this, several theoretical and methodological refinements were needed.

First, the research had to become much more molecular in focus. Instead of studying instruction across a school year or term and looking at changes in standardized achievement test scores, researchers needed to begin to focus more intensively on particular curriculum units or even individual lessons, taking into account the teacher's instructional objectives and assessing student learning accordingly. This meant knowing what the teacher was trying to accomplish, recording detailed information about classroom processes as they unfolded during the unit or lesson, and assessing learning using criterion-referenced measures keyed to the instructional goals. This implied more sophistication about curriculum and instruction in particular subject matter areas at particular grade levels than was typical of 1970s process-outcome research, as well as collection of thicker descriptions of classroom processes that would be analyzed in much greater detail.

Along with these changes came changes in theoretical sophistication. Early process-outcome work had been primarily empirical, concerned with showing that teachers make a difference and developing information about process-outcome relationships as a basis for formulating ideas about effective teaching. This approach did produce some useful ideas about relatively generic aspects of teaching. However, as investigators began to focus more on the teaching of particular content in particular subject matter areas, they began to draw on the literature on curriculum and instruction in these subject matter areas, and (often in collaboration with curriculum experts from these areas) to develop theoretical rationales (specifying hypotheses about worthwhile goals and effective methods for accomplishing them) to guide their research.

As more subject matter specialists began studying classroom teaching, they brought with them a concern for the nature of the learning goals that teachers were pursuing and the degree to which there was alignment among these goals, the content selected for focus, the methods used for teaching it, and the methods used for evaluating student learning. Unwilling to accept standardized tests as operational measures of student learning, these investigators stressed the importance of carefully analyzing the goals of instruction, determining the nature and depth of student understandings that should be taken as evidence that these goals had been accomplished, and the implications of this for the design of criterion-referenced evaluation methods.

In phrasing objectives and designing instruction, these investigators stressed the need to go beyond teaching facts in order to develop conceptual understanding of concepts and principles, as well as the need to go beyond teaching skills in isolation by developing the students' abilities to use the skills strategically under problem solving conditions. Instructional design and implementation would be guided by clear notions about the meaningful understanding of content and the strategic application of skills that were implied by the learning goals, so care would be taken to see that concepts were explained with clarity and precision and that the strategic application of skills to problem solving was modeled via "think aloud" demonstrations that made overt for the students the usually-covert strategic thinking that guides problem solving.

Assessment procedures would also reflect these learning goals. In addition to or instead of the familiar multiple-choice test, investigators began using more comprehensive assessment procedures that called for interviewing students individually at some length to determine the degree to which they could explain concepts and principles in their own words, as well as presenting them with application tasks to determine the degree to which they could apply their learning strategically under realistic problem solving conditions.

Developments in the psychology of learning and cognition also began to affect the conceptualization and design of research on teaching. Although there now was no longer any question about the fact that teachers play a vital role in stimulating student learning, attention began to focus once again on the student. Cognitive psychologists stress the fact that students do not merely passively receive or copy the input that they get from teachers but instead actively mediate that input by trying to make sense of it and to relate it to what they already know (or think they know) about the topic. Thus, although they are open to stimulation and guidance from teachers, students must develop new knowledge through a process of active construction. To the extent that they get beyond rote memorization to achieve meaningful understanding of the new input, it will be because they have developed and integrated a network of associations linking the new input to preexisting knowledge and beliefs anchored in concrete experience. Thus, teaching involves inducing conceptual change in students, not infusing knowledge into a vacuum. To the extent that they are accurate, students' preexisting beliefs about the topic facilitate learning and provide a natural starting place for teaching. To the extent that these beliefs include misconceptions, however, these will need to be confronted and corrected lest they persist and distort the new learning.

If the new learning is complex and multifaceted, the construction of meaning required to develop a clear understanding of it will take time and will be facilitated by the interactive discourse that occurs during classroom lessons and activities. Clear explanations and modeling from the teacher are important, but so are the opportunities to answer questions about the content, discuss or debate its meanings and implications, or apply it in critical thinking, problem-solving, or decision-making contexts. These activities allow students to process the content actively and "make it their own" by paraphrasing it into their own words, exploring its relationships to other knowledge and to past experience, appreciating the insights it provides, or identifying its implications for personal decision making or action. Increasingly, teacher-student and student-student discourse relating to academic content is being recognized as a crucial factor determining the degree to which classroom learning will be experienced by students as a personally meaningful sense-making activity rather than merely as an exercise in memorizing information for a test.

Finally, in conceptualizing the goals and processes associated with teaching and learning in any particular content area, many investigators have begun to stress the notion that complementary changes in the teacher and student roles should occur as learning progresses. Early in the process, the teacher will assume most of the responsibility for structuring and managing learning activities and will provide students with a great deal of information, explanation, modeling, or other input. As they develop expertise, however, the students can begin to assume responsibility for regulating their own learning by asking questions and by working on increasingly complex applications with increasing degrees of autonomy. The teacher will provide task simplification, coaching, and other "scaffolding" needed to assist the students with challenges that they are not yet ready to handle on their own, but this assistance will gradually be reduced in response to gradual increases in student readiness to engage in independent and self-regulated learning. To the extent that the goals of instruction include not only meaningful understanding of content but student ability to recognize and follow through on opportunities to apply the learning to a range of potentially relevant situations in and out of school, it will be important to develop student self-regulation through gradual transfer of responsibility from the teacher to the students.

THE RESEARCH DESCRIBED IN THIS VOLUME

The infusion of these and other theoretical and methodological innovations has created new forms of research on classroom teaching of academic content and skills in the 1980s that have begun to get at the qualitative aspects of good teaching that were not well addressed by the process-outcome research of the 1970s. This volume brings together state-of-the-art contributions reflecting these innovations in research on teaching in four content areas: reading comprehension, writing (composition), mathematics, and science.

Besides being exemplary contributions to the development of understanding of the nature of good teaching in their respective content areas, the various programs of research included in this volume share important characteristics that make them comparable to one another and that, taken together, represent a growing consensus about some of the relatively generic qualitative features of good teaching. Although no two research teams used precisely the same concepts or methods, each of them focused on particular learning goals to be accomplished with particular students in a particular content area, and proceeded by first articulating these goals in terms of students' meaningful understanding and self-regulated learning and then seeking to develop (or developing and then seeking to access the validity of) guidelines describing the nature of the teaching that would be required to accomplish these goals. The teaching and learning is seen as unfolding in phases, with teacher scaffolding decreasing and student assumption of responsibility for self-regulation increasing as student expertise develops. All aspects of the instruction are seen as goals-driven and the curriculum materials and general procedures are planned in advance, but the interactive discourse aspects of instruction are recognized as being only partly predictable. Therefore, besides following through on a planned agenda, teachers will need to be prepared to be responsive to student questions, comments, and mistakes that provide opportunities to correct misconceptions, link the content to the students' experiences, or elaborate on the content in productive ways. In studying and assessing the effects of such instruction, the emphasis is on thick description and microanalysis of processes and on assessment of the quality of the teacher's instruction and the students' learning.

The volume begins with two chapters on reading comprehension instruction. In Chapter 1, Gerald Duffy and Laura Roehler describe their research showing the importance of explicit teacher explanations and modeling of the strategic use of skills for extracting meaning from text, reinforced through responsive elaboration during interactions with the students. In Chapter 2, Annemarie Palincsar and Ann Brown describe their work on Reciprocal Teaching, a method in which students take turns acting as instructor and gradually assume more and more responsibility for their own learning as they work in small groups to comprehend and interpret text.

The next three chapters focus on writing instruction. Susan Florio-Ruane and Tim Lensmire provide an overview of recent research on the teaching of writing. They describe the features of various occasions for writing that occur in class-rooms and address the instructional role of the teacher during teacher-student discourse surrounding students' compositions and probe the issues involved in creating meaningful school writing tasks. In Chapter 4, Carol Sue Englert and Taffy Raphael describe their research on teaching students cognitive strategies for creating compositions. In Chapter 5, Cheryl Rosaen reviews and presents research findings on writing as a method of learning subject matter content.

Chapters 6 and 7 focus on mathematics instruction. In Chapter 6, Elizabeth Fennema, Thomas Carpenter, and Penelope Peterson present findings from research on their Cognitively Guided Instruction method for teaching children in the primary grades to acquire mathematical understanding. In Chapter 7, Magdalene Lampert describes her work on teaching for mathematical understanding in the middle grades, focusing on issues of finding ways to represent content that are both meaningful to the students and valid in the sense of being true to the discipline.

In Chapter 8, Charles Anderson and Kathleen Roth describe research on the Conceptual Change Teaching approach to science instruction. Finally, in Chapter 9, Linda Anderson considers the common elements in several of these programs and their implications concerning preparation of teachers to implement these programs effectively.

Following each chapter is a brief cross-talk section in which the authors respond to questions and comments raised by myself or by other chapter authors. Then, in a concluding section I describe some of the points of agreement and disagreement between chapter authors and identify additional issues needing research attention.

Jere Brophy
Editor

REFERENCES

Brophy, J., & Good, T. (1986). Teacher behavior and student achievement. In M. Wittrock (Ed.), *Handbook of research on teaching* (3rd ed., pp. 328-375). New York: Macmillan.

Coleman, J., Campbell, E., Hobson, C., McPartland, J., Mood, A., Weinfield, F., & York, R. (1966). *Equality of educational opportunity.* Washington, DC: U.S. Office of Health, Education, and Welfare.

Medley, D. (1979). The effectiveness of teachers. In P. Peterson & H. Walberg (Eds.), *Research on teaching: Concepts, findings, and implications.* Berkeley, CA: McCutchan.

ACKNOWLEDGMENTS

I wish to thank Martin Maehr for his suggestion that the series be initiated and his assistance in getting it started, the chapter authors for their willingness to cooperate in the crosstalk experiment, and June Smith for her assistance in manuscript preparation.

My contribution was supported in part by the Institute for Research on Teaching, College of Education, Michigan State University. The Institute for Research on Teaching is funded from a variety of federal, state, and private sources including the United States Department of Education and Michigan State University. The opinions expressed in this publication do not necessarily reflect the position, policy, or endorsement of the funding agencies.

Jere Brophy
Editor

THE TENSION BETWEEN INFORMATION-GIVING AND MEDIATION:

PERSPECTIVES ON INSTRUCTIONAL EXPLANATION AND TEACHER CHANGE

Gerald G. Duffy and Laura R. Roehler

When learning to read was viewed as a matter of mastering discrete sets of skills and answering comprehension questions, reading teacher effectiveness emphasized student engaged time on activities such as drill-and-practice exercise sessions and question-and-answer discussions of story content. Now, however, reading is understood to be a strategic process. Repeated exposure to skills or story content is no longer enough; readers must also understand how the reading system works, control the processing of text, and construct meaningful and well-organized understandings. This modified view of reading spawned instructional modifications. One of these is direct teacher explanation of reading strategies. This paper, based on our research establishing the effectiveness of such explanations, describes (1) the importance of both information-giving and mediation during instruction and (2) the implications our research has for teacher change efforts.

Advances in Research on Teaching, Volume 1, pages 1-33.
ISBN: 0-89232-845-2

INTRODUCTION

Three premises undergird this paper. The first is about expert reading; the second is about current classroom instructional reading practices; and the third is an instructional perspective triggered by the first two premises.

Reading As A Strategic Process

Recent research on reading establishes that text comprehension is a cognitive process. Initiated by "schema-theoretic" research (Anderson & Pearson, 1984), views of reading have recently been further influenced by research on the strategic nature of reading (Paris, Lipson & Wixson, 1983; Pressley, Forrest-Pressley, Elliott-Faust & Miller, 1985) and by research indicating that expert readers assume metacognitive control of strategy use (Baker & Brown, 1984; Flavell, 1981).

This research indicates that readers reason when combining prior knowledge with new text information to construct meaning. For instance, as readers begin to read they reason about what background knowledge to activate and what initial predictions to make about the meaning in the text; during reading readers reason about how to modify initial predictions; and when reading is completed they reason about the significance of what was read, about conclusions to draw, and about judgments to make. Additionally, good readers consciously activate certain kinds of strategic reading when they encounter difficult text. That is, they monitor comprehension and, when difficulties arise, consciously access and employ strategic reasoning as a means of regulating comprehension. In short, when the going gets tough, expert readers maintain cognitive control of the comprehension process rather than passively waiting for comprehension to occur.

Classroom Instructional Reading Practices

Current classroom instructional reading practices do not reflect this view (Duffy & McIntyre, 1982; Durkin, 1978-79). Instead, two sets of practices dominate. The first reflects a drill-and-practice model, in which teachers conceptualize reading as a hierarchical list of isolated skills to be mastered through supervised repetition, and tested using criterion measures such as those currently in vogue in state-wide accountability systems. A second view of reading instruction reflects a question-and-answer model in which teacher questioning about story content is emphasized on the assumption that high quality interactions about content help students infer how reading works. Current basal text programs, with a dual emphasis on questioning students about selections and on drilling them using workbook and skillsheet exercises, attempt to bridge both views.

As different as these two sets of practices are, they have one thing in common. Neither explicitly informs students about reasoning readers do when comprehending. The drill-and-practice model with its focus on activity completion sends to students the message, "Never mind how it works, just complete these isolated skill sheets and reading will follow." The question-and-answer model sends the message, "Never mind how it works, just participate in discussions after reading and you'll be a reader." The activity itself is the focus, not the mental processing that insures successful completion of the activity. In these approaches, teachers are not expected to explain the reasoning used by self-regulatory, strategic readers, and students are not expected to demonstrate awareness of such reasoning.

An Instructional Perspective on Strategy Instruction

This focus on activity completion rather than reasoning leaves students to figure out by themselves that regulatory control of strategic reasoning is the core of what we now understand reading to be. Because neither the drill-and-practice model nor the story discussion model explicates strategic reasoning, many students do not become aware of it. And because one cannot regulate what one is unaware of, use of such models does not result in the development of strategic readers except among some average and high ability students who possess enough background experience about language to infer the processes implicit in practice exercises and story discussions.

This is not to suggest that students are empty vessels to be filled or that they do not actively construct understandings about how reading works. To the contrary, students' mediation of instruction is crucial to what is ultimately understood. The point is, however, that learners need information to construct understandings. If they do not possess information about strategic reasoning while reading, teachers should help them by providing such information rather than waiting for students to stumble on it by themselves.

This instructional logic, however intuitively sensible, has not been readily accepted. There are three reasons for this. First, it conflicts with the entrenched drill-and-practice and story discussion models. Second, the results from research on teaching (see Brophy & Good, 1986), with its emphasis on student task engagement, are often interpreted to mean that drill-and-practice and question-and-answer activities should not only be encouraged but that they should be made even more structured so that more students will become more engaged. Finally, advocates of student involvement in learning are quick to fear that overt teacher information-giving will result in a transmission model of instruction which puts students in a passive role of mimicking teachers as opposed to a social mediation model of instruction which puts students in a position of actively constructing meaning.

However, findings from research in classroom reading practices demonstrate that social construction alone is not enough. It is also important for teachers to transmit knowledge, particularly when teaching low aptitude students. For instance, Anderson's work on first-grade seatwork (Anderson, Brubaker, Alleman-Brooks & Duffy, 1985) indicated that, in the absence of explicit information from teachers, low group students often draw incorrect conclusions about what is to be learned from typical reading seatwork tasks despite high rates of engagement.

Doyle (1983) and Winne and Marx (1982), in their studies of the "cognitive mediational paradigm," indicate that the reason students draw erroneous conclusions about instructional meaning is because they mediate instructional tasks in terms of prior experiences with similar tasks and infer from those experiences what they are to learn from the new task. For instance, when teachers teach strategic reading techniques without providing students with explicit information about what the strategy is, when to use it or how to do it, the students are free to infer from their previous experiences with drill-and-practice or question-and-answer activities that good readers are characterized by their ability to memorize rules for skills as opposed to their ability to engage in strategic reasoning and regulation of that reasoning. In short, students are more likely to construct meanings about strategic reading (i.e., be metacognitively aware of their reasoning and, hence, exert regulatory control over it) if teachers explicitly inform them about strategies and how to use them (Meloth, 1988).

This was the foundation for the research described here. Because expert readers reason strategically and are metacognitive about their reasoning when they encounter difficult text, teachers should provide students with explanations about such reasoning which are explicit enough to ensure that students will (1) draw accurate conclusions about what is to be learned, (2) become metacognitively aware of strategies, (3) use such awareness to assume regulatory control of their strategic thinking, and, in the process, (4) become better comprehenders.

THE RESEARCH

The research based on this foundation began in the late 1970s and early 1980s with observational studies (see, for instance, Anderson et al., 1985; Duffy & McIntrye, 1982; Roehler & Schmidt, 1979). These studies noted the absence of explicit teacher explanations during reading instruction. As a result, we asked the question: "Wouldn't students be more likely to read strategically if teachers explained how experts use strategies when *they* read?"

This question led to five years of study (for results from the initial years of study, see Duffy, Roehler & Wesselman, 1985). The culmination of this line of research was a naturalistic experiment conducted in 1984-85 (Duffy, Roehler, Sivan et al., 1987). This study was designed to determine whether teachers can be taught to explain reasoning strategic readers use to repair meaning blockages during reading and whether low reading group students who receive such explanations perform better on measures of metacognitive awareness and achievement than low reading group students who do not receive such instruction. Low reading group students were the targets because it was felt they would benefit the most. Twenty volunteer third-grade teachers, randomly assigned to treatment or treated-control groups, received extended inservice. Treated-control teachers were taught how to improve student engagement on academic tasks; treatment teachers were taught the same thing PLUS how to explain the reasoning associated with repair strategies. Both treatment and treated-control teachers were observed seven times throughout the year as they taught reading to their low reading groups. In treatment classrooms, teachers recast prescribed basal reading textbook skills as strategies and explained the reasoning employed in using these strategies while also insuring task engagement. In treated-control classrooms, teachers incorporated task engagement techniques but followed standard basal reading textbook procedures and prescriptions for skill teaching. Audio tapes of both treatment and treated-control teachers' explanations were rated for explicitness of explanation, and low group students in both groups were (1) interviewed following lessons to determine their metacognitive awareness of lesson content and (2) tested to determine their conceptual understandings and reading achievement.

The study was designed as a naturalistic experiment. It employed experimental research procedures such as random assignment of subjects to treatment or treated-control groups, provision of interventions for both treatment and treated-control teachers, administration of several measures to capture various aspects of student metacognitive awareness and achievement, and aggregation and treatment of data on the basis of the unit of treatment (the reading group). At the same time, however, the study was conducted under actual classroom conditions, using real teachers working in typical classrooms and in a typical urban school district where reading textbooks and curriculum were mandated. In short, every attempt was made to remain faithful to conservative principles of experimental research while simultaneously conducting the study under classroom conditions similar to those faced by teachers who would be expected to apply the findings.

Results established that classroom teachers, working in the context of normal curricular and instructional constraints, can learn to explain reasoning involved in using reading strategies, that students in low reading groups who receive such instruction demonstrate more metacognitive awareness of lesson content and of the need to employ repair strategies than students of teachers who do not provide such instruction, and that such students then demonstrate higher achievement on a variety of traditional and nontraditional reading achievement measures than students of teachers who do not provide such instruction. In short, low group students' metacognitive awareness and reading achievement improved as a function of explicit teacher explanation of reasoning involved in using reading strategies.

While this experiment was important, post hoc qualitative analyses were also conducted using teachers involved in that experiment and in earlier studies (see, for example Duffy, 1983; Duffy & Roehler, 1986; Duffy, Roehler, & Rackliffe, 1986; Roehler & Duffy, 1986). Data from such descriptive studies consisted primarily of transcripts of lessons and of teacher interviews. The usual procedure was to select a sample of more and less effective teachers (based both on the rated explicitness of their explanations and on their students' achievement and metacognitive awareness) and to analyze the transcripts of these teachers' lessons and interviews using modified microethnographic techniques (see, for example, Green & Wallat, 1981). These analyses resulted in findings not revealed by experimental results. This paper draws on both sets of findings.

This line of research answered in the affirmative the question posed following our early observational studies. Students *do* learn to read better when their teachers explain the reasoning involved in strategic reading. However, explanation itself is not a simple technique. Consequently, this paper examines the tension between information-giving and mediation during explanations, and considers implications these insights have for efforts to effect teacher change.

THE NATURE OF INSTRUCTIONAL EXPLANATION

Our findings indicate that reading teacher effectiveness involves a creative tension between information-giving and teacher mediation. Both are essential in order to achieve the best results. Consequently, effective instruction is neither transmission of knowledge nor social construction; rather, it is a fluid combination of both.

The Information-Giving Function of Explanation

Instruction is the teacher's intentional effort to help students build schemata for the curricular topic at hand. Information is needed to build schemata. While certain information can be inferred while completing academic activities, activities alone do not necessarily result in new schemata, particularly in the case of low aptitude students having misconceptions about how reading works because such students do not have rich enough background experiences to note the implied information and use it to correct a misconception or to build a new schema.

A major problem in instruction, then, is how students will receive information needed to build schemata for curricular goals. In reading, the approach has been one of engaging students in the aforementioned drill-and-practice and story discussion activities in the expectation that they will infer how reading works as they engage in these activities. At the other extreme, lecture approaches to instruction transmit information, but the information flow is one-way rather than reciprocal, and students are not active participants in the learning.

A potentially helpful way to think about providing needed curricular information may be a middle position between lecture-dominated and activity-dominated approaches. In such a middle position, teachers transmit information but do so in ways that (1) involve students in active building of schemata and (2) illustrate how the information is used. This is what we did in our research. Teachers provided information about when and how to use reading strategies through verbal statements and modeling, illustrating how the information was to be applied in a reading activity completed later in the same lesson or in the next lesson. Students were involved; they mediated information, restructured it in terms of their prior understandings, provided teachers information about restructuring as they engaged in the activity and gradually constructed schemata about curricular goals. However, the amount of inferencing students had to do was reduced by the explicit information the teacher provided. To avoid a tendency to associate such explanations with transmission models of instruction and with teachers who are unresponsive to students, we prefer to describe this as "reciprocal information-sharing" in order to convey (1) the interactive nature of the process and (2) the active role students play.

The effects of reciprocal information-giving were reflected in our research findings. Treated-control teachers, who focused mainly on task engagement using standard basal text activities, failed to get the results with low group students that their treatment group counterparts obtained when they implemented task engagement principles while *also* providing explicit information about when and how to use strategies. In short, engagement in activities alone did not work as well as engagement plus explanation because engagement in activities leaves students to infer whatever information is implicit in the activity while explanations reduce the amount of inferencing required of students by providing explicit information they can use in constructing an understanding of how and when to use the strategy in question. As a result, students tend to learn what the teacher intended.

Additional support for reciprocal information-sharing comes from two post hoc studies. First, discriminant analyses of teachers in our study indicate that effective teachers provided explicit information during initial lesson introductions, during modeling and during guided interactions while less effective teachers did not (Meloth & Roehler, 1987). Second, a study of instructional interaction patterns of teachers in our study using micro-analysis of lesson transcripts indicated that teacher questioning is effective only when teacher-student interactions are preceded by teacher-provided information (Vavrus, 1987). In short, standard teaching practices in which students complete drill-and-practice exercises or engage in question-and-answer dialogs without first receiving substantive information about what is to be learned are not as effective as teaching practices which provide such information. This seems to be the case even in instructional studies in which explanation is not emphasized. For instance, while journal reports on reciprocal teaching (Palincsar, 1986; Palincsar & Brown, 1984; Palincsar & Brown, 1986) refer only to the reciprocal dialog between teacher and students and attribute improved student outcomes to participation in that dialog, Palincsar (Palincsar & Brown, this volume, pp. 35-71) makes clear that students were provided with information about the activiites used during the dialog prior to the beginning of the study. Consequently, it is plausible that reciprocal teaching, like teacher questioning, is effective when preceded by explicit teacher-provided information. In sum, instruction is more effective when information is provided to reduce the amount of inferencing students must do as they attempt to build schemata about curricular goals.

Such reciprocal information-sharing may appear to be straightforward. However, its implementation when teaching strategic reading is complicated by three conditions. First, because the curricular goal is reasoning rather than simply knowing names of strategies or knowing routine steps to follow, the teacher must convey information about invisible mental processes, not information about tangible labels and steps. The declarative, conditional and procedural knowledge (Paris et al., 1983) conveyed about a repair strategy such as "context clues," for instance, emphasizes declarative knowledge about the *thinking* involved, not that the strategy is called "context clues"; it emphasizes when such thinking is called for as opposed to assuming that application is self-evident; and it emphasizes flexible and adaptable variations in reasoning according to the nature of the text rather than proceduralized steps or rules to be followed routinely. And because students' unique background experiences cause them to reason in idiosyncratic ways, the teacher must adapt information to individual students. Our studies indicate that teachers *can* deal with such flexibility. For instance, although both treatment teachers and treated-control teachers were mandated by the host school district to teach identical content from identical basal reading textbooks, the treatment teachers were able to recast this content and teach flexible reasoning which, in turn, resulted in better student awareness and achievement than obtained by treated-control teachers who emphasized standard drill-and-practice procedures and question-answer discussions of story content as prescribed by basal textbook teacher's manuals.

Second, information-sharing about strategic reading is difficult because the goal is to promote student metacognitive awareness. It is not good enough that students merely *do* strategic reasoning; they must also be in cognitive control of this reasoning so they can regulate its use when difficult text is encountered. Such control is tied to metacognitive awareness because once readers are aware of their reasoning, they are in a position to control it; if they have never been aware of their reasoning, however, they cannot impose control over it because one cannot consciously control that which has never been done consciously. For instance, good readers who seemingly are unconscious of their strategic reading under normal circumstances are able to exert regulatory control over complex comprehension problems encountered in difficult text if, during initial instruction, they were made aware of appropriate strategies to use in such situations. If instruction did not create such awareness, however, even good readers have difficulty regulating unusual comprehension problems because they are unaware of a strategy to apply in that situation. Consequently, teachers share information to promote metacognitive awareness. In our study, for instance, metacognitive awareness was accomplished by having teachers be as explicit as possible when providing information about strategies because the more explicit a teacher is, the more likely students will become aware. Findings supported this assumption. In post-lesson interviews, low group students of teachers who shared information in explicit ways demonstrated significantly more metacognitive awareness of what was taught, when to use it and how to do it than students of teachers who were less explicit.

Third, information-sharing about strategic reading is difficult because teachers must initially provide information about strategic reasoning while simultaneously conveying information about its ultimate application. This contrasts with conventional practice in which students engage in question-and-answer story discussions without first receiving information about strategies to use in answering questions, or drill on a strategy such as "context clues" without first receiving information about how to reason with context clues. In these situations, students show relatively little post-lesson metacognitive awareness of lesson content, responding to questions about when they would use a strategy by saying things such as, "Well, if you ever decide to be a teacher when you grow up, you will have to know this stuff." To combat such student misconceptions, teachers must present information about strategies in cohesive instructional experiences. In our research, for instance, we discovered early that standard lesson formats which move in an orderly fashion from explaining to guided practice to independent practice result in students who use strategies in practice situations but not when reading real text. Apparently, such lesson formats cause students to conclude that the only important thing to learn is the strategy in isolation because that product is what the teacher emphasized during the lesson. Consequently, we modified the standard lesson format so that it *began* with a basal textbook reading selection containing a situation requiring use of the repair strategy being taught that day. After establishing that the product of the lesson would be application of the strategy in real reading, the teacher provides information about the strategy and guides students as they come to understand how the strategy is used. Then, referring back to the introduction, the teacher says, "Okay, now let's use what we learned as we read today's story." In so doing, students receive information about a strategy in the context of its ultimate use, thereby reducing problems of transfer and increasing the likelihood that they will interpret instruction to mean that strategies are to be used in real reading. This complicates teachers' information-giving task not only because current instructional materials do not present strategies in the context of their use but also because they seemingly discourage it (see Duffy, Roehler, & Putnam, 1987).

The difficulties associated with information-giving highlight the need for good teacher modeling. Our findings indicate that straightforward, unambiguous and explicit modeling is an important element of strategy instruction for low group students. Presented in the form of "mental modeling" (Duffy, Roehler, & Herrmann, 1988), such information-sharing makes visible for novice readers the invisible mental processes of strategic reading by providing explicit examples of how expert readers reason when employing comprehension strategies. Such mental modeling tends to be used at the beginning of a lesson but is also used as needed throughout the lesson as teachers help students construct understandings. Students use these models as a basis for attempting the same reasoning on their own. Such modeling, if properly done, minimizes the above three difficulties by (1) illustrating for students the reasoning involved, (2) making them conscious of it, and (3) focusing them on application of the strategy.

A final point must be made about the information-giving aspect of instruction. Superficially, this looks a lot like the information-giving found in printed instructional materials such as textbooks. Textbooks transmit information students are expected to use to build schemata about curricular goals. However, there is a major difference between textbooks and explanations. The information flow in textbooks is one-way from text to readers, and students must take the information as written and adjust it to their particular backgrounds. The burden is totally on students. The information flow in explanation, however, is two-way. It includes both teachers and students. Teachers do not simply give information to students like a textbook does but also note information from students about the meaning they are constructing and adjust subsequent interactions accordingly. This judgment of students' emerging understandings on the spot and subsequent adjustment of instructional information accordingly is the second important component of explanation.

Teacher Mediation of Instructional Information

The teacher's function in adjusting instructional information to accommodate student idiosyncracies is often referred to as "teacher mediation" because teachers mediate between students' current understandings and the ultimate curricular goal. In doing so, teachers make adjustments in instructional interactions which help students progressively restructure their understandings in ways that move them closer and closer to the intended outcome. The emphasis on interaction reflects much more a social construction view of instruction than a transmission model. It is crucial because it not only distinguishes effective teachers of strategic reading from those who are ineffective teachers generally but also distinguishes effective teachers of proceduralized skill outcomes from effective teachers of strategic reading. Six illustrations of how effective teachers of reading strategies adjust instruction are presented.

First, when planning lesson introductions and modeling, effective reading strategy teachers think about particular students' prior experiences, understandings and difficulties and adjust information-giving accordingly. In Vygotsky's (1978) language, they consider students' "zones of proximal development." Teachers tailor instructional information to the group and to the group's past instructional experiences. Such adjustments, which are impossible for materials developers to anticipate when preparing reading programs or for textbook authors to anticipate when writing teacher's manuals, distinguish more effective from less effective teachers.

Second, effective reading strategy teachers adjust examples, nonexamples, analogies, and metaphoric illustrations as they present information, selecting those which they think will make curricular content vivid for the particular group being taught. For instance, a good teacher uses different examples when teaching repair strategies to Inuit students in a remote Alaskan village than when teaching students in a well-to-do suburb of Detroit. Less dramatic but equally true is the adjustment of examples during instructional dialog to the particular experiences of various reading groups of all ability levels in the same classroom, or to the events shared during that particular day. Such tailoring of examples, analogies, and metaphors also distinguishes more effective reading strategy instruction from less effective instruction.

Third, during instructional dialogs effective teachers adjust the explicitness with which they present information. While our research establishes that information must be presented explicitly in order to minimize the degree of ambiguity in instructional situations and, therefore, the amount of inferencing students need to do as they filter instructional information through their existing schemata, explicitness itself is relative. A level of explicitness which reduces ambiguity for one group of students may not be explicit enough to reduce ambiguity for another. Consequently, effective teachers mediate students' emerging understandings by adjusting the explicitness of their instructional statements to the backgrounds and experiences of students.

Fourth, because students always do some restructuring no matter how explicit the teacher is when initially presenting instructional information, effective teachers often modify the planned lesson to accommodate the need for spontaneously created elaborations and clarifications that were not anticipated in the plan. Characterized as "responsive elaboration" (Duffy & Roehler, 1987b) and as "alternative representations" (Wilson, Shulman, & Richert, 1987), teachers determine the need for such elaboration and clarification by creating opportunities for students to respond, using these responses as "windows" through which they observe students' mental processing, and then deciding what to insert into the instructional dialog to promote restructured student understandings which more closely approximate intended curricular outcomes. This instructional phenomenon has been observed in reciprocal teaching (Palincsar, 1987) and in writing instruction (Englert, Raphael, & Anderson, 1987), as well as in our work. It is another example of instructional mediation, and is a distinguishing characteristic of effective teachers.

Fifth, because students restructure instructional information over time, effective teachers adjust by gradually fading the amount of assistance provided to students. As a lesson progresses, effective teachers reduce the amount of explaining they do, the explicitness of the cues they provide, and the prompting they do. The objective is to move from a point at the beginning of a lesson where only the teacher possesses a coherent schema for the lesson goal to a point at the end of a lesson where the students have, through a series of guided restructurings of the instructional information, constructed for themselves a reasonably accurate schema. This process of transferring knowledge from teacher to student is alternately referred to as a "gradual shift of responsibility" (Pearson, 1985), as a period of "gradually diminishing teacher assistance (Roehler & Duffy, 1984), and as a movement from an 'inter-psychological to an intra-psychological plane" (Vygotsky, 1978). It requires considerable teacher on-the-spot mediation because decisions about how fast to move and precisely how to reduce explanations in subsequent interactions cannot be predicted totally in advance. This dimension of instruction is even more complex when one considers that student restructuring occurs not only within lessons but also across lessons. That is, teachers need to mediate not only the movement from teacher-directed to student-directed that occurs in the course of single lessons but also that which occurs across a series of lessons during which students construct more global schemata about strategic reading generally and its broader purposes (Roehler & Duffy, 1987). This longitudinal restructuring, combined with within-lesson "gradual shifts of responsibility," require great teacher sensitivity.

Finally, because reading strategy instruction is not simply a matter of presenting individual lessons but is, instead, much more like creating a conceptual mosaic, effective teachers capitalize on spontaneously occurring opportunities to communicate that the whole of strategy use is larger than the sum of the individual lessons or strategies taught. That is, the goal is to become a strategic reader, not to know a bunch of strategies. Consequently, effective teachers mediate students' understandings by using whatever opportunities present themselves to help students connect each new strategy in meaningful ways with previously learned strategies and with strategies to be taught in the future, and by utilizing all opportunities to engage students in using strategies in real reading (i.e., to be strategic readers). The goal is to have an overall mosaic of interrelated strategy use ultimately emerge as the outcome. To achieve this, teachers must look for opportunities to mediate students' understanding that reading requires not only knowledge about how to perform individual repair strategies but also an understanding of the global meaning-getting focus of reading, that strategies are interrelated, that strategies are used in combination, and that strategies are seldom used twice in the same way. Consequently, effective strategy teachers do not limit themselves to explanations of finite numbers of separate strategies. Rather, they use opportunities that arise during instructional dialogs to help students create organized networks of interrelated strategies (Roehler & Duffy, 1987).

Summary

Our research indicates that teacher explanation requires teacher sensitivity to the tension between information-giving and mediation of information—between instruction as transmission and instruction as social construction. First, because instruction is designed to build schemata, students must receive information they can use to build schemata. Second, because students are individuals who mediate instructional information idiosyncratically and construct their own meaning, teachers must adjust information to students' prior knowledge and emerging understandings to ensure a reasonably close match between curricular goal and student learning.

These two characteristics can be summarized in a model of instruction. This model, displayed in Figure 1, reflects an overall recursive pattern of teacher-issued challenge followed by teacher support for student growth. It begins with a goal, representing the teacher's overall conceptual understanding of the academic task (e.g., being a strategic reader). The particular group of students (e.g., the class or the reading group to be taught that year) is assessed in terms of their current status relative to the overall goal and, on the basis of the resulting data, the teacher modifies the goal to fit students' backgrounds and previous understandings (e.g., the strategic reading goal for the year will likely be different for a high fourth-grade reading group as opposed to a group of learning disabled fourth graders who demonstrate multiple misconceptions about how reading works). Once the goal is clear, the teacher initiates instruction by establishing the first challenge: an expectation that the product of instruction is the development of broad conceptual understandings about the curricular goal (e.g., controlling meaning-getting through conscious use of strategies in pursuit of real reading activities). This is supported by a classroom environment which involves students in the ultimate curricular product (e.g., being strategic readers while participating in uninterrupted sustained recreational reading, while pursuing projects of their choice which require reading, while engaging in language experience activities which dramatize the writer-reader relationship, and so on). Sometimes called a "literate environment" (Duffy & Roehler, 1987a), it supports students by providing conceptually consistent evidence of what is being learned and why we attempt to learn it.

Within this environment, the teacher initiates a series of challenges in the form of individual lessons (e.g., on particular reading strategies). These lessons are designed to move this particular group of students gradually closer to expert reader status not only by developing particular lesson outcomes but also by creating cohesive ties from lesson to lesson (e.g., all repair strategies are taught within the context of problems to be solved in the midst of reading, certain kinds of repair strategies are taught together, and so forth). The teacher longitudinally supports this series of challenges by gradually, over the course of the school year, releasing to students the responsibility for engaging in the ultimate goal (e.g., strategic reading). That is, the teacher progressively lessens the amount of assistance provided as students demonstrate greater and greater metacognitive awareness of the overall conceptual goal. In addition to this global support, the teacher offers "gradual release of responsibility" within individual lessons. That is, the teacher begins each lesson with a challenge (the objective) based on an assessment of students' previous understandings and bridges from the challenge to support by adjusting lesson information (e.g., the teacher introduces the story they will read which calls for the reading strategy to be learned, provides mental modeling, involves students in guided restructuring, monitors student metacognitive awareness of lesson content to assess student understanding, looks for opportunities to build cohesive ties to the overall mosaic being developed, supervises student application of the strategy to the story read that day, evaluates student acquisition of both the strategy selected for that day and the conceptual understanding of strategic reading as a whole, and provides additional instruction if student understanding is incomplete). This process of alternate challenges followed by support, which illustrates the tension between information-giving and mediation, continues indefinitely, with the teacher constantly adjusting the instructional dialog as students demonstrate misconceptions or understandings regarding the overall goal.

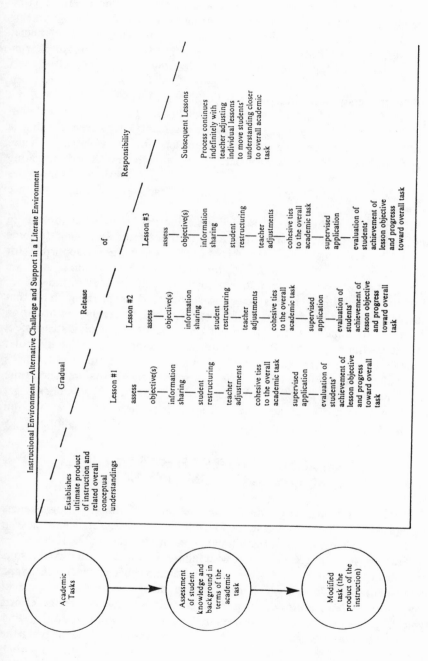

Instructional Environment—Alternative Challenge and Support in a Literate Environment

Establishes ultimate product of instruction and related overall conceptual understandings

Gradual Release of Responsibility

Lesson #1
assess
objective(s)
information sharing
student restructuring
teacher adjustments
cohesive ties to the overall academic task
supervised application
evaluation of students' achievement of lesson objective and progress toward overall task

Lesson #2
assess
objective(s)
information sharing
student restructuring
teacher adjustments
cohesive ties to the overall academic task
supervised application
evaluation of students' achievement of lesson objective and progress toward overall task

Lesson #3
assess
objective(s)
information sharing
student restructuring
teacher adjustments
cohesive ties to the overall academic task
supervised application
evaluation of students' achievement of lesson objective and progresss toward overall task

Subsequent Lessons
Process continues indefinitely with teacher adjusting individual lessons to move students' understanding closer to overall academic task

Academic Tasks

Assessment of student knowledge and background in terms of the academic task

Modified task (the product of the instruction)

Figure 1. Model for Instruction

15

Because instructional models possess a sequence, they are often criticized as being linear and, therefore, not representing the wholistic nature of strategic reading. To some extent this criticism is justified. The model IS linear. However, this is mitigated by two points. First, instruction is, in fact, linear. That is, instruction has a beginning (on the first day of school in the Fall) and an end (the last day of school in the Spring). Teachers are expected to teach reading one lesson at a time over this linear period. Given the nature of the school year and the fact that teachers normally only have one hour a day in which to teach reading, linear models reflect reality. However, reading is nevertheless a wholistic endeavor. It does not lend itself to isolated strategies or breaking the whole into smaller parts. Consequently, the second mitigating factor is the attempt to create a model in which conceptual wholeness is emphasized in a literate environment while simultaneously offering assistance one lesson at a time.

Models such as this are also sometimes criticized because they appear to emphasize one-way information flow from teacher to student. Again, to some extent, the criticism is just. In this model, teachers are responsible for transmitting to students substantive information about the nature of strategic reading. Again, however, two points mitigate the criticism. First, the essence of instruction is that teachers who know how to do something share that expertise with students who do not know how. Given this reality, information flow must to some extent be from teacher to student. Second, this model emphasizes the role of social construction of meaning, students' active roles in mediating and restructuring instructional information, and the teacher's responsibility to mediate and respond appropriately to that restructuring. Consequently, while teachers are responsible for seeing that students get information needed to create schemata for curricular outcomes, instruction ultimately revolves around students' restructuring of that information.

TRANSLATING TEACHER EFFECTS FINDINGS INTO CLASSROOM PRACTICE

Identifying characteristics of effective instruction is one thing; getting teachers to employ these characteristics in their teaching is another. Yet, achieving such classroom implementation is the ultimate goal of research on teaching.

However, such efforts often meet with failure or, at best, with mixed results (see, for instance, Stallings & Krasavage [1986] and other papers on the Napa Follow-Through Project which appeared in the November 1986 issue of *Elementary School Journal*). This may be because teacher change efforts typically emphasize "quick fix" procedures teachers can follow routinely. This perspective is reflected in reading's historical obsession with identifying the right "method" for teaching reading, in scripted approaches to instruction such as Distar, in prescriptions in teachers' manuals of basal textbooks, in lists of research-based instructional procedures which teachers are urged to follow, in the drive to package instructional innovations into commercial kits for teachers to follow, in lists of teacher behaviors currently being used to evaluate teacher performance and in interventions instructional researchers provide for teachers involved in instructional studies. The assumption in all these examples is that simplified techniques or packages or methods or formats listed in a few steps will result in teacher effectiveness.

However, our experience in providing an intervention for our treatment teachers (Putnam, Roehler, & Duffy, 1986), as well as subsequent experiences in conducting staff development projects based on the findings of our research, indicate that such procedural approaches to teacher change fail because (1) the complexities inherent in teaching teachers are not accounted for, (2) teachers are not expected to exert regulatory control over their instruction and (3) principles of effective instruction when teaching children are largely ignored when teaching teachers, not the least of which is the tension between information-giving and mediation. The following elaborates on each of these three reasons and suggests a model for effecting teacher change.

Complexities of Teacher Change

Teacher change is complex. Four kinds of complexity are described here.

Complexity of the Information to be Conveyed

First, instructional improvement efforts are difficult because of the amount and complexity of information teachers need. For instance, teachers must possess conceptual information about reading and instruction, procedural information which lightens the cognitive demands of instruction, pedagogical information regarding effective instructional actions and information about how to mediate instruction in order to make spontaneous adjustments as needed.

Conceptual information about reading and instruction develops teachers' understandings about the strategic nature of reading and instructional characteristics associated with teaching readers to be strategic. This information, based in educational research and development, establishes a rationale for undertaking an effort to change, informs teachers of the long-term goal, provides initial motivation for attempting change, and serves as a conceptual basis for adjustments teachers will ultimately make as they implement.

Procedural information helps teachers develop classroom routines which ease the demands of teaching. One example of procedural information is classroom management. By incorporating effective routines of classroom management (such as making clear the classroom rules and procedures), teachers create prerequisite conditions for effective instruction and minimize the amount of cognitive energy expended on student disruptions and discipline. Similarly, procedural information about lesson plan formats eases teachers' work loads by providing an organizational routine for expediting planning, thereby making it unnecessary for teachers to think through an organization for each lesson planned.

Pedagogical information focuses on techniques requiring teacher thought. Pedagogical information cannot, therefore, be reduced to procedures. For instance, pedagogical information includes information about how to select a reading assignment illustrating use of a repair strategy, how to decide what to say to model for students the declarative, conditional and procedural knowledge associated with a repair strategy, how to generate initial examples used, and how to move students from Vygotsky's (1978) "other-directed to self-directed" use of a strategy. Also in this category is information about how to decide whether an instructional situation calls for direct teacher explanation, reciprocal teaching techniques, collaborative groups, or combinations of these. Pedagogical information shows teachers how to make instructional decisions based on conceptual understandings about the nature of strategic reading, about the students involved and about effective instructional techniques.

The fourth and most difficult kind of information helps teachers mediate emerging student understandings. To mediate, teachers must be (1) comfortable enough with procedural and pedagogical information so they can expend cognitive energy on spontaneous adjustments and (2) knowledgeable enough about conceptual information that they can be comfortable with both the curricular goals and the variations in strategic reading individual readers employ in various texts. With cohesive and coherent knowledge about strategic reading, about the flexible, fluid way in which strategic readers operate, and about the ultimate goal of strategic reading, teachers can concentrate (1) on looking for stituations demanding adjustments in the instructional information presented and (2) on spontaneously making these adjustments.

The complexity of the information involved suggests five implications for teacher change. First, teachers must be helped to build coherent and cohesive knowledge structures based on concepts about both the nature of reading and the nature of instruction, and they should be made metacognitively aware of both how they are structuring information and how they are modifying as they learn. Second, information must be carefully organized and sequenced to reduce teachers' difficulties in processing it. For instance, substantive conceptual information about the over-all goals of an inservice project should be presented first to form a conceptual foundation upon which additional improvement can be based, procedural information should be presented next in order to ease teachers' burdens and to make available cognitive energy for pedagogical and adjustment information, pedagogical information should be presented next so teachers gain confidence in presenting information about strategic reading, and information about teacher mediation should be presented after teachers are comfortably using less demanding aspects of instruction. Third, despite the generally sequential presentation of information, staff developers must also help teachers create cohesive ties among the various kinds of information. Fourth, teacher change efforts must be longitudinal, because it takes time for teachers to develop conceptual understandings about such diversified information. Finally, teacher educators and staff developers must be as sensitive to the tension between information-giving and mediation when teaching teachers as teachers are when teaching children.

The Complexity of Teacher-as-learner

Second, instructional improvement efforts are difficult because of the complexity of the learners involved. Teachers learning to improve their instruction, like students learning to read, construct understandings reflecting their prior knowledge. Because many inservice teachers are veterans with strongly established knowledge structures about instruction, it is often more difficult to teach them to improve their instruction than it is to teach children to learn to read. Teachers, by virtue of going to school themselves, of years of actual teaching experience and of other preservice, graduate, and inservice education possess well-organized, firmly developed, and entrenched schemata about instruction. It is natural for them to filter new information about instruction through these well organized schemata and to restructure staff developers' messages to resemble their current practices.

Hence, teachers' old knowledge, understandings, and expectations established over the course of many years of teaching make it difficult for them to learn new instructional actions. Consequently, teacher change can only occur slowly through patient, intensive efforts that account for teachers' prior understandings and for the gradual way in which they, like all humans, integrate new knowledge with old knowledge. This puts a premium on the teacher educator's ability to mediate teachers' emerging understandings.

The Context of Instruction

Third, instructional improvement efforts are difficult because of the context in which teachers work. Two aspects of context are discussed: the external forces which mediate teacher acceptance of new ideas and the drive for smooth activity flow which impedes implementation of changes.

External forces include conditions such as accountability systems, school policies regarding teacher evaluation, competing staff development programs, and mandated commercial reading programs. Accountability systems mediate teacher acceptance of instructional improvement efforts because, since teachers' reputations depend on how well their students achieve on such measures, they resist any changes which threaten instructional routines associated with helping students score well. Teacher evaluation procedures mediate teacher acceptance of instructional innovations because, if innovations seem to vary to any degree from the criteria used in the evaluation system, teachers resist out of fear that they will receive lower evaluations. Competing staff development programs mediate teacher acceptance of instructional improvement efforts because, if the two efforts are not coordinated, they often end up contradicting each other, forcing teachers to choose one over the other rather than combining the best features of both. Finally, mandated commercial programs such as basal reading textbooks mediate teacher acceptance of instructional innovations because adoption of an innovation not included in the mandated program is technically a violation of school district policy.

Activity flow is a second contextual factor impeding teacher change. It refers to the fundamental teacher need for classroom order. All veteran teachers know that failure to keep students busy invites disaster, and that a routine of activities which move the class through the day smoothly is the key to activity flow. Instructional innovations endanger activity flow because they involve unfamiliar activities for which no routines exist. Consequently, implementation is often an awkward and inefficient period. Teachers avoid such disruptive periods and, hence, resist instructional innovations which threaten such disruptions.

Contextual influences suggest three implications for effecting teacher change. First, participating teachers should be excused for the duration of the teacher change project from pressures imposed by external conditions such as accountability procedures, teacher evaluation practices and central office mandates. Second, procedural information which helps teachers maintain activity flow during initial stages of implementation must receive priority. Finally, because of these complexities, in-service efforts must be sustained, coordinated and longitudinal. While brief in-service efforts may work when what is being taught is a relatively minor procedural alteration of the teachers' current practices (such as altering student seating patterns or turn-taking routines), the complexities involved in effectively teaching students to be strategic readers require extensive time commitments.

Human Resistance to Change

Finally, instructional improvement is difficult because teachers, like all humans, resist change. Change signals the end to comfortable practices of the past, the need to generate high levels of energy and the very real risk of failure. Simply stated, teachers resist change because it is energy sapping, emotionally draining and risky. To combat this natural human reaction, staff developers must bring patience and sensitivity to inservice projects, understanding that teacher resistance to change is natural, and providing emotional and physical support as teachers struggle to implement innovations.

Conceptualizing Teachers and Their Roles

Many teacher change efforts are based on the premise that instruction must be simplified for teachers. Two concerns seem to drive this premise. One, there is wide recognition of the difficulties associated with literacy instruction and a general agreement that teacher change efforts will work better if complexities are reduced. Second, curriculum and staff developers often perceive teachers as unable to deal with instructional subtleties, so they provide detailed directions and hold teachers accountable for following those directions.

Our research, however, suggests something else. Rather than reducing complexities and making teachers into technicians, teacher change must instead embrace the complexities, because effective instruction can occur only when teachers make multiple, on-the-spot adjustments while teaching. Consequently, just as the goal of strategic reading is to put readers in metacognitive control of the complexities associated with reasoning strategically while comprehending, the goal of teacher change efforts should be to put teachers in metacognitive control of the complexities associated with making instructional adjustments while teaching.

Conceptualizing teachers as metacognitive about instruction has implications for teacher change efforts. It is not enough to provide teachers with procedures to follow routinely. Instead, they must possess (1) conceptual understandings of the overall curricular mosaic represented by strategic reading and (2) the ability to make substantive interactive decisions about how to mediate instructional information to accommodate individual students' restructuring.

Similarly, the ultimate outcome is not that teachers will be observed implementing certain research-based instructional principles or that they adhere to certain lesson plan formats in organizing lessons or that they will otherwise implement in an intact form the information provided by the teacher educator. Rather, the ultimate outcome is that teachers be observed *modifying* research-based instructional principles, *adjusting* lesson plan formats and *altering* information provided by the teacher educator to fit the demands of the instructional situation, particularly as reflected in students' prior knowledge and emerging understandings.

In sum, teachers must be in regulatory control of their instruction just as readers must be in regulatory control of their comprehension. And staff developers must share with teachers information about teacher effectiveness findings in much the way that teachers share with students information about strategic reading. In short, staff developers must practice what they preach about what makes for instructional effectiveness, specifically as it relates to the tension between information-giving and mediation.

Instructional Effectiveness When Teaching Teachers

Teaching teachers involves many of the same instructional principles as teaching students. First among these is that instruction must be longitudinal. Like the students in our study whose responses to interview probes did not evidence metacognitive awareness of lesson content about strategies until after five months of instruction, teachers require time to accommodate new information to existing knowledge structures. That is, rather than the traditional "one-shot" afternoon session with a guest speaker from the university, change efforts must be conducted over a long period of time, with an academic year probably being the minimum.

Second, teacher change efforts must be characterized by emotional and physical support of teachers as they assume the risks associated with implementation while simultaneously managing on-going instructional programs. Examples of such support include tying of information-giving to teachers' existing understandings, freeing teachers from mandates associated with external factors, employing techniques such as collegial sharing, journal writing and one-on-one coaching to expedite teacher internalization, making instructional leaders, especially school principals, an integral part of the program, and displaying patience regarding teachers' individual rates of implementation.

Third, staff developers' information-giving must be sequenced so that the challenges presented to teachers are graduated in difficulty. Additionally, information must be spaced over extended periods of time to allow staff developers to mediate the gradual restructuring which is essential both to concept building and to accommodating teachers' individual differences in learning rate.

Fourth, standard principles of effective instruction must be routinely incorporated into teacher change efforts. For instance, instruction should be continually guided by assessment, information should be modeled and demonstrated, and teachers should progress from one stage of instructional expertise to the next by reference to evaluative data.

Fifth, staff developers should actively mediate, adjusting instructional information to teachers' backgrounds. That is, those conducting teacher change efforts must spontaneously note how teachers restructure information and provide spontaneous elaborations and modifications to accommodate such restructuring.

Sixth, teacher change efforts must be field-based. That is, staff developers must model instructional innovations in real classrooms so that teachers can see how it works outside the context of the ivory tower. Subsequently, staff developers must provide teachers with intensive field coaching as they implement innovations in their classrooms. Like all other aspects of effective teacher change efforts, the field-based component must be longitudinal in order to (1) demonstrate the day-to-day cohesion essential to effective instruction, (2) offer teachers supervised assistance in dealing with the many variations inherent in effective instruction and (3) provide a variety of supervised opportunities for teachers to experience the complexity and fluidity of strategy instruction.

Finally, staff developers should help teachers *adapt* instructional innovations, rather than adopt them. If teachers are to self-regulate instruction, they cannot rigidly parrot someone else's directions. Instead, they must fit directions to their existing knowledge structures. To accomplish this, staff developers must be explicit in communicating that such adaptation is desired and in providing assistance in making such adaptations. This step is essential if teachers are to exert metacognitive control over their own instruction.

Summary

Like instruction, teacher change can be summarized in a model for effecting teacher change (see Figure 2). Like the earlier-described model for reading strategy instruction, the teacher change model is based on findings about instructional effectiveness and on an overall cyclic pattern of teacher-issued challenges and support (or, in this case, staff developer challenges and support). Because effective classroom instruction is presumed to have much in common with effective instruction of students, the teacher change model resembles the instructional model. Both begin with broad conceptual goals, but the teacher change model begins with the staff developer's overall conceptual understanding of the academic task (e.g., developing strategic readers). The particular group of teachers (such as particular group of students in classroom instruction) is assessed and, on the basis of resulting data, the staff developer modifies the goal to fit teachers' background and previous understandings (e.g., the goal for the staff development project will be different for teachers operating in a context where they are not expected to follow mandated basal text practices as opposed to a group of teachers who are accountable for following exactly the mandates of such a system). Once the goal is clear, the staff developer introduces the first challenge: an expectation that the product of the staff development effort is students who read strategically and teachers who expedite this goal by being in metacognitive control of their instruction, an expectation that is maintained throughout the duration of the staff development project. To support this broad goal, constraints in the teachers' workplace which serve to counter the development of teacher metacognitive control of the development of strategic readers are suspended, thereby insuring that participating teachers' environments will be conceptually consistent with staff development goals. The staff developer then initiates a series of challenges, moving from conceptual information to procedural information to pedagogical information to spontaneous adjustments. While these challenges focus on

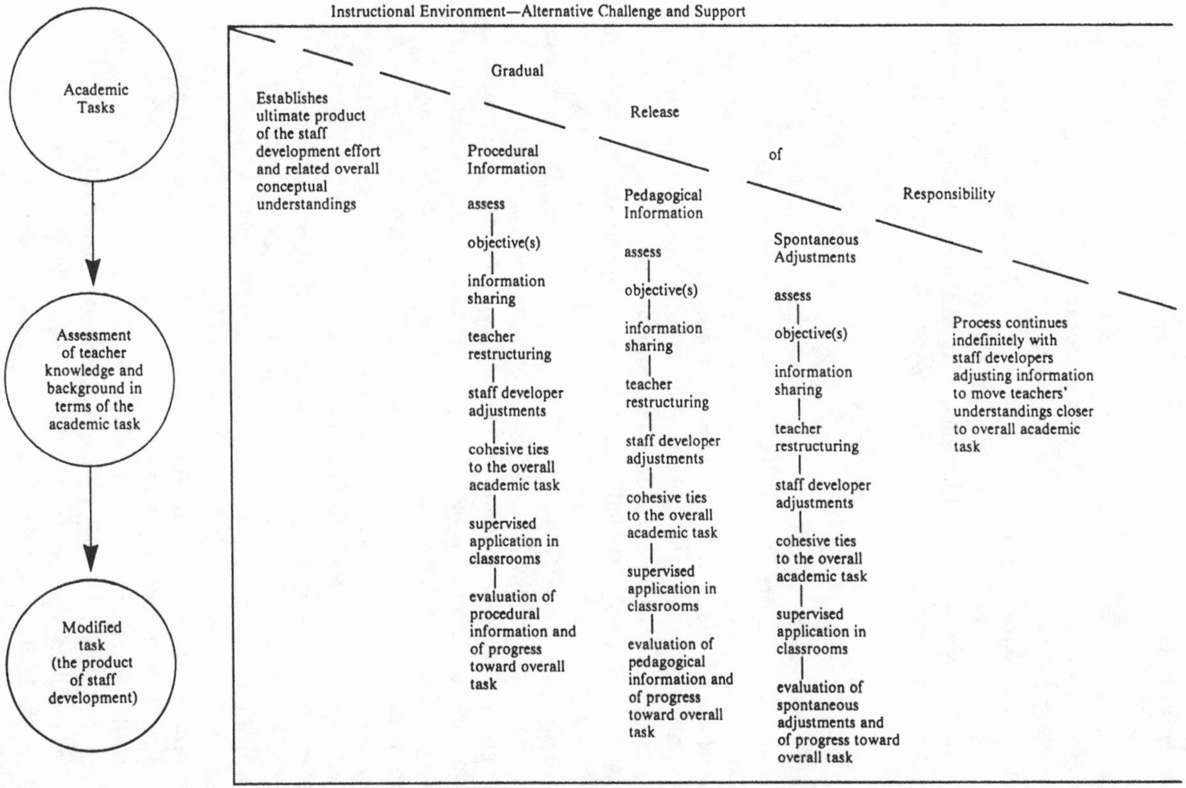

Instructional Environment—Alternative Challenge and Support

Responsibility   of   Release

| Gradual | Release | Spontaneous |
| Procedural Information | Pedagogical Information | Adjustments |

Establishes ultimate product of the staff development effort and related overall conceptual understandings

Procedural Information
assess
objective(s)
information sharing
teacher restructuring
staff developer adjustments
cohesive ties to the overall academic task
supervised application in classrooms
evaluation of procedural information and of progress toward overall task

Pedagogical Information
assess
objective(s)
information sharing
teacher restructuring
staff developer adjustments
cohesive ties to the overall academic task
supervised application in classrooms
evaluation of pedagogical information and of progress of progress toward overall task

Spontaneous Adjustments
assess
objective(s)
information sharing
teacher restructuring
staff developer adjustments
cohesive ties to the overall academic task
supervised application in classrooms
evaluation of spontaneous adjustments and of progress toward overall task

Process continues indefinitely with staff developers adjusting information to move teachers' understandings closer to overall academic task

Academic Tasks → Assessment of teacher knowledge and background in terms of the academic task → Modified task (the product of staff development)

Figure 2. Model for Teacher Change

specific types of information, they also promote the building of cohesive ties from one set of information to another. The series of challenges are supported by two things. First, they are supported by the staff developer's efforts over the course of the staff development project to gradually release to teachers responsibility for the development of strategic readers. Second, the staff developer offers a "gradual release of responsibility" within individual staff development sessions by beginning each session with a challenge (the objective) based on assessment of the teachers' previous understandings; by making adjustments designed to involve this particular group of teachers; by modeling the planning and implementation with children; by mediating teachers' restructuring; by monitoring teachers' metacognitive awareness of session content; by building cohesive ties to the overall conceptual mosiac; and by supervising teachers' application in their respective classrooms. Finally, because teachers as well as children need closure, the staff developer evaluates teacher achievement of the task of developing strategic readers, providing additional staff development if teacher understanding is incomplete. This sequence of alternate challenge and support continues indefinitely. In fact, if the staff developer is successful in developing teachers' metacognitive control of instruction, teachers will continue to modify and adjust their instructional practices well beyond the end of the staff development project itself.

Like the instructional model described earlier, the teacher change model is partly linear and depends initially on providing teachers with information. Just like that model, the teaching of teachers requires a linear sequence of specific objectives developed within the framework of a wholistic conceptual understanding of the ultimate goal. That is, the teacher change model, like the reading strategy instructional model, must help teachers develop wholistic conceptual understandings about the interrelated and cohesive aspects of instructional effectiveness, and staff developers must spontaneously respond to teachers' emerging understandings about instructional effectiveness.

CONCLUSION

Effective reading strategy instruction requires both transmission of information and socially constructed mediation of that information. That is, teachers must insure that students, particularly low aptitude students, receive substantive information with which to build a schema for using strategies and, because students restructure all experiences, teachers must spontaneously adjust subsequent instructional information in light of students' emerging understandings. Commercial programs and instructional scripts that tell teachers what to say are limited in their effectiveness because what they transmit cannot be tailored to students and because prescriptions cannot be adjusted to mediate emerging student understandings. Only teachers can do these things.

Hence, it is the teacher operating on the spot—not the master developer preparing materials in advance—who is the real key to instructional effectiveness. Given this, it is crucial that teachers be helped to engage in both the transmission role and the mediation role. Unfortunately, helping teachers develop flexible, fluid blends of transmission and mediation is complex and difficult. To accomplish it, we must apply the same combined principles of transmission and mediation to teacher education. This paper is a beginning in that regard.

REFERENCES

Anderson, L., Brubaker, N., Alleman-Brooks, J., & Duffy, G. (1985). A qualitative study of seatwork in first grade classrooms. *Elementary School Journal, 86*(2), 123-140.

Anderson, R., & Pearson, P.D. (1984). A schema-theoretic view of basic processes in reading comprehension. In P.D. Pearson (Ed.), *Handbook of reading research* (pp. 255-292). New York: Longman.

Baker, L., & Brown, A.L. (1984). Metacognitive skills and reading. In P.D. Pearson (Ed.), *Handbook of reading research*. New York: Longman.

Brophy, J., & Good, T. (1986). Teacher behavior and student achievement. In M. Wittrock (Ed.), *The handbook of research on teaching* (3rd ed., pp. 328-375). Riverside, NJ: Macmillan.

Doyle, W. (1983). Academic work. *Review of Educational Research, 53*(2), 159-199.

Duffy, G.G. (1983). From turn-taking to sense-making: Broadening the concept of teacher effectiveness. *Journal of Educational Research, 76*(3), 134-139.

Duffy, G., & McIntyre, L. (1982). A naturalistic study of instructional assistance in primary grade reading. *Elementary School Journal, 83*(1), 15-23.

Duffy, G., & Roehler, L. (1986). Constraints on teacher change. *Journal of Teacher Education, 37*(1), 55-59.

Duffy, G., & Roehler, L. (1987a). Building a foundation for strategic reading. *California Reader, 20*(2), 6-10.

Duffy, G., & Roehler, L. (1987b). Improving classroom reading instruction through the use of responsive elaboration. *Reading Teacher, 40*(6), 514-521.

Duffy, G., Roehler, L., & Herrmann, B.A. (1988). Modeling mental processes helps poor readers become strategic readers. *The Reading Teacher, 41*(8), 762-767.

Duffy, G., Roehler, L., & Putnam, J. (1987). Putting the teacher in control: Instructional decision making and basal textbooks. *Elementary School Journal, 87*(3), 357-366.

Duffy, G., Roehler, L., & Rackliffe, G. (1986). How teachers' instructional talk influences students' understanding of lesson content. *Elementary School Journal, 87*(1), 3-16.

Duffy, G., Roehler, L., Sivan, E., Rackliffe, G., Book, C., Meloth, M., Vavrus, L., Wesselman, R., Putnam, J., & Bassiri, D. (1987). Effects of explaining reasoning associated with using reading strategies. *Reading Research Quarterly, 22*(3), 347-368.

Duffy, G., Roehler, L., & Wesselman, R. (1985). Disentangling the complexities of instructional effectiveness: A line of research on classroom reading instruction. In J. Niles & R. Lalik (Eds.), *Issues in Literacy: A research perspective* (34th yearbook of the National Reading Conference, pp. 244-250). Rochester, NY: National Reading Conference.

Durkin, D. (1978-79). What classroom observation reveals about reading comprehension instruction. *Reading Research Quarterly, 14*, 481-533.

Englert, C., Raphael, T., & Anderson, L. (1987). *Discourse for learning about writing strategies.* Paper presented at the National Reading Conference, St. Petersburg Beach, FL.

Flavell, J.H. (1981). Cognitive monitoring. In W.P. Dickson (Ed.), *Children's oral communication skills*. New York: Academic Press.

Green, J., & Wallat, C. (1981). Mapping instructional conversations. In J. Green & C. Wallat (Eds.), *Ethnography and language in educational settings*. Norwood, NJ: Ablex.

Meloth, M. (1988). *The improvement of metacognitive awareness and its contribution to reading performance of third grade low group readers who receive explicit reading instruction*. Unpublished dissertation. Michigan State University.

Meloth, M., & Roehler, L. (1987). *Dimensions of teacher explanation*. Paper presented at the annual conference of the American Educational Research Association, Washington, DC.

Palincsar, A.M. (1986). The role of dialogue in providing scaffolded instruction. *Educational Psychologist, 21*, 73-98.

Palincsar, A.M. (1987). *Discourse for learning about comprehending text*. Paper presented at the National Reading Conference, St. Petersburg Beach, FL.

Palincsar, A., & Brown, A. (1984). Reciprocal teaching of comprehension-fostering and comprehension monitoring activities. *Cognition and Instruction, 1*(2), 117-175.

Palincsar, A., & Brown, A.L. (1986). Interactive teaching to promote independent learning from text. *Reading Teacher, 39*(8), 771-777.

Paris, S., Lipson, M., & Wixson, K. (1983). Becoming a strategic reader. *Contemporary Educational Psychology, 8*, 663-672.

Pearson, P.D. (1985). Changing the face of reading comprehension instruction. *The Reading Teacher, 38*(3), 724-738.

Pressley, M., Forrest-Pressley, D., Elliot-Faust, D., & Miller, G. (1985). Children's use of cognitive strategies, how to teach strategies and what to do if they can't be taught. In M. Pressley & C. Brainerd (Eds.), *Cognitive learning and memory in children* (pp. 1-47). New York: Springer-Verlag.

Putnam, J., Roehler, L., & Duffy, G. (1986). *The staff development model of the Teacher Explanation Project*. East Lansing: Institute for Research on Teaching, Michigan State University.

Roehler, L., & Duffy, G. (1984). Direct explanation of comprehension processes. In G. Duffy, L. Roehler, & J. Mason (Eds.), *Comprehension instruction: Perspective and suggestions*. New York: Longman.

Roehler, L., & Duffy, G. (1986). Why are some teachers better explainers than others? *Journal of Education for Teaching, 12*(3), 273-284.

Roehler, L., & Duffy, G. (1987). *Characteristics of instructional responsiveness associated with effective teaching of reading strategies*. Paper presented at the National Reading Conference, St. Petersburg Beach, FL.

Roehler, L., & Schmidt, W. (1979). *Quarterly report–Language Arts Project*. East Lansing: Michigan State University, Institute for Research on Teaching.

Stallings, J., & Krasavage, E. (1986). Program implementation and student achievement in a four-year Madeline Hunter Follow-Through Project. *Elementary School Journal, 87*(2), 117-138.

Vavrus, L. (1987). *The functional role of teacher elicitations in instructional sequence interactions during low group reading skill lessons of more effective and less effective fifth grade teachers*. Unpublished dissertation, Michigan State University.

Vygotsky, L.S. (1978). *Mind in society: The development of higher psychological processes* (M. Cole, V. John-Steiner, S. Scribner, & E. Souberman, Eds. and Trans.). Cambridge, MA: Harvard University Press.

Wilson, S., Shulman, L., & Richert, A. (1987). "150 different ways" of knowing: Representations of knowledge in teaching. In J. Calderhead (Ed.), *Exploring teacher thinking* (pp. 104-124). London: Cassell.

Winne, P.H., & Marx, R.W. (1982). Students' and teachers' views of thinking processes for classroom learning. *Elementary School Journal, 82*, 493-518.

*   *   *

CROSS-TALK

What is the nature of reading instruction, the relative role of skills and strategies? Can all strategies be explained?

Skills are no longer really an issue in reading; neither is our former advocacy of skills. Reading has been fundamentally changed by cognitive research. Whereas 15 years ago reading was seen to be primarily skill-driven and we wrote a book about teaching skills, it is now seen to be primarily strategy-driven and we write about teaching strategies. The change is conceptual. We advocate reading instruction which emphasizes conscious reasoning about the process of comprehension, not mechanical skill responses (Duffy & Roehler, 1987a).

Comprehension of difficult text requires even expert readers to be conscious strategy users. That is, when faced with text for which they do not possess rich prior knowledge backgrounds, even expert readers engage in reasoned problem solving: they determine the nature of the comprehension problem, access a strategy appropriate to the problem, adapt the strategy to the specific textual situation, and construct meaning. In order to do this, however, they must be conscious of what they are doing. It is not enough that students learn strategy labels or develop isolated strategy use; rather, they must be in conscious control of strategic reasoning, particularly the conditional knowledge which empowers them to be adaptive in their reasoning. Consequently, rather than simply learning "a bunch of strategies" in a declarative sense, readers learn when and how to consciously adapt strategies to an infinite number of textual situations.

This is not to say that reading is a totally conscious act. Some aspects of reading are routine and rarely require conscious thought, such as moving the eyes from left to right across the page and recognizing many words instantly. Neither do we deny that reading is automatic when the reader possesses rich prior knowledge for the text being read. We do, however, argue that a hallmark of true literacy is comprehending texts for which one does *not* possess rich prior knowledge. Comprehending unfamiliar text requires use of strategies; in order to access strategies one must be aware of them; and the genesis of such awareness is the original instruction (Derry & Murphy, 1987). Hence, for readers to be literate in unfamiliar as well as familiar text, instruction must develop conscious awareness of strategic reasoning.

Consequently, the bulk of reading instruction is not skills but, rather, strategies which research has identified as useful (see, for instance, Pearson, Dole, Duffy, & Roehler, in press; Pressley, Johnson, Symons, McGoldrick, & Kurita, in press). No one yet knows all the strategies a good reader might use or whether all strategies can be explained; however, that is not a viable reason for withholding explanations of those we *do* know are useful and explainable (while simultaneously expecting future research to suggest additional and/or different strategies).

In sum, while reading instruction has traditionally been characterized by skill instruction embedded in narrowness, procedures, drill, and automaticity, modern reading instruction is characterized by strategies embedded in breadth, thoughtfulness, flexibility, and sense-making; while the product of reading instruction has traditionally been the mastery of isolated skills as measured by tests, the product of modern reading instruction is adaptive strategy use focused on constructing meaning from real text in genuine literacy situations. Distinguishing strategy instruction from skills instruction is fundamental to understanding our position.

Would an emphasis on explaining strategies not cause students to learn isolated strategies at the expense of genuine comprehension?

We do not emphasize means at the expense of ends. Instead, we propose a "process-into-content" instructional approach (Roehler, Duffy & Meloth, 1986) in which "process" refers to the reasoning processes good readers use (the means) and "content" refers to the textual message (the ends). We argue that instruction which emphasizes process only is doomed to failure because students will learn isolated strategies and therefore will be unable to transfer that knowledge to problem solving and strategy adaptation in real reading. Likewise, instruction which emphasizes content only is doomed to failure because students are left to infer for themselves how good readers use strategies to get text messages. A process-into-content format, in contrast, in which strategies are taught and immediately applied in real reading situations, provides a balance. Further, we argue that this balance must be reinforced by embedding strategy instruction within the context of a "literate environment" (Duffy & Roehler, 1989a) which provides students with literacy experiences they can use as the raw material for building conceptions of reading. For instance, if classroom reading experiences emphasize isolated worksheets, students conceptualize reading as an essentially meaningless school task; if classroom reading experiences emphasize genuine literate events, students conceptualize reading as functional and enjoyable. Stated in terms of the means-ends question, in a nonliterate classroom environment emphasizing only strategies (the means) students interpret strategies to be meaningless school tasks but in literate environments emphasizing strategy use in conjunction with worthwhile literate pursuits (the ends), students interpet strategies to be meaningful and useful. Balance is the key.

This balance is crucial because the purpose of reading instruction is not only comprehension of specific content (the ends) but also comprehension of an infinite variety of text through an ability to self-regulate the reasoning involved in comprehension. Being able to comprehend specific content by participating in discussions with the teacher and/or peers (as is the case in most standard reading instruction) is not the same as independently comprehending a wide variety of text by self-regulating one's comprehension processes. Of the two, independent reading is most important since reading in the real world is normally a solitary act. Consequently, helping students employ in self-regulated ways strategic reasoning processes (the means) as they construct meaning from text (the ends) is an important goal of reading instruction.

This does not mean that teachers do not sometimes teach to content-only goals. For instance, when a science teacher wants students to comprehend the specific content of a specific text on a specific day, a content-only approach is effective. However, "comprehension" in this situation is limited to the specific text in question; there is no expectation that students are learning how to self-regulate their use of strategies when they encounter an infinite variety of text throughout their lives. To achieve that goal requires a process-into-content format.

In sum, our intent is to help students self-regulate their comprehension in a wide variety of textual situations. To do so, we emphasize putting students in control of the *processes* of comprehension as they construct meaning (as opposed to a content-only approach that focuses solely on the ends). Hence, we argue for reading instruction that is presented in a process-into-content (or "means-into-ends") format.

Our theory is not limited to reading. To the contrary, a balanced emphasis on process and content is applicable to any other curricular area where development of self-regulated reasoning is valued. Writing is a clear example. Composing text requires mental processes, often described as planning, drafting, revising, and editing processes. Good writers reason as they engage in these processes. If the intent is for students to be self-regulated writers (i.e., to be in conscious control of what they are doing as they compose text), it is both prudent and efficient to inform them of these processes and to mediate their understanding of them in a balanced process-into-content format in which writing processes are taught in conjunction with real writing activities (see Englert & Raphael, this volume, pp. 105-151). Similarly, if in mathematics we want students to be able to reason about solving mathematical problems, we should inform them of appropriate reasoning and mediate their understanding of this reasoning in conjunction with solving real mathematical problems (which is what we interpret to be the approach of Lampert, this volume, pp. 223-264); if in science we want students to be able to draw scientific conclusions, we should inform them of how scientists draw conclusions and mediate their understanding of this strategy in conjunction with studying real scientific phenomena, and so on. In sum, we believe that achieving a delicate instructional balance between process and content is as crucial as achieving a balance between information-giving and mediation, and that balance between means and ends is applicable to all curricular areas where self-regulated "higher order thinking" is an important outcome.

Who Should Receive Explanations?

Several questions were asked about whether direct teacher explanation is a technique appropriate only for at-risk students, because we refer in our chapter only to low-group students. Our answer is that explanation is appropriate at each student's "zone of proximal development" (Vygotsky, 1978).

Our research focused on at-risk students for political reasons associated with gaining access to the schools. Our hypothesis was that when teachers provide direct explanation (i.e., information giving and mediation of student understanding) about strategic processes within their low group students' zones of proximal development, those students would be aided in constructing intended curricular understandings and would become better readers. Results substantiated the hypothesis.

There is no reason to think that average and high group students would profit any less from explanations provided at their zones of proximal development. The zone of proximal development is not limited to low group development. It is just that the zone is more advanced for high aptitude students. Consequently, direct explanation will be helpful to high aptitude students as long as it is provided within their zone of proximal development. We hypothesize, for instance, that the national concern for the lack of "higher order thinking skills" in average and high ability American youth can be explained, at least in part, by a failure to provide these students (at their zone of proximal development) information and mediation about such thinking processes; further, we hypothesize that the absence of substantive teacher decision making in observational studies of classrooms can be traced to a failure by teacher educators and staff developers to provide teachers (at their zone of proximal development) with information and mediation about how to engage in such thinking. If we want students and teachers to possess such reasoning ability, we should explain it to them; wanting students and teachers to possess the reasoning while refusing to explain it to them is inefficient at the very least.

How Does the Explanatory Dialogue Work?

Space prohibits providing examples of dialogue here (although examples are available in Duffy, Roehler, & Herrmann, 1988; Duffy, Roehler, Meloth, & Vavrus, 1986; Duffy & Roehler, 1987b; Roehler & Duffy, 1986). Our qualitative analyses of lesson dialogues reveal that explanation involves subtleties not normally associated with traditional views of explanation where information is presented in a one-way, teacher-dominated lecture. We have explored these subtleties in depth elsewhere (see Duffy & Roehler, 1986a; Duffy & Roehler, 1989b) but two brief illustrations may suffice to make the point. First, dialogues reveal that the tension between information-giving and mediation is not sequential in the sense that first the teacher gives information and then mediates but, rather, is recursive in that information-giving and mediation occur throughout the lesson in a responsive interaction between teacher and students. It is not, therefore, a rigid procedural pattern but, rather, a subtle interaction between the mind of the teacher and the minds of the students. Second, teacher sensitivity to student restructuring is crucial. Effective teachers understand that students do not necessarily learn what was explained in exactly the intended way and constantly examine student responses for evidence of what is understood. Student cues such as partial responses, incorrect responses, hesitations, and inflexibility of strategy use are all used by the teacher as assessment data from which hypotheses are formulated about what students are understanding, and spontaneously generated statements, questions, and probes are provided which mediate students' understandings and move them closer to the intended outcome.

Our conclusion, based on our study of such dialogues, is that explanation cannot be proceduralized. It is, like strategy use itself, a reasoning process requiring teachers to be in regulatory control of professional knowledge so that adaptive, flexible decisions can be made.

Can Teachers Learn to be Decision Makers?

Clearly, it is not easy for teachers to maintain a balance between information-giving and mediation, to say nothing of maintaining the balance between means and ends, teaching to students' zone of proximal development and engaging in spontaneous explanation in the midst of classroom interactions.

Currently, there is no definitive answer to questions about whether teachers can be self-regulated decision makers because little research has been done in this area. However, our teacher explanation research has led us to conclude that the development of self-regulated teachers takes priority over all other concens. Specifically, we believe that teachers *can* learn to be self-regulated users of knowledge *if* teacher educators and staff developers apply to teacher education the same principles associated with successful efforts to teach children to be self-regulated strategy users. That is, teacher educators and staff developers must abandon "quick-fix" and "teacher-proof" approaches to instructional improvement in favor of the more demanding, long-term commitment to putting teachers in cognitive control of their instructional actions.

We have no illusions about the difficulty of achieving this goal (see, for instance, Duffy & Roehler, 1986b; Duffy, Roehler, & Putnam, 1987). In our experience, for instance, it is particularly difficult for teachers to explicitly convey conditional knowledge because they are so accustomed to using artificial tools of school to present reading as "work" as opposed to making reading a meaningful pursuit in the context of the real world. Nevertheless, recent concern about society's failure to accomplish substantive school reform (see, for instance, Elmore & McLaughlin, 1988) dramatizes once again how important it is that we help teachers learn to do such difficult things. Accordingly, our personal research agenda for the next five years is the study of substantive teacher change.

References to Cross-talk

Derry, S., & Murphy, D. (1987). Designing systems that train learning ability: From theory to practice. *Review of Educational Research, 56*(1), 1-39.

Duffy, G., & Roehler, L. (1986a). The subtleties of instructional mediation. *Educational Leadership, 43*(7), 23-27.

Duffy, G., & Roehler, L. (1986b). Constraints on teacher change. *Journal of Teacher Education, 37*(1), 55-59.

Duffy, G., & Roehler, L. (1987a). Teaching reading skills as strategies. *The Reading Teacher, 40*(4), 414-421.

Duffy, G., & Roehler, L. (1987b). Improving reading instruction through the use of responsive elaboration. *The Reading Teacher, 40*, 514-521.

Duffy, G.D., & Roehler, L.R. (1989a). *Improving classroom reading instruction: A decision making approach* (2nd ed.). New York: Random House.

Duffy, G., & Roehler, L. (1989b). Why strategy instruction is so difficult and what we need to do about it. In C. McCormick, G. Miller, & M. Pressley (Eds.), *Cognitive strategy research: From basic research to educational applications.* New York: Springer Verlag.

Duffy, G., Roehler, L., & Herrmann, B. (1988). Modeling mental processes helps poor readers become strategic readers. *The Reading Teacher, 41*(8), 762-767.

Duffy, G., Roehler, L., Meloth, M., & Vavrus, L. (1986). Conceptualizing instructional explanation. *Teaching and Teacher Education, 2,* 197-214.

Duffy, G., Roehler, L., & Putnam, J. (1987). Putting the teacher in control: Basal textbooks and teacher decision making. *Elementary School Journal, 87,* 357-366.

Elmore, R., & McLaughlin, G. (1988). *Steady work.* Santa Monica, CA: The Rand Corporation.

Pearson, P.D., Dole, J., Duffy, G., & Roehler, L. (in press). Developing expertise in reading comprehension: What should be taught and how should it be taught? In J. Farstrup & J. Samuels (Eds.), *What research says to the teacher of reading* (2nd ed.). Newark, DE: International Reading Association.

Pressley, M., Johnson, C., Symons, S., McGoldrick, J., & Kurita, J. (in press). Reading comprehension strategies that can be taught efficiently. *Elementary School Journal.*

Roehler, L., & Duffy, G. (1986). Why are some teachers better explainers than others? *Journal of Education for Teaching, 12,* 273-284.

Roehler, L., Duffy, G., & Meloth, M. (1986). What to be direct about in direct instruction in reading. In T. Raphael (Ed.), *Contexts of school-based literacy* (pp. 79-96). New York: Random House.

Vygotsky, L. (1978). *Mind in society: The development of higher psychological processes* (M. Cole, V. John-Steiner, S. Scribner, & E. Souberman, Eds. & Trans.). Cambridge, MA: Harvard University Press.

CLASSROOM DIALOGUES TO PROMOTE SELF-REGULATED COMPREHENSION

Annemarie Sullivan Palincsar and Ann L. Brown

DIALOGUE, PRIVATE SPEECH, AND THE DEVELOPMENT OF SELF-REGULATORY BEHAVIOR

Recently, 5-year-old Danielle received a game with the ominous words, "some assembly required," printed on the package. Within earshot of her parents but not in their presence, Danielle removed and lined up the pieces. She began to mutter: "Hm, it's in four pieces," "What does the picture say it should look like?" "Which one goes first?" "Does this fit here?" This linguistic event is interesting in several aspects. Strictly speaking, Danielle was engaged in a monologue; her remarks were directed at no one; in fact, there was no one present and no one responding. Yet, there was something strikingly dialogic about the nature of her remarks. She commented and paused. She self-questioned and paused. She verbally directed her own activity. Furthermore, the remarks she made bore a remarkable similarity to a dialogue in which she had recently participated as she and her mother put together a doll house.

To explore the possible relationship between Danielle's independent problem-solving activity with its accompanying monologue and the joint problem-solving endeavor and dialogue in which she participated, it is useful to examine a sociohistorical approach to cognitive development, particularly

Advances in Research on Teaching, Volume 1, pages 35-71.
ISBN: 0-89232-845-2

as represented by the work of the Soviet psychologist, Lev Semenovich Vygotsky (1896-1934).

The role of dialogue in problem-solving activity is central to Vygotskian tenets that the inner speech that is used by humans to plan, as well as to regulate, their own activity is a consequence of earlier participation in social activity (Vygotsky, 1962, 1978; Wertsch, 1980). Vygotsky maintained that the strategic patterns of reasoning exercised at the *intrapsychological* plane (within the individual) were a reflection of the strategies which the child was encouraged to follow earlier as a participant at an *interpsychological* plane (between or among individuals). Indeed, Vygotsky argued that through social dialogue it is possible for a child to participate in strategic activity without understanding it completely. Through repeated and shared social dialogues, the child comes to discover the import of the more experienced individual's utterances and his or her own responses. Having experienced this social dialogue, the child is then able to engage in private speech or speech that is spoken aloud but addressed to himself or herself for the purpose of directing cognitive activity. This private speech finally leads to inner, self-guiding speech which, with maturation and expertise, is internalized as verbal thought. Reflecting this perspective on cognitive development, Bruner (1978) observed, "One of the most crucial ways in which culture provides aid in intellectual development is through a dialogue between the more experienced and the less experienced" (p. 171).[1]

In this paper we discuss the use of dialogue between teachers and students for the purpose of teaching children to engage in self-regulatory activity while comprehending text. We will suggest that the supportive features of naturally occurring dialogue, which many young children experience prior to entering school, offer interesting instructional opportunities in classroom settings. Furthermore, dialogue can serve as a window on the verbal thought in which children are engaged as they attempt to understand text. Finally, dialogue fosters collaborative problem solving among peers.

The Role of Dialogue in Cognitive Development

Studies of parent-child interaction have provided rich data documenting the role of dialogue in the acquisition of language and problem-solving skill. For example, Snow (1977) provides delightful accounts of mothers carrying on conversations with their 3- to 18-month-old babies. With the youngest children the mothers made discriminating use of burps, coos, laughs, and yawns (but not kicking or arm waving) to carry on "conversations." Questions were posed so that they required only the most minimal responses. However, over time, the mothers began to treat only certain vocalizations, for example, babbling, as responses from the child. Wood and Bruner introduced the term "scaffold" to characterize the manner in which adults provide and adjust assistance to children's language development (Bruner, 1978; Ninio & Bruner, 1978; Wood, Bruner, & Ross, 1976; Wood & Middleton, 1975).

There are several ways in which this scaffolding occurs. Scollon (1976) uses the term "vertical constructions" to describe a pattern of conversation in which the child says something, the adult asks a question about the topic, and the child responds, essentially elaborating or commenting upon the initial topic. Over time, the child independently generates single utterances that include both the topic and the comment. Cazden (1983) identified a second form of interactional scaffolding that occurs when adults and children engage in games (e.g., "The lady rides the horse"; "peekaboo") and picture-book reading. In these language events there are scripts that are initially produced in their entirety by the adult. Over time, as the child develops the ability to participate, the parents encourage the child to speak more of the script.

Similar research has been conducted observing parent-child interactions during problem-solving activity to assess the manner in which adult guidance facilitates cognitive development on the part of the child. For example, Rogoff, Ellis, and Gardner (1984) observed mothers preparing their children to engage in a classification task. They observed that the adults assisted the children with novel problems by guiding transfer of knowledge and skills from more familiar contexts. This transfer occurred, not through observation of the adult or explicit instruction by the adult but rather through a collaborative effort in which the parent scaffolded the participation of the child, gradually transferring responsibility to the child over the course of the interaction. Furthermore, parents modified their instruction as a function of the child's age and the familiarity of the task, providing the most assistance to young children working on unfamiliar tasks.

The Role of Private Speech in Cognitive Development

Vygotsky (1962) observed that young children emit private speech initially after a given activity, as an afterthought. As expertise is acquired, the timing of the speech, in relationship to the activity, changes. The speech begins to accompany the activity and, in time, precedes the activity. It is when the speech precedes the activity that it begins to assume the functions that are typically associated with self-regulation: orienting, planning, guiding, and monitoring. In the final transition, Vygotsky maintained that private speech "goes underground" to constitute verbal thought. This private speech commonly resurfaces, even among adults, when the individual confronts a novel or complex problem. Hence, an adult lost while driving might mumble: "Which direction am I going now?" "Was that the third or second traffic light?" "I wonder if I should just go back to the last familiar spot."

Attempts to empirically validate Vygotskian theory regarding the extent to which private speech facilitates problem-solving activity have met their fair share of obstacles. Researchers have been able to document that the frequency of private speech increases when children are confronted with difficult tasks (Berk & Garvin, 1984; Deutsch & Stein, 1972; Goodman, 1981). Verbalizations also increase when adults are not present to exert control over children's activity (Kohlberg, Yaeger, & Hjertholm, 1968). However, when investigators examined the relationship between private speech and quality of task performance, the relationship has often been determined to be nonsignificant (Fuson, 1979), if not negatively correlated (Frauenglass & Diaz, 1985; Zivin, 1972). For example, in the study by Frauenglass and Diaz (1985) the problem solving of preschoolers, who used a considerable amount of private speech, was observed to be poorer than that of children who used little private speech. However, one cannot conclude that these results refute Vygotsky's theory because the amount of private speech might have been indicative of task difficulty and associated with immediate failure; but over the course of time, may well relate to increases in task peformance.

In addition to the unclear relationship between the nature and frequency of verbalizations and performance, the sheer incidence of private speech in this body of research has been problematic. In a review of studies investigating private speech, Fuson (1979) reported that only half the children serving as subjects engaged in private speech. Furthermore, the occurrence of private speech, even among this population, was quite minimal. However, as Frauenglass and Diaz (1985) point out, the majority of research regarding the incidence of private speech among children and the relationship of speech to performance has been conducted with tasks that are generally nonverbal in nature (mazes, block design) and has been conducted in situtations that are not conducive to talking aloud. That is, the children were in formal and unfamiliar settings that might well have inhibited talk-alouds.

A study recently conducted by Berk (in press) was designed to compensate for the obstacles traditionally encountered in private speech research. Berk compared the private speech of first and third graders. The children were observed in a naturalistic setting; in their classrooms engaged in mathematics seatwork. Furthermore, the problems were selected as typically challenging to children; therefore maximizing the production of private speech. In addition, Berk examined the influence of both age and aptitude (as measured by I.Q. tests) on the production of private speech. Observers recorded each child's private speech, motor accompaniment to the task, and level of attention over four seatwork periods.

Berk's results indicated that the overall incidence of private speech was high, with 98.7% of the children uttering self-guiding comments, responding to their own verbalized questions, and otherwise commenting on their performance or the nature of the task. Furthermore, while externalized speech decreased between grades one and three, internalized (subvocal) speech increased between grades one and three. IQ was positively related to the incidence of private speech for first graders and negatively related for third graders. Finally, private speech did relate to task performance; task-relevant private speech predicted achievement similarly for high-I.Q. first graders and average IQ third graders. In this naturalistic study, Berk's findings offer clear support for Vygotsky's theory regarding the functional significance of private speech in children's cognitive development and self-regulation.

During the past decade there has been a considerable amount of interest in the role that private speech might play in regulating the cognitive as well as social behaviors of adolescents and adults. Interventions have been designed that involve teaching students to make a number of self statements that will guide them in the attainment of a particular goal. These statements generally represent a series of steps or reminders in the completion of a task. The statements are initially modeled for the students; the students are then taught to make these statements aloud while completing a task, and finally to fade the verbal statements to subvocalizations, which are also faded over time. These interventions, identified as cognitive behavior modification (Meichenbaum & Goodman, 1971), have been implemented effectively in the improvement of children's handwriting (Robin, Armel, & O'Leary, 1985); composition (Harris, Graham, 1985); and reading comprehension (Meichenbaum & Asarnow, 1978).

The Role of Self-regulation in Reading Comprehension

We have maintained, thus far, that dialogue is an important means of acquiring private speech and that private speech is related to the regulation of cognitive activity. Before proceeding to describe the use of dialogue to teach self-regulated comprehension activity, it is appropriate to define what is meant by self-regulated learning (cf. Anderson, this volume, pp. 311-343; Duffy & Roehler, this volume, pp. 1-33).

The self-regulated learner possesses and is able to use, in a flexible way, three types of knowledge: (1) knowledge of strategies as heuristics that enable one to accomplish learning tasks efficiently; (2) knowledge of one's own learner characteristics as well as knowledge of the task demands one confronts, often called metacognition; and (3) knowledge of the content or the factual knowledge that one possesses about specific domains as well as the world (Brown, Campione, & Day, 1981; Pressley, Borkowski, & Schneider, 1987; Schoenfeld, 1985). Theoretical treatments of comprehension activity suggest that the following types of strategy knowledge facilitate successful reading comprehension (Brown, Palincsar, & Armbruster, 1984): (a) clarifying the purposes of reading to determine the approach taken to reading; (b) activating background knowledge to create links between what is known and the new information to be presented; (c) allocating attention to the major content of the text at the expense of trivia; (d) critically evaluating content for internal consistency and compatibility with prior knowledge as well as common sense;

(e) monitoring to determine if comprehension is occurring; and (f) drawing and testing inferences of many kinds, including interpretations, predictions, and conclusions.

The success with which the learner selects and orchestrates the use of these self-regulatory strategies is, in large measure, a reflection of metacognitive knowledge. Knowledge of oneself and the demands of the activity in which one is engaged facilitates the selection, employment, monitoring, and regulation of these strategies.

Thus far, we have characterized the factors that contribute to self-regulatory behavior during reading as types of knowledge. However, in addition to possessing knowledge, the self-regulated learner is motivated to employ this knowledge. Current research examining the relationship between self-regulation and motivation portrays a complex picture in which individuals' performance reflects the value attached to the task, as well the learning activity, feelings of self-competence regarding the task, and attributions regarding success or failure with the task (Brophy, 1987; Paris & Oka, 1986; Schunck, 1986). Moreover, this picture changes with age and ability. Paris and Oka and their colleagues have determined that, while comprehension strategies are critical for young and poor readers, awareness and attitudes toward reading better correlate with reading achievement among older students and better readers. Finally, while underachieving readers indicate negative views toward reading and have lower expectations for themselves, more successful readers have positive self-perceptions regarding reading and are optimistic regarding their reading performance.

The preceding characterization of self-regulated reading suggests that students should learn: (1) a repertoire of strategic approaches to interacting with text; (2) how to monitor their comprehension activity for the purpose of flexibly using strategy knowledge; and (3) the relationship between strategic activity and learning outcomes so that they are, in fact, motivated to engage in self-regulated learning.

USING DIALOGUE TO TEACH SELF-REGULATION OF COMPREHENSION ACTIVITY

Earlier in this paper we discussed the role of social dialogue in the acquisition of language and problem-solving activity. The examples given were derived exclusively from adult-child interactions; generally parent-child interactions outside of school settings. In this section we will address the use of teacher-child and child-child dialogue in classroom settings.

Since the 1970s, considerable attention has been paid to the forms and functions of language in the classrooom (see reviews of this literature by Bloome & Green, 1984; Cazden, 1986; Green, 1983; see also Heath, 1981; Mehan, 1979).

The work conducted by linguists, anthropologists, and sociologists has enhanced our understanding of such issues as social relationships and participant structures in the classroom, teaching styles, and cross-cultural communication. A subset of this research has examined classroom discourse in cognitive terms, typically by categorizing teacher talk and student talk. This research indicates that verbal interactions in school settings differ strikingly from conversations outside of school. For example, teachers generally focus on the development of specific skills and simple attribute concepts. Teacher-child interactions are dominated by adults, in terms of both the amount and direction of the conversation. Most "discussion" that is held in classrooms is, in fact, recitation where there are recurring sequences of teacher questions and student responses, with most questions of the "known-answer" variety where there is little opportunity for the exchange of ideas and opinions (Gall, 1984). In short, dialogue assumes little prominence in typical classroom practice. There are, of course, numerous explanations for this situation. Generally speaking, many teachers express concern over the management of dialogue and find the tension between sustaining the attention of the group while sustaining a meaningful learning dialogue to be problematic. Our interest in identifying an instructional procedure by which teachers could use learning dialogues led to the development of *reciprocal teaching*.

Reciprocal Teaching:
An Example of Instructional Use of Dialogues in Classrooms

Over the past eight years, we have conducted research with a number of teachers, from primary grades through high school, for the purpose of determining the outcomes of an instructional procedure that is principally dialogic in nature. The procedure is called *reciprocal teaching*. In the process of reciprocal teaching, students and their teachers take turns leading discussions about shared text. These are not, however, open-ended discussions. Similar to the "scripts," referred to earlier in this chapter, that are inherent in word games that adults play with children, there is a degree to which reciprocal teaching is also "scripted." The scripting occurs with the use of four activities that are practiced as strategies: *predicting, questioning, summarizing*, and *clarifying*. Before discussing the role these strategies play in the discussion, we will explain why they were selected to structure the dialogues.

These four activities were selected on the basis of several features. First, they are examples of strategic activities that good readers routinely bring to bear when learning from text (cf. Bereiter & Bird, 1985), but poor readers fail to use (Garner, 1987). Second, when employed intelligently, they both improve comprehension and provide the alert reader an opportunity to monitor for understanding. For example, if one attempts to paraphrase a section of text and fails, this may be a good indication that comprehension and retention have not been achieved and remedial action, such as rereading, is required. Finally, as we will illustrate, these particular strategies lend themselves well to scaffolding (i.e., supporting) a discussion.

When groups initially engage in reciprocal teaching dialogues, the discussion is "text driven" (Mosenthal, in press). When working with a new story or passage, the discussion begins by generating *predictions* about the content of the text based upon: the title, the group's prior knowledge of information suggested by the title or their expectations driven by questions they have regarding the topic or by experiences they have had with similar kinds of text. Following the discussion regarding the group's predictions, the group reads and/or listens to a portion of text.

One individual is invited to lead the discussion for each portion of text the group reads. The discussion leader begins by asking *questions* pertinent to the information read. Other members of the group respond to these questions and suggest additional questions, which are also answered. The discussion leader then *summarizes* the same segment of text and other members of the group are invited to comment or elaborate on the summary. If there were points in the text that were unclear (e.g., concepts or vocabulary), these are discussed for the purpose of attempting to achieve *clarity*. Finally, if the text provides sufficient clues, the group generates additional predictions. The following dialogue illustrates a text-driven discussion that occurred among a group of first grade students and their teacher.[2]

> The teacher reads the following text:
> > The pipefish change their color and movements to blend with their surroundings. For example, pipefish that live among green plants change their color to a shade of green to match the plants.
>
> Clare, the child leading the discussion, begins:
> > One question that I had about this paragraph is: What is special about the way that the pipefish looks?
>
> Keith (clarifying):
> > Do you mean the way that it is green?
>
> Andy (elaborating):
> > It's not just that it's green; it's that it's the same color as the plants around it, all around it.
>
> Clare resumes:
> > Yes. That's it. My summary is this part tells how the pipefish looks and that it looks like what is around it. My prediction is that this is about its enemies and how it protects itself and who the enemies are.
>
> Monty adds on to her summary:
> > They also talked about how the pipefish moves. . .

To which Keith rejoins:
  It sways back and forth.

Andy adds:
  Along with the other plants.

Ms. Mackey, the teacher, interjects:
  What do we call it when something looks like and acts like something else?
  The way that the walkingstick was yesterday? We clarified this word when
  we talked about the walkingstick.

Angel:
  Mimic.

Ms. Mackey:
  That's right? We said/ we would say/ that the pipefish mimics the . . .

Students:
  Plants.

Ms. Mackey:
  O.K.! Let's see if Clare's predictions come true.

  While the strategies serve to structure and support the dialogue, the teacher
supports the children's participation in the dialogue. This support varies,
naturally, according to such features as the ability of the students and the
difficulty of the text.

  Over time, as the children internalize the use of these activities, there are
two shifts that occur in the dialogue. The first is that the dialogue is increasingly
"discourse driven" (Mosenthal, in press) as opposed to exclusively text driven.
The strategies are used in a far more flexible fashion and the dialogue becomes
less routinized. Simultaneously, the role of the adult teacher also changes. The
teacher is consciously attempting to turn over more responsibility for leading
and sustaining the dialogue to the student participants. Initially, the teacher
instructed, provided explanations to the students, and modeled strategy use.
Over time, the teacher engages more in coaching the students' participation
in the discussion.

Collaborating With Teachers In the Use of Reciprocal Teaching

Because teachers seldom possess meaningful levels of experience in
classroom use of dialogue for instructional purposes, either as teacher or
learner, a critical step in the implementation of reciprocal teaching has been
the preparation of the teachers. Over the years, with our teachers' advice, we
refined this process to include the following steps.

First, the teachers were encouraged to reflect on and discuss their current
instructional goals and activities related to improving students' comprehension

of text (cf. Peterson, Fennema, Carpenter, & Loef, 1989). Similarities between the processes and outcomes of their current programs and reciprocal teaching were highlighted. For example, most teachers with whom we worked already engaged in the teaching of strategies. The differences between teaching strategies as isolated skills and teaching strategies for the purpose of self-regulating one's learning activity were discussed and demonstrated (for a comprehensive treatment of this issue, see Duffy & Roehler, this volume, pp. 1-33; Duffy et al., 1986; Duffy et al., 1987).

Second, the theory informing the design of reciprocal teaching was introduced to the teachers. The following points were emphasized:

1. The acquisition of the strategies employed in reciprocal teaching is a joint responsibility shared by the teacher and students.
2. The teacher initially assumes major responsibility for instructing these strategies (i.e., the teachers "think aloud" how they generate a summary, what cues they use to make predictions, how rereading or reading ahead is useful when encountering something unclear in the text); but gradually transfers responsibility to the students for demonstrating use of the strategies.
3. All students are expected to participate in this discussion; that is, all students are to be given the opportunity to lead the discussion. The teacher would enable the students' successful participation by supporting the students in a variety of ways. For example, the teacher might prompt the student, provide the student additional information, or alter the demand on the student.
4. Throughout each day of instruction there is a conscious attempt to release control of the dialogue to the students.
5. The aim of reciprocal teaching is to construct the meaning of the text and to monitor the success with which comprehension is occurring.

Following this explanation and description, the teachers were shown tapes in which reciprocal teaching was demonstrated with students of an age comparable to those with whom the teachers would work. Following these introductory activities, the teachers participated in several sessions where the reciprocal teaching dialogues were role-played, simulating situations that had arisen in previous research. Transcripts of reciprocal teaching sessions were shared for the purpose of discussing some of the fine points of the dialogue; for example, how teachers adjusted the support given to individual members in the instructional group. Finally, there was a demonstration lesson in which the investigator and a teacher conducted a reciprocal teaching lesson followed by a debriefing with all of the teachers involved in the study. Following these formal sessions to prepare the teachers, additional coaching was provided to each of the teachers as they implemented the dialogues in their respective settings.

Introducing Students to Reciprocal Teaching

In the initial investigations of reciprocal teaching (Palincsar & Brown, 1984), instruction started with the dialogues. When we began to investigate its use with larger instructional groups and younger children, we added a procedure to introduce the students to reciprocal teaching.

The procedure included: discussion regarding the purpose of reciprocal teaching, the features of reciprocal teaching, and a structured overview of each of the strategies that would be used in the discussions. Each strategy was introduced with the use of teacher-led activities. For example, questioning was introduced by discussing the role that questions play in our lives, particularly in our school lives. The students then generated information-seeking questions about everyday events. This activity permitted the teacher to evaluate how well their students could frame a question. The students then read or listened to simple informational sentences about which they were to ask a question. Next, the students were asked to evaluate questions that were written about short segments of text; and finally the students were to generate their own questions from segments of text. Similar activities were conducted for each of the four strategies.

These actitivites were included principally to introduce the students to the language of the reciprocal teaching dialogues and to provide the teacher with diagnostic information suggesting how much support the individual children in the group might need in the dialogue, based on their performance with these isolated activities.

Evaluating the Effectiveness of Dialogic Instruction. The initial research on reciprocal teaching was conducted with junior high students who were adequate decoders but poor comprehenders (Palincsar & Brown, 1984). Implementing the reciprocal teaching procedure on a small group basis (the groups averaged five students) with remedial reading teachers, for a period of twenty days, we observed that: (a) students' ability to summarize, generate questions, clarify, and predict improved markedly; (b) quantitative improvements on comprehension measures were large, reliable, and durable; (c) the benefits of the intervention generalized to classroom settings; and (d) there was transfer to tasks that were similar but distinct from the instructional tasks.

Having determined that reciprocal teaching was an effective intervention for poor readers in junior high school, we began a series of comparative studies to determine the essential features of reciprocal teaching. In the first of this series we compared reciprocal teaching with other interventions that included instruction regarding the same strategies but were not conducted in a dialogic manner. We compared reciprocal teaching with: (a) modeling, in which the teacher modeled the four strategies as she read the text while the students observed and responded to her questions; (b) isolated skill practice, in which the students completed worksheet activities on each of the four strategies and received extensive feedback from the teacher; and (c) reciprocal teaching/ practice, during which the students received the reciprocal teaching intervention for the initial four days of instruction, followed by eight days of independently applying the strategies, in writing, to segments of text. Only the traditional reciprocal teaching procedure resulted in large and reliable gains (Brown & Palincsar, 1987).

In the second comparative study we asked whether the four strategies were necessary to effect improvement on the comprehension measures or whether a subset of the strategies would suffice. Ten days of reciprocal questioning alone and ten days of reciprocal summarizing alone did not result in the same gains as ten days of the full reciprocal teaching procedure (Brown & Palincsar, 1987).

Satisfied that this was not a procedure that could be streamlined readily and still maintain the same degree of effectiveness, we implemented the reciprocal teaching procedure in a series of classroom studies in which all six middle school remedial reading teachers from an urban district, working in groups that ranged in number from 7 to 15, compared reciprocal teaching with an individualized program of reading skill instruction. Although the results were not as dramatic as our earlier work, over 70% of the students participating in the experimental groups met our criterion as compared with 19% of the control students (Palincsar, Brown & Samsel, work in progress).

Our focus is on our most recent work, conducted with first grade students. This research was motivated by our interest in determining what comprehension instruction might look like when conducted with students who were, as yet, nonreaders (in the sense that they were not yet decoding words). We chose to work with students who are often identified "at-risk" for academic difficulty (i.e., children from disadvantaged families, children referred for special education or remedial services). We were particularly interested in these children in light of the evidence that, while considerable educational efforts are spent on teaching them decoding skills, such instruction is often at the expense of comprehension instruction. This focus on decoding activity may well foster the notion among these young children that the purpose of reading is "saying the words right and fast" (Allington, 1980; Collins, 1982; McDermott, 1976). Our intention was to provide these children with early (school) lessons on the nature of reading as a meaningful activity.

In keeping with the theoretical perspective of this paper, we will discuss the results of a portion of this first grade work by first considering the activity that occurred between the children and teachers and then characterizing the concomitant changes that were observed on the part of the children in these instructional groups.

The students were selected by asking each of the three first-grade teachers to nominate at least 12 of their 27-30 students who might be at risk for academic difficulty, based on previous school histories, referrals for remedial education, and current classroom performance. The teachers were also asked to identify up to four students who were not experiencing any school-related difficulty who might serve as catalysts to the discussions. All nominated children were then assessed using an array of procedures. The students were first administered the *Stanford Early Assessment of School Achievement Test* (SESAT). This test measures listening comprehension by asking the students to circle the picture that best represents the statement that has been read to them. The children were below the fiftieth percentile on the *SESAT*. To collect a measure of listening comprehension in a task more representative of learning from extended text, the children were administered a series of comprehension assessments in the following manner. The children were told that they were going to hear a story and that, as the story was read, they would be asked to answer questions about what they were learning. The stories were read, paragraph by paragraph. The mean length of each story was five paragraphs with each paragraph averaging 80 words. There were a total of 10 questions designed to assess recall as well as the ability to draw inferences from the text. These questions were interspersed so that the children generally answered two questions per paragraph. In addition, following the story, the students were asked one question that required them to identify the gist of the passage and one question that measured their ability and inclination to use information that had been presented in the story to solve a novel problem. For example, following a passage that described the unique characteristics of spiders, the children were told about a man in Chicago who climbs very tall buildings and calls himself "the spider man." The children were asked why that was a good name for the man to choose. Three of these comprehension assessments were administered to each child before the instruction began. On the recall and inference questions the children were averaging about 50% correct. On the gist questions, they averaged 27% correct and on the application questions, 25% correct.

As an additional measure of listening comprehension activity, we asked the students to engage in the isolated use of the four strategies that would be used to structure the dialogue. First, we read the title of the passage to the children and asked them to tell us three things they would expect or would like to hear about in a story with this title (predicting). Then we asked the students to listen carefully as we read the first part of the story and to think of a question they might ask other children to make sure they understood the story (questioning). We then asked the children to listen once again so that they could tell us what the story was mainly about (summarizing). The students were told, with each reading, that they should ask for help if there were any words or ideas that they could not understand (clarifying). Each story was constructed to include one difficult vocabulary word for young children. There were two such assessments of strategy knowledge administered during pretesting. The students earned 26% of the total points possible for executing each of these strategies.

To increase our understanding of these children's listening comprehension activity, we asked them what they did while listening to the stories to help them to understand and remember what they were hearing. Typical responses for the majority of our students included: "I don't know this. I'm only seven years old!" "I do nothing." "I stay still." "I be quiet." These responses contrast with a few of the students selected by their teachers as potential catalysts to the discussion who answered: "I keep thinking about it." "I keep running my mind over it." "I picture it in my head, I catch the picture."

Following this evaluation, the 10 children whose individual composite scores suggested that they were most in need of instruction to increase comprehension were matched and randomly assigned to either the experimental or control groups for each of the three teachers. In addition, two students (generally from the four each teacher had nominated as possible catalysts to the discussions) who fared well on the assessments were selected and randomly assigned to either the experimental or control group. Each of the three instructional and control groups then consisted of five at-risk children and one child not experiencing difficulty.

The three teachers in this replication had each taught for more than 15 years in the primary grades and had successfully participated in two earlier studies of reciprocal teaching. Instruction took place in each teacher's classroom during that time of day when the teachers generally met for small-group instruction. Prior to beginning the dialogues, the children in the experimental groups were introduced to reciprocal teaching using the activities described earlier in this chapter. The introductory activities required five consecutive days of instruction, each lasting 20-30 minutes.

The teachers then began the dialogues. Once again, instruction was held for 20-30 minutes a day for a total of 20 consecutive school days. The teachers read expository passages derived from third grade basal reading materials and covering a range of topics such as plants that glow, chimps that use sign language, and the production of cartoons.

Examining the Dialogues

Each day the teachers audio-recorded the reciprocal teaching dialogues. Days 1, 5, 10, 15, and 18 through 20 were transcribed for each teacher. In addition, the teachers were invited to asterisk any tape they would like transcribed for their own interest.

We used different sets of questions to guide our examinations of the transcripts. The patterns of interaction that emerged during the initial exploration became the focus of the second and third sweeps of the transcripts. In previous research (Palincsar, 1986) we asked such general questions as: How does the dialogue change over time? What differences are observed among the groups engaged in the dialogue? Recently, we have begun to ask: What opportunities are created when instruction features dialogue that features the use of strategies and attends to the transfer of control for the learning activity to the students?

For the purposes of this paper, we are particularly interested in the manner by which assistance provided in the dialogue permitted the children to participate in constructing the meaning of the text in a way that would not be possible if they were unassisted. We also examined the transcripts for evidence of scaffolded instruction (when the dialogue was used to provide temporary and individualized support to the students so that each student might participate in the dialogue and, over time, the students could achieve independence from their teacher as well as from the group in comprehension activity).

Within this framework, the dialogues afforded opportunities for the more experienced teacher to model those processes that underlie successful comprehension; for example, self-inquiry, paraphrasing, and monitoring for understanding. Furthermore, dialogue permits the teacher the opportunity to evaluate the learners' status with regard to these self-regulatory processes and to guide them in the acquisition and application of these processes. Finally, dialogue facilitates a collaborative effort among the participants to construct the meaning of the text, break down these constructions when confronted with contrary evidence, and reconstruct them. In the following sections we provide examples of this dialogue, highlighting the role of teacher and peer collaboration in this instruction.

Modeling the Processes Underlying Successful Comprehension

In the following discussion the teacher, Ms. Derber, is reading an expository piece about a relative of spiders, "Daddy Longlegs." She begins to read:

> Daddy longlegs spend much of their time cleaning or preening their long legs

when a child interrupts her to ask:
> What does preening mean?

This interruption illustrates the spontaneity with which the students begin to use the strategies (in this case, clarification) while listening to the text. Ms. Derber inquires of the children:
> Now then, the question is, what does preening mean?

The children offer a number of possible explanations:
    taking care of it
    not doing bad things to it
    giving it special air and food

The teacher comments:
    These are all good things that you would do for the whole body.

She then calls their attention to the text again. . .
    Let's read again and listen for a word that is used in the sentence that might
    give you a clue. [rereading] Daddy longlegs spend much of their time
    cleaning or preening their long legs.

Meara interjects:
    cleaning?

The teacher responds by indicating how she could use the text to assist her
to figure out the meaning of the word, preening:
    Yes. Did you hear that little word that they used after cleaning? Cleaning
    or preening. When I hear that little word, "or" I know that it is saying,
    another word for this is, and so, cleaning or preening. You are exactly
    right. Preening does mean cleaning.

In this example, Ms. Derber has made explicit how she could use the text
to define an unfamiliar word. To do this, she has had to deautomatize her
reading of the text. A number of our teachers have noted that this is an
important key to using the dialogue for the purpose of modeling their reading
of the text; having the knowledge of an expert but experiencing the
comprehension activity as a novice might. That is, the teachers ask of
themselves how they would proceed to infer meaning if they did not know
the meaning.

Evaluating and Guiding the Acquisition and
Application of Self-Regulatory Strategies

The following dialogue illustrates two children taking turns leading the
dialogue: Sara and Dan. Sara, who had done very poorly on the pretest
measures required a considerable amount of support from the teacher to lead
the discussion. Ms. Mackey provided this support by, for example, modifying
the requests she makes of Sara and providing additional modeling. Dan was
selected to join this group because of his success with language related activities.
He required little assistance from the teacher in his turn as discussion leader.

    The teacher, Ms. Mackey, reads:
        One thing you need is an air tank. The air tank gives you air to breathe
        underwater. You wear the tank on your back. A short hose from the tank
        brings the air to your mouth. Before you dive, a lot of air is pumped into

your tank. The tank can hold enough air for you to breathe under water for about an hour.

Your hour is almost over. It's time to go up. As you swim slowly to the top, the pressure gets lighter. The water is warmer too. The top of the water looks like a wavy mirror. At last your head comes out. Now you can take off your mask. You can breathe the air around you.

Ms. Mackey then asks:
Now when it says "you" who are they talking about?

Students:
The aquanauts.

Ms. Mackey:
Yes. Now Sara, think about what the section was about and a question you might ask us. [pause]

When Sara is unable to generate a question, Ms. Mackey modifies the task:
Well, maybe you could think of a summary. What did this paragraph tell us about?

Sara suggests:
About whenever that tank is not filled up, he has to come up.

Ms. Mackey:
Yes! Now we could make up a question about that, couldn't we?

This is still not enough assistance to Sara and so the teacher models such a question, using the information that Sara has suggested:
We could say, we might say, "Why does the aquanaut have to come up?" Would you like to ask that question?

and Sara repeats the teacher's question:
Why does the aquanaut come up? and calls another child, "Candy!"

Candy:
Because it didn't have enough air.

Sara:
That's right.

Rather than proceed with the discussion, Ms. Mackey then asks Sara to try for another question, providing more opportunity for assessment and scaffolded instruction:

Let's try for another question. Let me read a part of this again.

Ms. Mackey then rereads the second paragraph and asks:
Can you think of a question?

Sara, while not able to generate a question does, on this turn, identify a topic in the text at hand:
I know. They can see themselves.

Ms. Mackey:
Aha! You could ask a question about that couldn't you? [pause] Start the question with the word, "how."

Sara has now suggested the topic of the question but still appears unable to generate her question, so Ms. Mackey suggests the question word she might use. With Ms. Mackey's assistance, Sara then generates a question:

Sara:
How can the . . .

Ms. Mackey:
aquanauts. . .

Sara:
see themselves in the mirror?

Ms. Mackey:
O.K.! That was close! You answered your own question. What is the mirror, Sara?

Sara:
The water.

Ms. Mackey:
So you might ask. "How could the aquanauts see themselves?" or "What was the water like?" Let's go on now. What do you suppose, Sara, we will learn about next?

Sara:
More about breathing in the water.

Ron:
About the other things you will need in the water.

Ms. Mackey:
Fine! Let's go on and see. Dan will you be the teacher?

The next portion of the discussion is led by Dan. The reader will notice how independently Dan functions from the teacher.

Ms. Mackey [reading]:
Some aquanauts have already lived and worked under water for many days. Wearing their gear, they went out of the underwater houses. They took pictures of coral. They gathered rocks from the ocean floor. They looked for signs of oil and minerals. They watched fish feed and lay their eggs. They learned a lot about life in the sea.

Dan:
How does the aquanaut get air in his house?

Bobby:
By the hose.

Dan:
Yes. And what did the aquanauts do under the water?

Devon:
Gather rocks.

Dan:
And take pictures of the coral.

Ms. Mackey:
Well, you've covered that section very well.

Dan:
Also, what did the aquanauts build under water?

Candy:
Houses.

Dan:
Yes. And my summary: This was about that they build houses under the water.

The teacher then elaborates upon Dan's summary:
Excellent. And they told us what they used them for, to observe the life underwater. Dan did an excellent job being our teacher. Let's go ahead.

Collaborating to Construct the Meaning of the Text

In the following dialogue, Ms. Hagerman's children are reading and discussing a story about glow worms. There are two points illustrated in this discussion. First, there are many instances of opportunistic use of the strategies in the reading/discussion and second, there are numerous occasions when the discussion is very collaborative in nature. These occasions are the result of the skillful manner in which Ms. Hagerman invited the children's participation in the dialogue.

Ms. Hagerman [reading]:
Some glow worms live in caves. They hang from the ceilings of caves.

Kim interjects:
I have a good question. Where do they live?

Students:
In the ceilings of caves.

Kim:
That's right.

Ms. Hagerman:
[reading] And they spin sticky fishing nets.
What else do we know that spins a net?

Molly:
A spider.

Ms. Hagerman:
That's right.
[reading] These nets are like spider webs. Some insects that live in these caves see the bright lights.
Oh! What do you think they do?

Lou:
Die.

Ms. Hagerman:
O.K. The glow worm will spin a little net. And another insect sees the little light. And, what's it going to do? [pause] What do insects do when they are near the light? [pause] It's dark out and you're at a ball game and you look up at the lights. What do you see?

Students:
Bugs.

Joe:
Bugs like the light.

Ms. Hagerman:
So, we're back at the cave. Are you back in the cave?

Students:
Yeah.

Ms. Hagerman:
The insects are outside. They look in the cave and see the lights. . .

Angel:
They go in there to get under the lights.

Lou:
And they get caught in the nets.

Ms. Hagerman:
That's right and then what happens?

Molly:
The glow worms come out and pull them in and eat them.

Ms. Hagerman:
Let's see what it says.
[reading] Small insects that live in the caves see the bright lights and fly up to them. On the way they are caught in the glow worm's fishing lines.

What does it mean, fishing lines?

Students:
> The net.

Ms. Hagerman:
> Yes. The net.
> [reading] The successful glow worms pull in their sticky threads and gobble up the insects. Then they lower their fishing lines again to catch another insect.
>
> Let's summarize the story so far. We are learning about insects that glow and the last part told us about. . .

Joe:
> glow worms.

Angel:
> They are lightening bugs without wings.

Ms. Hagerman:
> Yes, without wings. And where do they live?

Molly:
> In caves.

Teacher:
> Where?

Angel:
> In New Zealand.

Ms. Hagerman:
> And how do they catch their food?

Joe:
> They hang from the ceilings of the caves.

Lou:
> And they get the bugs under the. . .

Angel:
> . . .light.

Kim:
> The bugs try to get in and then they get caught.

Ms. Hagerman:
> And then what happens?

Students:
> They get eaten by the glow worms.

Collaborative Reconstruction of Text Meaning

The role that schema plays in comprehension activity initially called our attention to the facilitative effects of background knowledge on the construction of meaning. We are now beginning to understand how partial or inaccurate prior knowledge or beliefs can serve to impair comprehension (cf. Anderson & Roth, this volume, pp. 265-309; Alvermann, Smith, & Readance, 1985; Brown, Smiley, Day, Townsend, & Lawton, 1976). Simply stated, problems arise when learners permit their previous knowledge or beliefs to override incompatible information in the text instead of using the new information to correct their existing knowledge or beliefs, or at least to recognize the discrepancies and realize that resolution is needed.

In the following discussion, Ms. Derber elicits a number of predictions from the children based on the title of the passage, "Lions in the Grass." The children begin the text with very clear expectations that they will be hearing about animal lions. The dialogue allows one to see how tenaciously the children cling to their prior expectations despite the contrary evidence posed by the text.

Ms. Derber:
Today's story is, "Lions in the Grass." I wonder what that would be. Does anyone have a prediction for us?

Phillip:
It might tell about. . .lions in the grass.

Ms. Derber:
Well, tell me more. That's what the title is.

Phillip:
It might tell where they live.

Ron:
It might tell that they eat the grass.

Ethan:
It might tell that they sleep in the grass. . .

Meaghan:
. . .that's where they get their shade.

Ms. Derber:
The lions get shade from the hot. . .

Students:
Sun.

Ms. Derber:
Great. Ron?

Ron:

It might tell us about what the lion eats.

Ethan:

It might tell us that the lions eat insects that live in the grass.

Ms. Derber:

Alright. So, it might tell us what lions eat, where they live, and what they do there in the grass. Well, let me start reading and let's see if your predictions are correct.

[reading] Did you know that there may be lions in the grass all around you? Yellow lions with green teeth?

Ethan [clarifying]:

I know what all around you means. It means that there are lions all around, all around people.

Ms. Derber:

Hmmm. Have you noticed lions all around you, here in Springfield?

Students [resoundingly]:

NO!

Ms. Derber:

Well, that's what the story says. Listen, Yellow lions with green teeth.

Meara:

Oh, I know how they got their green teeth. Because they were eating grass.

Despite the fact that the children, as a group, have recognized that there is something in the text that is incongruous with their expectations, Meara continues to think about the topic as animal lions. Interestingly, however, she is the first to "catch on":

Ms. Derber:

Maybe that's it. Let's read a little further and see if Meara is right.

[reading] But these lions do not roar. And, they cannot walk.

Meara:

Oh! They are called dandelions!

Ms. Derber:

Oh. What are dandelions? Amy? Are they animals?

Amy:

No. Flowers.

Kim:

Yes. Flowers.

Ms. Derber:
And flowers are not animals. They belong to the group called . . . plants. Well, let's see if that's right. It would seem to match wouldn't it? Terrance, lions that are yellow with green teeth?

Dan (clarifying):
What's the green teeth?

Ms. Derber:
That's a good question. Dan. Do flowers have teeth?

Phillip, who is apparently still thinking along the lines of the initial predictions suggests a possible explanation, but in the process of providing this explanation experiences a shift:

Phillip:
They might need to clean them because they eat grass . . . and like . . . where they eat it . . . NO! It might be green like their stem.

Ms. Derber:
So, at first Phillip was thinking about lions that eat, but do dandelions eat grass?

Kim:
Yeah!

A surprised Ms. Derber:
Dandelions eat grass?

Kim [states firmly]:
Yes, because they kill grass if they are near it.

Ms. Derber:
Oh, they might kill grass, but have you ever seen a dandelion munching and eating like we do?

Students [giggling]:
No.

Ms. Derber:
It would have to be a different kind of eating, I guess.

Meara:
Maybe the teeth are the leaves.

Ms. Derber:
What about that? Could their teeth be the leaves?

Students:
Yeah.

Ms. Derber:
Let me read a little further and let's see.

At this point in the discussion the issue is resolved; however it is interesting to note how much discussion was necessary to achieve this simple change and how the dialogue promotes this change.

Evaluating the Outcomes of Dialogic Instruction

We maintain that by participating in dialogue, children can learn a problem-solving and self-regulatory approach to comprehending text. We suggest that, from a sociohistorical account of learning, what the child learns while participating in the dialogue is internalized over time. To examine this hypothesis, we will discuss data provided by the transcripts, anecdotes, and posttests for the children in the three instructional groups from which the transcripts were selected.

The transcripts for these three groups suggest that the discussions, over the course of the twenty days of instruction, became more spontaneous, less labored, and less teacher-directed. Furthermore, the children increasingly monitored their understanding of the text (e.g., by requesting clarifications with greater frequency or asking the teacher to reread). Finally, the transcripts indicate that the children began to make distinctions regarding the information that was provided in the text and information that either was derived from personal experience or would have to be sought elsewhere.

This last observation requires some explanation. In contrast to the seventh graders with whom we had done the earliest reciprocal teaching research, one of the difficulties experienced by these first graders was distancing themselves from the text as a source of information (cf. Mason, McCormick, & Bhavnagri, 1986). This difficulty manifested itself in two ways. First, the children often would indicate that they could not answer a question (either in the discussion or in the assessment sessions) because of the relationship between this information and their personal experience. For example, after hearing a story about chimps that had been taught to use sign language, the children were asked several general questions about the story. It was not uncommon for children to indicate that they knew nothing about this since they had never seen chimps that could talk, or to indicate that they ought to know something about this because they had seen some chimps in the zoo on a school trip. Second, when these first graders initially began to generate their questions, an unusual number of these questions (compared once again with those generated by seventh graders) could not be answered from the text but rather seemed to reflect general knowledge the children possessed related to the topic of the text. The teachers were careful to acknowledge these question types as "good and interesting questions" and then ask the children to indicate whether this was a question that could be answered using the text, or rather the knowledge the children already possessed. Over time, the children began to distinguish between text and background knowledge; they asked more text-based questions. However, at the same time, they began using their background knowledge to make predictions about the text.

Anecdotal evidence of internalization on the part of the students is indicated in the teachers' reports that the children began to use the strategies employed in the dialogue, unprompted, in contexts other than the listening comprehension lessons. For example, all three of the teachers in this replication indicated that the children attempted to engage them in the same discourse during small-group reading time and asked for clarifications during whole-class discussions (greatly impressing some "community helpers" who were presenting to the classes).

In addition to this collective evidence, individual students' response to the intervention is reflected in the results of the comprehension assessments administered throughout the intervention. These were the assessments in which the children listened to an expository passage and answered ten questions that were interspersed throughout the story and one gist and application question following the story. These assessment materials were independent from the materials that were used during the instruction. The results of these assessments indicate that during baseline, on the three assessments that were administered prior to instruction, the mean for the three experimental groups was 51.2% and for the three control groups: 48.6%. Following the first half of intervention, the experimental mean was 62.2% and the control was 48.7%. The experimental mean for the last phase was 72.1% and the second phase mean for the control students was 55%. Multivariate analyses of variance, using a design on dependent measures and decomposing the gains made from baseline to the first half of intervention and from the first to the second half of intervention indicated that there was a significant difference between the gains of the experimental and control students following the first half of the intervention $F(1,33) = 4.75, p < .02$. While there were no significant differences detected on the gist questions as a function of the intervention (both the experimental and control groups showed gains on this measure, simply as a function of practice answering these questions), there were significant differences indicated on the analogy questions (i.e., those questions that required the students to use information in the text to solve a novel problem). The gains made by the experimental students between the first and second half of intervention were significantly greater than those indicated by the control students on these measures, $F(1,33) = 5.02, p < .02$.

Finally, we have suggested that, while mastering the strategies is not the principal goal of instruction, the ability to engage in independent use of the strategies is certainly a desirable by-product of instruction. While both groups were earning about 26% of the total points possible on the pretest measure, the experimental group earned 48% of the points possible on the posttest measure and the control group earned but 33% of the points possible. This represents a significant difference between the experimental and control groups, $F(1,33) = 4.16, p < .03$.

Students participating in the collaborative and supportive context of reciprocal teaching dialogues outperformed matched, control children on measures of independent listening comprehension, strategy use, and ability to use the information in text to solve novel problems.

Examining Variability in Dialogic Instruction and Instructional Outcomes

Evaluating the discussions and determining the reasons for successful and less successful dialogue is not an easy undertaking. There is always a certain degree of crudeness to the method employed. The interactive nature of the dialogue makes it difficult to ascertain where the breakdown is occurring when the dialogue is not going well; principally, it is difficult to tease apart the skill of the teacher and the ability and heterogeneity of the students in the group. However, there are two indices that we have found helpful in analyzing student/ teacher dialogues.

One is to label the kinds of statements that teachers make in three broad categories: *instructional/modeling statements* (e.g., "As I summarize, I am going to think first, what is the topic of this part?"); *prompting statements* (e.g., "Why don't you ask us about. . .";); and, *reinforcing statements* (e.g., "Good for you, that was an important idea to clarify"). Interesting trends emerge from this kind of analysis. Teacher A was a teacher whose group dialogues afforded many of the opportunities discussed earlier in the previous section of this chapter. On Day 5 of instruction, the proportion of statements this teacher made that were categorized as instructional in nature was 45%, while prompting statements consisted of 43% of her statements and only 13% could be characterized as praise statements. This is in contrast to Teacher B whose instructional statements on Day 5 represented only 12% of her statements, while 81% were prompting, and 7% were reinforcing statements. Teacher A is actively engaged in modeling and instruction at this time, while Teacher B is already engaged in the type of instructional activity we associate with coaching. Interestingly, by Day 8, while Teacher A has reduced the proportion of her instructional statements to 33%, Teacher B has increased hers, although only to 17%. Teacher A is now relying more on prompting and reinforcing statements to sustain the dialogue. Toward the conclusion of the intervention, Teacher A has once again reduced the proportion of her instructional statements to 17% while concurrently increasing prompting and reinforcing statements. Teacher B continues to make a high proportion of prompting statements.

A second index is to determine the extent to which the students are able to function more independently of the teacher over time. For example, when we juxtapose the interchanges between Teachers A and B and their students, an interesting profile emerges. The pattern for Day 5 looks quite similar across both groups with the teachers and students turn-taking in a predictable pattern.

The teacher's turn is followed by a student's turn, which is followed by the teacher's, and so on. However, on Day 18, Group A's pattern looks quite different from Day 5 as well as quite different from Group B's pattern. On Day 18, the students in Group A are able to attain as many as ten exchanges independently of their teacher. In contrast, on Day 18, Teacher B remains pivotal to the lesson. In almost every instance, her turn is followed by a child's turn, followed by the teacher's turn, maintaining a pattern very similar to the one identified for Day 5.

Is this instructional variability reflected in the performance of the students? The results of the comprehension assessments that were administered throughout the intervention suggest that there are indeed differences in the gains reflected by the students. While Group B students showed some initial response to the instruction for the first third of the intervention, there is no further change over time (comprehension assessment scores maintained at 52% accuracy or less throughout the duration of the intervention), while Group A continues to make gains throughout the course of instruction and, in fact, the group mean indicates 75% accuracy with the comprehension questions for the last third of the intervention phase.

Examinations regarding qualitative differences in dialogue and concommitant differences in the gains indicated by students suggest the need to tease apart further discrete characteristics that can be shared with teachers who are interested in using dialogic activities to scaffold learning.

ISSUES AND AGENDAS

Reciprocal teaching is a collaborative learning procedure developed to improve children's ability to understand text. The theoretical underpinnings of reciprocal teaching attribute conceptual change to the process of internalizing cognitive activities that were originally experienced in a social context. The results of eight years of research testify to the robustness of this theory. However, there are numerous issues emanating from this research that remain largely unexplored and constitute an interesting research agenda. These issues include: the strategies used to bolster dialogic instruction across content areas; the preparation of teachers to engage in learning dialogues; and the role of peer collaboration in cognitive instruction.

The strategies used in reciprocal teaching—questioning, summarizing, predicting, and clarifying—were derived from theoretical and empirical treatments of comprehension activity. There has a been a degree of refinement in the application of these four strategies in the dialogue over recent years, reflecting current research. For example, we incorporated the instruction of story grammar to strengthen the summaries of young children working with narrative text. Basically, however, these strategies have remained the same. It is certainly worth asking whether these are, in fact, the most efficacious comprehension strategies with which to structure the dialogues to enhance text comprehension.

With the current emphasis on teaching critical thinking skills across the curriculum, the use of learning dialogues across content areas presents an important area of inquiry. To date, we have been concerned principally with children's learning of naturally occurring grade-appropriate expository text. These texts, covering a range of issues, permit little opportunity for the children to accumulate information and the assessments that accompany them are tests of encapsulated knowledge. In our most recent work we used a series of passages that contain basic biological principles, such as camouflage, animal adaptations, and biological deterrents (Brown, Palincsar, Ryan & Slattery, work in progress). The content promotes discussions where children are using bodies of knowledge over time. Preliminary analyses of the dialogues and assessment data indicate that the children are accumulating, using, and transferring this knowledge. In addition, long-term maintenance checks (conducted six months after instruction was completed) support that the children retain both the strategies used in the dialogues as well as the content of the discussions.

Investigating the use of dialogue across the curriculum will be faciliated by the burgeoning of cognitive research across the content areas revealing more about the strategic activity good learners routinely bring to mathematical and scientific problem solving. Research of this nature will identify potential strategies for structuring learning dialogues in these domains.

The teacher's role in supporting the students' participation in the learning dialogues is, without question, a demanding one. For example, as we have suggested, the dialogue process provides rich opportunities for the teacher to conduct diagnoses of the impediments to comprehension and the chance to model the processes of successful comprehension. However, to engage successfully in this diagnosis and modeling, the teacher must possess some degree of pedagogical knowledge (Shulman, 1986) regarding, for example, comprehension processes, the demands of comprehension tasks, and the variables that interact in reading/listening activity. We have but mere glimpses of the role this knowledge plays in a teacher's success with dialogic instruction.

There is a significant amount of research to be done, exploring how, at both the preservice and inservice levels, teachers' knowledge of learning and teaching can be nurtured. At the inservice level, we are currently collaborating with teachers who have been involved in reciprocal teaching research as they educate other teachers regarding the procedure (for example, by conducting demonstration lessons). Furthermore, teachers who are new to the procedure are working in pairs, observing one another and debriefing with one another. These implementation models are being investigated to determine how teachers might learn the effective implementation of instructional dialogues in a supportive environment.

The role of peer collaboration in supporting the learning dialogues is the one about which we currently know the least. This is, in part, a consequence of how little is known regarding peer interaction for cognitive development. In reciprocal teaching research, the peer groups have been fairly homogeneous to the extent that all or virtually all of the participants were from remedial or at-risk populations. However, we noticed very early in our work that there are interesting implications when there is a diversity of ability present in the group. The diversity is catalytic to the extent that peers can serve as additional models of comprehension monitoring. Furthermore, we are aware of occasions when peers more successfully identified the source of difficulty in text than did their teachers. However, there are limits to the diversity that can be successfully handled by a teacher. For example, issues regarding the level of difficulty of the text and the pacing of the lesson become more critical as the group membership becomes more diverse. If there is too much diversity, it is difficult to identify reading material that is equally challenging to all members and difficult to maintain a pace to the dialogue satisfactory to all.

As reciprocal teaching has been conducted traditionally, the peers share the work of constructing the meaning of the text. There are no designated roles for the individuals beyond the turn-taking as "discussion leader." In an exploratory study in which we prepared students to tutor their peers in reciprocal teaching, there were some interesting implications (Palincsar, Brown, & Martin, 1987). The peers took the ascribed role of teacher very seriously and were acknowledged in this role by their tutees. This situation served to constrain the interaction of the group to a degree. For example, there was much less co-construction of text than is typical for reciprocal teaching dialogues. As learning dialogues are investigated across problem-solving domains, it will be interesting to contrast the value of having students share the problem-solving activity with the value of assigning legislated responsibilities, such as explaining, questioning, and monitoring. Observations of children who have received instruction and guidance with regard to learning in group interactions will provide important insights into the mechanisms by which children acquire self-regulatory knowledge.

ACKNOWLEDGMENTS

The research reported in this paper was supported by PHS Grant 05951 from the National Institute of Child Health and Human Development and OSE Grant G008400648 from the Department of Eduation. Special thanks are due Kathryn Ransom, Reading Coordinator, School District #186, Springfield, Illinois; her enthusiastic support of reciprocal teaching has contributed enormously to the success of this research program. In addition, we wish to acknowledge the many fine teachers who have participated in our research, including Mrs. Derber, Ms. Hagerman, and Mrs. Mackey who have given us permission to "listen in" on their instruction via the transcripts of dialogue occurring in their classrooms.

NOTES

1. After about seven minutes of unproductive activity on Danielle's part, her musings erupted into strident declarations: "Look at all these damn pieces! They should have put it together for you!" These remarks bore a remarkable similarity to another dialogue in Danielle's recent history; one she observed occurring between her parents as they struggled to assemble a Christmas tree stand. As any parent knows, it is not always "intellectual development" that is fostered through dialogue.

2. The children's names have been changed to maintain their anonymity; however, the teachers have granted us permission to use their names.

REFERENCES

Allington, R. (1980). Teacher interruption behavior during primary-grade oral reading. *Journal of Educational Psychology, 72,* 371-377.

Bereiter, C., & Bird, M. (1985). Use of thinking aloud in identification and teaching of reading comprehension strategies. *Cognition and Instruction, 2,* 131-156.

Berk, L.E. (in press). Relationship of elementary school children's private speech to behavioral accompaniment to task, attention and task performance. *Developmental Psychology.*

Berk, L.E., & Garvin, R.A. (1984). Development of private speech among low-income Appalachian children. *Developmental Psychology, 20,* 271-286.

Bloome, D., & Green, J. (1984). Directions in the social sociolinguistic study of reading.In P.D. Pearson, M. Kamil, R. Barr, & P. Mosenthal (Eds.), *Handbook of reading research* (pp. 395-421). New York: Longman.

Brophy, J. (1987, April). *Teachers' strategies.* Paper presented at the Annual Meeting of the American Educational Research Association, Washington, D.C.

Brown, A.L., Campione, J.C., & Day, J.D. (1981). Learning to learn: On training students to learn from texts. *Educational Research, 10,* 14-21.

Brown, A.L., & Palincsar, A.S. (1987). Reciproal teaching of comprehension strategies. A natural history of one program for enhancing learning. In J. Borkowski & J.D. Day (Eds.), *Intelligence and cognition in special children* (pp. 81-132). New York: Ablex.

Brown, A.L., Palincsar, A.S., & Armbruster, B. (1984). Inducing comprehension-fostering activities in interactive learning situations. In H. Mandle, N. Stein, & T. Trabasso (Eds.), *Learning from texts* (pp. 255-287). Hillsdale, NJ: Lawrence Erlbaum.

Brown, A.L., Smiley, S.S., Day, J.D., Townsend, M.A.R., & Lawton, S.C. (1976). Intrusion of thematic idea in children's comprehension and retention of stories. *Child Development, 48,* 1454-1466.

Bruner, J.S. (1978). The role of dialogue in language acquisition. In A. Sinclair, R.J. Jarvella, & W.J.M. Levelt (Eds.), *The child's conception of language* (pp. 241-256). New York: Springer-Verlag.

Cazden, C.B. (1983). Adult assistance to language development: Scaffolds, models, and direct instruction. In R.P. Parker & F.A. Davis (Eds.), *Developing literacy*. Newark, DE: IRA.

Cazden, C.B. (1986). Classroom discourse. In M.C. Wittrock (Ed.), *Handbook of research on teaching* (pp. 432-463). New York: Macmillan.

Collins, J. (1982). Discourse style, classroom interaction and differential treatment. *Journal of Reading Behavior, 14*, 429-437.

Deutsch, F., & Stein, A. (1972). The effects of personal responsibility and task interruption on the private speech of preschoolers. *Human Development, 15*, 310-324.

Duffy, G.G., Roehler, L.R., Meloth, M.D., Vavrus, L.G., Book, C., Putnam, J., & Wesselman, R. (1986). The relationship between explicit verbal explanations during reading skill instruction and student awareness and achievement: A study of reading teacher effects. *Reading Research Quarterly, 21*, 237-252.

Duffy, G.G., Roehler, L.R., Sivan, E., Rackliffe, G., Book, C., Meloth, M.S., Vavrus, L.G., Wesselman, R., Putnam, J., Bassiri, D. (1987). Effects of explaining the reasoning associated with using reading strategies. *Reading Research Quarterly, 22*, 347-368.

Frauenglass, M.H., & Diaz, R.M. (1985). Self-regulatory functions of children's private speech: A critical analysis of recent challenges to Vygotsky's theory. *Developmental Psychology, 21*, 357-364.

Fuson, K.C. (1979). The development of self-regulating aspects of speech: A review. In G. Zivin (Ed.), *The development of self-regulation through private speech* (pp. 135-218). New York: Wiley.

Gall, M.D. (1984). Synthesis of research on questioning in recitation. *Educational Leadership, 42*(3), 40-49.

Garner, R. (1987). *Metacognition and reading comprehension*. Norwood, NJ: Ablex.

Goodman, S. (1981). The integration of verbal and motor behavior in preschool. *Child Development, 52*, 280-289.

Green, J. (1983). Research on teaching as a linguistic process: A state of the art. In E. Gordon (Ed.), *Review of research in education* (Vol. 10). Washington, DC: American Educational Research Association.

Harris, K.R., & Graham, S. (1985). Improving learning disabled students' composition skills: Self-control strategy training. *Learning Disability Quarterly, 8*, 27-36.

Heath, S.B. (1983). *Ways with words: Language, life, and work in communities and classrooms*. Cambridge: Cambridge University Press.

Kohlberg, L., Yaeger, J., & Hjertholm, E. (1968). Private speech: Four studies and a review of theories. *Child Development, 39*, 691-736.

McDermott, R. (1976). *Kids make sense: Ethnographic account of the interactional management of success and failure in one first grade classroom*. Unpublished doctoral dissertation, Stanford University.

Mason, J.M., McCormick, C., & Bhavnagri, N. (1986). How are you going to help me learn? Lesson negotiations between a teacher and preschool children. In D.B. Yaden, Jr. & S. Templeton (Eds.), *Metalinguistic awareness and beginning literacy: Conceptualizing what it means to read and write* (pp. 159-172). Portsmouth, NH: Heinemann.

Mehan, H. (1979). *Learning lessons*. Cambridge: Harvard University Press.

Meichenbaum, D., & Asarnow, J. (1978). Cognitive behavioral modification and metacognitive development: Implications for the classroom. In P. Kendall & S. Hollon (Eds.), *Cognitive behavioral interventions: Theory, research, and procedure* (pp. 11-32). New York: Academic Press.

Meichenbaum, D., & Goodman, J. (1971). Training impulsive children to talk to themselves: A means of developing self control. *Journal of Abnormal Psychology, 77*, 115-126.

Mosenthal, J.H. (in press). The comprehension experience and teaching to it. In D. Muth (Ed.), *Children's comprehension of narrative and expository text: Research into practice.* Newark, DE: IRA.

Ninio, A., & Bruner, J. (1978). The achievement and antecedents of labelling. *Journal of Child Language, 5,* 1-15.

Palincsar, A.S. (1986). The role of dialogue in providing scaffolded instruction. *Educational Psychologist, 21* (1 & 2), 73-98.

Palincsar, A.S., & Brown, A.L. (1984). Reciprocal teaching of comprehension-fostering and comprehension-monitoring activities. *Cognition and Instruction, 1,* 117-175.

Palincsar, A.S., & Brown, A.L. (1988). Teaching and practicing thinking skills to promote comprehension in the context of group problem solving. *Remedial and Special Education, 9,* 53-59.

Palincsar, A.S., Brown, A.L., & Martin, S. (1987). Peer interaction in reading comprehension instruction. *Educational Psychologist, 22,* 231-352.

Palincsar, A.S., Brown, A.L., & Samuel, M. (in progress). *From skill builders to building skills: The adoption of reciprocal teaching by a middle-school district.*

Paris, S.G., & Oka, E.R. (1986). Self-regulated learning among exceptional children. *Exeptional Children, 53,* 103-108.

Peterson, P.L., Fennema, E., Carpenter, T.P., & Loef, M. (1989). Teacher's pedagogical content beliefs in mathematics. *Cognition and Instruction, 6* (1), 1-40.

Pressley, M. Borkowski, J.G., & Schneider, W. (1987). Good strategy users coordinate metacognition, strategy use, and knowledge. In R. Vasta & G. Whitehurst (Eds.), *Annals of child development* (Vol. 4, pp. 89-130). Greenwich, CT: JAI Press.

Robin, A.L., Armel, S., & O'Leary, D. (1975). The effects of self-instruction on writing deficiencies. *Behavior Therapy, 6,* 178-187.

Rogoff, B., Ellis, S., & Gardner, W. (1984). Adjustment of adult-child instruction according to child's age and task. *Developmental Psychology, 20,* 193-199.

Schunk, D.H. (1986). Verbalization and children's self-regulated learning. *Contemporary Educational Psychology, 11,* 347-369.

Scollon, R. (1976). *Conversations with a one year old: A case study of the developmental foundation of syntax.* Honolulu: University Press of Hawaii.

Schoenfeld, A.H. (1985). *Mathematical problem solving.* Orlando: Academic Press.

Shulman, L.S. (1986). Paradigms and research programs in the study of teaching: A contemporary perspective. In M.C. Wittrock (Ed.), *Handbook of research on teaching.* New York: Macmillan.

Snow, C.E. (1977). The development of conversation between mothers and babies. *Journal of Child Language, 4,* 1-22.

Vygotsky, L.S. (1962). *Thought and language.* Cambridge, MA: MIT Press.

Vygotsky, L.S. (1978). In M. Cole, V. John-Steiner, S. Scribner, & E. Souberman (Eds.), *Mind in society: The development of higher psychological processes.* Cambridge, MA: Harvard University Press.

Vygotsky, L.S (1986). In A. Kozulin (Ed.), *Thought and language.* Cambridge, MA: MIT Press.

Wertsch, J.V. (1980). The significance of dialogue in Vygotsky's account of social, egocentric, and inner speech. *Contemporary Educational Psychology, 5,* 150-162.

Wood, P. Bruner, J., & Ross, G. (1976). The role of tutoring in problem solving. *Journal of Child Psychology and Psychiatry, 17,* 89-100.

Wood, D., & Middleton, D. (1975). A study of assisted problem-solving. *British Journal of Psychology, 66,* 181-191.

Zivin, G. (1972). Functions of private speech during problem solving in preschool children. *Dissertation Abstracts International, 33,* 1872.

*   *   *

CROSS-TALK

Are there contradictions between the instructional procedures recommended by Duffy and Roehler (this volume, pp. 1-33) and the instructional recommendations in this paper?

Our approaches do not represent contradictions as much as they do differences. Perhaps the most significant distinction between responsive elaboration and reciprocal teaching is the proleptic nature of reciprocal teaching. Proleptic instruction refers to instruction in anticipation of competence (Stone & Wertsch, 1984). In proleptic instruction, the plan is for the child to come to an understanding of the cognitive task via participation in completing the task. Proleptic instruction can be contrasted with responsive elaboration to the extent that there is no attempt to make the task explicit before engaging the learners in the task. Proleptic instruction maximizes the *active participation of the learner in constructing an understanding of the task.* All students are expected to participate in the dialogue with the support of the teacher and with the support of one another. From a Vygotskian perspective, this opportunity to construct shared meanings of the task through social interaction is critical to meaningful learning (Vygotsky, 1978). The differences between proleptic instruction and explanation provide rich grounds for empirical research.

Regarding the "Lions in the Grass" dialogue, why did the teacher not simply begin with a "didactic" introduction to the story telling the children that they were going to be hearing about dandelions?

We respond to this question by identifying three of the significant opportunities that might well have been lost had the teacher simply told the children "up-front" the topic of the story. First, consider the engagement of the children as they work to reconcile differences between the preconceived ideas that have been activated through their predictions with the information that is presented in text. There is a high degree of involvement on the part of the students; they spontaneously interrupt the reading to reflect on what they have heard, they take issue with one another, and elaborate upon one another's contributions. Second, keeping in mind that the purpose of this lesson was not to teach children about dandelions, but rather to teach children about the task and activity of comprehension, this provided a powerful lesson on the need to monitor one's understanding; to actively test the connections between one's prior knowledge and the new knowledge presented in the text. The final opportunity we describe relates to what the teacher learned from this dialogue. The teacher was struck by the tenacity the children displayed in this discussion and the skill of the children in providing warrants and backings for their interpretations (e.g., "dandelions do eat grass . . . they kill the grass that is all around it").

Without this dialogue there would not have been such a diagnostic oportunity. Furthermore, as we know from the work of Anderson and Roth (this volume, pp. 265-309), and Alvermann and her colleagues (cf. Alvermann, Smith, & Readance, 1985), simply telling the children that they were going to hear a story about dandelions would not have ensured that the children would not persist in their belief that they were hearing about lions whose teeth are green because, after all, they eat grass.

Is an important goal of dialogic instruction "helping students to conceive an appropriate goal for reading?"

This is a very important issue that I believe is related to the *co-construction of task* regardless of the content area. It is a feature of instruction that is presented in the majority of chapters in this volume.

What about the interaction between dialogic instruction and the social environment of the classroom?

The points that Linda Anderson raises are particularly relevant to this issue (this volume, pp. 311-343). Unfortunately, it is only recently that we have begun, in our research, to systematically and formally attend to teachers' beliefs and implicit theories and the relationships among these and implementation of dialogic instruction.

The preliminary work that we have conducted (Palincsar, Stevens, & Gavelek, 1989) supports that teachers' beliefs, specifically with regard to the process of knowledge acquisition, have an important role to play in determining the potential role for dialogic instruction. To illustrate this point, consider the following responses two of our teachers made to the question, "Are there some learning outcomes that are best achieved by having students learn from one another?" One teacher responded that there were some types of learning that could occur *only* among children while a second teacher responded that, "given a strong teacher, I can imagine nothing that would not be better learned from the teacher." When examining the dialogues in these two teachers' classrooms, there were several striking differences: The turn-taking patterns in the dialogues were different. There were twice the number of opportunities for the students to contribute to the dialogue in the first teacher's class and, while the ratio of student to teacher exchanges increased dramatically in the first group, the ratio remained static for the second group.

What is the relationship between content instruction and reciprocal teaching instruction?

This is a very important issue and one that we have talked with teachers about considerably as we have attempted to strike a satisfactory balance between comprehension instruction and content instruction. We have been guided in our recommendations to teachers in the following way: Reciprocal teaching is, first and foremost, a way of teaching children how to interact with text, how to construct meaning from text. At the point where the teacher initiates reciprocal teaching dialogues, teachers are making conscious decisions to forfeit content coverage in at least two respects. First, very simply, the time that it takes to work through the text implies that less content will be covered. Furthermore, the teacher makes decisions that render the immediate goals of reciprocal teaching apparent. For example, there is no attempt to build background knowledge prior to having the children read the text beyond the activity of the children and teacher (initially) generating predictions for the purpose of activating background knowledge and setting up expectations of the text. Instructionally, this would probably not be the most advised procedure if the principal concern were content acquisition. Typically, if content acquisition were the chief goal, then we would expect that teachers would probably "build" (not just activate) background knowledge prior to reading the text. However, if the goal of instruction is to enable the students to independently read and make sense of text, then teaching children the desirability of and means to activate their own knowledge and frame expectations becomes important.

I do not want the distinction made above to suggest that we intend to divorce comprehension and comprehension monitoring instruction from learning. Typically, the purpose for reading texts in school is for the purpose of learning. I would suggest that the type of learning in which R.T. children are engaged is the assimilation of new knowledge, not the kind of learning that requires restructuring of knowledge.

But I also think it is possible that dialogic instruction can be useful, is perhaps even essential, to knowledge restructuring. My impression, not based on empirical data, but rather based on foreshadowings from the little biological themes work we attempted is that the first step might be to teach students sense-making for the purpose of knowledge retention and assimilation and then proceed to knowledge restructuring.

What are the variables that seem to operate in reciprocal teaching dialogues among peers?

We have found in our work that the single best predictor of successful peer/peer dialogues is the success that the teacher has engaging the students in teacher/student dialogues. Our teachers have suggested that the most important elements to sustain peer/peer dialogues include: establishing a climate in which everyone's ideas are listened to and taken seriously, children feel comfortable disagreeing with one another and with the teacher, and "wait time" is recognized as valuable "think time." In addition, the teachers report that the support for the dialogue that is provided by the strategies used to scaffold the discussion enables peer exchanges because the agenda is understood by all the participants. Finally, we have observed that from a sociological perspective, it is simply easier to get first graders to talk with one another than it is seventh graders, for whom there seems to be a norm against peer/peer dialogues (at least around academic learning).

References to Cross-talk

Alvermann, D.E., Smith, L.C., & Readance, J.E. (1985). Prior knowledge activation and the comprehension of compatible and incompatible text. *Reading Research Quarterly, 20*(4), 420-436.

Palincsar, A.S., Stevens, D.D., & Gavelek, J.R. (1989). Collaboration with teachers in the interest of student collaboration. *International Journal of Educational Research, 13*, 41-53.

Stone, C.A., & Wertsch, J.V. (1984). A social interactional analysis of learning disabilities remediation. *Journal of Learning Disabilities, 17*, 194-199.

Vygitsky, L.S. (1978). In M. Cole, V. John-Steiner, S. Scribner, & E. Souberman (Eds.), *Mind in society: The development of higher psychological processes.* Cambridge, MA: Harvard University Press.

THE ROLE OF INSTRUCTION
IN LEARNING TO WRITE

Susan Florio-Ruane and Timothy Lensmire

OVERVIEW

This paper reviews recent research on writing and relates it to advances in instruction. Background information about cognitive, developmental, and social research is offered to show that written literacy involves higher order thinking and meaningful communication. This view of literacy influences our conceptions of teacher, learner, and instruction. The chapter focuses on writing research in relation to two important but often neglected aspects of teaching: the instructional role of teacher/student talk about student texts and the creation of meaningful school writing tasks. A description of instruction is offered which supports the development of higher order thinking and writing skills and leads to students' gradual attainment of independence and self-regulation as authors.

TOWARD AN INSTRUCTIONALLY USEFUL
DEFINITION OF WRITING

How we define writing significantly influences the way we think about the teacher, the learner, and teaching. Thus a good place to begin an examination

Advances in Research on Teaching, Volume 1, pages 73-104.
Copyright © 1989 by JAI Press Inc.
All rights of reproduction in any form reserved.
ISBN: 0-89232-845-2

of writing instruction and the teacher and learner's roles within it is by defining written literacy. While definitions of literacy change with history and circumstance, contemporary educational theorists and practitioners in our society define writing as a complex and meaningful sociocognitive process (see Scardamalia & Bereiter [1986] for a review of this current research).

Most of us can remember when research on writing was limited primarily to categorizing and describing genres and when instruction stressed the drill and practice of rules and procedures for producing well-formed texts. In contrast, contemporary research and practice in writing emphasize the composing process—its nature, development, and social functions. In this regard, Frederiksen and Dominic (1981) propose a taxonomy of theoretical perspectives on writing which "emphasizes different aspects of writing processes and influences on them; yet are all concerned centrally with understanding the writing process" (p. 2). The four views of writing offered in their taxonomy of current research help us to define writing as:

1. a cognitive activity;
2. a particular form of language and language use;
3. a communicative process; and
4. a contextualized, purposive activity.

Written literacy involves the ability to use higher order thinking skills to create text that is meaningful within particular social situations and institutions. We shall see that this view of writing exerts powerful influences on current instructional roles and practices.

Mature Writing as the Goal of Instruction

Writing theorists see mature writing as the goal of instruction. Research on the thinking of mature writers finds that their writing involves mastery of the technical skills of written language production, knowledge of higher order intellectual processes such as planning and revision, and an understanding of textual forms and functions. While technical skills are essential and knowledge of text structure is central to literacy, current views suggest that far more than this is involved in becoming a mature writer.

Mature writing is thinking about and manipulating text to make it expressive of an author's intentions and meaningful to a reader. An author is able to realize writing's purposes and fulfill them in text. To do this he or she needs to know the graphic, lexical, syntactic, and semantic tools of written language. Moreover, he or she needs to consider purpose, topic, and audience, and relate decisions about text production to these considerations. Finally, written literacy involves assuming the role of author in social situations where writing is one or even the most appropriate of expressive alternatives.

Both mature writers and those learning to write may be called upon to collaborate in producing texts. Moreover, they may find themselves writing in fulfillment of purposes set by others. This is particularly the case when writing is undertaken in the public, institutional settings of school and workplace. In these situations, writing is an act of social rather than private invention (LeFevre, 1987). Yet written literacy depends on knowing how to write toward a range of situations and purposes—some private and self-initiated, others collaborative and public—and assumes a considerable degree of independence and self-regulation.

Learning to write involves not only achieving propositional and procedural knowledge of language structure and norms, but also acquiring beliefs, values, and attitudes about self, others, and text. A mature writer can perceive and use writing as a tool for communicating and also as a means of furthering his or her own thinking and learning of new subject matter (Rosaen, this volume, pp. 153-194). This expansive definition of mature writing is complex and multifaceted. A great deal needs to be taught and learned in the gradual transformation of beginner to experienced writer. How to support and extend learners' development on the way to the attainment of written literacy challenges and expands the horizons of instruction.

INSTRUCTION AND WRITING GROWTH

Applebee (1986), summarizing across many recent studies of writing and how it is learned, cites three general findings which seem to have particular relevance to instruction. They highlight writing as a cognitive activity whose development is supported by the social process of instruction:

1. Writing involves a number of recursively operating subprocesses (for example, planning, monitoring, drafting, revising, editing) rather than a linear sequence.
2. Expert and novice writers differ in their use of those subprocesses.
3. The processes vary depending upon the nature of the task. More recent studies have suggested that the processes also vary depending on the instructional context, personal history, and knowledge the writer has about the topic. (p. 96)

The writing instruction most of us remember did not necessarily lead to meaningful communication or to our becoming efficient, autonomous composers. It typically involved the creation of grammatically correct written products to fulfill a limited menu of teacher-assigned purposes and topics. The ability to produce these products was thought to derive from step-wise drill and practice of writing sub-skills (i.e., first letter formation, next spelling, then forming sentences, and finally structuring paragraphs and longer texts).

Contemporary instruction, largely influenced by research on cognition and oral language development, dwells less on direct teaching of isolated rules and sub-processes or on a narrow set of written forms and functions. Instead, teachers and researchers take a holistic approach to the composing process stressing gradual shifts in thinking and writing as novices become more expert. Writers learn and practice many subskills within the context of varied and meaningful writing tasks and enjoy the opportunity to participate in defining at least some of those tasks. Writing growth is seen in this context as a consequence of development supported by teaching.

The Development of Writing

Scardamalia and Bereiter (1986) have demonstrated in numerous studies that beginning writers differ from experienced ones in their approaches to writing and in their realization of its sub-processes. Yet while novices appear to differ greatly from experts in most aspects of writing, even very young children tackle writing as a purpose-driven symbolic activity. They practice the means of text production, not piecemeal and out of context, but by creating whole and meaningful work. This work initially takes the form of scribbles, pictures, or invented spellings because children write even before they have learned to form letters or words (Sulzby, 1986). This view of the acquisition of written language mirrors in many respects what we know of children's acquisition of oral language.

Young children openly and eargerly use written or drawn symbols to represent ideas and realize a limited range of purposes. Gundlach (1985) argues that they are building bridges to mature writing from childhood symbolic activities such as drawing, play, story telling/listening, and imitation of adults. Once in school, formal instruction supports and extends children's learning of the conventions and appropriate uses of written language in our society. Summarizing the instructionally-relevant features of this process as it relates to the learning of both speech and writing, Temple, Nathan, and Burris (1982) make the following assertions:

1. Children normally take a great deal of initiative in learning to talk and in learning to write;

2. Children must be surrounded by language used in meaningful ways if they are to learn to talk; the same is true of written language if they are to learn to write (and read);

3. Children learn to talk by formulating tentative rules about the way language works, trying them out, and gradually revising them. At first, they make many mistakes in speech, but they gradually correct them. In writing we see errors of letter formation, spelling, and composition occurring as children make hypotheses about the rules that govern the writing system; errors give way to other errors before they arrive at correct forms;

4. Children generally do not start using correct forms of speech as a result of direct teaching; speech forms change only gradually. In writing, too, spelling forms and composition strategies will not be immediately improved by corrective teaching but through gradual conceptual learning that is controlled by the child as much as by the teacher;

5. Children learn to talk to meet a range of personal needs, and they learn to vary their use of language as their needs and purposes change and as they have opportunities to use language functionally. Writing serves different purposes, too; and there are unique forms of writing for each function. Children must have opportunities to use writing meaningfully to serve different purposes in order to develop complete literacy;

6. Any spoken language is an immensely complicated thing; no one yet has succeeded in writing down all of the rules that explain how any natural language works. Thus it is absurd to suppose that we could teach our children to talk by explaining the language to them—we don't understand the language well enough ourselves to do that. People somehow learn spoken language on a working level, but this does not enable them to explain their knowledge of it to others. Written language has never been fully understood, either. None of us understands writing well enough to explain to someone else how to write, unless that other person exerts his powers to learn for himself. (pp. 9-10)

These research-based assertions by no means diminish the importance of the teacher or instruction, but they do transform our traditional views of what is taught and how to teach it. Because teachers cannot teach writing simply by explaining it as a process or body of rules, and because they must share responsibility for literacy acquisition with learners, they are challenged to provide meaningful occasions for learners to practice a myriad of writing skills and a broad range of written language functions. Moreover teachers serve an essential role as diagnosticians who read and make instructive responses to learners' written work.

THE ROLE OF INSTRUCTION IN LEARNING TO WRITE

When teaching toward higher order thinking and independent learning in literacy education and elsewhere, teachers must manage a dynamic tension between observing the learner's work and intervening in it. Temple et al. (1982) put the matter simply saying: "The best teacher responds to what the child is trying to do" (p. viii). However, that sentence oversimplifies the teacher's role because it leaves out awareness of instructional goals. Hawkins (1974) elaborates usefully on both the matter of teacher response and on instructional responsibility. He says,

The function of a teacher, then, is to respond diagnostically and helpfully to a child's behavior, to make what he considers to be an appropriate response, a response which the child needs to complete the process he's engaged in at a given moment. (p. 53)

But, recognizing the teacher's responsibility to plan the curriculum and teach beyond the task at hand so that ultimately the learner will be able to complete similar tasks and continue to learn unaided, Hawkins adds,

> When *you* give a child a range from which to make choices, the choices *he* makes in turn give you the basis for deciding what should be done next, what the provisioning should be for him. This is *your* decision, it's dependent on *your* goals, it's something *you* are responsible for. (p. 57, emphasis in original)

To make instructional responses to students' work is a process of decision making that requires the teacher to understand both learner and curricular goals—and the instructional means likely to help the learner attain those goals.

Embedded in the tasks and talk about writing which teachers and students jointly create are many of the conditions, resources, and social supports necessary for learners to acquire the writing system and use it meaningfully and freely. The fact that writing is jointly created by teachers and learners is not simply a social fact of life. While adult participation provides social mediation and support for the learner's growth (what Bruner [1975] called "instructional scaffolds"), students' opportunities to influence writing tasks enable them gradually to practice and assume a full range of the author's rights and duties.

This realization is a significant one for teachers. In early descriptive studies of classroom writing, for example, Clark and Florio et al. (1981) found that although students wrote a great deal to fulfill both social and academic tasks in classrooms, their responsibility to craft text or identify purposes for writing was greatly limited. As Figure 1 illustrates, authorship was a right and obligation students had limited opportunity to experience. Moreover, writing was used primarily as a means to other social and academic ends. Using primarily published worksheets and lacking a clear sense of a writing curriculum, teachers and students were observed to have the following instructional problems:

1. teachers often missed opportunities to teach about the writing process within the very writing tasks they were requiring students to complete;
2. students were not provided social or academic support gradually to assume more responsibility for the composing process.

This pattern was found at both elementary and middle schools and operated largely outside the awareness of either teachers or students. When brought to participating teachers' attention by means of conversations about research

Function Type	Sample Activity	Initiator	Composer	Writer/Speaker	Audience	Format	Fate	Evaluation
						Distinctive Features		
Type I: Writing to participate in community	classroom rule-setting	teacher	teacher & students	teacher	student	by teacher and students: drafted on chalkboard; printed in colored marker on large white paper	posted; referred to when rules are broken	no
Type II: Writing to know oneself and others	diaries	teacher	student	student	student	by teacher: written or printed on lined paper in student-made booklets	locked in teacher's file cabinet or kept in student desk; occasionally shared with teacher, other students, or family	no
Type III: Writing to occupy free time	letters and cards	student	student	student	other (parents, friends, family)	by student: printed or drawn on lined or construction paper	kept; may be given as gift to parents or friend	no
Type IV: Writing to demonstrate academic competence	science lab booklets	teacher	publisher	publisher & student(s)	teacher	by publisher: printed in commercial booklet	checked by teacher; filed for later use by student; pages sent home to parents by teacher	yes

Source: Clark and Florio (1983). Reprinted with permission.

Figure 1. Functions of Writing and Their Distinctive Features

79

findings, however, heretofore unperceived opportunities to teach about writing within meaningful occasions were identified. In those occasions students could begin to become independent and self-regulated writers (Clark and Florio, 1983). Some of those occasions for writing will be described in a later section of this paper.

CHANGES IN WRITING INSTRUCTION LEAD TO NEW QUESTIONS

Recent research on writing as a sociocognitive process has influenced instructional practice in swift and sweeping ways (Hayes and Flower, 1986). Many teachers are, for example, providing more time for students to practice the writing process. Instead of writing one draft to be evaluated by the teacher, students often have an opportunity to plan, draft, revise, and edit their texts. Some teachers have introduced peer and group meetings in which young writers can discuss their drafts. Many classrooms contain an author's chair where any student may sit and lead a discussion of his or her own text or a favorite book. Teachers often provide writing folders in which students can collect interesting topics and notes for possible drafts. Students have greater liberty to select the topics about which they will write. The educational literature is currently replete with innovative instructional ideas and claims about their power to prompt more fluent and meaningful writing (see Calkins [1986] and Graves [1983] for summaries of these innovations).

Problems and Possibilities of Process-Oriented Instruction

At its best, Applebee asserts, instruction sensitive to the development of the composing process can be "more effective in fostering good writing and breadth of form, and also in encouraging a more reasoned and disciplined thinking about the (writing) topics themselves" (Applebee, 1986, p. 97) . In other words, instructional sensitivity to the writing process and students' developmental work to master it enables both learning to write and writing to learn. Process-oriented instruction can foster the development of technical skills of writing while it expands students' writing repertoires to admit of more purposes and audiences for writing than are typically available either inside or outside school. In addition, application of process-oriented instruction in writing across the curriculum encourages the use of writing as a tool for thinking and learning about academic content in many subject areas (Rosaen, this volume, pp. 153-194).

Transformations of the Teacher's Role

Transformation of the classroom environment and activities for writing instruction has implications for the teacher's role. Teachers of the writing process do not tend to spend the bulk of their instructional time presiding over drill and practice of isolated composition skills or correcting errors on students' written texts. Their roles have become more complex and diversified as they have tried to combine skill instruction with meaningful writing tasks and a more holistic approach to composing. Among their diverse responsibilities are the following:

1. teachers provide *models* of text, the writing process, and the thinking underlying composition;
2. teachers plan *occasions* for the meaningful practice and use of writing in school;
3. teachers make *responses* to students' written work by serving as coaches, tutors, and audiences;
4. teachers offer *direct teaching* in specific composition skills.

As our conception of written literacy has grown to embrace new understandings of the composing process, our views of instruction and the teacher's role have also grown and become more complex. Instruction includes but is not limited to the direct teaching of the skills and subskills of written language production. Teachers who want to help students become independent and self-regulated writers offer models of text itself and the composing process. Often these models mirror or expand and extend the composing work children are already attempting. Additionally, teachers have two unique opportunities to help the young learn to write: They are empowered by our society to create for and with students occasions to use and practice writing as meaningful communication. They are also responsible to guide learning by reading and talking about texts with students.

Unanswered Questions About Instruction

To transform writing instruction for higher order thinking and authorship among students requires changes in classroom procedure and teaching methods. However, these changes do not by themselves provide the full realization of the goals we have set for writing instruction. Opening up the classroom task environment to permit more time and topics for writing, encouraging young writers to talk with peers and teachers about their written work, and embedding skill instruction in meaningful composition are necessary conditions for effective writing instruction. But, by themselves, they are insufficient. The changes described above simply create opportunities for teachers and students to reorient themselves to the writing process. They do not tell teachers how to read and respond to learners' texts or how to design writing tasks likely to lead to meaningful understanding and self-regulated learning among learners. In that sense, process-oriented instruction raises more educational questions than it answers. It raises them particularly in two key instructional areas of talk and task. Of these areas it is worthwhile to ask:

1. What kinds of communication should teachers and students be engaging in so that students can come ultimately to be independent writers?
2. What kinds of tasks should students be asked to accomplish if they are to learn and practice writing as higher order thinking and communication?

We do not have conclusive answers to these questions, although they are of growing interest to educational researchers (Duffy & Roehler, this volume, pp. 1-33; Palincsar & Brown, 1989). Perhaps one of the contributions of writing process research and instruction has been to prompt our asking them. But a great deal of conceptual work remains for both researchers and practitioners. In this vein Applebee (1986) comments that

> Writing processes in general, and the nature of process-oriented instruction in particular, have been underconceptualized. In the first flush of enthusiasm, process-oriented instruction was embraced simplistically and naively; in the next wave we must carry it toward a more sophisticated maturity. (p. 97)

In line with Applebee's challenge, the following sections of this chapter explore two important aspects of writing instruction heretofore underconceptualized in the research and teaching literature: instructional talk about text and meaningful occasions for writing in school.

WRITING INSTRUCTION AS TALK ABOUT TEXT

The work of researchers in several traditions converges on the instructional importance of talk when discussing the teaching and learning of higher order thinking skills. While these scholars differ in their theoretical biases and entering assumptions, there is a growing consensus that writing, like speaking, is a complex cognitive process whose development is dependent on commuication with others. Those with whom a beginner might talk when learning to write are typically members of the culture who are more experienced with rules, conventions, and uses of writing as a tool for communication. Additionally, however, research suggests that a beginner's peers can be powerful audiences for his or her work. In this instance learning to write and learning to read become entwined as beginning authors and audiences talk with one another about how they have made sense of a text and how it might be revised.

A Developmental Perspective

By talking with students about their plans, difficulties, and strategies as they compose text, teachers can provide what Bruner (1975) calls "scaffolds," or instructional supports for writing development (Calkins, 1983). Moreover, by organizing the classroom environment to encourage peer discussions of text, teachers can enhance learning of both reading and writing, increase the range and variety of audiences for student text, and provide more frequent and immediate responses to written work than might otherwise be possible (Freedman and Sperling, 1985; Gere and Stevens, 1985). From the developmental perspective, it is claimed that conversations about writing (often called "writing conferences"), either between teacher and student or among student peers, offer personal and immediate audience response. This helps very young writers over one of composition's greatest hurdles—the problem of taking the perspective of an absent and often unknown reader. The presence and immediate reaction of a reader eases the cognitive burden on young writers and helps them learn to take the perspective of another on their written work. This experience potentially aids in the learning of how and why to revise one's text (Daiute, 1985; Kroll, 1978).

A Cognitive Psychological Perspective

Cognitive psychologists also believe that dialogue about text is important to writing growth but cite slightly different reasons why this might be the case. They argue that the dialogic structure of the conference is gradually internalized as a set of strategies or heuristics. With time and practice, writing strategies are gradually internalized by the beginner so that he or she can have an inner dialogue representing both the writer's intentions and the reader's interpretations. While this process may occur between peers, it may happen most powerfully when a less experienced writer discusses his or her draft with a more experienced one. Particularly in the areas of topic selection, planning, and revision, writing has been viewed by language educators and researchers as dependent to a great degree on the mediation of text production by talk (Daiute, 1985; Graves, 1983; Murray, 1979).

A Sociolinguistic Perspective

A third approach to the study of writing is sociolinguistic. Researchers who study writing from this perspective are interested in the role of written expression in a culture at large. They also study the local situations in a culture or community in which writing is learned and used (Basso, 1974). Here they observe that dialogue is more the rule than the exception in many of life's occasions for writing. In short, talk about text is important in children's acquisition of knowledge about what text is and how it is used (Heath, 1983).

The instructional nature of response to writing is a broad and complex topic. Establishing a classroom climate supportive of peer response and teaching children about how to read and discuss one another's work are among the responsibilities of the teacher (Englert & Raphael, this volume, pp. 105-151). This chapter focuses on teacher response to students' written work both because it is an important aspect of instruction and because with a repertoire of responsive strategies in hand, a teacher may be more likely to foster instructive talk about text among students.

Teacher and Student Involvement in Writing Instruction

In all three views of the social mediation of writing development previously described one important assumption is made—that author and respondent alike will be highly involved in the writing process. This mutual involvement is not self-evident even in classrooms putatively embracing a holistic approach to teaching the writing process. Involvement is sensitive both to social relations (the rights and responsibilities of author and respondent as they are defined or negotiated in the classroom) and to the nature of the writing task (what the author is writing and how and why the respondent reads it). It is not always the case that students will be engaged with their teachers or peers in writing tasks which occasion high mutual involvement. In some cases, less than optimum conditions may exist for writers to discuss their work with others in ways which help them learn more about the writing process. In short, social mediation may be precluded either by the task itself or by the social relations of task participants.

Calkins (1986) offers a helpful figure (attributed to Edward Chittenden) which illustrates four categories of involvement which might occur in a writing classroom (see Figure 2). Paraphrasing and expanding upon Calkins' analysis, note that the figure contains four quadrants representing instructional conditions which might be present in a classroom.

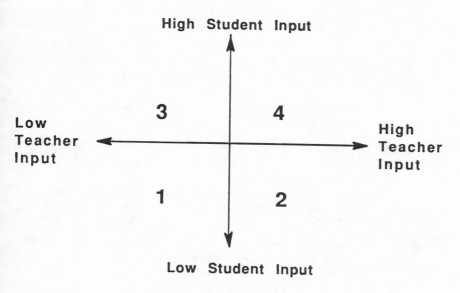

Source: Calkins (1986). Reprinted with permission.

Figure 2.   Four Categories of Involvement in Writing Classrooms

Quadrant 1: Low Teacher and Student Input

Quadrant 1 contains classrooms in which the input or involvement of both teacher and students in the writing process is low. This may be the case for a variety of reasons. For Calkins (1986),

> Classrooms where writing is taught through ditto sheets and langauge arts textbooks belong in quadrant one. In these classrooms, published materials lead students into whatever writing they do, and neither the students nor their teachers invest much energy in written work. (p. 164)

Ethnographic research in elementary and middle school classrooms conducted by Clark et al. (1981) offers another scenario for Quadrant 1. As illustrated in Figure 1, writing in the classrooms they studied had a kind of invisibility—although much writing was undertaken by teachers and students in the course of daily school life, it was taken for granted as a means toward other ends. Thus writing was not explicitly discussed by either teachers or students, and their involvement in writing instruction was low.

Another example of low teacher and student involvement in writing was found in the secondary schools of both Great Britain (Britton, Burgess, Martin,

McLeod, & Rosen, 1975) and the United States (Applebee, 1981). In large surveys of secondary school teachers and students about writing across the content areas, it was found that writing occurs infrequently. The absence of writing on the part of teachers or students in the course of a day, week, or term in school ensures low instructional involvement and little opportunity to learn writing.

Quadrant 2: High Teacher Input and Low Student Input

Quadrant 2 presents another classroom scenario. In this case, teacher input is high, but student input is low. Of this quadrant, Calkins (1986) says,

> Many teachers will probably identify with the second quadrant: high teacher input and low student input. During my first years of teaching, my classroom would have fallen into this category. I wanted to be a creative, committed, and skillful writing teacher, and so I spent long hours writing story starters and responding at great length to everything my students wrote. It never occurred to me that I was one of the only people in that room investing a great deal of energy in writing. (p. 134)

An alternate way to think about the second quadrant is illustrated in Bereiter and Scardamalia's (1987) description of a type of teacher (Teacher B) who attempts to support student writing growth by carefully selecting and sequencing reading and activities to build on students' background knowledge as follows:

> Teacher B emphasizes students' writing about what they know best. If a topic is to be assigned, the class will often spend a week before the writing begins, reading, discussing, drawing, acting, taking trips—any variety of activities to insure ample and available information to draw on in writing. Most often, however, students select their own topics, Teacher B conferring with them individually to help them focus on a topic in which they have genuine interest, and to formulate goals and plans. Teacher B usually does this through Socratic dialogue, in which students are questioned about their interests, experiences, intentions, and so on. Similar conferences are conducted after the first draft has been written, so as to help the student produce a richer second draft. (p. 10)

This approach may, indeed, produce well-formed drafts. However, it is so teacher-directed that it is unlikely to produce the underlying instructional goal of "trying to teach students to do it for themselves" (Bereiter & Scardamalia, 1987, p. 10).

Thus one might observe a classroom in which activity flows smoothly and where students are busy. But the tasks are defined and the social relations organized in such a way as to preclude student participation in shaping the broader conditions of their own writing and learning. In short, task definition is the exclusive domain of the teacher and, as a result, dialogue between teacher and student (or among students) which gradually would permit the student to assume more of the rights and duties of authorship is unlikely.

Another reason why over-determination of the writing task limits learning is illustrated in the work of Flower (1987) and Moffett (1968/1983). Flower reasons from pilot research on task representation in writing classrooms that there are occasions in which it is important for teachers to determine the definition of situation and for students to come to share that definition with teachers via direct instruction. This is a part of how one learns a new written form or function. We must be careful, however, to avoid instruction which suggests that forms and genres and the functions they serve are somehow fixed and easily defined. Moffett (1968/1983) warns against believing too rigidly in what accepted forms and genres look like, saying,

> Though perhaps the best classification of literature so far, genres are too cavalierly equated with form and structure. Actually the structure of a novel or play is at least as much unique to itself as it is shared by other novels and plays. And some stories are poems, some poems stories, some plays essays, and some essays are stories or poems. Perhaps more than anything else, genres are marketing directives. As such, they provide convenient rhetorical bins. Pedagogically, they constitute a hazard by making both teachers and students feel that they have to "define" what a short story or a poem is, i.e., find something similar in all the examples. Even if this were not futile, one would be left with only a definition, another substantive reduction that does not help one to read or write, or even appreciate. (pp. 5-6)

Consistent with Moffett's view of genres, Flower (1987) implies that an important part of mature writing is the capacity to define a writing situation for oneself and mobilize appropriate strategies to write effectively within it. Thus genre, topic, audience, and purpose might be usefully discussed—or even negotiated—between teacher and student as a part of writing instruction (Florio, 1987).

The importance of students and teachers discussing and negotiating what is called for in a writing task becomes more pronounced when we recognize that students from different ethnic backgrounds come to school with differing experience and knowledge in various forms of oral and written discourse. In a study of instructional talk in a multiethnic urban kindergarten, for example, Michaels (1981) found that children from different backgrounds responded to the task of sharing a personal narrative in oral "sharing time" (an activity intended by the teacher to provide practice in literate discourse) with different kinds of discourse. At one level, the teacher and students may have shared a view of the task (or definition of situation) as one of telling personal narratives. For the teacher, however, there was a second, unstated definition of task—the practice in speech of the language of text.

Some children's story-telling matched the teacher's schemata for literate prose in that their talk was topic-centered. For them, sharing time did, indeed, become an "oral preparation for literacy" (Michaels, 1981, p. 423) in the sense that student and teacher collaborated in the construction of a more complex narrative than the child could create by her/himself. But, for the students whose narrative styles did not match the teacher's, sharing time was a frustrating experience. They were responding to the task of oral storytelling and using discourse strategies appropriate to their nonschool experience. They may have missed both the teacher's unstated schemata for text structure and, along with their peers, been unaware of the speaking-reading connection the teacher was drawing. The teacher's responses to these students' narratives assumed that the children knew both her discourse structure and how to share experiences of the school-literate style of topic and supporting detail. In other words, the teacher assumed that she and the students were working on simliar tasks. As these students chained associated topics in extended narratives, they received from the teacher not collaboration to expand their narratives, but limiting corrective responses to a task they did not even share with her.

It was not inappropriate for the teacher to want children to build bridges to the language of school books by oral sharing—children bring from their backgrounds a great deal on which to build in literacy education. But the culture-bound differences in what they bring can lead to differential treatment which limits some students' access to knowledge of higher order composing skills.

Teachers need to be thoughtful of the meaning children are intending to make and the discourse forms they may have already learned for the expression of that meaning. Children whose discourse knowledge does not match the school's very well may find themselves at a disadvantage, not because of incompetence in communication, but because of a difference in style. The instructional importance of student participation in shaping writing tasks, then, not only is in the service of making those tasks more meaningful but addresses the possibility that teachers and students may go about the tasks in different ways and with different background knowledge and assumptions. These differences need to be addressed, discussed, and clarified by teacher and students if all students are to have an opportunity to use the competencies they already possess while working toward new ones.

Quadrant 3: Low Teacher Input and High Student Input

Searching for greater student ownership or responsibility to define and fulfill the writing task, Calkins asserts that many classrooms fall into the third quadrant in Figure 2. Here student input is high but teacher input is low. In contrast to teacher overdetermination of task and social relations, in Quadrant 3 classrooms, students are left primarily to themselves. They are free to determine their own topics, pace, and composing strategies. Moreover, though they talk with others about their texts, teachers, not wishing to appropriate students' rights as authors, effectively withhold helpful and necessary instruction. This quadrant holds many of the classrooms in which the currently popular process approach to teaching writing has been adopted as a method, but where the teacher's instructional role and the goals of the curriculum are not clearly specified. Of this type of classroom Calkins (1986) writes

> Students write up a storm and eargerly share their work in reponse groups. Many students willingly revise. They write in a range of genres, and they write for a variety of purposes. Teachers are amazed at the interest in writing. But the curious thing is that often the writing does not improve with revision, or even over time. Students are apt to write rough draft after rough draft, but they do not know how to hone their strengths or to select what works best in their pieces. Because they lack a sense of what good writing is like, they have no compass to steer by as they write. Meanwhile, out of fear of "taking ownership," teachers desperately avoid teaching. Sometimes, on the sly, they make coy comments such as, "I wonder if there is another sentence you could use as a lead?" This, of course, convinces the students that their teachers have the "right answers" but are hiding them, and so the students try all the harder to wrangle judgments and suggestions out of their teachers. (p. 165)

Documentation of this sort of response to students' work is widespread in the research on writing conferences. Researchers find not only the withholding of strategic instruction as described above, but the subtle insinuation of the teacher's interpretive framework on student work. Entering an unspoken compact in which the teacher and student assume the teacher has the "answer" to a composing problem but will not disclose it, students can spend much time and many drafts scuttling about trying to arrive at the best word or construction to satisfy the teacher (Sperling and Freedman, 1987). All of this occurs without explicit discussion of why the text is being revised as it is. Moreover, as in Quadrant 2 classrooms, where teachers overdetermine writing tasks for students, in Quadrant 3, students' understandings of the writing task are also not discussed but are subordinated here to the search for the answer the teacher is thought to have but will not disclose.

Quadrant 4: High Teacher and Student Input

For Calkins, the fourth quadrant of Figure 2 is the optimum instructional environment. In this quadrant both teacher and student input is high. Note that in other quadrants it may appear that all participants are actively engaged, but in terms of task definition or opportunities for students to talk about their texts and receive helpful responses, meaningful input may be very low. Ideally, in Quadrant 4, teachers and students work together to frame meaningful writing tasks and instruction. This means that students will not only have opportunities to help identify the purposes, topics and audiences for writing, but that their concerns, intentions, and meanings can be voiced and will help shape the nature of the instruction they receive.

Bereiter and Scardamalia (1987) assert that this type of teaching "is only beginning to emerge out of experimental instructional studies specifically concerned wtih the fostering of higher order competencies" (p. 11). In this kind of instruction, students learn not just how to fulfill teachers' tasks and purposes, but how to write and think for and by themselves. Students reach the goal of being their own teachers, however, by being taught in engaging, challenging, and meaningful ways. Despite our lack of research on instructional strategies, Calkins (1986) makes a broad instructional recommendation based on her own practice and descriptive research:

> We should not relinquish our identities as teachers in order to give students ownership of their craft. If we have a tip to give about good writing, why not give it? If we think students need instruction in quotation marks, why not teach them? We need not be afraid to teach, but we do need to think carefully about the kinds of teacher input which will be helpful to our students. (p. 165)

Thinking carefully about teacher input is not simply a matter of thinking about what to *say* to students. It is also a matter of what teachers and students *do* together. What is said about writing inside classrooms is influenced by social norms for participation (who may say what to whom?) and by the writing task being undertaken (what are the participants talking about?). Thus a second aspect of instruction—the tasks we ask students to complete—must be carefully considered when we attempt to teach writing for meaningful communication and self-regulated learning. Ultimately talk about text is embedded in socially organized writing occasions. Thus talk leads to a consideration of task, and the two cannot be fully understood in isolation from one another.

CREATING MEANINGFUL OCCASIONS FOR WRITING

The writings of John Dewey on schools and the learning activities children should experience within them are especially appropriate for the overall themes of this book and discussions of occasions for writing. In general terms, Dewey was concerned with describing the type of schooling necessary for students to understand and act competently and responsibly in their ongoing relations with the social and physical world. This book addresses similar concerns in its focus on instruction for meaningful comprehension and self-regulated learning.

More specifically, the definition of "discipline" Dewey developed in *Democracy and Education* (1944/1966) captures what meaningful comprehension and self-regulated learning entails. Dewey wrote:

> A person who is trained to consider his actions, to undertake them deliberately, is in so far forth disciplined. Add to this ability the power to endure in an intelligently chosen course in face of distraction, confusion, and difficulty, and you have the essence of discipline. Discipline means power at command; mastery of the resources available for carrying through the action undertaken. (p. 129)

Discipline as Dewey defines it is acquired by engaging in purposive, meaningful activities. For Dewey, reading and writing were cultural tools to be developed and utilized in working through such activities. In *School and Society* (1899/1980) he describes reading and writing as powerful *means* of extending and controlling experience, as tools for intellectual pursuits, as keys to knowledge (p. 77). Dewey believed that development in reading and writing did not occur simply by the study of them as communication tools. Rather, children's literacy developed in the use of these tools in genuine communication.

This perspective is not unique to Dewey. Writers on literacy have begun to emphasize meaning and purpose as essential considerations in instruction and development. Goodman (1986), writing for the NCTE Reading Commission, asserts that "language is learned best when the focus is not on language but on what it is used for" (p. 359). Applebee (1986) reminds us that the process of writing is not independent of purpose—instruction that is based on a generic, mechanical model of the writing process ignores the research finding that expert writers shape and subordinate the writing process to the *purpose* for which they are writing. He argues that instruction needs to take into account the fact that writing is purpose-driven. Florio (1979) expresses this conception of writing development when she writes:

> Children, in effect, *practice* the use of language not as preparation or training for social life, but as social life itself. (p. 3, emphasis in original)

Features of Occasions for Writing

A major challenge for teachers who would help children develop as writers, then is to devise or find writing tasks that are functional within the life of the classroom and school. This would create genuine opportunities for students to play the role of author. Addressing this pedagogical problem, Florio and Clark (1981) developed a construct they called the "occasion for writing." Derived out of their descriptive research on teacher planning and classroom instruction, the construct was useful in portraying and analyzing extended writing activities. The researchers noted five features distinguishing occasions for writing from the other instructional forms present in the classrooms they studied:

1. Occasions for writing are of sufficient duration to permit linking of multiple activities in the composing process.
2. Activities constituting occasions for writing arise in the context of (or are planned with reference to) real events of classroom and/or community life.
3. Activities within an occasion for writing are driven by the broad purpose for the writing and are therefore linked thematically over time.

4. Activities in occasions for writing are expressive in nature and may involve multiple modes along the continuum of oral-written expression (e.g., writing, drawing, speaking, reading, and so forth).
5. Participants (teacher and students alike) collaborate and play multiple roles in accomplishing the social and academic goals of an occasion for writing.

In the following sections of this paper, examples of occasions for writing are presented to illustrate the five distinctive features and show how these features support meaningful and self-regulated writing in the classroom.

Examples of Occasions for Writing

An essential characteristic of occasions for writing in classrooms is that they be meaningful to the participants. This means that students have something to express to an audience and the possibility of response from that audience. In order that the purpose for writing be more than just the completion of academic work in which the teacher overly determines the task and acts as sole audience—Dewey (1899/1980) noted that there is "all the difference in the world between having something to say and having to say something" (p. 35)—the occasion for writing should allow for some shaping of the task by the student and involve audiences in addition to the teacher. Three examples of occasions for writing which involved meaningful communication follow.

Safety Posters

The first example comes from Florio and Clark (1982). They describe an occasion for writing created by Ms. Donovan (pseudonym) and the students of her combined second/third grade classroom. The occasion for writing began with an unexpected school assembly in which members of the local police force gave a presentation on bicycle and pedestrian safety. During the assembly, Ms. Donovan decided to use the experience of the assembly as the basis of a writing activity.

Later in the day, in a whole-class discussion, Ms. Donovan asked the students to recall the safety rules that they had heard at the assembly. With the help of Ms. Donovan, who acted as class scribe, the students collectively reconstructed the presentation by the police officers and created a list of ten rules which were written on a large piece of white paper in multi-color magic marker. During this activity, students suggested safety rules to be written down by Ms. Donovan. They were encouraged orally to revise their statements on their own or with the help of other students, until they came up with versions of rules which satisfied them. Ms. Donovan said: "Sometimes does it take a couple of times to get out what you want to say? That's OK . . . take your time and re-state it, how you want to say it" (Florio & Clark, 1982, p. 276).

Once the list of rules was completed, Ms. Donovan asked each student to choose a safety rule and to draw a picture illustrating the rule. The pictures, with the safety rules as captions, would eventually be posted in the hallways as a service and a reminder to the other students in the school.

Several days later, Ms. Donovan arranged for her students to share their posters with the kindergarten class. Several small groups of student authors showed and explained their posters to the morning kindergarteners. When they came back to Ms. Donovan's room, some said that they thought it would be a good idea to practice sharing the posters before returning to the kindergarten room. Thus the remaining students who would present their posters to the afternoon kindergarten decided first to practice in front of those who had presented in the morning. Ms. Donovan encouraged the students to help their classmates by asking questions they thought the kindergarteners would ask. Although some reported being nervous (one student complained of a stomachache), the remaining students shared their posters that afternoon.

The practice session illustrates many things about meaningful occasions to learn writing. First, it was a student-generated strategy to improve communication with an audience. Second, the teacher did not lead this activity but supported it with time, encouragement, and suggestions. Third, participants played a variety of roles including author, coach, and proxy audience. Fourth, there was also a real audience outside the classroom walls whose presence increased students' concern that their work made sense. Finally, the occasion tapped a genuine topic of school and community concern and integrated various parts of the curriculum in addressing that concern.

Sunday's Project

The next example, from a high school classroom in London, England, again illustrates some of these features but adds new dimensions appropriate to the age and background of the students and the teacher's curricular and instructional goals.

McLeod (1986) describes his collaborative research with John Hardcastle, Head of English Department at Hackney Downs School, and an all-male class of students Mr. Hardcastle worked with for five years. McLeod asserts that Hackney is probably the poorest borough in London. More than half of Hardcastle's students were London-born children from families of formerly British Caribbean countries. The class had a "reputation for trouble, even in comparison with other classes in all-male London schools" (p. 38). Mr. Hardcastle was the Humanities (combined program of English, history, geography, social studies, and drama) teacher the first three years, and the class's English teacher the remaining two years.

A significant aspect of Mr. Hardcastle's instruction was the role that discussion played in his classes. Discussions were far-ranging, intense, and tied to the world outside the classroom walls. They explored nuclear arms, racism, neutrality, the Falkland Island crisis, Afro-Caribbean history, school policy, and other topics. Hardcastle often started such discussions with a question. In the ensuing conversation among students, the teacher would intervene not to alter the discussion's course, but to insist on clarification or to assure the right of someone to be heard. Otherwise the discussions were largely carried by the students. Furthermore, the discussions carried over into one another and topics were revisited from different viewpoints over time. McLeod (1986) comments that it is "not possible to 'deal with' issues like racism, unemployment, war, and exploitation, and then move on to something else" (p. 41).

McLeod finds that discussion was often the starting point for the writing that students did in class. Of this he writes:

> Typically . . . topics were brought to focus in a conversation with John Hardcastle. He would remind a student of something he had contributed to a discussion, possibly weeks or even months before, and ask whether he would like to extend the idea into a piece of writing. They would make notes of the conversation, sometimes, to provide the student with a framework. (p. 44)

As an example, McLeod discusses the writing of a young man named Sunday during the class's third year work in Humanities. Sunday's parents came from Nigeria. One of the units during the third year was a study of migration in and out of Britain. The final section of the unit explored the migration by Caribbean, African, and Asian peoples to Britain.

As part of the unit, Sunday collaborated with another student in writing about slave trade and the exploitation of Caribbean agriculture. Sunday soon began expressing his anger with the way Nigeria and other African countries were portrayed in the media, especially TV. John Hardcastle suggested that Sunday work on an extended writing project on Nigeria. The purpose of the project was two-fold. First, Sunday's project would inform his fellow students because student writing was read and discussed by the class as part of the curriculum. Second, Sunday's writing would become part of his course work for assessment at the end of the year. Thus Sunday's text helped shape the social studies and writing curricula for himself and his peers. Moreover he was assessed on the basis of extensive written work on a topic of personal significance.

Sunday worked at his project for over two months, and after five revisions of large portions of this text, produced 66 pages. About half of his text was report-like, providing information on Nigerian history, geography, economy, and politics. The other half was a more personal account based on six months he had spent in Nigeria when he was eleven.

McLeod (1986) reports that the project gave Sunday high status in the class. He was considered an expert on Africa and Third World politics, and played the roles of teacher and critic in class discussions of those topics. Sunday's experience was not unique. Mr. Hardcastle's other students similarly researched, wrote, and taught others about important topics. McLeod (1986) concludes:

> So it was not only a matter of the discussion providing starting points for writing. This work, by Sunday and Robert and all the others was read and talked about when it was done, and then became a resource for discussion and argument for some time afterwards; it was a two-way process by which talk fed writing, and was in turn fed by it. (p. 48)

The discussion in Mr. Hardcastle's classroom is a good example of the transformation Dewey hoped the traditional recitation would undergo in classrooms dedicated to meaningful learning. Instead of being a "place where the child shows off to the teacher and the other children the amount of information he has succeeded in assimilating from the textbook," Dewey (1899/1980) envisioned the recitation as a "social clearing-house, where experiences and ideas are exchanged and subjected to criticism, where misconceptions are corrected, and new lines of thought and inquiry are set up" (pp. 33-34).

The ongoing nature of the writing-related discussions in Hardcastle's classroom suggests several other important characteristics of occasions for writing. They are extended opportunities to write. Moreover they integrate a variety of language skills and tasks with academic content such as social studies. In addition, they demand high levels of participation among writer and peers. All participants play important and varied roles (e.g., assistants, audience, co-authors, and so forth).

Writing is a process greater than the sum of its parts. It is neither a set of sub-skills nor a chain of procedures. It is a complex whole. This is the case in a very rudimentary sense for beginners and in a more elaborated sense for experts. Beginners tend to approach and produce whole texts (or scribbled "pseudotexts") before they differentiate their knowledge of writing into categories such as letter, word, sentence. In addition, Gundlach (1985) finds that they

> discover significant uses for writing by building bridges from the familiar activities of speaking, drawing, and playing to the new activities that writing makes possible. Children write to name and organize parts of their worlds, to capture and savor their experiences, to tell stories, to try out voices and roles, to fulfill family and school responsibilities, to communicate messages to readers near and far, and to make lists that will help them remember what they have to do. (p. 145)

Gundlach's perspective on the importance of speaking, drawing, and play to children's development in writing is similar to that of Vygotsky (1978). Vygotsky argues that the prehistory of writing in children includes their attempts at symbolism in play and drawing—eventually, children master writing, which Vygotsky characterizes as the drawing of speech (p. 115). Drawing, speaking before an audience, discussion, and reading remain important for the development of writing after children come to school. In the first example involving the creation of safety posters, the drawings and oral language of the students were essential to the fulfillment of the writing occasion and were integrated with the writing itself. In the second example from the British high school, discussion and reading were language activities essential to the creation of meaningful student text.

Pen Pals

The development of writing, then, involves more than just writing. Consequently, if occasions for writing are to support writing development, they must be of sufficient duration and complexity to permit the linking of multiple activities. The final example reported in this chapter concerns this feature of occasions for writing. It is a description of a pen pals activity studied by Florio and Clark (1981).

Two second/third-grade teachers in different schools, Ms. Donovan and Mr. Donizetti (pseudonym), arranged for the students in their classes to exchange letters. The occasion for writing would eventually stretch over five months. At the beginning of the activity, Ms. Donovan, who taught a second- and third-grade class, and Mr. Donizetti, a second-grade teacher, assigned pen pals randomly within sex groups. Mr. Donizetti's students received the names of their pen pals in early February and wrote the first letters. Most of the letters were descriptions of their authors and were three or four sentences long.

Ms. Donovan's students were initially critical of the letters they received. They seemed short, uninformative, and replete with errors in spelling and punctuation. Ms. Donovan took instructional advantage of her students' responses to the letters they had received. She reminded them that their own letters would soon be read by Mr. Donizetti's students. What could they do to make certain their letters did not elicit such criticism from their pen pals? This was an occasion for direct instruction (what Calkins [1986] calls "mini-lessons") in various aspects of revision and editing. Multiple drafts of the letters were written. Students worked both with one another and in small groups with Ms. Donovan to make sure letters contained enough detail to be interesting and were edited for correctness of surface features such as spelling, handwriting, and punctuation.

In responding to the letters, Ms. Donovan's students described themselves in words and pictures. They grew more understanding of their pen pals when they experienced difficulty writing extended and interesting descriptions to readers whom they did not know. They also were challenged in writing the letters by the fact that their pen pals had written brief and stilted self-reports.

There was not much in the first letters requiring or even suggesting a reply. In short, the students confronted the difficulty of getting a "writing conversation" going with correspondents they did not know. Ms. Donovan helped her students get started by requiring that each person write at least one personal question in his or her letter to the pen pal. In the longer run, she helped the writing conversations along by arranging with Mr. Donizetti an opportunity for the pen pals to meet and talk with one another.

In March, when Mr. Donizetti's class was invited to sing in a nursing home across the street from Ms. Donovan's school, the two teachers decided to hold a meeting of their classes. Ms. Donovan's class would host the event, and subsequently spent much time planning and writing in preparation. Planning for the event required deliberation, discussion, drawing, writing, and cooking on the part of Ms. Donovan's class. The students decided on and prepared art activities which could be shared with the pen pals at centers around the room. They also made Rice Krispie treats and created name tags. The name tags featured student signatures and drawings expressing something interesting about the wearer.

When the two classes met, the pen pals talked, ate snacks, sang for each other, took tours of the school, exchanged phone numbers, and worked and played at the art and game centers. Many social and academic skills were practiced on the occasion of this writing-related event. In addition, the event was granted high status within Ms. Donovan's school by the principal. She visited the pen pal meeting, listened to the singing, and offered Ms. Donovan's students the privilege of taking their pen pals on a tour of the building.

The pen pal visit proved to be an important event for the ongoing correspondence between the two classrooms. Florio and Clark (1981) note that, in addition to more letters being written and the letters being longer and more complex, the students expanded the purposes which the letters served beyond the "simple declaratives about him/herself" and "one question to the recipient" types in the earliest letters (p. 17). New purposes included exchanging gifts, commenting on the visit, describing school and home life, exchanging home addresses and telephone numbers, flattering and joking, and sharing problems and feelings.

> To achieve some of these purposes requires only one letter. Others require one letter and a reply. Still others are worked out in several rounds of letters where the children appear to chain topics. In some of the letters the children share information about themselves that would ordinarily not be shared in face-to-face communications. In many we can see the effort to establish shared experience and understandings. (Florio & Clark, 1981, p. 17)

This example illustrates the importance of multiple and integrated activities linked over time by a common theme—in this case, writing to pen pals—in support of writing that is meaningful and increasingly self-regulated among learners. It also illustrates the importance of teacher planning, assessment, and provisioning. The teacher decides what resources—instructional, temporal, material, and social—to provide in helping students proceed with the written work at hand and with the larger project of becoming thoughtful and independent writers.

CONCLUSION

This paper suggests that writing instruction might be usefully conceived of as involving three interrelated components: direct instruction, response to student writing, and meaningful occasions for writing.

If writing is a cultural tool with a history, then teachers can help students learn the conventions of writing through direct instruction. In this capacity, teachers can instruct students in skills they will need to craft texts. They can also provide models drawn from literature to help students learn the convention of written language. In addition, teachers can encourage discussion among students attempting to solve textual problems and leading to the discovery of various writing strategies.

Children learn to write in the practice of meaningful communication and through participation in social relationships, not in practice for them. The nature of children's development demands that writing instruction go beyond explanation. Direct instruction in the rules of language must be subsumed and become strategic moments within the larger components of response to text and occasions for writing.

If writing becomes self-regulated by means of the internationalization of social and cognitive dimensions of the composing process, then instructional response to children's text can enhance development. Teachers can respond directly to student authors in writing conferences. They can also organize peer and group response activities in which students teach and learn from each other. Finally, teachers can design writing tasks and activities rich enough to provide response from other audiences or collaborators and from the task itself.

Finally, if writing is goal-driven, then teachers can offer student writers complex and diverse goals toward which to write. They can also help students identify their own writing goals. In either case this can occur through the crafting of meaningful occasions for writing. By engaging students in such occasions, teachers can greatly expand the expressive repertoire of beginning writers to include writing for diverse purposes and in varying genres. Within such occasions students can learn to use writing not just as a tool for communicating with others, but also as a way to think and learn about new subjects.

REFERENCES

Applebee, A.L. (1981). *Writing in the secondary school: English and the content areas* (Research Report No. 21). Urbana, IL: National Council of Teachers of English.

Applebee, A.L. (1986). Problems in process approaches: Toward a reconceptualization of process instruction. In A.K. Petrosky & D. Bartholomae (Eds.), *The teaching of writing: 85th yearbook of the National Society for the Study of Education* (pp. 95-113). Chicago: University of Chicago Press.

Basso, K. (1974). The ethnography of writing. In R. Bauman & J. Sherzer (Eds.), *Explorations in the ethnography of speaking*. London: Cambridge University Press.

Bereiter, C., & Scardamalia, M. (1987). An attainable version of high literacy: Approaches to teaching higher-order skills in reading and writing. *Curriculum Inquiry, 17*(1), 9-30.

Britton, J.N., Burgess, T., Martin, N., McLeod, A., & Rosen, H. (1975). *The development of writing abilities, 11-18*. London: Macmillan.

Bruner, J. (1975). The ontogenesis of speech arts. *Journal of Child Language, 2*, 1-19.

Calkins, L.M. (1983). *Lessons from a child: On the teaching and learning of writing*. Portsmouth, NJ: Heinemann.

Calkins, L.M. (1986). *The art of teaching writing*. Exeter, NH: Heinemann.

Clark, C.M., & Florio, S. (1983). The written literacy forum: Combining research and practice. *Teacher Education Quarterly, 10*(3), 57-87.

Clark, C.M., & Florio, S., with Elmore, T.L., Martin, J.M., Maxwell, R.J., and Metheny, W. (1981). *Understanding writing in school: A descriptive study of writing and its instruction in two classrooms* (Final Report, Grant No. 90840 of The National Institute of Education). East Lansing: Michigan State University, Institute for Research on Teaching.

Daiute, C. (1985). Do writers talk to themselves? In S.W. Freedman (Ed.), *The acquisition of written language: Response and revision* (pp. 133-159). Norwood, NJ: Ablex.

Dewey, J. (1966). *Democracy and education*. New York: The Free Press. (Original work published 1944)

Dewey, J. (1980). *School and society*. Carbondale: Southern Illinois University Press. (Original work published 1899)

Florio, S. (1979). The problem of dead letters: Social perspectives on the teaching of writing. *Elementary School Journal, 80*(1), 1-7.

Florio, S. (1987, December). *How ethnographers of communication study writing in school*. Paper presented at the annual meeting of The National Reading Conference, St. Petersburg, FL.

Florio, S., & Clark, C.M. (1981, October). *Pen pals: Describing an occasion for writing in the classroom*. Paper presented at the Midwest Regional Conference on Qualitative Research in Education, Kent State University, Kent, OH.

Florio, S., & Clark, C.M. (1982). What's writing for?: Writing in the first weeks of school in a second/third grade classroom. In L. Cherry-Wilkinson (Ed.), *Communicating in the classroom* (pp. 265-282). New York: Academic Press.

Flower, L. (1987). *The role of task representation in reading-to-write* (Tech. Report No. 6). Berkeley: University of California-Berkeley, Center for the Study of Writing.

Frederiksen, C.H., & Dominic, J.F. (1981). Introduction: Perspectives on the activity of writing. In C.H. Frederiksen, & J.F. Dominic (Eds.), *Writing: The nature, development, and teaching of written communication* (Vol. 2). New York: Erlbaum.

Freedman, S.W., & Sperling, M. (1985). Written language acquisition: The role of response and the writing conference. In S.W. Freedman (Ed.), *The acquisition of written language: Response and revision* (pp. 106-130). Norwood, NJ: Ablex.

Gere, A.R., & Stevens, R.S. (1985). The language of writing groups: How oral response shapes revision. In S.W. Freedman (Ed.), *The acquisition of written language: Response and revision* (pp. 85-105). Norwood, NJ: Ablex.

Goodman, K.S. (1986). Basal readers: A call for action. *Language Arts, 63,* 358-363.

Graves, D.H. (1983). *Writing: Teachers and children at work.* Exeter, NH: Heinemann.

Gundlach, R.A. (1985). Children as writers: The beginnings of learning to write. In M. Nystrand (Ed.), *What writers know: The language process and structure of written discourse.* New York: Academic Press.

Hawkins, D. (1974). I, thou, and it. In D. Hawkins (Ed.), *The informed vision: Essays in learning and human nature* (pp. 48-62). New York: Agathon Press.

Hayes, J.R., & Flower, L.S. (1986). Writing research and the writer. *American Psychologist, 41,* 1106-1113.

Heath, S.B. (1983). *Ways with words: Language, life, and work in communities and classrooms.* London: Cambridge University Press.

Kroll, B.M. (1978). Cognitive egocentrism and the problem of audience awareness in written discourse. *Research in the Teaching of English, 12*(3), 269-281.

LeFevre, K.B. (1987). *Invention as a social act.* Carbondale: Southern Illinois University Press.

McLeod, A. (1986). Critical literacy: Taking control of our own lives. *Language Arts, 63*(1), 37-50.

Michaels, S. (1981). "Sharing time": Children's narrative styles and differential access to literacy. *Language in Society, 10,* 423-442.

Moffett, J. (1983). *Teaching the universe of discourse.* Boston, MA: Houghton Mifflin. (Original work published in 1968)

Murray, D.M. (1979). The listening eye: Reflections on the writing conference. *College English, 41,* 13-18.

Scardamalia, M., & Bereiter, C. (1986). Research on written composition. In M.C. Wittrock (Ed.), *Handbook of research on teaching* (3rd ed., pp. 778-803). New York: Macmillan.

Sperling, M., & Freedman, S.W. (1987). *A good girl writes like a good girl: Written responses and clues to the teaching/learning process* (Tech. Report No. 3). Berkeley: University of California, Berkeley-Center for the Study of Writing.

Sulzby, E. (1986). Young children's concepts for oral and written text. In K. Durkin (Ed.), *Language development during the school years* (pp. 95-116). London: Croom Helm.

Temple, C.A., Nathan, R.G., & Burris, N.A. (1982). *The beginnings of writing.* Boston, MA: Allyn & Bacon.

Vygotsky, L.S. (1978). *Mind in society: The development of higher psychological processes* (M. Cole, V. John-Steiner, S. Scribner, & E. Souberman, Eds.). Cambridge, MA: Harvard University Press.

*   *   *

CROSS-TALK

What are the key similarities and differences in the treatment of dialogue and literacy learning in your paper and those by Englert and Raphael and Palincsar and Brown?

These papers have all been strongly influenced by Vygotsky's social historical theory of cognitive development. In this regard, as Palincsar and Brown explain, learning is socially mediated such that beginners move from dialogue with more experienced persons to private speech and, ultimately, to independent cognitive activity. Because these papers embrace the idea that cognition is interpersonal before it is intrapersonal, it is not surprising to see that each stresses the importance of dialogue in literacy acquisition. The talk which occurs between teacher and student or among students is treated in detail in instructional research on both composition and comprehension by these authors (and by others in the volume including Rosaen and Duffy and Roehler).

The papers by Englert and Raphael, Palincsar and Brown, and ourselves are concerned with the communication underlying meaningful understanding and self-regulated learning. Thus, they share a concern for teachers creating learning environments which foster talk about text in the completion of genuinely meaningful reading and writing tasks so that students may internalize and apply elsewhere strategies for successful reading and writing.

It seems to us that all three papers acknowledge multiple instructional activities for teachers who want to foster higher order thinking in literacy instruction. All the authors note that teachers can, do, and must teach some skills, concepts, and strategies by direct explanation. In addition, however, all three papers describe other ways teachers can support literacy learning by means of idea exchange between teacher and student (or among students) in writing or reading situations.

Each paper describes a different kind of expressive activity for the teacher who wishes to support literacy learning by dialogue. Teachers can orally offer models of their own thinking as in Englert and Raphael's concept of the "think aloud." They can present written, formal models of text structure or teach discourse supportive of the cognitive strategies entailed in writing and reading as in Englert and Raphael's "think sheets." They can engage students in the carefully planned conversational moves and sequences of Palincsar and Brown's "reciprocal teaching." (We also note that teachers can use the discussion of literature as a source of models for text structure, as do Englert and Raphael in other publications.)

In contrast to these discourse-level interventions, the focus of our paper is on the teacher's work to create meaningful curricular units for the discourse we all believe will support literacy learning. We, therefore, describe in some detail extended sequences of time and activity which interweave the social and academic dimensions of school talk and writing. We discuss the ways teachers can create or capitalize upon social occasions for the use of literacy in pursuit of a meaningful communication goal. We do not, however, offer detailed scripts or scenarios for the structure or content of the talk embedded in those occasions.

It seems to us that rather than any fundamental differences or disagreements in these three chapters, what we have are differences in figure and ground. The other authors acknowledge that literacy has meaning and that it is learned and practiced by means of social interaction. They stress, however, the internalization of cognitive strategies by means of communication and elaborate on what that communication should contain. They spend relatively less time dealing with classrooms and their social norms as constraining or enabling contexts for communication or for the knowledge subsequently internalized.

Palincsar and Brown report on interventions by teachers at the level of discourse moves in discrete literacy events (i.e., comprehension discussions). For Englert and Raphael, the intervention is both written and oral and is keyed to the phases of the composing process as well as to the strategies needed to produce expository text with particular, prespecified forms and functions. Perhaps because our training and research have been ethnographic, our paper deals with interventions at the broader level of the social "occasion," or those writing events linked to one another by topic and purpose. In our paper, the social organization of writing into occasions provides the opportunity for teachers and students to co-create text and discuss the knowledge needed to craft it. Thus, although they stress different parts of the complex activity of teaching, all of the three papers deal with certain essential issues in the transformation of talk about text to inner speech and, ultimately, to independent and self-regulated literacy in the particular social context of the classroom and in the special relationship of teacher to student.

Is your paper really about instruction?

The most troubling aspect of our paper seems to be its treatment of instruction. E. Fennema suggests that our paper's title might be misleading, saying that what we have written about has little to do with "traditional" definitions of instruction. G. Duffy and L. Roehler comment that our paper makes only "hesitant" acknowledgment of the teacher's active participation in instruction. J. Brophy and C. Rosaen ask for elaboration on the teacher's instructional decisions and role. Apparently we have used the term "instruction" in an unusual way, have underspecified what we mean by the term, or both.

If we have misled our readers and ourselves, perhaps it has been in confusing "teaching" with "instruction." Therefore, we begin our response with a definition of "teaching" which captures what we had intended by the term "instruction." Teaching is, according to Oakeshott (1972),

> a variegated activity which may include hinting, suggesting, urging, coaxing, encouraging, guiding, pointing out, conversing, instruction, informing, narrating, lecturing, demonstrating, exercising, testing, examining, criticizing, tutoring, drilling, and so on—everything, indeed, which does not belie the engagement to impart an understanding. (pp. 25-26)

Oakeshott's definition of "teaching" mentions "instruction" as one of its many constituent activities. Given this definition, we suspect that E. Fennema is correct in implying that our paper is misleading. A narrow view of instruction, it seems to us, limits its power greatly. When Webster is consulted, for example, to "instruct" is:

> to give knowledge or information; to impart knowledge in a systematic manner; to direct authoritatively and on the basis of informed awareness. (Woolf, 1979, p. 594).

Notice that in this traditional definition the relationship is unidirectional. The instructor gives, imparts, and directs from of her/his greater information and awareness. The instructor also plans the system by which the giving should take place. The problem with this definition is that it does not say much about the other parts of the teaching relationship—the learner or the content. While writing surely is comprised of many conventions and strategies which should be instructed to students, it is also a social process of invention, one in which the student may have great stake in and responsibility to determine such important matters as topic, audience, and purpose.

In their chapter in this volume, Palincsar and Brown (citing Duffy, Roehler, et al.) state that, for literacy learning, we know very little about how much instruction should be "delivered" from teacher to student in an explicit manner (p. 39). This concern is echoed by Lampert's chapter where, in the case of mathematics, we see considerable teacher deliberation about how to balance delivery of information with the joint construction of solutions to problems by teacher and students. It also arises in Rosaen's description of an American History unit, where there is a gradual expansion of the students' rights and obligations to shape the course of their research.

Where there is a discipline to be learned, a teacher must certainly know that discipline and its conventions. Teachers must impart knowledge which will support and extend learners' intellectual growth. However, in fields such as writing, where there has, perhaps been too much "imparting" of rules and maxims and too little focus on either the learning process or the meaning and purpose of literacy, we feel a need to expand our traditional definition of instruction. Moreover, in writing and other fields where invention is important, part of the school curriculum involves learning *that one can invent* as well as that one can build on existing knowledge or use available tools. We see a need for teachers to mitigate their social and disciplinary authority on these occasions and participate, in Buchmann's words, in a "letting go of certainty" (1984, p. 40). This is an instructional choice teachers can make so that learners may be challenged to undertake problem-solving within their own texts.

The "letting go of certainty" to which we refer should not be confused with teachers being ignorant of their discipline nor should it be interpreted as *laissez-faire* pedagogy. What we attempt to show in our paper is that instruction is highly systematic and teacher-directed and that it requires teachers to know both their discipline and their students. However, to say that instruction is teacher-designed, systematic, and discipline-based does not mean that it is necessarily teacher-directed or that it is always at its best when the teacher is showing or telling. Like Murray (1979) who wrote about writing teachers needing a "listening eye," or Hawkins (1974) who argued that teachers need to be "diagnostic" providers for their learners, we think that learners need to have more opportunities to speak about their thinking and their texts—to hypothesize, question, to attempt solutions, and revise. Teachers are understandably eager to show and tell. However, there is danger that in their efforts to explain and help, they may miss the point of what children are trying to do and learn within the medium of text. There is also danger that the process of invention which is essential to writing will be truncated in the service of mastery of isolated skills and strategies.

We do not make a "hesitant" acknowledgment of teacher's direct participation in instruction. Without teachers' thoughtful work, school writing would be neither systematic nor instructive. What we are cautious about, however, is the tendency to stress teachers' talk over their listening. Teachers need to listen to learners talk about text. They need to read learners' drafts carefully and diagnostically. They need to read many other texts with learners so that together they can discover how authors make meaning with words. All this is part of an expansive definition of instruction we have used in our paper.

In our paper we offered at least several ways in which teachers "instruct," or lead systematically on the basis of their knowledge of both writing and pedagogy. They are (1) direct explanation of skills, concepts, and strategies needed by young authors to craft texts (what Calkins [1986] called "mini-lessons"); (2) listening/reading and response to the young writer who has questions to frame, solutions to try out, and purposes to clarify (what Graves [1983] called "writing conferences); and (3) designing for and with children rich and meaningful occasions for the practice of literacy—occasions enlivening and instructive in their own right which offer teachers ample opportunity to understand their young writers' needs and provide continued instructional support (what Clark & Florio [1983] called "occasions for writing").

References to Cross-talk

Buchman, M. (1984). The priority of knowledge and understanding in teaching. In L.G. Katz & J.D. Raths (Eds.), *Advances in teacher education* (Vol. 1). Norwood, NJ: Ablex.

Calkins, L.M. (1986). *The art of teaching writing.* Exeter, NH: Heinemann.

Clark, C.M., & Florio, S. (1983). The written literacy forum: Combining research and practice. *Teacher Education Quarterly,* 10(3), 57-87.

Graves, D.H. (1983). *Writing: Teachers and children at work.* Exeter, NH: Heinemann.

Hawkins, D. (1974). I, thou, and it. In D. Hawkins (Ed.), *The informed vision: Essays in learning and human nature* (pp. 48-62). New York: Agathon Press.

Murray, D.M. (1979). The listening eye: Reflections on the writing conference. *College English, 41,* 13-18.

Oakeshott, M. (1972). Education: The engagement and its frustration. In R.F. Dearden, P.H. Hirst, & R.S. Peters (Eds.), *Education and the development of reason.* London: Routledge & Kegan Paul.

Woolf, H.B. (Ed.). (1979). *Webster's new collegiate dictionary.* Springfield, MA: G.&C. Merriam Company.

DEVELOPING SUCCESSFUL WRITERS
THROUGH COGNITIVE STRATEGY
INSTRUCTION

Carol Sue Englert and Taffy E. Raphael

Research and theories of cognitive psychology have increasingly influenced studies of the development of written literacy skills (Pearson, 1986). With this influence has come greater understanding of cognitive processes underlying written literacy (e.g., Anderson & Pearson, 1984; Flower & Hayes, 1981; Samuels & Kamil, 1984; Scardamalia & Bereiter, 1986). Understanding of the processes themselves has led to an increased focus on current instructional contexts and their impact on students' performance (e.g., Anthony & Anderson, 1986; DeFord, 1986; Raphael, Englert, & Anderson, 1987).

Related theoretical development in the areas of learning and development has recognized the social nature of cognitive development, emphasizing the social mediation fundamental to acquiring cognitive skills in nonformal Rogoff, 1986) and formal instructional contexts (Gavelek, 1986). This instruction has been referred to under different labels, including "cognitive apprenticeship" models (Collins, Brown, & Newman, in press), "scaffolded" instruction (Applebee & Langer, 1983; Wood, Bruner, & Ross, 1976), and "reciprocal teaching" (Palincsar & Brown, this volume, pp. 35-71). A consistent theme across these studies is the inability to separate social process from the

Advances in Research on Teaching, Volume 1, pages 105-151.
Copyright © 1989 by JAI Press Inc.
All rights of reproduction in any form reserved.
ISBN: 0-89232-845-2

study of cognitive development. Features fundamental to socially-mediated instruction include: (1) modeling of the to-be-learned skill or strategy by a more experienced, more expert adult or peer, (2) emphasis on dialogue and conversation as the expert models and thinks-aloud while engaged in the use and regulation of the strategy, and (3) focus on problem-solving while engaged in the activity.

Our purpose here is to explore the social-mediation underlying the acquisition of expository writing skills. We begin by discussing research on the writing process, including both writers' knowledge and their ability to control the process, and on the instructional context in which writing instruction occurs. Second, we consider how writers' metacognitive knowledge about writing and the instructional context have each contributed to current problems exhibited by young, developing writers. Third, we present an instructional model based on current conceptions of the writing process, and the importance of socially-mediated instruction in the acquisition of cognitive strategies for expository writing. Finally, we examine the impact of participation in this program on children's knowledge about and ability to apply and control strategies in the generation of expository text.

Interview data and writing samples from two students in the Cognitive Strategy Instruction in Writing (CSIW) project of the Institute for Research on Teaching at Michigan State University (Englert, Raphael, & Anderson 1985; Raphael, Englert, & Kirschner, in press) help set a context for this paper Spencer, a fourth grade LD student, and David, a high achieving fifth grader illustrate the importance of strategies for successful, independent writing. The following is a portion of Spencer's interview in which he was asked to advise Sally, a hypothetical child, who had difficulty writing a report.

> I: Sally has been asked to write a report about a wild animal. What are the steps Sally should follow in writing a report about an animal?
>
> S: She should think.
>
> I: What should she think about? What's the first thing Sally should do?
>
> S: Okay, when I was a second grader we have to get a piece of paper and get it out. I guess I was the last or the middle person or last person done
>
> I: Okay, so the first thing you tell her to do is to think. What should she think about?
>
> S: What she's writing.
>
> I: Okay what's the second thing she should do to write a report?
>
> S: What she's gonna write about. ...As soon as she writes one page she should just go up and (have) her teacher correct that page. That's what I did. Go up to the teacher and let her correct that again, whatever she misspelled She could get another piece of paper, write the whole thing over.

I: How will Sally know when her paper is finished?

S: When she goes up to the teacher and the teacher crosses out something and she write ...whatever she crosses out of it and ....she should take another piece of paper and write what she crossed out and write up to the top.

I: Well, how does Sally know when she's finished? Before she takes it to the teacher, how does she know she's finished?

S: She doesn't...When she's done with one....Like if the teacher say you have to write on one whole page...one page.

Spencer's comments indicate lack of knowledge about the writing process, related strategies, audience, and purpose. He has a poorly developed concept of control of the process, indicated by his assumptions that the teacher has responsibility for decisions, and that trivial external criteria such as page length should guide his writing. These misconceptions and lack of understanding impact his ability to successfully generate text of his own. When given the opportunity to write about a topic of his choice, and to share his paper with someone who knew little or nothing about the topic, he chose to write an explanation of how to play "one-on-one."

Basketball

This is how to play 1 on 1. You would have to check that person up and try to make the basket. If I made it, I will have to go back to that line and check him or her up again.

Whereas each of Spencer's individual sentences is comprehensible, his explanation does not succeed. His topic is explicitly stated but he fails to generate the step-by-step explanation that would enable a naive reader to understand or play the game. His text is not "reader friendly" because the reader is left to infer important information related to "checking," "going back to the line." and so forth. Consistent with his interview comments, his text indicates a lack of understanding of audience and purpose, and lack of internal criteria for evaluating the success or completeness of his text.

David's text illustrates similar problems, in spite of his obviously more sophisticated understanding of writing strategies (e.g., organizing ideas, informing his reader). He, too, apparently lacks an understanding of purpose, and the abrupt topic change midway through his paper suggests that he was driven by a goal of filling up a page.

Lansing and Chicago

First, I will compare/contrast Chicago and Lansing. Chicago and Lansing are different because Chicago has more buildings, highways, pollution, people, and doesn't have as much forests and woods as Lansing. Chicago and Lansing are alike because they both have houses, buildings, people, highways, sight-seeing places, etc. Now I shall compare/contrast Monopoly and Clue. Monopoly and Clue are alike because in both games you move around the board getting stuff to help you win the game. They are different because in Monopoly you go around the board collecting money and buying property, as in Clue you go around the board looking for clues and guessing.

These examples illustrate the importance of writing strategies and sensitivity to audience and purpose in the writing process. Our goal is to consider potential contributors to the problems typical students such as Spencer and David have in developing successful writing strategies. We consider problem sources such as the complexity of the writing process itself and the instructional environment in which writing instruction occurs, and potential benefits of using a socially-mediated instructional approach.

RESEARCH IN THE WRITING PROCESS: HOW DO EXPERTS AND NOVICES DIFFER?

One reason students exhibit writing problems may be attributed to the complexity of the cognitive processes involved. Writing research has detailed a nonlinear process that includes activities during prewriting, drafting, revising and editing (Applebee, 1984; Flower & Hayes, 1981). During planning, skilled writers employ strategies that aid in setting goals and determining the content and organization of the paper (Hayes & Flower, 1980). During drafting, writers consider evolving internal plans while translating ideas into printed sentences, instantiate plans with details, arrange related ideas together, and insert signals that convey the relationships among the planned ideas. During revising and editing, writers monitor the success of the draft in meeting goals, and if needed, modify the draft to reflect their goals and audience needs.

Learning to write is further complicated since not only is the process nonlinear, but not every component process is involved in each writing activity (Applebee, 1986). Thus, students must learn the process as a whole, the component subprocesses, and the appropriateness of each in meeting the purposes of their current writing activity. In this section we detail the component subprocesses, related task specific strategies, and differences in successful and less successful writers' performances.

The Component Writing Subprocesses

Planning

Planning requires that writers access relevant ideas from background knowledge, reflect upon topics and ideas, invoke metamemorial search routines to initiate and sustain their thinking about the topic, and research topics to gather new information. When writers plan, they generate a set of ideas, then cull and organize these ideas to create a relevant body of information that fits the constraints of the written genre and the needs of the intended audience (Graham & Harris, in press; Hayes & Flower, 1987; Scardamalia & Bereiter, 1986). Planning involves at least four knowledge sources including: (1) knowledge of writing purposes and goals, (2) knowledge of the topic, (3) knowledge of text structure genre or organizational patterns, and (4) knowledge of problem-solving strategies when current plans are found to be inadequate, including procedures for reinitiating idea generation and establishing new goals or plans when new ideas or purposes are discovered (Hayes & Flower, 1987).

As Spencer's and David's papers suggest, skilled and novice writers are not equally effective in using these knowledge sources. In terms of knowledge about writing purposes and goals, skilled writers are aware of a range of possibilities, including writing to communicate ideas, to learn or acquire new information, and to reflect on information read (Atwell, 1983). Novice and poor writers have much narrower views of writing. Raphael, Englert, and Kirschner (in press) found that elementary students frequently viewed writing as a source of evaluation or assessment, consistently stating that their teacher was the audience. These students generally viewed writing as a decontextualized school activity designed to test their content knowledge, or their knowledge about ways to present information. This view of writing is reflected in Spencer's focus on the teacher as the ultimate judge of students' compositions, and in David's writing to complete a school task, rather than to communicate.

A second knowledge source important during planning is topic knowledge. This knowledge drives the generation of relevant ideas that eventually can be organized into a well-developed text. While skilled writers use strategies for idea generation designed to exhaust their fund of knowledge, poor writers demonstrate a lack of such ability. Englert, Raphael, Fear, and Anderson (1988) interviewed students who had produced inadequate texts. The interviews revealed that they had far more topic knowledge available than was indicated in their texts. However, without external prompting (e.g., from a teacher or more experienced peer) these less successful writers ended their idea generation process well before they had exhausted their fund of relevant ideas. This is similar to the problems less able readers evidence during comprehension in which inferencing is involved (Paris & Lindauer, 1977). In the writing literature, this has been referred to as a problem of inert knowledge; knowledge poor writers possess is not activated in applicable situations (Bereiter & Scardamalia, 1985).

The third knowledge source important to planning is writers' knowledge of text structures. This encompasses writers' knowledge of the questions different types of texts are designed to answer (Anderson & Armbruster, 1984) and the key words and phrases used in text to signal the location of information. Text structure knowledge contributes to less skilled writers' difficulties during planning in two ways: (1) lack of knowledge of text structures in general, and (2) overreliance on the narrative and descriptive structures.

David's comparison/contrast text is unique in that it both illustrates a successful application of text structure (i.e., comparison/contrast), while simultaneously providing an example of a less sophisticated strategy (i.e., knowledge telling) often used by less skilled workers. David's knowledge of text structure and related questions is clear in the type of information included as he compares and contrasts two cities, then two games. The paper reflects knowledge of four questions that can be used to guide the generation of information for comparing and contrasting two places or things: What is being compared and contrasted? On What? How are they alike? How are they different? To a degree, however, David's text also reflects the use of the less sophisticated knowledge-telling strategy. This occurs when writers generate everything they know about a topic in whatever order the ideas come to mind (i.e., brainstorming). While such a strategy may be an effective first step in identifying potentially relevant information, poor writers frequently ignore the need to make decisions about the relevance of information and the importance of organizing the information by grouping, categorizing, and sequencing. Thus, poor writers using such a strategy during planning may produce texts generated in an associative fashion. In the case of David's paper, when he ran out of ideas for comparing and contrasting Chicago and Lansing, rather than ending the paper or getting additional information from external sources, he merely thought of the next comparison/contrast topic for which he had some information. More typically, students adhering to the knowledge-telling strategy generate a text in which each word or sentence stimulates the construction of the next idea, with little attention to the organization of the whole text or the organization best suited for their writing purpose and audience.

A second problem manifested during planning that relates to text structure knowledge is an overreliance on narrative and descriptive text structures. Our current research suggests that a majority of upper-elementary students have particular problems creating well-organized expository or informational texts. Such students generate text using the more familiar descriptive or narrative structures, or personal experience reports rather than structures suited for informational prose. These strategies enable writers to generate ideas to complete a paper, but without intervention, many young writers continue to have difficulties gathering, retrieving, and organizing information to create informational text (Scardamalia & Bereiter, 1985, 1986).

The fourth knowledge source contributing to the planning problems of poor writers involves knowledge of problem-solving strategies. Problem-solving strategies are critical to self-regulation particularly during writers' revision activities, whether these revisions are applied to connected texts or drafts, or to plans found to be inadequate. Lack of problem-solving strategies during planning may surface because: (1) students do not realize their plan is inadequate and thus make no effort to identify means for solving the problem, (2) students realize their plan is inadequate, but may not recognize when to apply known task-specific strategies that could solve the plan's problem, or (3) students may lack knowledge of the problem-solving strategies themselves.

Thus, during planning, successful writers use their knowledge of topics, audience, purposes, and problem-solving strategies to generate a viable plan for a paper that communicates information to a real audience for a meaningful purpose. Lack of such knowledge about any of these aspects relevant during planning can inhibit writers' ability to produce successful text.

Text Organization and Text Structure

A second component writing subprocess, organizing, is an extension of the planning process previously described. Just as in planning, knowledge of text structures or discourse schema plays a critical role as writers cull and organize relevant ideas to achieve their purpose and meet the needs of their audience. Based upon the content, purpose, and audience, they identify an organization that structures their ideas both into the global text structures they plan to use in their paper and into the local or topical groupings or categories.

Research suggests that a number of text structures underlie the organization of text, including explanation, comparison/contrast and problem/solution (Meyer, 1985), and that each of these text structures answers a different set of questions. In addition to addressing questions specific to different text structures, successfully organized texts signal the location of the answers to these questions through cueing devices known as key words. Words such as "in contrast to" or "similarly" signal comparison/contrast information, while words such as "first" or "next" signal the steps in the explanation text structure. David's paper reflects the questions and key words addressed in a comparison/ contrast paper. In contrast, Spencer's paper, although less successful, represents an attempt to address questions relevant to an explanation text structure. However, the failure of his paper to communicate this basic information (e.g., What are the materials? What are the steps?) and his omission of key words (e.g., first, second) provide two reasons for the paper's lack of success.

The structural problems evident in children's writing often can be attributed to two organizational difficulties including: (1) problems of categorizing and labeling related ideas, and (2) difficulties constructing a global text structure. The first problem reflects an inability to group or categorize ideas by topics and provide relevant conceptual or superordinate labels (Englert, Stewart and Hiebert, in press). For example, students interviewed by Englert et al. (1988) were asked to help generate ideas for Sally, the hypothetical student having problems generating information to include in her written report, responding to questions such as "What information would you include in an animal report?" "Do you think any ideas (in the animal report) go together?" "What can you call this set of related ideas?" Learning disabled and low-achieving students differed from normally-achieving students in their ability to generate categories of information. Learning disabled and low-achieving students tended to generate low-level details (e.g., it is black, it has a tail) in contrast to normally-achieving students who generated categories of information (e.g., what it looks like, where it lives).

The second organizational difficulty reflects poor writers' difficulties constructing an appropriate global text structure in which to embed the information generated during planning (Scardamalia & Bereiter, 1986). This is true during both comprehension and composition. Meyer, Brandt, and Bluth (1980) and Taylor and Beach (1984) reported that middle-grade students had difficulty using common expository text structures to aid their comprehension and recall. Similarly, Englert, Raphael, Anderson, Gregg, and Anthony (1987) studied the writing performance of upper elementary students. The study revealed students' difficulties in adhering to common text structures in generating expository text. Low-achieving students' texts, in particular, lacked both global coherence as well as quantity of information included. These findings suggest that students need to acquire a working knowledge of expository frameworks that can help them systematically retrieve and organize ideas for better performance on literacy tasks.

Lack of knowledge of text structures is also apparent when writers are interviewed about expository texts. For example, when we interviewed Spencer about the comparison/contrast text structure, we found that his concept was incomplete. In the interview, Spencer was asked to read and edit the following paper in which Pamela, a hypothetical child, was asked to compare and contrast two restaurants (e.g., McDonalds and Hot and Now). The original text presumably written by Pamela is shown in regular type, the revisions Spencer made to the text are written in italics.

> Some ways McDonalds and Hot and Now is alike. McDonalds has a playground it is fun. They go out and *look at* the flowers. *Hot and Now you get food there cheaper. When you add it up, it's not cheap. You can't go inside Hot and Now. It's like a car wash. Hot N Now is not a playground.*

Spencer's changes suggest partial understanding of the comparison/contrast text structure. He uses the words "cheaper" to suggest a contrast and he alludes to other contrasts (e.g., going inside, playground), but be cannot control these text structure processes to effectively signal similarities and differences. His interview corroborated his lack of awareness of text structure. When he was asked whether the paper was done, he replied "Yes. Because that's all Hot and Now." When his answer was probed with the question, "If you were Pamela, would you turn the paper in now?", he replied "If that's all I have to write, yeah." Thus, Spencer uses the external criteria of assignment length to determine whether or not the paper was complete, rather than using text structure criteria.

Drafting

A third component writing subprocess is drafting. Once writers have gathered and organized their ideas, they translate their evolving plans into print. Drafting requires that writers instantiate plans with details, group related ideas, and insert signals that convey relationships among the planned ideas. The drafting of tentative writing plans into formal prose requires cognitive effort (Hayes & Flower, 1987). Writers must explain briefly sketched ideas, interpret nonverbal material in verbal form, and carry out mental instructions (Hayes & Flower, 1987). In addition, writers must continually attend to their readers' needs, providing additional details and information, creating an interesting text, and meeting their own writing goals.

However, less successful writers are not always successful in organizing their ideas for a naive audience and often lapse into using the knowledge-telling strategy during drafting. Table 1 presents Tom's paper, representative of those who mechanically complete the writing process. In this composition, Tom begins to describe what one needs to play football, but changes course by stating that he is the best player in football, and his friend is the quarterback. He concludes his paper by implying that there are steps in playing football (e.g., the persons throw the ball and he catches it). Tom's paper is characteristic of the compositions produced by students employing the knowledge-telling strategy. Tom generates ideas linearly, each idea stimulating the construction of the next idea with little attention to the relationships among the ideas. Tom also exhibits a problem with inert knowledge, as he is unable to provide substantive information explaining his topic to his reader, despite the fact that the directions had emphasized that he should try to give his reader as much information about the topic as possible.

Table 1.   Tom's Paper

Football

In football you have to wear pads and a cup, shoulder pad, pants, and shirt. The best thing you have to wear is a helmet. The helmet is made out of metal. I am the best player in football, but sometimes I get tackled. My friend is the quarterback. The persons throw the ball then I catch it.

Editing and Revising

The remaining writing subprocesses involve writers' abilities to monitor the success of their plans, and to modify their draft to better meet their own goals, the needs of their audience, and the constraints of text structure. To do so, successful writers engage in processes related to editing and revising. In contrast, beginning and less skilled writers engage in a limited amount of such activities (Bridwell, 1980; Perl, 1979). There are four potential causes underlying students' inability to monitor the success of their papers and focus on such constraints.

First, one skill fundamental to successful revision is the ability to distance oneself from one's writing, to read it through the eyes of a naive reader. This shift in perspective is difficult for many writers. In fact, knowledge of one's own text makes it difficult for a writer to detect its faults. Hayes, Schriver, Spilka, and Blaustein (1986) found that revisers who read a well-written text before they evaluated an unclear version had difficulty detecting problems in the text relative to revisers who did not have access to the well-formed version. Not surprisingly, therefore, research suggests that young writers perform better in detecting errors in the less familiar texts produced by other writers than in detecting errors in their own, more familiar text (Bartlett, 1981).

Second, poor writers' editing problems may stem from an inability to distinguish relevant from irrelevant information. Young writers may be particularly susceptible to problems related to this ability which Brown and Smiley (1977) found to be developmental in nature; and poor writers may be particularly disadvantaged (Hillocks, 1986). That is, having produced an idea, poor writers have difficulty evaluating its relevance or discarding it from their first or final drafts. Data from our current research with fourth- and fifth-grade students suggests that editing for textual relevance based upon communicability, audience, purpose, and text structure is such a difficult process for most young writers that there are no significant differences in the kinds of editing strategies used by learning disabled, low-achieving, or high-achieving students (Englert et al., 1988). LD, low-achieving, and high-achieving students are similarly successful in their ability to detect one or more mechanical errors, and all groups are equally unsuccessful in their recognition of coherence problems related to text structure. Thus, young and less successful writers are preoccupied with technical matters in revision (Hillocks, 1984), frequently at the expense of more meaningful revisions that would improve the communicability of their text.

The third potential problem arises from the innate differences between oral and written language (Rubin, 1987). Lack of direct interaction between author and reader(s) places great demands on the writer to tailor discourse to meet the needs of the potentially unknown reader. Yet, young writers' previous experiences in oral discourse may not prepare them to anticipate the needs of a reader distant in time or space. In conversation, when speakers begin conversations without setting an appropriate context, listeners help speakers monitor the success of the conversation by requesting clarification. In written language, however, the writer must anticipate potential areas of confusion and breakdowns in the communication process without this on-line or continual feedback from the listener. Because the writer's audience is generally indeterminate, Rubin suggests that the writer's own social cognition, the process of inferring others' thoughts, feelings, and beliefs, may be more critical to successful written than oral communication. The writer must become adept at imagining a reader and mentally role-playing this reader's state of mind and difficulties.

Summary

The writing subprocesses related to planning, organizing, drafting, and editing represent language skills that generally have not been required during oral communication. In conversation, for example, a listener provides continual communication prods to the speaker that stimulate new memory searches; listeners also provide feedback to the speaker that conveys when information is unnecessary or irrelevant (Bereiter & Scardamalia, 1982, 1985; Rubin, 1987). In written composition, however, writers must use their own resources, initiate their own communication prods, and monitor the adequacy of their generated ideas. The training of successful writers, therefore, places a great demand for the development of students' writing strategies and the self-regulating mechanisms to determine the efficacy of chosen writing strategies.

CONTRIBUTIONS TO PROBLEMS OF SELF-REGULATION IN WRITING

Given the complexity of the writing process, it is not surprising that many students experience difficulties as they learn writing strategies. In the previous section we described the process itself and differences between successful and novice writers. In this section we focus on selected causes of these differences, with particular attention to two categories of variables that directly affect the ability to regulate and control the cognitive activities related to successful writing: metacognitive knowledge and the instructional context in which writing is taught.

Metacognitive Knowledge

Metacognitive knowledge includes both the writer's knowledge of component processes and strategies, and their ability to regulate and control the writing process. Such knowledge is one of the foundations required for self-regulation of cognitive processes (Pressley, Goodchild, Fleet, & Zajchowski, 1989), and research has demonstrated that metacognitive knowledge influences learners' performance in such activities as memory, reading comprehension, and problem-solving (e.g., Brown, 1980; Flavell, 1976; Palincsar & Brown this volume, pp. 35-71). The research on students' metacognitive knowledge about writing suggests similar influences on writing performance (Englert et al., 1988; Raphael et al., 1986).

Three types of metacognitive knowledge (i.e., declarative, procedural, and conditional) have been described (Paris, Lipson, & Wixson, 1983). Declarative knowledge involves "knowing that," knowledge about task structure and goals. This includes knowledge that writing involves subprocesses such as planning, organizing, drafting, and revising. Procedural knowledge involves "knowing how," knowledge about how to perform the various actions or strategies related to each of the writing subprocesses. In prewriting, for example, procedural knowledge includes the writer's ability to implement strategies for generating information from background knowledge and gathering information from external reference sources. Conditional knowledge refers to "knowing when and why," and includes the application and adaptation of strategies to various writing conditions and circumstances. Thus, conditional knowledge is perhaps best identified as those strategies actually implemented during the writing process, as opposed to strategies discussed in the abstract.

Beginning and poor writers' difficulties in writing may be traced to lack of metacognitive knowledge and related strategies for addressing audience needs, determining purpose, identifying relevant strategies for use in the writing process, and knowing when to implement known strategies (Englert et al., 1988). In a study of normally-achieving fifth and sixth grade students' metacognitive knowledge and performance levels in writing narrative and expository text, Raphael et al. (in press) administered group questionnaires and individual interviews to students to assess their knowledge about audience, purpose, and the writing process. Prior to an instructional intervention, students showed limited understandings of audience (e.g., identifying teachers as the primary audience and occasionally mentioning their parents or a friend). In discussing purposes, most students centered their reasons around the teachers' need to assess what they know. For example, Dawn indicated that she wrote reports so her teacher could "see if I had read the book good, the pages, and to see if I understand what she was saying," while she wrote stories "to get practice on writing and to learn more about the guy. To see how much I know" (Raphael et al., in press, p. 39).

Students' limited metacognitive knowledge of the writing process itself is seen in another example. Terry was asked to explain what he did when he wrote a story. His response suggests an overemphasis on text conventions typical of many elementary students, stating, "When I write a story this is how I first start off, write the title, and the write the beginning of it. First step I do is write the major story. And then I go all the way through and stop at periods and when I ask a question, I write a question mark. And if it's exciting, I put an exclamation mark. Put a period [at the end]" (Raphael et al., in press, p. 44). These typical young writers demonstrate an overall lack of declarative knowledge about what strategy to use, lack of procedural knowledge about how to perform the task, and lack of conditional knowledge that helps them determine strategies appropriate to varying audiences, purposes, and writing circumstances.

Predictably, instruction in the utility of and the procedures for performing new writing strategies must provide for students' acquisition of the strategies and the specific support to enhance their conditional knowledge of when and why a learned strategy may be effective. In short, if young and disabled writers exhibit less control of the writing process and are more dependent on external criteria and resources (e.g., teachers) than on their own internal resources, then strategy instruction must emphasize the writing procedures as well as develop students' knowledge of how to flexibly activate, adapt and monitor the strategy in different writing circumstances.

The Instructional Context

The instructional context in which writing instruction occurs is as complex as the process itself. For example, L. Anderson (this volume, pp. 311-343) explains this complexity in terms of five dimensions that determine the instructional environment, including such variables as the teachers' instructional goals, nature of the academic tasks, and the social environment. Others (e.g., Bloome & Greene, 1984; Raphael, 1984; Raphael et al., 1987; Roehler & Duffy, 1987) describe how teachers' use of language can create variance in the implementation of ostensibly similar lessons. From this literature, we identify four instructional problems that impede the development of self-regulation and that must be considered in the design of writing curricula: (1) failure to establish a literacy-promoting environment in which students write for meaningful purposes and real audiences, (2) separation of instruction in writing processes from the content in which they are applied, (3) insufficient attention to the development of students' conditional knowledge about writing, and (4) procedural rather than dialogic instructional approaches.

First, teachers often fail to establish a social context for writing that places students in control of their writing and develops their social cognitions for their audience. Research suggests that the social context in which students write has a major effect on their social cognition and the quality and nature of their writing (Calkins, 1983; DeFord, 1986; Graves, 1983; Hansen, 1983; Rubin & Bruce, 1986). One important aspect of social context that influences children's activities is audience. Audience provides the forum for one's ideas, and it communicates to children the purpose of prewriting, drafting, editing, and revising activities. Audience can be created in several ways, such as sharing finished products (Graves & Hansen, 1983), peer-conferencing and publishing written works (Graves, 1983), or transmitting work via microcomputer networks (Rubin & Bruce, 1986).

A second important aspect of the social context is the potential for multiple purposes of writing. Purpose affects the ideas generated during prewriting, how those ideas are communicated and eventually revised. For example, students learn that different writing purposes (e.g., imaginative, fictional, argumentative) determine what types of information can be included and alternatives for arranging those ideas. Publishing class books for placement in the school or classroom library (Deford, 1986) or sharing ideas with teachers in the form of dialogue journals (Atwell, 1983) provide students with opportunities to work toward different purposes and to see the relationship between purposes and audience. When both purpose and audience are emphasized in the writing curriculum, students are more likely to be aware of the social and communicative purpose of writing (e.g., meaningful nature of writing), see the importance of controlling the writing process, and eventually assume responsibility for their own writing activities.

Unfortunately, several studies have shown that teachers often fail to establish a social context that emphasizes audience and purpose. Most often, teachers select writing purpose and formats, focus on surface features, and consider writing as a private rather than as a social experience (Florio-Ruane & Dunn, 1985). In these circumstances, students often write to complete school tasks defined by the teacher rather than write for real audiences and purposes. A remark made by one of our CSIW classroom teachers illustrates the misconceptions teachers can promote. The teacher told her students that because their audience included university researchers, they should be carefuul "with their grammar and mechanics." Unfortunately, despite this teacher's surface attempts to establish a meaningful environment through peer-editing conferences and publication of students' writing, she continued to emphasize a more distant and evaluative adult audience rather than the more immediate audience of their peers.

The absence of writing for real audiences and purposes, when students write to complete assignments for an audience who merely is evaluating, has an effect on their metacognitive knowledge and related control of the writing process. In such an environment, students construe writing as test-taking or matching the teacher's criteria for good writing rather than employ internalized criteria (cf. comments by Dawn & Terry, p. 116). Under these circumstances, many students fail to take ownership of the writing process, and fail to develop the necessary metacognitive knowledge to monitor their own texts with a firm sense of their audience and purpose.

A second instructional problem is the separation of process from content. Roehler, Duffy, and Meloth (1986) stress the importance of integrating both process and content during reading lessons, teaching students meaningful strategies with immediate opportunities for their application to relevant content lessons. Similar principles apply to writing instruction. In content-only instruction, skill and strategy instruction is isolated from extended writing opportunities. Thus, students learn writing strategies such as brainstorming, categorizing ideas, or editing skills in lessons designed to build procedures for each of the strategies. Although there is nothing inherently problematic in teaching skills that are relevant to eventual regulation of the writing process, without opportunities to apply learned strategies flexibly according to the constraints imposed by the choice of topic, audience, and purpose, students are not likely to become independent in their application of learned strategies.

For example, during a classroom visit to a fourth grade participating in the CSIW program, we observed a teacher instructing students in organizing ideas they had generated for an explanation text. Two boys in the class had chosen to write explanations about mythological subjects rather than a more typical explanation of a process. Instead of taking advantage of the opportunity to show them how the strategies they were learning could be adapted to different topics, she told them to start over with another topic that better met her lesson objectives. Teaching the strategy out of context, as in this rigid lesson, discourages students from flexibly and strategically applying their knowledge to different writing problems.

Creating an appropriate environment and teaching process strategies within the environment is not sufficient to solve the instructional problems. Such instruction must highlight the conditional knowledge underlying the effective application of learned strategies. That is, instruction should focus on the strategy to use, why it is effective, and under what conditions it can be applied. Pressley et al. (1989) suggest that if students are to acquire conditional knowledge about strategies, teachers must make explicit the strategy's goals and objectives, tasks for which the procedural information about strategy use is important, the strategy's range of applicability, learning gains expected from consistent use of the strategy, and the amount of effort associated with strategy development. Duffy et al. (1986) have found that such instruction enhances students' metacognitive knowledge about reading and enhances their comprehension performance on a variety of measures. Without such instruction, students remain unconvinced of the utility of learned strategies, and rather than developing into self-regulated learners, may remain dependent upon the teacher to cue appropriate strategy use.

Finally, teachers often approach instruction in a procedural rather than a dialogic manner. Pressley et al. (1989) discuss the difficulty teachers have presenting cognitive strategies, and suggest that strategy instruction is very demanding since teachers must tailor their instructional efforts to a range of pupils and learning situations. Similarly, Roehler and Duffy (Roehler & Duffy,

1987; Roehler et al. 1986) and Palincsar (1986) discuss the difficulties teachers have modeling the thinking processes that underlie strategy use through the use of dialogue.

Teachers' use of language to model, think-aloud, and dialogue about cognitive strategies is particularly critical to instruction in cognitive activities such as reading and writing. Unlike motor activities such as tennis or artistic techniques such as printing, there are no visible models or products that are observable for the developing writer. Students cannot "see" the cognitions underlying planning, monitoring, or revising activities. Their only window into such cognitions is that of the teacher's use of language in her dialogue with students. For this reason, it is not sufficient for students to examine a paper on which revisions have been indicated, for it is not the lines, arrows, or carets that make the revision. Rather, it is the thoughts and inner dialogue that generate these surface level features that guide the revision process.

Through teacher dialogue, therefore, students can begin to internalize the self-talk and thinking that guides writing performance. However, dialogue about writing generally, and writing strategies particularly, are seldom observed in writing lessons (Anthony & Anderson, 1987). The following lesson in which a fifth-grade teacher discussed the concept of purpose was observed as part of the CSIW project (Raphael et al., 1987). Notice how the teacher/ students' dialogue deemphasizes the underlying cognitive activities determining one's purpose for writing, instead stressing assessment, judgment, and an indeterminant audience for writing.

T: When you are doing a rewrite, you have to remember your audience and some of you didn't for Calbery and I was a bit disappointed. If you are going to write for professors or judges, you have to be careful with your grammar and mechanics. When we write a compare/contrast, you will also have a purpose. You know that an explanation paper has a purpose. Why do we write explanations?

S: To see if we know how to write an explanation.

T: What if I was 30 and writing an explanation paper. Why would I be writing it?

S: To help younger kids learn.

T: Anyone else?

S: To tell someone how to do something.

T: What do you think is the purpose of a compare/contrast?

S: To show the differences between a bike and a motorcycle.

T: [Writes on board: To show how some things are alike and different] I want you to think what you know about compare and contrast [writes "compare and contrast" on the board]. Which word will show likenesses?

The entire recitation pattern suggests that there are correct answers that the students are to indentify. There is little use of dialogue to suggest what the teacher is thinking about when she considers establishing purposes, neither is there little elaboration when students identify meaningful purposes (e.g., "to tell someone how to do something") in contrast to superficial reasons (e.g., "to see if we know how to write an explanation"). The teacher conveys equal value for both responses.

A second teacher was observed discussing purposes of comparison/contrast texts. While more effective than the previous example, there is still an aura of recitation pattern designed to elicit correct answers, rather than thinking aloud or modeling congitive activities.

> T: The purpose, does anyone remember why I decided to write about movies?
>
> S: It's better than watching them at home.
>
> T: Yes, it's better at home. I don't like going to movies at the theater and my husband does. Maybe I can convince him it's better to be at home.
>
> T: [after brief review that there is more than one purpose for writing c/c] Who can describe one of these purposes? Robin?
>
> S: To introduce someone, or to compare a known to an unknown.
>
> T: Can you give an example?
>
> S: A mother and child. A compare/contrast would help you know one of them.
>
> T: [writes on board, "comparing a known and an unknown"] You remember this well. ...A student—that's the known—with an unknown—that's your mom or a parent...another purpose?
>
> S: To convince an audience that one thing may be better than another.

Despite the recitative nature of the dialogue, this sample indicates more promise. For example, she is more responsive to the students' responses, elaborating to elicit a supporting example or to provide additional clarification of terms used. She also reveals her underlying thinking when she explains that her purpose is to convince her husband that watching movies at home is better than watching them at the theater. Thus, while these two examples represent a range of effective teacher talk and dialogue, both reflect the need to help teachers better understand what is meant by modeling, thinking aloud, and using dialogue to help students develop the strategies for self-regulation.

THE COGNITIVE STRATEGY INSTRUCTION
IN WRITING PROGRAM

The Cognitive Strategy Instruction in Writing (CSIW) project represents one program designed to provide an alternative instructional model based in the tradition of socially-mediated instruction. The research agenda of CSIW has involved several studies of writing instruction designed to integrate and extend the research literature on strategy instruction, self-regulated learning, and effective teaching. The overall goal of these studies was to provide an alternative instructional context that emphasized how dialogue and scaffolded instruction could be used to: (1) improve students' understanding of expository text structures, (2) improve students' metacognitive knowledge about the writing process, (3) encourage students' application of expository writing strategies, (4) increase students' self-regulation of the writing process and of writing-to-learn strategies, and (5) extend students' understanding of writing strategies to comprehension, particularly in content area subjects.

The CSIW program has evolved based on a line of research that began with the teaching of a single text structure to enhance comprehension and moved to instruction that embeds learning about text structures within a context that emphasizes the writing process, writing for meaningful purposes, and real audiences (see Raphael et al., 1989). In this paper, we focus on the features of CSIW, the most current program (see Englert, Raphael et al., 1988).

CSIW is illustrative of instructional models that focus on strategy instruction of cognitive processes, using language (i.e., teacher talk, teacher/student dialogue and student/student dialogue) to make the invisible visible. The social-mediation model in which this language is used has been described as *apprenticeship* (Collins et al., in press). A primary feature of the apprenticeship model is the role of a master craftsman or expert who models the skill for the novice. Initially, the master craftsman has absolute control of the skill. However, the craftsman imparts his or her knowledge about the skill through modeling while explaining the steps of the procedure in a think-aloud. Gradually, the novice takes over responsibility for the performance of the skill as he or she attempts to complete the task while being monitored and coached by the master teacher. Eventually, the novice "solos" while performing the skill under the close supervision and guidance of the master. This gradual assumption of control by students has been discussed by Pearson (1986; Pearson & Gallagher, 1983) in terms of the acquisition of reading comprehension strategies, and is directly relevant to acquisition of writing strategies.

Another primary characteristic of the apprenticeship model is an emphasis on making "invisible" cognitive processes "visible" to students through dialogue. Vygotsky (1962) suggests that learning occurs first in a social plane, between individuals (i.e., the expert and the novice). Initially, as a new strategy or concept is introduced, the expert or teacher talk takes the form of a monologue rather than a dialogue, with the teacher "thinking-aloud." This provides students with a window into the skilled writer's thought processes. This talk gradually becomes a teacher/student dialogue, the teacher "coaching" students and guiding their strategy use. Finally, as students begin to assume control of the writing process, the teacher uses language to model collaborative processes, encouraging student/student dialogue from planning and idea generation to discussions of written products. This student/student dialogue provides teachers with a window into the learners' cognitive processes, and provides students with opportunities for feedback from their teacher and their peers. Eventually, the intraindividual dialogue that directs learning becomes internalized.

Peer collaboration and mediation by peers is another important feature of CSIW which provides the opportunities for internalization of cognitive processes and writing dialogue. Peer collaboration and mediation fosters self-regulation in three ways: (1) providing students with opportunities to practice using the dialogue appropriate to writing, (2) providing opportunities in an oral language setting for immediate feedback on writing plans or text, (3) providing individual opportunities for students to rehearse and discuss alternative problem-solving strategies, and (4) providing an opportunity for students to share ideas with a meaningful audience.

Opportunities for students to use the language and writing dialogue occur primarily during peer-editing conferences. Because strategies exist first on an interpsychological plane, between individuals, prior to moving to the intrapsychological plane where they are internalized (Vygotsky, 1962), peer conferences serve the interpsychological function as students rehearse and articulate their knowledge, eventually leading to the internalization of problem-solving strategies.

Within the context of the conferences, social interactions among peers also provide opportunitites for students to receive immediate feedback on plans and text. Peers serve as external monitors for what "works" and what does not because they are more able than the author to distance themselves from the product. Peers note comprehension difficulties in ways that provide immediate feedback to writers. Writers gradually assume increasing responsibility for ensuring that breakdowns in communication will not occur, resulting in greater ownership of the writing process and the processes that regulate strategy use. Thus, peer collaboration provides writers with an external monitor to identify communication breakdowns until that time when the criteria and perspective of the reader has been internalized by the author. In the process, the communications between author and editor help establish a social context in which writers write for real audiences (e.g., peers) and purposes (e.g., conferencing with peers to share ideas and gain assistance in preparing papers for publication).

Peer conferences also enhance self-regulation by providing opportunities for students to dialogue about writing strategies and to constructively apply problem-solving strategies in collaborative ways. Students jointly consider various writing alternatives and problem-solving strategies for resolving communication breakdowns in the classroom dialogues and in peer conferences. Thus, students learn and practice not only strategies for monitoring and identifying breakdowns, but also strategies for fixing-up or remedying breakdowns to restore communication. Collaboratively, students rehearse the cognitive strategies as they dialogue about ways to prevent and construct solutions to text problems. Gradually, students apply similar internalized criteria in generating problem-solving alternatives in response to questions about how to improve their own and others' written texts. In this way, students' assumption of the roles of producer and critic is incremental, with students taking over more and more of the dialogue, monitoring, and problem-solving processes from other students and teachers as their skills improve. This direct teaching and internalization of criteria for self-evaluation, collaboration, and revision are important features of successful writing programs (Hillocks, 1984).

To summarize, the CSIW program cycles students through an instructional process that begins with the teacher in control of strategy use and concludes with the transfer of responsibility to students for strategy use and regulation. As previously stated, teachers initially control the process, using talk to reveal expert thinking about the different writing subprocesses. The teacher does this by modeling and thinking aloud while engaging in each writing subprocess, from planning through final draft. Next, teacher and students jointly plan, organize, write, edit, and revise a class paper emphasizing teacher/student dialogue. Third, students practice the dialogue and strategies, collaboratively and individually, as they develop their own papers through the procedural assistance of the CSIW curriculum materials (i.e., think-sheets) that cue and scaffold students' strategy use. Student ownership of the writing experience is fostered by the establishment of a social context in which students write for real audiences (e.g., peers) and purposes (e.g., publication of their papers). Ideally, students eventually control the writing process independently, no longer needing the support of the teacher or curriculum materials. Instead, they use inner speech to guide their own appropriate application of strategies, monitor their success, and seek help as needed.

In this section, we describe the specific features of CSIW designed to foster the development of students' metacognitive knowledge and independent strategy use. First, we present the CSIW curriculum components that support teachers' implementation of effective strategy instruction in writing. Second, we consider the effects of the CSIW program on writing performance and students' metacognitive knowledge.

CSIW Curriculum

The CSIW curriculum materials include two elements that contribute to the development of self-regulation through the meaningful presentation of teaching strategies. These curriculum elements include the use of think-sheets and samples of effective writing lessons.

Think-sheets

CSIW think-sheets are curriculum materials designed to make writing processes and strategies explicit to students. The term, think-sheet, was selected to underscore their differences from traditional worksheets. Worksheets are typically used in elementary classrooms to promote students' independent practice of learned skills. They are generally instruments for practice and later assessment by the teacher, and are often the basis for determining when a student is ready to "move on" to the next skill. They are rarely used to promote peer interactions, with the one exception of when students are asked to check each other's papers for accuracy. In contrast, think-sheets were developed as a tool for use during modeling and peer interactions. Their purpose is to provide support for teachers during modeling of writing component subprocesses, and later, to serve as reminders to students of appropriate strategy use during the subprocess in which they are engaged. Thus, they are tools used as a paper is developed, and are not evaluated as final products at any time. For teachers who elect to examine individual students" think-sheets as the students develop their papers, the think-sheet serves as a "window" into the cognitive activities of the students, rather than as an evaluation source.

Each think-sheet contains procedures specifically correlated to strategies related to each writing subprocess. Think-sheets serve as a form of procedural facilitation, providing students with help in carrying out more sophisticated composing strategies while directing their attention to specific cognitive activities (Scardamalia & Bereiter, 1986; Collins et al., in press). Think-sheets are designed to possess seven features designated by Langer (Langer & Applebee, 1986) as important to procedural facilitation: (1) emulate mature monitoring processes using simplified routines, (2) reduce attention students need to coordinate their monitoring and executive routines, (3) provide a finite set of strategies and choices, (4) structure activities to by-pass rather than support immature composing behavior, (5) foster metacognition by making cognitive operations more overt, (6) provide labels to make tacit knowledge about strategies and procedures more accessible, and (7) incorporate procedures used by expert writers that are adjusted in complexity to match the evolving needs of different writers.

Using Bereiter and Scardamalia's (1985) discussion of the development of procedural facilitation devices as a guide, we completed four preparatory steps prior to the final design of each think-sheet. First, we identified self-regulatory functions that appear in expert performance but occur in attenuated form in students' performance. Specifically, we identified important writing activities underlying successful planning, organizing, drafting, editing, and revising. For example, accessing information from background knowledge and grouping related ideas were identified as important prewriting strategies related to successful planning and organizing. Second, we defined the self-regulatory functions in terms of mental operations or strategies fundamental to successful performance in each writing subprocess. For example, we targeted self-questioning and self-instruction as important metacognitive activities that help writers activate and monitor the effectiveness of writing strategies. Third, we devised a cueing system that signaled the onset of the mental operation being taught (e.g., think-sheets). Fourth, we designed external supports or teachable routines (e.g., teaching scripts) to decrease the information-processing burden of the teachers' mental operations. Elements such as the think-sheets were important both to teachers during the instructional process and students as they worked independently. Elements such as the teaching scripts were used solely by the teachers.

Each think-sheet reflects the thinking and self-regulatory processes suggested by the writing research as being critical to skilled writing, but that are used in an attentuated fashion by poor or novice writers. For example, the *Plan* think-sheet was developed to cue students to consider their writing purpose or goals, their intended audience, and their background knowledge related to their selected topic. The *Plan* think-sheet contained such questions as: "Who am I writing for?" (audience); "Why am I writing this?" (purpose); "What do I know?" (memory search and activation of background knowledge); and "How can I group my ideas?" (categorizing ideas). These questions were used to prompt students to perform specific planning activities, while emphasizing the development of self-instructional statements important to the activation and control of planning strategies (see Table 2).

Each of the writing subprocesses was similarly delineated to direct students' attention to specific strategies and mental operations for performing the subprocess. For example, the *Organize* think-sheet consisted of a set of pattern guides that cued students to consider organizational groups and the relationships among ideas as they further developed their writing plan. Initially, pattern guides that matched well-formed text structures were used to prompt students to consider the text strucure questions. For example, the *Organize* think-sheet for explanation prompted students to order their groups of ideas into categories related to: "What is being explained?" "What are the materials?" "What are the steps?" "What happens first?...last?" In contrast, the *Organize* think-sheet for writing comparison/contrast papers used a different visual pattern with questions specific to comparing and contrasting (see Table 3). Whereas such "pure" structures may rarely occur in students' textbooks or in

Table 2. Plan Think-sheet

PLAN

Name _____ Date _____

TOPIC: _____

WHO: Who am I writing for?

_____
_____

WHY: Why am I writing this?

_____
_____

WHAT: What do I know? (Brainstorm)

1._____
2._____
3._____
4._____
5._____
6._____
7._____
8._____

HOW: How can I group my ideas?

```
┌──────────────────┐          ┌──────────────────┐
│                  │          │                  │
└──────────────────┘          └──────────────────┘
```

_____   _____

_____   _____

```
┌──────────────────┐          ┌──────────────────┐
│                  │          │                  │
└──────────────────┘          └──────────────────┘
```

_____   _____

_____   _____

How will I organize my ideas?

_____ Comparison/Contrast   _____ Problem/Solution
_____ Explanation   _____ Other

127

Table 3. Comparison/Contrast Organization Form

What is being compared/contrasted?

On what?

Alike?	Different?

On what?

Alike?	Different?

On what?

Alike?	Different?

library resources (Schallert & Tierney, 1981), our experience suggests that it may be easier to introduce children to text structures through the use of these well-formed texts with well-defined text structure categories.

A third *Organize* think-sheet was used to demonstrate that text structures do not always conform to the well-organized explanation or comparison/contrast text structure, but may in fact, incorporate multiple text structures in a single passage. For example, when authors write about a country, they may write about its climate, topography, resources, and culture. While these categories may lead the author to explain the steps in mining resources, or compare/contrast one country with another, the categories of information rather than the explanation or comparison/contrast text structure drive the composing process. To communicate to students the idea that texts have shifting text structures, students were introduced to a form of writing called "expert writing", which is centered on categories of information (e.g., superordinate and subordinate information). For this structure, the expert *Organize* think-sheet prompted students to group their ideas into categories with appropriate superordinate labels, and to order their ideas in preparation for their first drafts. An expert *Organize* think-sheet is shown in Table 4.

Once students had learned to plan and organize their ideas, they learned new strategies associated with drafting their paper, as prompted through the use of the *Write* think-sheet. This think-sheet was a lined colored paper, signaling writers to record their prose in draft form. Colored paper, rather than white lined paper, was used to underscore the notion that a draft is not a final copy (i.e., neatly written on clean white paper). The emphasis on a draft also was designed to signal students to focus on content and organization rather than mechanics or grammatical conventions. The specific strategies utilized by students in composing their first drafts involved those associated with the translation of their plans into formal prose, tactics to engage their readers through their introductions and conclusions, the use of key words as signals to cue the location of specific types of text information, and strategies for fleshing out their text to conform to their plans, audience, and writing purpose. Furthermore, by referring to their pre-draft plans, students' reliance on the knowledge-telling strategy was diminished as they learned to compose texts after developing writing goals and organizational plans.

The fourth think-sheet, *Edit*, guided students to reflect on their papers in terms of both the content and organization, and to prepare for a peer-editing session. The first set of prompts on the think-sheet directed students to reread their paper, placing a star next to the parts they liked and did not wish to change, and explaining why they liked the parts indicated; then to put question marks by the parts that might be confusing to their readers or that required clarification, and explain why the section might cause confusion. In this way, students were encouraged to focus on the content of their papers from the perspective of their reader, and to interact directly with their first drafts in

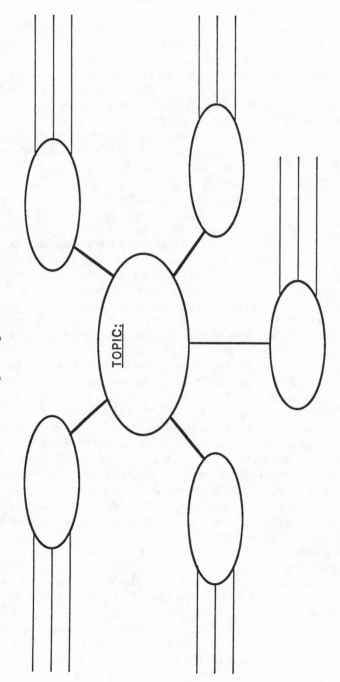

Table 4. Expert Organization Form

TOPIC:

1. How can I group my ideas into categories?

2. How can I order my ideas?

identifying their papers' strengths and weaknesses. The second set of prompts on the *Edit* think-sheet focused students' attention on their paper's organization and its potential interest to their audience. Prompts for organization asked them to rate the extent to which they used the criterion text structure features in their papers (e.g., Did I ... "Tell what was being explained? Tell what materials you need? Make the steps clear? Use key words?"). To address audience interest, the prompt asked them to rate how interesting their paper was to their reader. For each of the prompts, students rated themselves according to three simple self-rating choices ("Yes," "Sort of," and "No"). By responding to each of these questions and locating the information in their own papers, students learned to perform text analysis strategies that underlie successful writing. These strategies included the use of text cues to identify important information, procedures related to monitoring the clarity and integrity of the meaning being constructed, and fixup strategies to remedy communication breakdowns.

The third set of prompts on the *Edit* think-sheet helped writers explicitly prepare for their peer-editing session by: (1) identifying problem areas in their papers by reviewing their ratings and their papers to locate places that have been marked confusing or unclear, and (2) writing two or more questions to ask their peer editors, thus reinforcing peer editing as a collaborative process.

The fifth think-sheet, *Editor*, paralleled the fourth. It guided peer editors to reflect on the paper they were editing, again focusing on both content and organization, and helping writers plan revisions based on constructive suggestions from their editor. Editors placed stars next to their favorite parts, placed question marks where they were confused, and brainstormed with the author about ways to improve the paper. This think-sheet provided extended work in text analysis, monitoring, collaboration, and problem-solving skills fundamental to the CSIW program.

After students completed both the editing and peer editing proceses, they considered how to revise their own text with the aid of the *Revision* think-sheet. This think-sheet guided students to reflect on their first drafts by using their *Edit* and *Editor* think-sheets to identify areas of concern. This think-sheet stressed the need for the writer to again assume control over the paper, listing all the suggestions generated and received, and deciding on the changes to implement. Following this think-sheet, students returned to their drafts and implemented their revision plan. When completed, they then moved to final copy, a lined sheet of white paper.

In summary, the use of think-sheets provided procedural facilitation designed to prompt students' use of appropriate strategies. Think-sheets emulated mature thinking and monitoring processes, and helped reduce the attention students needed to coordinate executive routines by prompting and sequencing strategy use. Initially, self-questions served to externalize the control process for students, while freeing students from the burden of remembering the specific strategies and questions. Later, students' reliance on the think-sheet's self-questions was faded as teachers focused on the internalization of the questions and the types of strategy adaptations that writers make in response to different writing purposes and problems. In this way, think-sheets fostered metacognition by making cognitive operations more overt, and provided labels for strategies to make tacit knowledge more accessible.

Sample Writing Lessons

Another important component of the CSIW curriculum was a set of writing lessons of teachers modeling the thinking, problem-solving, and self-regulatory processes that underlie the component processes of writing, developed for participating teachers to illustrate appropriate dialogue and critical lesson elements. One sample was developed for each of the following aspects of the writing process: (1) recognizing and analyzing specific text structures (e.g., introducing students to explanations or comparison/contrast texts), (2) planning (i.e., one sample lesson each for explanation, comparison/contrast, and expert), (3) organizing ideas, (4) writing the first draft, (5) editing, (6) peer editing, and (7) revising.

The following sample lesson illustrates the introduction of the comparison/contrast structure. The lesson includes teacher/student dialogue and a set of four writing samples. The writing samples were papers produced by fourth and fifth grade students in a previous study (Englert et al., 1987). The four writing samples for each text structure were selected to represent the range from very effective to poorly written papers. The papers were placed on overhead transparencies and the quality of each paper was rated in terms of the degree to which it answered the relevant text structure questions (e.g., for an explanation paper, did the author tell what was being explained, who or what materials were needed, and the steps?), the degree to which key words and phrases were used appropriately to cue the important information, and the degree to which the paper captured and maintained the reader's attention. This lesson provided students with a basis for internalizing a text structure schema they could use as a guide in retrieving, organizing, signaling, and monitoring ideas.

The accompanying teaching script focused on how teachers could introduce their students to text structures. In the script, teachers introduced a text structure using the student writing samples, beginning with the most to least successful example. For each example, the teacher led a classroom discussion about the purpose of the paper, the critical elements or text structure features of the paper, the author's use of key words, and the degree of interest or audience appeal of the paper.

Initially, teachers were prompted to think aloud about relevant features found in the writing example, leading students in identifying text structure features e.g., the set of questions the text structure was able to answer and the presence of key words), and features related to audience and purpose. However, the script gradually led teachers to relinquish responsibility to students for identifying these elements and evaluating the quality of the text. For example, teachers were guided to invite the students to identify text structure features (e.g., "Does the text tell … What is being explained? What materials do I need? What are the steps?), as well as features of the paper that they particularly liked or had questions about, or that made the paper interesting to the reader. When problems were identified, teachers and students were encouraged to hold classroom dialogues about writing strategies and solutions, collaborating in generating problem-solving strategies and hypothesizing ways the author could have used alternatives to solve the problem.

Implementing the CSIW Curriculum

The following lesson transcript represents one adaptation of the CSIW curriculum to teach comparison/contrast texts. The fourth grade students in the class had already learned about and produced explanation texts, and thus were already familiar with the components of the writing process. In this lesson, the teacher introduces her students to the new text structure.

> T: (after identifying the new structure to be introduced as a comparison/ contrast) We use comparison all the time in our lives. A lot of times we make decisions, we are really comparing and contrasting two things to see which is better. I remember last night talking to my husband, and saying that we should get a movie to play at home in the VCR. He wanted to go to a movie. I can picture our discussion. I said, "It's cleaner at home, and quieter. In the movies, it's dirty because the floors have popcorn and are sticky from spilled cokes. In the movies people sit behind us and talk, but at home it's quiet unless we *want* to talk." He said, "They have good snacks in the movies, like popcorn, candy, and drinks. At home you only serve oranges and bananas." I think we talked a lot about the similarities and differences between the two, until I convinced him to stay home.
>
> Think about the last time you made a decision. What were you comparing and contrasting?

In this example, the teacher first modeled one purpose for writing a comparison/contrast paper, to convince an audience that one point is better than another. She used terms such as "I remember," "I can picture," and "I think" to indicate the inner dialogue that the skilled writer and problem solver uses. She also indicated sources of ideas, provided a concrete example, then guided students to consider relevant experiences from their own background. After discussing students' ideas, she introduced a second reason for comparing and contrasting.

T: These are all good examples of comparing and contrasting to convince someone one person, place, or thing is better than another. I'm wondering if that is the only reason to compare and contrast, and I'm thinking I've heard too many comparison/contrasts for that to be the only purpose. I'm thinking of the last time I was talking to one of my friends. My friend was asking what my brother is like, and I think I compared him to me. She knew me well, but didn't know my brother, so I said things like "Well, he is little like me in some ways, but different in others. In looks, we are both tall, with dark curly hair, but he is taller. His eyes are different than mine because mine are blue and his are brown. We're different in athletic ability in some ways. We both like to swim and ski, but he is better at them. One way we are really different. He can fly a plane, and I not only don't fly one, I don't like to be in one!"

In this example, I used a comparison/contrast to tell this person about someone they didn't know by comparing him to someone they did know—me. That's different than trying to convince them one of us is better! Can you think of a time you compared two things, one that was familiar to one that was less familiar to someone?

After a discussion of students' ideas, the lesson moved on to critiquing examples of comparison/contrast texts through the use of the four student writing samples. The sample writing passage presented to students in leading this discussion is shown in Table 5.

T: (placing the sample text on Burger King and McDonald's on the overhead projector) I'm going to read this aloud as you follow along with me. I wonder what the author is going to say about Burger King and McDonald's? Why is he writing this? [Reads text aloud]

I'm thinking that the author is telling me about two different places. I think he really likes Burger King better than McDonald's. I wonder if that's why he's writing this? To make me like Burger King better? I notice that there are several clues in this to tell me it's a comparison/contrast. My first clue was the title where there were two things mentioned. My next clue is that the words 'similar' and 'different' were used a lot. I remember that in explanations, there were certain kinds of words used to help us find important information. In an explanation we used key words like "steps," "first," "second," are there any key words that you notice in this paper that help you find important compare/contrast information?

S: "but"

S: "alike," "both have"

The lesson continued with the teacher sharing her thoughts and reactions to the text, beginning with a focus on sense-making and question-asking ("

Table 5.   Sample Writing Passage

McDonalds is a big place it even has a playground for the kids. That's probably why the kids gobble up their food and run outside. The father gets up grab the kid by the hair and says were are you going? He say swallow your food. So theirs a point that McDonald is a good place for the kids. Well the only think I like is the Big Mac and the Strawberry Shake. The other place I'm comparing is BurgerKing. BurgerKing is a place that has the Whopper. That's what I like.

The End

---

wonder what the author meant by ..." "Do you have any other ideas or questions for the author?"), then moving on to a discussion of the quality of the text in terms of the features of comparison/contrast texts: (1) identifying what was compared and contrasted, (2) identifying features on which they were to be compared and contrasted, (3) using key words and phrases appropriately, (4) describing both similarities and differences for the features named, and (5) level of interest generated by the author. In this particular lesson, the teacher rated the paper fairly well on the first four features; however, both students and teacher agreed it lacked interest.

The teacher increased students' contribution to the discussion by inviting them to help determine ways that the paper could be improved. The students suggested a way to make it more interesting, adding a conversation between the teacher and her husband about going out for dinner. They composed a short argument with one wanting to go to Burger King, the other to McDonalds, and ended with a brief conversation that was a compromise, e.g., going to Burger King "tonight" and McDonald's on another evening. In this way, students practiced strategies related to comprehension-monitoring and question-generating, and practiced fix-up routines to remedy communication breakdowns.

After introducing students to a text structure, the teacher then modeled how to use the various think-sheets by creating a group paper. The following lesson illustrates how one teacher used the ideas from the lesson script to model the *Plan* think-sheet for developing a comparison/contrast paper. In this lesson, the models purpose, frequently thinking aloud to explain why she is writing a particular item. She also models how to brainstorm topics, how to use the space on the *Plan* think-sheet, the content to include when responding to each prompt, and alternatives to what she herself is including in her example.

> T: The reason I'm writing these topics down, even if you have to read to find out more information, they might give you an idea for another idea. Like top hat and bowler made me think of a baseball hat, and maybe I could compare that to some other hat.
>
> Everyone write down the topic you chose. I'll write my topic down. [Writes: Watching movies at home and at the theater.]

Think about who is going to read your paper. I want my husband to read mine, but our audience can be anyone from one person, like mine, to thousands of people, like for people that write in newspapers (Writes "my husband" on think-sheet after question, "Who will read my paper?)

Now let's think about purpose. Probably the most important part of the first page of the Plan Think-sheet is purpose. When I compare and contrast, I might want to convince my reader that one thing, like one restaurant, is better than another one. Maybe I'd want to compare something that is unknown to something that is known. Can anyone think of another example?

S: a mother and a child, how you'd know one of them.

T: I'm impressed! You might want to compare a student—that's the known— with an unknown. Like your mother, or like one of your parents. Then we would know who your mother or parent is when we met them!

For my paper, my purpose is "I'm going to convince my husband that watching movies at home is lots more fun than watching movies in a theater." I'm going to need to keep referring back to my purpose. I'm going to be careful to remind myself so when I write, I won't forget my purpose, and maybe start talking as if they are both equally fun. Notice that my purpose takes up several lines. This is a sheet to help you remember and plan your ideas; it's a note-taking tool. You don't have to worry about whether your ideas are in complete sentences or written on printed lines.

The rest of the lesson continued with the teacher modeling the other aspects of the *Plan* think-sheet. She modeled how to brainstorm ideas (e.g., popcorn, noise, big theater, large screen) in response to the question "What do I know?", and she showed how to group her brainstormed ideas into categories (e.g., types of food, setting, people).

Teachers' dialogue in CSIW served two functions. First, it helped students understand that think-sheets were tools that aided writers in composing. Adaptations to think-sheets were modeled by teachers so that think-sheets were implemented by students in a strategic rather than mechanical way. Second, dialogue was used to make the cognitive operations explicit (e.g., I am going to ...refer back to my purpose ...when I write), helping students become more metacognitively aware of cognitive processes. Specifically, teachers guided students to become more metacognitively aware as they modeled, from the writer's perspective, the inner speech and reflective thought that directed the writing process. Such self-talk was evident in the planning example when the teacher verbalized her inner speech, making frequent reference to her own problem-solving strategies (e.g., "I remember that ... I can picture..."). These references to one's inner thinking can include references to activating strategies (e.g., "I should ask myself the planning questions), implementing strategies e.g., "I'll brainstorm as many ideas as I can. I don't have to worry about using complete sentences or the order of my ideas"), monitoring strategies (e.g., "How am I doing? Have I thought of everything the reader needs to know?"), and task management (e.g., "It's okay if I haven't remembered everything. I can come up with more ideas when I organize or draft my ideas").

Summary of Writing Lessons

These lessons illustrate how teachers made visible the thought processes, purposes, and procedures for performing each subprocess cued by the think-sheet. In turn, these subprocesses were designed to correspond to specific writing strategies important to skilled writing. The sample teaching scripts were an important tool in helping teachers understand these writing strategies, as well as the instructional dialogue that they could use to communicate strategy use. Through this dialogue, students began to internalize processes related to the regulation of the writing process.

EFFECTS OF COGNITIVE STRATEGY INSTRUCTION ON STUDENTS

Although we are still in the early stages of analyzing the complete data set from the intervention year of the CSIW project, there are several areas in which we are exploring changes in students' knowledge and performance, including: (a) expository writing performance, (b) metacognitive knowledge about writing, and (c) dialogue about writing processes and strategies. In this section, we use writing samples and interviews to explain the types of changes observed in these areas.

Expository Writing Performance

At the beginning of the chapter, we described the writing performance of David. David began the CSIW program with a fairly sophisticated knowledge of text structure, insofar as his comparison of cities and games successfully reflected his knowledge of the text structure questions (e.g., What is being compared and contrasted? On What? How are they alike? How are they different?). His comparison/contrast paper failed, however, in the mechanically-driven way that he attempted to fill up the page, showing a general insensitivity to both his purpose for writing and his audience.

With the scaffolded assistance of the CSIW program (e.g., teacher modeling, think-sheets, peer conferencing), David's first published comparison/contrast begins with an introduction to his purpose (e.g., to compare and contrast apples and oranges). The dialogue and humor he uses to introduce his topic conveys a personal involvement with and enthusiasm for his topic. Thus, David's writing now has a great deal of author's voice and suggests an emerging awareness of writing purpose and audience. However, these changes do not come at the expense of his ability to control text organization. Notice the detailed information he provides about his topics, the topical groupings he includes, and the text structure signals he uses to signal the comparison/contrast information.

Compare/Contrast Apples and Oranges

"Hey, Bob!"
"Yeah, what do you want?"
"Do you want an apple or orange?"
"Sure!"
"Which one?"
"Gee, I don't know Pete, I like them both."
"Well, I'll compare/contrast them to help you figure it out."
"Thanks."

"First I'll compare/contrast them on their growth. Apples and oranges both grow in orchards. Both have blossoms and both blossom are white, both grow in trees, and both have seeds! But oranges grow in warm climates and apples grow in temperate regions."

"Wow, tell me more, Pete!"
"Second, I'll compare/contrast their texture and taste. Oranges have a rough skin and apples have a smooth skin. On the apple you can eat the skin, on the oranges you can't. The orange is a citrus fruit and the apple isn't. The orange is sweet or sour. The apple is sweet or tart. The only thing alike about them is that they can both be made into juice!"

"Neat, so which one are you recommending so far?"
"I'm not tellin!"

"Thirdly, I'll compare/contrast their design. Both are round and edible. Both have skin and both can be made into drinks!" They're both loaded with vitamin C and they both have seeds! But the orange has a thick skin and an apple has very thin skin. Very few oranges are seedless, but apples are never seedless!"

"One more thing to compare/contrast and then you can make your pick.."

"Whew."
"Their color ..."
"Oh, wow."
"Finally, the orange is, guess, orange. The apple is red or green on the outside and white in the middle."

"So which one are you recommending to me?"
"The apple."
"Why?"
"Because I like the orange better!"

At the time of the posttest, David continues to show a greater sensitivity to his purpose and audience, although his establishment of purpose and his author's voice is somewhat diminished in the more formal, first-draft testing situation.

Have you ever heard of a football or a baseball? If you have, I'm going to tell you the likenesses and differences of them. If you haven't, I'm still going to tell you.

First, I'll compare/contrast their weight and size. A baseball is round, has a 4-5 inch diameter, and weighs around 5-10 pounds. A football is oval with roughly pointed ends, is usually 7-10 inches long and can weigh anywhere from 5-12 pounds.

Second, I'll compare/contrast them on their structure. A baseball has a cork center. Around the center, there is a tightly wrapped ball of string. On the outside, there is a leather covering to keep everything together. A baseball is very hard. A football has an air-filled inside with a hard leather outside with six or seven grip notches. A football is hard, and of course, a football and a baseball are both balls.

Well, now you know, if you already knew or not!

David's posttest paper is well organized. He clearly introduces each subtopic (e.g., weight and size, structure), and he makes effective use of key words (e.g., first, second, both) to signal the location of the attributes he is comparing and contrasting. Further, David's paper contains far more information about his topic than his pretest. He is more successful in accessing background knowledge and organizing it for his reader. In addition, David talks directly to his audience, using questions to engage them and using pronominals (e.g., you) to acknowledge an awareness of his readers. Although David functioned at a level higher than most students in his knowledge of text structure at the beginning of the program, he makes strong progress in his acquisition of strategies for accessing and organizing ideas, as well as drafting text to inform a naive audience. Although David still displays some insensitivity to the information needs and interest of his audience (e.g., "Well, now you know, if you already knew or not!"), he is now approaching writing as a communicative process rather than a school-based task.

Larry is an example of a fifth-grade student who displayed poor-to-average writing skills at the beginning of the program. At the time of the pretest his explanation of how guys become cool is unrecognizable because his text does not answer the text structure questions (e.g., What is being explained? What are the steps that explain it? What happens first? second?), and he fails to include key words.

Guys

Well guys are cool as you see they are acully the best in town right budy. Well that is all right you now.

With the scaffolded assistance of the CSIW program, Larry writes an explanation that conveys both his purpose for writing, as well as a concern for his audience's participation (e.g., "Eat well and hardy"). Notice that Larry's paper is not only a well-organized and detailed explanation, but an interesting one as well.

How to Boil an Egg

"Boy, I'm hungry, aren't you? Ya. All I have is eggs. That's O.K., let's boil an egg. How about one at a time? Cool with me.

Now let's boil an egg. First these are the things you need: a pot of cold water, a spoon, an egg, and don't forget you need a stove. Secondly, put the cold pot of water on the stove. Then put the egg in the pot. Put the pot on left rear, then turn left rear dial of the stove for 20 minutes. After 20 minutes turn the dial off. Drain the water off the eggs. Let it cool off. When it's cool crack the egg and peel the shell off and eat the delicious egg. Mmm mmm, yum yum. Eat well and hardy.

The progress indicated by these writing samples tends to parallel the results found in preliminary analyses of the CSIW data. In comparison to control students who received regular writing instruction, CSIW students made significant gains in their ability to produce well-organized expository compositions (Englert et al., 1987). In addition, they showed an increasing sensitivity to their audience, as indicated by the growing author's voice in their compositions, the increasing presence of purpose-setting statements, and an enhanced ability to engage their readers through dialogue, humor, and questions.

Metacognitive Knowledge

In addition to writing performance, a small subset of students in the study were interviewed to determine whether their knowledge about the writing process and their ability to monitor and regulate writing had changed. The transcript below contains selected questions and comments of a pretreatment interview administered to a fourth-grade student, Megan. Megan's pretreatment interview suggests a very naive conception of the writing process. Her description suggests writing consists of thinking of the title, writing the paper, and looking the paper over. When she is asked to edit a comparison/contrast paper written by a hypothetical student named Mary, she focuses on surface-level mechanical and meaning errors, but overlooks the more global violations to text structure.

I: Can you tell Sally the steps she can follow in writing her report?

S: Well, first, decide on a topic and see if you really like that topic or else it's not that great.

I: After she decides on a topic, what should she do?

S: She could start out by saying "This story is about whales."

I: Then what should she do?

S: Well, after she writes it she could look it over.

I: Here is a story written by Mary. Mary's question today is whether she is done with her paper or not. She wants us to read what she has written and see if we can give her any advice. Let's read the story.

> Thair are meny steps you must follow to mak cukies. You mak them outside. Joe likes cookies.
> Makeing cukies is different in many ways from makeing cakes. I loke chocolate cake best. Do you?
> When I mak cukies, I sometimes have a problem. I go and ask myu big brother. Then every thing is ok. We eat our cake before dinner.

I: Do you think Mary is ready to turn her paper in?

S: No. there are a lot of misspellings. And this sentence really doesn't make sense: "You make them outside." She really didn't stick to her topic here. "When I make cookies," and then, "We eat our cake before dinner." Cake and cookies are two different things; yet, they're talked about in the same paragraph.

I: Anything else?

S: Indent, indent, indent.

In the posttreatment interview administered one year later, Megan has a much more refined understanding of the writing process. When questioned about the process, she conveys an understanding that the author gets feedback from the teacher and peers, but that the author remains in control of decisions involving his or her paper. Similarly, when asked to make suggestions to the hypothetical student, Mary, she poses questions to Mary rather than tell Mary what to do. Her comment that Mary should decide what to do suggests that the author regulates and controls the writing process. Unlike her pretreatment interview, Megan now shows a keen awareness of text structure and how these structures can be used to organize, monitor and revise written text. Megan also strategically uses her knowledge of the writing subprocesses and text structures to initiate planning and generating activities during editing (e.g., "to make cookies you need so hot an oven, you need so hot an oven for cakes").

I: What steps can Sally follow to write her paper?

S: She could use POWER. She could plan, organize, write, edit, peer edit, adult edit, revise, like rewrite it.

I: What does plan mean?

S: Plan. Just thinking of everything you need in organizing it, writing it, [and]writing it in your organized form ... You just think, well I know about this and this, and this and this and I need to do this about this. ... And you just brainstorm everything [you] know.

I: Is there anything else you do when you plan?

S: You sort of start organizing because you have those little topic things. To organize a paper you take all your ideas and you rearrange them and arrange them until you are happy with them.

I: And how does she edit her paper?

S: Edit it yourself is like check [be]fore your peer editor [to see] if everything is spelled right, if you've got periods, if it is understandable. Well, you probably should try your peer editor first, because sometimes it is hard to see what you are doing wrong.

I: How does she revise her paper?

S: I remember it as rewrite, but revise her paper. Revise should be rewrite, like write it again, so it will be your final copy.

I: What do you do when you revise?

S: Well, you think back what the peer, the adult -- that everybody -- has told you. And you say, well this really doesn't fit. They all said that and I agree with it. This really doesn't fit. So I think I'll take this out and I'll put this in and write it all down in sequence or whatever.

I: Well, let's actually give a student some editorial advice. This is a story written by Mary. Mary's question today is whether she is done with her paper or not. She wants us to read what she has writen and see if we can give her any advice. Let's read the story (see story on page 141). Do you think Mary is ready to turn her paper in?

S: No. I'm not sure if this is supposed to be a compare and contrast or what.

I: What would you do then?

S: Well, I would probably say like if there are many steps you must follow to make cookies, you make them outside. No, two things, they don't tie together.

I: What would you do then?

S: By tie together, I mean like there are many steps you make cookies, now you make them outside, okay. Where outside? How do you bake them outside? Like if it is just a really sort of different. ... You make them outside. Joe likes cookies. In the first place, who is Joe?

I: Okay, let me write some of your questions down here. "Who is Joe?"

S: How do you make cookies outside? How do you make cookies?

I: Okay any other questions about the first paragraph?

S: Not really.

I: Okay, let's look at the next paragraph. "Making cookies is different in many ways from making cakes. I like chocolate cake best. Do you?"

S: Now before this sound[ed] like an explanation, now it sounds like a compare and contrast.

I: Okay, what should she do?

S: She should decide which one she is going to do, like .... Making cookies is different in many ways than making cakes." She should like say, "Well, cookies versus cakes or something like that." ... And tell to make cookies you need such and such and such and such; to make a cake you need such and such and such and such. To make cookies you need such a hot an oven, you need so hot an oven for cakes.

I: Which one would that be?

S: That would be a compare and contrast.

I: Okay.

S: *If* she wants to compare and contrast.

I: Would she do both in the same paragrah?

S: No.

I: What should she do then?

S: She would decide on either an explanation or compare and contrast.

This example illustrates the growth in students' knowledge about the writing process and the component processes related to text analysis and revision. Whereas Megan's pretreatment interview indicated little sensitivity to text structure and coherence, her posttreatment interview demonstrated a growing sensitivity to text structure as well as to the author's right to make editorial decisions about his/her own text (e.g., "If she wants to compare and contrast). Since the ability to revise and recognize problems in text was one of the less developed skills of students prior to the intervention, this change represented an important cognitive growth.

Children's Dialogue about Writing Strategies and Processes

Finally, students' ability to dialogue about writing processes and to experiment with writing strategies was examined through observations of students as they engaged in writing and peer conferencing. Since CSIW focused on dialogue, we expected change in students' ability to talk about writing processes, principally in the context of the peer conferences where students had the greatest opportunities to practice using the dialogue appropriate to writing, and various problem-solving alternatives.

There was strong evidence that CSIW did contribute to the active rehearsal and development of self-regulation, self-talk, and active experimentation with written language. For example, in one CSIW special education classroom where students were beginning their second explanation paper, Carla and Chris (two learning disabled students), conferenced with each other about their plans for their introductions. Carla's first explanation about washing a dog had begun rather abruptly (i.e., "I'm going to explain how to wash a dog for people who have a dog. First, you need materials. . ."). However, Carla told Chris that she was going to start this explanation about taking care of fish by telling how she got interested in fish (e.g., Meijer's was giving away free fish to children on Kid's Day and she received a free fish). Carla's second explanation began as follows:

> One day I went to the store with my friend. We went to Meijer's. It was Kid's week and we got to get a fish free. And that's how I got to like fish. I'm going to explain how to take care of fish. First, you should buy a bowl. You have to buy a bowl. Then you should get gravel and some plants so they feel at home . . . .

This introduction suggests that Carla was experimenting with setting up a context for her explanation, and that she was actively testing different writing patterns from her first to second explanation. In her dialogue with Chris, she verbally rehearsed a writing strategy that she subsequently implemented in her written draft.

Chris was concerned with a different writing problem. His first explanation had an introduction that rambled and contained much irrelevant information as he attempted to set his context:

> One day I was in Frandor with my mom, brother, and my two sisters. And me and my brother went into the Hobby Hub. The problem was—he had money and I didn't. And he got the game Car Wars that he had wanted for a long time, and a book for the game that has weapons for the car. And now I will tell you how to play. First, you need to read the instruction book.

When Chris heard Carla's plans for her second explanation, he responded by stating that he had "tried that the last time and now I am going to get right to the point." Notice how Chris begins his second explanation, getting right to the point as he had explained to Carla.

> I'm going to get right to the point. I'm going to explain how to take care of a kitten or cat. First, I'm going to tell you how to feed a kitten or cat. When you get your kitten, check if it has big or little teeth. If it has little teeth, give it soft cat food. If it has medium teeth, mix hard cat food and soft cat food. Then when it is a full grown cat, give it just hard cat food. Give it a cat food it likes.

Although Chris' explanation begins abruptly, like Carla, he is experimenting with written language and new writing patterns. Chris may ultimately create introductions somewhere between his first and second attempts, learning from his active construction of different writing patterns and later analyzing their effects. Thus, children seemed to be flexibly applying strategies to solve the particular problems they saw in their own texts.

This exchange illustrates the nature of student dialogue during conferencing. Children were experimenting with language, going beyond the intended lessons of the teachers by fine-tuning aspects of their text that were of particular concern to them. Furthermore, without direct teacher intervention, writers were studying how other students composed their texts and they tried out these procedures in their own texts. Thus, the CSIW program and peer collaboration provided an important stage for cognitive rehearsal of plans and strategies, and for the study of alternative writing patterns. Additionally, by collaborating with their peers and serving as readers of other children's writing, writers saw what worked and what didn't, prompting them to try out new strategies and procedures. In seeing how others failed to take them into consideration as audiences in their writing; writers learned to hypothesize about the problems their audiences will face, and internalize their readers' perspective. In this way, interactive sessions did seem to help writers begin to preplay the communicative cycle between writers and their audience, and to apply problem-solving strategies to real problems.

SUMMARY

This paper examined sources of writing problems of elementary students and explored the potential of socially-mediated instruction in addressing these problems. Features fundamental to this type of socially-mediated instruction include: (1) modeling of the writing strategy by teachers and peers, (2) emphasis on classroom dialogues and conversations about the use and regulation of writing strategies, and (3) focus on problem-solving responses to writing problems. CSIW is one example of an instructional program that fosters self-regulation and internalization of writing subprocesses. With the development of a curriculum that uses procedural facilitation to foster strategy acquisition and an emphasis upon socially-mediated instruction (e.g., teachers and peers), CSIW guides teachers and students to better understand the writing process and the strategies for regulating writing performance.

Existing evidence suggests that CSIW enhances students' performance on measures of expository writing performance and metacognitive knowledge. Students' compositions were better organized and showed a greater awareness of their writing purpose and audience. Interviews with students suggested an increasingly sophisticated knowledge of the writing process and strategies for analyzing, monitoring, and revising text. Informal observations of students further suggested that students were acquiring problem-solving strategies that could be flexibly applied to their own and others' writing problems.

In summary, learning to write can be assisted through an instructional model that focuses on the development of children's strategies through a socially-mediated model that emphasizes teacher dialogue, modeling of component subprocesses, and student/student dialogue about writing. Further, the instructional context is enhanced by a literacy-promoting environment in which students write for meaningful purposes and audience, and in which teachers emphasize the development of students' declarative, procedural and conditional knowledge about writing. The literacy knowledge that develops through these methods can empower students to learn and develop throughout their school career and beyond.

REFERENCES

Anderson, R.C., & Pearson, P.D. (1984). A schema-theoretic view of basic processes in reading comprehension. In P.D. Pearson (Ed.), *Handbook of reading research* (pp. 255-291). New York: Longman.

Anderson, T.H., & Armbruster, B.B. (1984). Content area textbooks. In R.C. Anderson, J. Ostborn, & R.J. Tierney (Eds.), *Learning to read in American schools* (pp. 193-226). Hillsdale, NJ: Erlbaum.

Anthony, H.M., & Anderson, L.M. (1987). *The nature of writing instruction in regular and special education classrooms.* Paper presented at the Annual meeting of the Council for Exceptional Children, Chicago, IL.

Applebee, A.N. (1984). *Contexts for learning to write: Studies of secondary school instruction.* Norwood, NJ: Ablex.

Applebee, A.N. (1986). Problems in process approaches: Toward a reconceptualization of process instruction. In A.K. Petrosky, & D. Bartholomae (Eds.), *The teaching of writing: Eighty-fifth Yearbook of the National Society for the Study of Education* (pp. 95-113). Chicago: University of Chicago Press.

Applebee, A.N., & Langer, J.A. (1983). Instructional scaffolding: Reading and writing as natural language activities. *Language Arts, 60*(2), 168-175.

Atwell, N. (1983). Writing and reading literature from the inside out. *Language Arts, 61,* 240-252.

Bartlett, E.J. (1981). *Learning to write: Some cognitive and linguistic components.* Washington, DC: Center for Applied Linguistics.

Bereiter, C., & Scardamalia, M. (1982). From conversation to composition: The role of instruction in a developmental process. In R. Glaser (Ed.), *Advances in Instructional Psychology* (Vol. 2, pp. 1-64). Hillsdale, NJ: Erlbaum.

Bereiter, C., & Scardamalia, M. (1985). Cognitive coping strategies and the problem of "inert knowledge." In S. Chipman, J. Segal, & R. Glaser (Eds.), *Thinking and learning skills: Current research and open questions* (Vol. 2, pp. 65-80). Hillsdale, NJ: Erlbaum.

Bloome, D., & Greene, J. (1984). Directions in the sociolinguistic study of reading. In P.D. Pearson (Ed.), *Handbook of reading research* (pp. 395-421). new York: Longman.

Borkowski, J.G., Johnston, M.B., & Reid, M.K. (1987). Metacognition, motivation, and controlled performance. In S. Ceci (Ed.), *Handbook of cognitive, social, and neurological aspects of learning disabilities* (Vol. 2, pp. 147-174). Hillsdale, NJ: Erlbaum.

Bridwell, L.S. (1980). Revising strategies in twelfth grade students: Transactional writing. *Research in the Teaching of English, 14,* 197-222.

Brown, A.L. (1980). Metacognitive development and reading. In R.J. Spiro, B.C. Bruce, & W. Brewer (Eds.), *Theoretical issues in reading comprehension* (pp. 453-481). Hillsdale, NJ: Erlbaum.

Brown, A.L., & Smiley, S.S. (1977). Rating the importance of structural units of prose passages: A problem of metacognitive development. *Child Development, 48,* 1-8.

Calkins, L.M. (1983). *Lessons from a child.* Exeter, NH: Heinemann Educational Books.

Collins, A., Brown, J.S., & Newman, S. (in press). The new apprenticeship: Teaching students the craft of reading, writing and mathematics. In L. Resnick (Ed.), *Cognition and instruction: Issues and agendas.* Hillsdale, NJ: Erlbaum.

DeFord, D. (1986). Classroom contexts for literacy learning. In T.E. Raphael (Ed.), *The Contexts of School-Based Literacy* (pp. 163-180). New York: Random House.

Duffy, G.D., Roehler, L.R., Meloth, M.S., Vavrus, L.G., Book, C., Putnam, J., & Wesselman, R. (1986). The relationship between explicit verbal explanations during reading skill instruction and student awareness and achievement: A study of reading teacher effects. *Reading Research Quarterly, 21,* 237-252.

Englert, C.S., Raphael, T.E., & Anderson, M. (1985). *Teaching cognitive strategies to the midly handicapped: A classroom intervention study.* Project funded by the U.S. Department of Education, Special Education Programs, Office of Special Education and Rehabilitative Services.

Englert, C.S., Raphael, T.E., Anderson, L.M., Gregg, S.L., & Anthony, H.M. (1987, December). *Implementing cognitive strategy instruction: Impact on elementary students' composition and comprehension of expository text.* Paper presented at National Reading Conference, St. Petersburg, Florida.

Englert, C.S., Raphael, T.E., Fear, K.L., & Anderson, L.M. (1988). Students' metacognitive knowledge about writing informational texts. *Learning Disability Quarterly, 11,* 18-46.

Englert, C.S., Stewart, S.R., & Hiebert, E.H. (1988). Young writers' use of text structure in expository text generation. *Journal of Educational Psychology, 80,* 143-151.

Flavell, J.H. (1976). Metacognitive aspects of problem-solving. In L.B. Resnick (Ed.), *The nature of intelligence* (pp. 231-235). Hillsdale, NJ: Erlbaum.

Florio-Ruane, S., & Dunn, S. (1985). *Teaching writing: Some perennial questions and some possible answers* (Occasional Paper No. 85). East Lansing: Michigan State University, Institute for Research on Teaching.

Flower, L., & Hayes, J.R. (1981). A cognitive process theory of writing. *College Composition and Communication, 35,* 365-387.

Gavelek, J.R. (1986). The social contexts of literacy and schooling: A developmental perspective. In T.E. Raphael (Ed.), *The contexts of school-based literacy* (pp. 3-26). New York: Random House.

Graham, S., & Harris, K. (in press). Cognitive training: Implications for written language. In J. Hughes & R. Hall (Eds.), *Handbook of cognitive behavioral approaches in educational settings.* New York: Guilford.

Graves, D.H. (1983). *Writing: Teachers and children at work.* Exeter, NH: Heinemann Educational Books.

Graves, D.H., & Hansen, J. (1983). The author's chair. *Language Arts, 60*(2), 176-183.

Hansen, J. (1983). Authors respond to authors. *Language Arts, 60,* 970-977.

Hayes, J.R., & Flower, L. (1980). Identifying the organization of writing processes. In L. Gregg & E. Steinberg (Eds.), *Cognitive processes in writing* (pp. 31-50). Hillsdale, NJ: Erlbaum.

Hayes, J.R., & Flower, L.S. (1987). On the structure of the writing process. *Topics in Language Disorders, 7,* 19-30.

Hayes, J.R., Schriver, K.A., Spilka, R., & Blaustein, A. (1986, March). *If it's clear to me it must be clear to them.* Paper presented at the Conference on College Composition and communication, National Council of Teachers of English, New Orleans.

Hillocks, G. (1984). What works in teaching composition: A meta-analysis of experimental treatment studies. *American Journal of Education, 93,* 133-170.

Hillocks, G. (1986). The writer's knowledge: Theory, research, and implications for practice. In A.K. Petrosky, & D. Bartholomae (Eds.), *The teaching of writing: Eighty-fifth Yearbook of the National Society for the Study of Education* (pp. 71-94). Chicago: University of Chicago Press.

Meyer, B.J.F. (1975). *The organization of prose and its effects on memory.* Amsterdam: North-Holland.

Meyer, B.J.F., Brandt, D.H., & Bluth, G.J. (1980). Use of author's textual schema: Key for ninth-graders' comprehension. *Reading Research Quarterly, 16,* 72-103.

Palincsar, A.S. (1986). The role of dialogue in providing scaffolded instruction. *Educational Psychologist, 21,* 73-98.

Paris, S.G., & Lindauer, B.K. (1977). Constructive aspects of children's comprehension and memory. In R.V. Kail, Jr., & J.W. Hagen (Eds.), *Perspectives on the development of memory and cognition* (pp. 333-349). Hillsdale, NJ: Erlbaum.

Paris, S.G., Lipson, M.Y., & Wixson, K.K. (1983). Becoming a strategic reader. *Contemporary Educational Psychology, 8,* 293-316.

Pearson, P.D. (1986). Changing the face of reading comprehension instruction. *Reading Teacher, 38*(8), 724-738.

Pearson, P.D., & Gallagher, M.C. (1983). The instruction of reading comprehension. *Contemporary Educational Psychology, 8*(3), 317-344.

Perl, S. (1979). The composing process of unskilled college readers. *Research in the Teaching of English, 13,* 317-336.

Pressley, M. Goodchild, F., Fleet, J., Zajchowski, R. (1989). The challenges of classroom strategy instruction. *Elementary School Journal, 89,* 301-342.

Raphael, T.E. (1984). Teacher explanations and student's understanding of sources of information for answering questions. In J.A. Niles & L.A. Harris (Ed.), *Changing Perspectives on Research in Reading/Language Processing and Instruction* (pp. 214-222). Rochester, NY: National Reading Conference.

Raphael, T.E., Englert, C.S., & Anderson, L.M. (1987, December). *What is effective instructional talk? A comparison of two writing lessons.* Paper presented at the National Reading Conference, St. Petersburg, FL.

Raphael, T.E., Englert, C.S., & Kirschner, B.W. (1989). The acquisition of expository writing skills. In J.N. Mason (Ed.), *Reading and writing connections* (pp. 261-290). Newton, MA: Allyn & Bacon.

Raphael, T.E., Englert, C.S., & Kirschner, B.W. (in press). Students' metacognitive knowledge about writing. *Research in the Teaching of English.*

Roehler, L.R., & Duffy, G.G. (1987, December). *Characteristics of responsive elaboration which promote the mental processing associated with reading strategy use.* Paper presented at the National Reading Conference, St. Petersburg, FL.

Roehler, L.R., Duffy, G.G., & Meloth, M.B. (1986). What to be direct about in direct instruction in reading: Content-only versus process-into-content. In T.E. Raphael (Ed.), *Contexts of school-based literacy* (pp. 79-95). New York: Random House.

Rogoff, B. (1986). Adult assistance of children's learning. In T.E. Raphael (Ed.), *The Contexts of School-based Literacy* (pp. 27-40). New York: Random House.

Rubin, A., & Bruce, B.C. (1986). Learning with QUILL: Lessons for students, teachers and software designers. In T.E. Raphael (Ed.), *Contexts of school-based literacy* (pp. 217-230). New York: Random House.

Rubin, D.L. (1987). Divergence and convergence between oral and written language. *Topics in Language Disorders, 7,* 1-18.

Samuels, J., & Kamil, M.L. (19840. Models of the reading process. In P.D. Pearson (Ed.), *Handbook of Reading Research* (pp. 185-224). New York: Longman.

Scardamalia, M., & Bereiter, C. (1985). Fostering the development of self-regulation in children's knowledge processing. In S.F. Chipman, J.W. Segal, & R. Glaser (Eds.), *Learning and thinking skills* (Vol. 2, pp. 563-577).

Scardamalia, M., & Bereiter, C. (1986). Written composition. In M. Wittrock (Ed.), *Handbook of research on teaching* (3rd ed., pp. 778-803). New York: Macmillan.

Schallert, D.L., & Tierney, R.J. (1982). *Learning from informational text: The interaction of text structure with reader characteristics.* NIE-G-79-0161. Final report submitted to the National Institute of Education.

Taylor, B.M., & Beach, R. (1984). The effects of text structure instruction on middle grade students' comprehension and production of expository text. *Reading Research Quarterly, 19,* 134-146.

Vygotsky, L.S. (1962). *Thought and language.* Cambridge, MA: MIT Press.

Wood, D.M., Bruner, J.S., & Ross, G. (1976). The role of tutoring in problem-solving. *Journal of Child Psychology and Psychiatry, 17*(2), 89-100.

*   *   *

CROSS-TALK

Do differences among perspectives in the writing chapters reflect fundamental or more superficial differences in beliefs about writing?

In addressing this question, perhaps it might be useful to picture the following scenario. Several scholars who have studied the writing process and writing instruction are in a conference room discussing the research findings and implication for practice. A number of points are raised for which consensus is easily reached. First, all agree that the writing is a social activity involving communication about personally relevant and meaningful topics. Second, all agree that writers produce greater quantities of well-organized and interesting information when selecting topics that are meaningful. Third, all agree that teachers of writing themselves should be experienced in the writing process. Fourth, all agree that writing is a nonlinear process consisting of several subprocesses (i.e., prewriting, drafting, revising), and each of the subprocesses has strategies that can ease and enhance the overall writing activity. Such is the scenario that might exist if the authors of the chapters in this volume participated in such a discussion. The discussion continues harmoniously as such points of agreement are easily reached. How these points are implemented in classrooms is at the center of the discussion.

Whether any disagreement is considered fundamental depends on the perspective from which the discussion is viewed. Historically, the so-called fundamental differences existed between the *product* and *process* views of writing. All of the contributors to this volume are quite similar in their advocating of a process approach: writing is a process that can be taught, not a talent available to the chosen few. Thus, if a continuum delineating approaches to writing were available, we would probably all be toward one end. However, the degree to which instruction is child- or teacher-directed seems to be the basis for existing differences. The questions raised by others in cross-talk help us focus on these existing differences.

We see CSIW fitting within a literate environment that emphasizes writing as a communicative process. In fact, our experience suggests that CSIW is more successful when it is introduced in process-writing classrooms. Teachers more successful with the program are those who have a firm understanding of and experience teaching from a process-writing perspective. Furthermore, these teachers were those who provided writing experiences in addition to CSIW across the curriculum. Thus, the real question is, "What does CSIW add to process writing programs?"

Process writing approaches assume that teachers have a well-developed understanding of the writing process and how to teach it. However, our experience suggests that teachers trained in a process writing approach relate feelings of inadequacy when making decisions about what to instruct. They express satisfaction with the motivational aspects of their process-writing program, but voice concern about students' development as successful writers. CSIW provides a framework within which teachers can model specific writing strategies to help their students develop writing skills. With this framework, teachers feel more confident in their ability to help their students develop into mature writers.

What is the role of background knowledge, subject matter knowledge, and extensions to content area instruction?

In addition to providing a framework within which teachers can model writing strategies, CSIW provides opportunities for teachers to make connections between the writing program and content area learning. For example, in a fourth-grade classroom, for a social studies unit on plains around the world, students were assigned to groups. Each group selected one geographic region in which a plain was located, then planned, drafted, and presented information about the people, resources, and so forth. Students spontaneously used the planning think-sheet to organize their activities and decide who within the group would be responsible for each aspect of their report. The planning and organizing think-sheets guided their search for information and their decisions about what information was important to include in subsequent drafts. In a fifth-grade classroom, students who had written essays following an expository passage from their basal reader used a self-edit think-sheet to self-evaluate how well they had met the goals of the assignment. Other related examples of extensions of CSIW to content learning include using think-sheets to record notes during reading, development of alternative formats for organizing information, and so forth.

Is there difficulty in maintaining a separation of think-sheets as *means* versus *ends* in and of themselves?

The distinction between means and ends may be thought of as the difference between a think-sheet and a worksheet. As we indicated in the chapter, worksheets are designed as independent activities that serve to evaluate the students' development of particular, isolated skills. If think-sheets are misinterpreted by some teachers and used as worksheets, little or no improvement in writing will occur. Worse, students may believe that writing itself is a series of discrete and isolated skills that lead in a linear fashion to an assigned product. The solution to this potential problem is not to deprive teachers and students of the availability of these support materials, but rather, to educate them as to their approriate use. Thus, in introducing think-sheets, the emphasis is on their thoughtful and strategic use, their modifiability, and the importance of internalizing the ideas such that the think-sheets themselves are no longer needed. Further, focus should be on making explicit connections between strategies learned as a part of the writing process and use of these strategies during other learning activities.

What is the teacher's metacognitive control of the instructional dialogue and the role that think-sheets serve in promoting or inhibiting such control?

We recognize that writing and writing instruction is complex. Teachers need both knowledge and personal experience in writing and teaching writing. The think-sheets served to guide teachers in terms of what they should be thinking aloud about. The sample lessons provided teachers with alternative ways of expressing their inner thinking about various writing strategies and various activities within the writing subprocesses. However, in spite of such support, teachers experienced difficulties because they were, in fact, learning two distinct bodies of knowledge. First, they themselves were developing their own knowledge of writing strategies. Second, they were also learning a new way to dialogue with students that focused on thinking aloud about invisible mental processes. Teachers who were most successful tended either to know a great deal about writing or to use modeling or thinking aloud in other content area subjects. Internalization of appropriate instructional dialogue to help develop successful independent writers was a long and difficult process that took teachers at least two years before they acquired and owned the new instructional model.

It is our intention that CSIW be interpreted as a set of guidelines compatible with writing for meaningful purposes and real audiences, whether the topics be of the students' own choosing or part of the broad goals of specific content area curricula. Our goal is to provide teachers and students with the support necessary to learn, implement, and own the complex process of writing to learn.

WRITING IN THE CONTENT AREAS:
REACHING ITS POTENTIAL
IN THE LEARNING PROCESS

Cheryl Rosaen

INTRODUCTION AND OVERVIEW

As educators have searched to find more effective ways to teach subject matter knowledge, they have identified writing as a possible means to help students develop and refine understanding in the content areas and develop higher order skills with which they approach content area learning (e.g., critical thinking, problem-solving skills, self-regulatory behavior). Shifting the instructional focus of classroom writing activities from teaching students how to create particular written forms or to use writing to demonstrate their academic competence to teaching students to use the writing process to explore and develop their thinking about subject matter is a complex undertaking that requires careful and studied implementation. The purpose here is to examine what is currently known or understood about writing to learn in the content areas, to identify instructional issues that are central to teaching students to successfully use writing to develop understanding of subject matter content, and to offer principles that classroom teachers can use as a framework for teaching writing in the content areas.

Advances in Research on Teaching, Volume 1, pages 153-194.
Copyright © 1989 by JAI Press Inc.
All rights of reproduction in any form reserved.
ISBN: 0-89232-845-2

First, writing in the content areas is defined and current theories that account for how writing in the content areas promotes meaningful comprehension and self-regulated learning are examined. Current research on writing is used to explain hypotheses about how writing to learn should be carried out. What has been learned from research in elementary and secondary classrooms about the complex interaction between students' writing knowledge and skill and their content knowledge is explained. Then, four sets of issues classroom teachers face in trying to successfully teach students to use writing as a means to learn are outlined. The complexities of the issues are illustrated with a series of examples from a research study that focused on writing about subject matter in an elementary classroom. Finally, guidelines are offered for classroom teachers to help them manage the complexities of teaching students to use writing as a means to understand subject matter.

WRITING IN THE CONTENT AREAS: BEYOND "KNOWLEDGE TELLING"

The purpose of this section is to make clear the potential power of writing in the content areas. Writing in the content areas is defined as it pertains to helping students understand subject matter and develop higher order thinking skills. Then, current theories are examined that account for how writing as a form of communication helps students understand subject matter better and helps students improve their thinking skills and ability to learn.

Writing to Learn

The notion of writing in the content areas typically evokes images of the essay test in social studies, the lab report in science, or the research report in English or history. These common forms of writing in the content areas share an emphasis on having students use writing to show what they know about a topic to the teacher, who is the sole audience for the piece of writing. Using writing for this purpose has been labeled a *knowledge telling* activity which contrasts with other purposes for writing that are referred to as *knowledge transforming* experiences. Knowledge telling writing is called a *developmental dead end* (Scardamalia & Bereiter, 1986) in that students only report knowledge they already possess or have ready access to (through cursory reading of text material, for example), instead of using the writing process to explore, develop, and enrich their understanding of subject matter (knowledge transforming). Thus, there is no guarantee that improved learning occurs simply because students write about subject matter. Rather, research on the writing process has shown that teaching students to "write to learn" about subject matter entails teaching students to use the writing process for a particular purpose (see Florio-Ruane

& Lensmire [this volume, pp. 73-104] for a discussion of additional purposes for writing). Moreover, instruction in using the writing process for this purpose may look different from instruction in using writing for other purposes (e.g., personal expression or display of academic competence). Given particular subject matter to be learned, different aspects of the writing process (e.g., generating ideas) may require greater instructional emphasis, while other aspects (e.g., learning to correctly produce a particular written form) may be de-emphasized in the instructional process. In addition, various aspects of the writing process (generating ideas and learning to express them in particular forms to particular audiences) interact with one another in complex ways, and the interaction may require special instructional support, as will be described later.

Teaching students to write in the content area will refer to teaching them to "write to learn subject matter," where the main purpose of engaging in writing activity is to help learners better understand subject matter or develop higher order thinking skills that they can habitually apply to future learning situations (e.g., critical thinking, problem-solving, self-regulatory behavior). The forms of such writing are not necessarily limited to the expository forms that typically occur in content area classes today (essays, fill-in worksheets, or reports); such writing might also include more expressive forms such as journals, narrative, or other creative forms in which the purpose goes beyond personal expression. Thus, instruction in writing to learn differs *in emphasis* from other types of writing instruction in that its *primary purpose* is to engage students in cognitive activity that promotes the use and development of higher order thinking skills for learning subject matter. Accordingly, writing instruction will require providing opportunities for students to *develop* (and not merely display) knowledge and skill in three areas: (1) knowledge of subject matter content and skill at gaining access to one's understanding; (2) writing knowledge and skill (integrating knowledge of topic, knowledge of audience, language conventions, and writtern forms); and (3) metacognitive knowledge of how one approaches a writing-to-learn activity, and skill at strategically using skills to manage the writing process. Here, I explore ways in which the first area, *development* of subject matter knowledge and understanding, can be given greater emphasis in writing instruction so that the use of content area writing in classrooms can go beyond finding out what students know to helping them construct new knowledge during the writing process. Such emphasis does not diminish the importance of providing appropriate instruction in developing knowledge and skills in writing and metacognition. Instead, it requires figuring out how to effectively manage instruction across all three areas.

Why Use Writing as a Means to Learn?

Why do researchers think the writing process will promote improved understanding of subject matter and students' abilities to monitor and develop their understanding of subject matter content? In this section I explain current theories about ways in which writing as a unique form of communication holds potential power in the learning process.

As one of four basic language processes in human development, writing has characteristics that point out its unique potential as a means to learning. Unlike speaking, listening or reading, writing is a more tangible, concrete means of using representational symbols. It is thought, for example, that younger children use writing as an extension of other activities in which they use representational symbols such as drawing, drama, and symbolic play (Emig, 1981; Gundlach, 1982; Vygotsky, 1982). Writing's visible, concrete form enables users to make external to themselves their thoughts, knowledge, and understandings in a medium that can be examined and re-examined by themselves and others for further clarification or exploration. Moreover, such examination can take place at a pace suitable to the writer (Emig, 1977). In addition to its more concrete form compared to other language processes, the act of writing brings about cognitive activity that can promote learning. Psychologists such as Vygotsky (1962) and Bruner (1971) have argued that expanding inner speech *requires* making systematic connections and relationships and therefore makes writing a powerful learning tool. Moreover, writing down their thoughts requires writers to represent a problem to themselves, or decide what they are writing about, to whom, and for what purpose (Flower & Hayes, 1980a). This type of cognitive activity is an integral part of knowledge construction, whereby learners must organize or make sense of new knowledge in light of how it relates to prior knowledge and understanding (Posner, Strike, Hewson, & Gertzog, 1982). Thus, while writing shares with other forms of language processes (speaking, listening, reading) the benefits of requiring learners to draw out for examination, exploration, and clarification their prior knowledge (Barnes, 1969; Cazden, 1986), it also has unique characteristics that make it especially suited for developing meaningful understanding of subject matter (Emig, 1977).

Using the writing process as a tool for understanding holds the potential for helping learners monitor their own learning processes. Yet how effectively writers approach a writing task will affect how much they learn from the process. By studying and describing writers' cognitive processes, researchers have developed hypotheses about how writers can learn to pay attention to their cognitive activity as they write, and subsequently improve their abilities to use writing as a means to learn (e.g., de Beaugrande, 1984; Flower & Hayes, 1980a; Hayes & Flower, 1980). It is also argued that opportunities for learners to plan reflectively so that they have occasions to progressively shape goals and ideas during the writing process will help learners take advantage of the interaction between rhetorical goals (e.g., what is being written and for whom) and content goals (e.g., how the writer wants to affect the reader, the writer's attempt to create meaning), much like expert writers do (Flower & Hayes,

1980a; Scardamalia & Bereiter, 1986). In this way, opportunities to engage in goal-directed strategic planning before and during the writing process hold the potential for fostering metacognitive awareness of the learning process and improved approaches to understanding subject matter content (Scardamalia & Bereiter, 1986).

These benefits of the writing process imply a close relationship between writers' content area knowledge and their writing knowledge and skill. Much of the research on which the above claims are based is research that focuses more closely on writers' knowledge and skill, and less on their content area knowledge. In the next section, I summarize what researchers have learned about the complex interaction between the two areas and identify the complexities and difficulties the classroom teacher faces in designing and implementing writing activities in the content areas.

WRITING TO LEARN AS A DUAL PROCESS

How can students who are still learning to write successfully use writing as a tool to learn? In the following discussion, I examine the contributions of research on the writing process to our understanding of how writers' knowledge of subject matter content interacts with their writing skill and knowledge of the writing process. If writing-to-learn activities are to be appropriately designed and supported, we must know more about the nature of the cognitive activity in which students engage when they write about subject matter. The section concludes with a discussion of implications from the research for creating successful writing-to-learn opportunities.

The Interaction Between Content and Writing Knowledge

Writing is an extremely complex cognitive activity, and writers draw on different kinds of knowledge and skill as they write. In discussing research conducted with elementary and secondary students, two main subprocesses are identified that are central to writing to learn: developing subject matter knowledge, and developing writing knowledge and skill. These two broad categories and ways in which they interact are discussed below.

Making Sense of Subject Matter

Constructivist theories of learning claim that learners actively shape and make sense of activities in the environment. Furthermore, learners interpret new knowledge in light of their prior knowledge and skills (Barnes, 1979; Bruner, 1982; Posner et al., 1982; Vygotsky, 1962, 1978). Learning is facilitated when students have the opportunity to connect new information with prior knowledge, and are required to construct (as opposed to receive) knowledge

(Armento, 1986; Wittrock, 1977). Writing in the content areas is an opportunity for students to bring together their prior knowledge with new ideas or information and thereby construct new meaning through the act of writing (Van Nostrand, 1979). A key claim here is that students will go beyond mere "knowledge telling" to "knowledge transformation," where they bring to bear cognitive operations (e.g., discrete cognitive operations, complex processes, and critical appraisal) that allow them to go beyond mere comprehension and recall to analysis, synthesis, evaluation, and critical appraisal of knowledge. However, there is little research that documents how development of knowledge and reasoning skills comes about during the writing process (Applebee, 1984). Therefore, I will briefly summarize the available research that does investigate this aspect of content area writing, and identify potential areas of difficulty for students as they write about subject matter.

If writing is to help students link their prior knowledge with new ideas or information in meaningful ways, students' ability to generate content, or think of what they know (and, therefore, think of what to say) is an important subprocess during the writing process (Burtis, Bereiter, Scardamalia, & Tetro, 1983; Hayes & Flower, 1980; Scardamalia & Bereiter, 1986). Content generation involves two main areas: one's knowledge level about a topic, and one's ability to gain access to the knowledge one has. Scardamalia & Bereiter (1986) report that when trying to gain access to their knowledge of a topic, children lack effective metamemorial and heuristic search strategies for looking at the information they have available, and are therefore left to using trial-and-error or exhaustive searches. Effective metamemorial search allows writers to generally determine what they know about a topic without having to exhaustively retrieve, measure, and evaluate their knowledge. Effective heuristic search occurs when writers are able to reduce the range of search through memory by using partial knowledge of a topic to search for further knowledge. That is, effective metamemorial and heuristic search enables writers to quickly survey the breadth and depth of their knowledge about a topic to decide if they know enough about a topic to write about it and determine ways in which they can focus on their topic that will efficiently aid in information retrieval. Scardamalia and Bereiter also suggest that children experience difficulty with "cognitive overload" because of having to monitor the composing process while at the same time monitoring and using strategies for knowledge retrieval. Thus it appears that requiring students to write about content can interfere with thinking about content when the writing task demands more resources of children than they currently have (Scardamalia, 1981).

A second aspect of content generation, one's knowledge level about a topic, also influences the writing-to-learn process. Chi (1985) investigated the issue of how students' existing knowledge affects their use of cognitive strategies, and postulated that young children's categorical knowledge is not unlike adults' knowledge (as was previously believed). Instead, their categories are smaller, and the set of members is more restricted. Therefore, as children are taught retrieval strategies, the strategies must take their existing knowledge structure into account and not simply teach to a different knowledge structure with which students are unfamiliar. Similarly, Langer (1985) found that with high school students, different kinds of knowledge are predictive of success with different kinds of writing tasks. She concluded that there may be instances where an exploratory writing assignment is not helpful in developing students' knowledge if they do not have an adequate base or knowledge structure on which to build. In such instances, further study of the content might be more helpful to students' knowledge development than asking them to extend knowledge they do not currently have. Finally, Rowland (1986) studied the role writing took in elementary children's developing understanding of subject matter, and found that the form of writing children chose (e.g., poetry, narrative, personal essay) shaped which details and information children paid attention to during the writing process, and, therefore, influenced the nature of their knowledge development.

Thus, while claims are made that writing should be viewed as "revision of inner speech" (Moffett, 1979), or that writing should become an "integral part of thought" instead of a product of thought (Bereiter, 1980), students' current knowledge level and their ability to gain access to that knowledge will affect the amount and quality of the thinking about the content that takes place.

Writing Knowledge and Skill

Students' development of writing knowledge and skill is a second subprocess in content area writing. By studying writers' thought processes during the writing process, researchers have learned that writers use schemata that allow them to write according to a certain form such as narrative, exposition, or argument (Scardamalia & Bereiter, 1986). Yet it is unclear as to whether adult writers consciously use abstract knowledge of discourse forms (e.g., Chafe, 1977), or whether such knowledge is implicitly incorporated into the writing process (e.g., Botvin & Sutton-Smith, 1977; Stein & Trabasso, 1982). It does seem apparent that knowledge of written form will affect students' ability to produce specific types of written products, and explicit instruction in the use of particular forms can help students organize their knowledge of a topic (see Englert & Raphael, this volume, pp. 105-151).

In addition to knowledge of written forms, Applebee's (1982) investigation of school writing practices identified three areas of knowledge that writers must bring to bear in school writing tasks: knowledge of the topic, knowledge of language, and knowledge of the audience. He argued that language skills at the sentence and word level are emphasized at the expense of text level learning; that factual recall of content is emphasized at the expense of examining and extending knowledge; and that audiences are restricted to those who know more than the author at the expense of learning to assess and extend a reader's knowledge of a topic. He concluded that current school practices are mere exercises in producing what students already know, and focus on low-level writing skills. Moreover, focusing on low-level writing skills restricts students' opportunities to use the writing process to expand and develop their knowledge of the topic.

Based on their understanding of bringing writing knowledge and skill to bear on the writing-to-learn process, some researchers have investigated ways in which teachers might try to actively develop writers' awareness of and ability to monitor their own processes and subsequently improve their own abilities to take control of the writing process. For example, by studying more and less skillful writers, Flower and Hayes (1980b) developed a model of elements of the rhetorical problem writers represent to themselves when composing. These elements include the rhetorical situation (the writing task, audience) and the writer's own goals (how the writer wants to affect the reader, how he or she perceives him or herself, the writer's attempt to create meaning). Teaching students to be aware of all elements of the rhetorical problem instead of just letting them focus on text features such as length and format allows them to treat their topic in greater depth and breadth. Similarly, Scardamalia & Bereiter (1985) experimented with instructional methods that promote "procedural facilitation," or self-regulatory mechanisms for planning and evaluating the writing process, and "goal concretization," which helps students head toward goal-directed writing. Implicit in these examples is the close tie between students' developing writing knowledge and skill and their developing content knowledge. What they know and understand about one subprocess shapes their knowledge and understanding of the other, and shapes their ability to interconnect the two to create coherent written pieces that will change their understanding of subject matter content. I turn now to discuss the interconnection between the two subprocesses.

A Tension in Cognitive Focus

The tension between focusing on "idea production" (content) and "text production" (form) as subprocesses in writing (Collins & Ginter, 1980) raises the issue that if writing is to serve as a means to learn, it must be an effective, usable tool that serves the learning process. The issue of "cognitive overload" is salient when one considers how a writer's ability to work on developing ideas interacts with his or her ability to work comfortably with the conventions of writing as a tool to aid in thinking. At this point, researchers are extremely cautious in their claims about how useful writing can be to children as a tool in content development because of the potential problem of asking them to attend to too many demands at once. In addition, children naturally attempt to simplify the dual problem spaces placed on them as novice writers (idea production and text production), and convert writing tasks into tasks of telling what they know about a problem, regardless of the rhetorical problem offered to them (Bereiter & Scardamalia, 1985). Unless opportunities for "reprocessing" are provided during the writing process, where writers have the opportunity to use what they produce from one writing episode of text creation (e.g., text, notes, thoughts) as input to another cycle of processing that involves transforming what was previously produced, students will not have the opportunity to learn to use goal directed strategic planning in their learning processes (Scardamalia & Bereiter, 1986).

It is also difficult for teachers to know where students' difficulties in managing this tension lie by looking at a written product. For example, when researchers examined how students' developing understanding of science content interacted with the process of writing about it (Ammon & Ammon, 1987), they found several possibilities as to ways in which writing knowledge and skill and content knowledge could influence one another. It may be that difficult conceptual content interferes with a student's ability to use a particular written form to express ideas or understanding, resulting in incoherent writing. Difficulties with or confusion over content may also cause students to skirt issues that they do not fully understand. Others may resolve confusions through the writing process, or at least identify confusions and state them as dilemmas in their writing. This range of possibilities underscores the difficulty for teachers in knowing when and how to focus on the interaction between idea and content production, and when students need help with expressing ideas or content in a particular form.

Not only do students' content knowledge and writing knowledge and skill interact to shape the writing experience, but there are additional factors that enter into the tension as well. When researchers looked at post-test measures of high school students' knowledge of social science and science concepts (Newell, 1984) and students' understanding of literature (Marshall, 1987), the nature of the writing task was particularly important. In both instances, more extensive written forms (e.g., essay writing, personal analytic writing, and formal analytic writing) proved to be much more profitable in helping students develop and extend their knowledge than shorter written forms such as note-taking, study questions, and short answer writing tasks. Finally, Mosenthal, Conley, Colella, and Davidson-Mosenthal (1985) investigated the relative influence of writers' prior knowledge and teachers' classroom lesson structure on students' narrative production. They pointed out that the important issue to consider is what teachers allow students to do with their prior knowledge. They argued that if teachers' classroom structures only permit knowledge reproduction, then that is what writers will do; if they are encouraged to reconstruct as well as reproduce, then knowledge reconstruction will become apparent in narrative writing.

Understanding the nature of cognitive activity makes teaching students to write to learn a complex and confusing undertaking. Teachers must address students' knowledge levels in the areas of writing and subject matter, in addition to attending to the nature of the tasks they provide and the context in which they offer the tasks. In the following section, I summarize implications of research on the writing process regarding what teachers should pay attention to when designing writing-to-learn activities.

The Nature of Writing Activities That Contribute to Content Area Purposes

Researchers have begun to suggest necessary characteristics of writing tasks and conditions conducive to the particular use of writing as a means to learn subject matter that address complexities in the process. I will briefly characterize what content area writing activities might be like if knowledge and understanding from research on the writing process are taken into account. This discussion will provide a backdrop for the ensuing discussion where I identify instructional issues teachers face in trying to successfully implement writing-to-learn activities in complex classroom settings.

Writing-to-learn activities should center around the *primary purpose* of providing opportunities for students to engage in and develop cognitive processes that promote development of higher order thinking about subject matter as well as skills and dispositions necessary to carry out such thinking. Given this requirement, purposes or outcomes of engaging in writing activity must be clearly defined. Teachers must specify the nature of the "thinking skills" involved in composing a written piece and decide what kind of support students need to develop and use the skills. This might entail teaching students to use discrete thinking operations such as recall, comprehension, application, analysis, synthesis or evaluation of subject matter. Or the writing activity might require teaching students problem-solving or decision-making strategies. Or it might center around developing and using critical thinking to appraise the accuracy of knowledge claims or arguments related to subject matter. The point is that writing-to-learn activities should provide occasions for students to think about subject matter, to restructure it in ways that help them see new relationships or interpret new knowledge in light of prior knowledge, and the teacher must clearly define what these opportunities are in order to provide appropriate instruction.

Another area to consider is how writing activities should be *structured*. Instead of expecting students to somehow manage the tension between idea production and text production, teachers need to pay attention to two areas to teach students ways to manage it (Bereiter, 1980; Calkins, 1983; Collins & Ginter, 1980). First, teachers need to make and clearly communicate decisions about how students will receive credit for engaging in thinking processes during the writing process, and how they will assess the extent to which students engage in the desired thinking processes (Doyle, 1983). Second, teachers need to make and clearly communicate to students decisions about what they expect regarding the eventual written product. Too often teachers only evaluate and reward the written product without finding ways to evaluate and reward students' developing thinking skills or the quality of the thought students engage in during the composing process.

Teachers also need to provide actual support or strategies that help students cope with the cognitive demands of writing to learn. Teachers should not assume that just because a writing activity requires a certain type of thinking, that students can or will successfully engage in it. Rather, students need to be taught how to develop ideas, see relationships, solve problems or make judgements (Beyer, 1979; Giroux, 1979; Ventre, 1979). For example, teachers need to structure activities to aid students during the composing process to help them learn how to capture ideas (e.g., brainstorming, free-writing, using resource material) and manipulate ideas (e.g., identify variables, generate critical cases, use analogies, contrast or differentiate, simulate, see taxonomies) (Collins & Ginter, 1980). Similarly, metacognitive awareness must be developed regarding ways to control the writing process. For example, teachers must teach students strategies for juggling text production issues such as how they should selectively focus on their knowledge of the topic, knowledge of written language, and knowledge of their audience while they simultaneously bring their knowledge together in a written form (Applebee, 1982; Flower & Hayes, 1980b).

Finally, writing to learn must be conceived as *full-fledged authoring* so that the composing process requires original, authentic expression of students' ideas, where they have synthesized or created them themselves (Moffett, 1979). This means getting away from having students use lower-level operations such as recall or comprehension of subject matter in their writing, and heading toward opportunities to apply ideas, analyze, evaluate, critically appraise knowledge, and define and solve problems (Applebee, 1986; Scardamalia & Bereiter, 1986). In addition, full-fledged authoring allows for authentic communuication with a real audience. Students need opportunities to use goal-directed strategic planning so they can learn to choose and develop appropriate written forms to examine and extend their knowledge as they define and write for particular audiences with varied knowledge levels (Applebee, 1982, 1986; Flower & Hayes, 1980a; Scardamalia & Bereiter, 1986).

This set of requirements follows logically from the research findings, and yet it poses many challenges for classroom teachers who wish to implement these recommendations. In the section that follows, I identify four broad areas where issues regarding difficulties in implementation arise, and illustrate the complexities of the issues with an extended example from classroom research.

WRITING TO LEARN IN AN ELEMENTARY CLASSROOM: ISSUES TO DELICATELY BALANCE

Writing to learn makes a great deal of sense, although current research over the past decade claims there is not enough of it in schools (Applebee, 1981, 1982; Britton, Burgess, Martin, McLeod & Rosen, 1975; Graves, 1978; Perrin, 1984; Sunflower & Crawford, 1985). How can we explain the contrast between the claims for its use and success, and the lack of evidence that writing to learn takes place in classrooms or that when it does that it actually succeeds? In this section, I examine this issue from the viewpoint of the classroom teacher and the learner. I identify four problem areas teachers and students face when writing to learn is taken on as a primary goal: (1) curriculum problems, (2) problems of teacher-student relationships, (3) scaffolding problems, and (4) problems of developmental limitations. Throughout this discussion, examples are used from a research study I conducted in an early elementary classroom (Rosaen, 1987a) to illustrate how teachers and students balanced the tensions they faced in relation to the four areas. I discuss ways the classroom teachers addressed the instructional problems, and offer alternative ways to think about solving them.

Curriculum Issues: The Problem of Defining Subject Matter

Recent evaluations of teachers' instructional practices reveal that when the process approach to teaching writing is used at all, the activities are often divorced from the purposes they are meant to serve. For example, a high school science teacher used a process approach to writing laboratory reports, but only rewarded the traditional product, and therefore students did not value or focus on the composing process itself (Applebee, 1986). This brief example illustrates a curriculum problem teachers must solve: What counts as subject matter in the curriculum, and how will students be rewarded for learning the defined subject matter? It may be that the way school curricula are organized and how teachers and students perceive curricula interfere with effectively teaching students to use the writing process as a means to develop understanding of subject matter and higher order thinking skills. First, I examine the concept of curriculum, and identify a basic tension in the "what counts as knowledge" issue in curriculum. This discussion is followed by an illustration from my research that shows how this curriculum issue plays out in the classroom.

Curriculum as a Message System

How does one's conception of curriculum influence the learning process? Bernstein (1975) argues that educational knowledge is a major regulator of the structure of experience. That is, educational knowledge shapes people's ways of seeing and interpreting the world.

Formal educational knowledge can be considered to be realized through three message systems: curriculum, pedagogy and evaluation. Curriculum defines what counts as valid knowledge, pedagogy defines what counts as a valid transmission of knowledge, and evaluation defines what counts as a valid realization of this knowledge on the part of the taught. (Bernstein, 1975, p. 85)

Each of these message systems contains a spectrum of possibilities. For example, Bernstein defines two major types of curricula. The "collection type" of curriculum is characterized by strong boundaries between subject areas, with strong classification, or strong boundary maintenance, between subjects. A second type of curriculum, the "integrated type," is characterized by weak or blurred boundaries between subjects. With the collection type of curriculum, *states of knowledge* count as a valid realization of knowledge, whereas with the integrated type of curriculum, *ways of knowing* are emphasized. Out of these underlying message systems arises the pedagogical relationship, or frame, between teacher and student. Frame refers to the range of options available to the teacher and student in the *"degree of control over the selection, organization, pacing and timing of the knowledge transmitted and received in the pedagogical relationship"* (Bernstein, 1975, p. 89, emphasis in original). A tight frame refers to more teacher control in these areas, while a loose frame refers to less control. All three of these message systems interact to structure or influence the learner's experience. I envision a spectrum or range of possibilities as to where particular learning activities might lie within these three message systems, instead of seeing them as forced-choice categories.

I will examine two of the three message systems, curriculum and evaluation, as Bernstein has defined them, and reveal areas of potential difficulty for teachers who wish to implement writing to learn in the content areas. Writing to learn subject matter necessarily blurs the boundaries between teaching of writing and teaching subject matter. Learners must draw on their writing knowledge and skill as well as on their knowledge of subject matter content to write about subject matter. Accordingly, teachers must figure out how to focus their instruction across both areas. When teachers have students write to learn, they move closer on the curriculum spectrum to the integrated type of curriculum than to the collection type of curriculum. It follows then, that ways of knowing would count as a valid realization of knowledge as well as states of knowledge. Aspects of the writing process such as the quality of the thinking that goes into the process and the nature of the change or development of ideas throughout the process would count as well as the finished product. This is consistent with the advice researchers give to classroom teachers about the nature of writing-to-learn activities, but is not consistent with what researchers generally find in classrooms. Why is it that such an approach is so difficult to implement? What are the complexities that teachers and students face? These questions are examined in the following section.

Curriculum in Action

I conducted a study in an early elementary classroom, where I focused on the last 7 weeks of a 12-week unit of American history (Rosaen, 1987a). The purpose of the study was to describe how students and teachers interpreted learning activities (with a particular focus on writing activities), and how the meaning students assigned to learning activities shaped opportunities for knowledge development. This study serves as a vivid illustration of the complexities of the curriculum and evaluation issues pertaining to writing to learn subject matter.

The classroom was in a private school that contained a multi-age group of 36 children ranging from 6 to 9 years old. Two teachers, Mr. and Mrs. Stanford,[1] were responsible (along with two full-time aides) for teaching this class and an upper elementary class of 18 children. The 12-week American history unit was divided into four time periods: (1) the pre-1600s; (2) the 1600s and 1700s; (3) the 1800s; and (4) the 1900s. Famous people and events were organized by time periods as a way for the children to "sort out" or be able to place what they read and wrote about in a chronological framework. The two teachers focused on subject matter in this way so that students could learn to figure out when an event occurred and see significant ways it tied in with other events the class discussed or read about. Mr. and Mrs. Stanford viewed the learning process during the history unit to be much like solving a puzzle, where the teachers showed students the "pieces" of American history, and helped them learn to fit them together into a coherent shape and design.

Reading, writing, drawing, and participating in discussions about historical figures and events were a means by which students were to accomplish the teachers' two major goals. The first goal was to broaden the students' exposure to American history. That is, before they could make sense of events in relation to each other, Mr. Stanford (the teacher responsible for the history unit) felt the students needed to know about an array of people and events. Second, Mr. Stanford wanted students to learn how to place these events or people in a chronological framework. This did not mean memorizing names and dates. It meant students should think about the characteristics of a time period and learn to logically reason how or why an event would occur in a certain time period, or how an event would logically relate to another event the students knew about. Thus, the teachers wanted the students to use the research process as a means to go beyond mere retention and recall of facts and learn to analyze, synthesize, and evaluate information they read and wrote about. This meant they faced the problem of providing writing activities and a work structure that equally emphasized and rewarded knowledge states and ways of knowing.

To accomplish the teachers' goals for the history unit, students completed a series of activities each week that I call *the research cycle*. For the research cycle, students were to: read several selections about historical events or people or a time period; write a rough copy of a research report about one of the elections, and hand it in; make corrections on the rough draft and write a final copy; draw an illustration to accompany the final copy. These independent activities were organized and paced by a weekly checklist students followed, and all students were accountable for finishing the various steps in the research cycle sometime between Monday and Friday. In addition to these independent activities, students participated in group discussions after lunch and special activities (field trips, simulation games, music) that were also intended to help students reach overall goals of the history unit.

Thus, content goals for the unit were intended to focus on helping students develop ways of knowing rather than simply focusing on developing knowledge bases. The teachers wanted students to have the opportunity to identify interest areas, learn to logically connect facts about one topic to facts about others, and make judgments about how events fit together and helped shape the development of our nation. In addition, the classroom routines were organized in a way that attempted to emphasize and reward inquiry. For example, students were given a minimum requirement of selections to read for a certain time period, but latitude was allowed (and encouraged) for students to read more than the minimum amount. The flexible schedule allowed students to make decisions about the extent to which they wanted the develop their knowledge base and their rough copy of their research, as well as how much they wanted to refine their rough draft before creating their final copy.

When I looked closely at how students interpreted the routines associated with the research cycle, I found that despite the emphasis in the teachers' intentions and organized routines on providing opportunities for and rewarding inquiry (or ways of knowing), students interpreted and implemented the routines differently. While the teachers wanted students to focus on the quality of their inquiry and make rich connections about their reading topics through the reading and writing activities, the students often interpreted participating in the research cycle in a timely manner as a goal in itself, rather than as a means to the teachers' intended learning goals. In the way many students carried out the task, finishing the written product overshadowed their focus on their knowledge development. Thus, completing the assignments on their checklist became a goal for many students, instead of a tool for realizing other content-related goals. Many students translated the set of guidelines and routines for conducting research that the teachers provided as a set of discrete steps to follow that looked quite uniform across students in all phases of the process. Despite the teachers' intended emphasis on the inquiry process, the students focused more on the "product" of finishing their weekly research on time. In addition, there was greater student concentration on creating a corrected finished form (a final copy that contained no errors) than on the revision process (using the writing process to develop and refine understanding).

Mr. and Mrs. Stanford were troubled by the students' emphasis on "getting done" that overshadowed their efforts to develop their inquiry skills. They reported that they constantly struggled with the "fine line" between having the students use the checklist activities as a tool for their learning, and yet knowing that students needed some means of pacing their work and breaking it down into smaller, manageable parts. It may be that the concreteness of finishing a written product was a more easily visible, tangible measure for the students to know they were in tune with their classroom requirements. At first glance, they could see the written product much more easily than the process of generating ideas. The intangible goals of thinking about the subject matter and developing their ability to associate various pieces of knowledge together so that they fit into a coherent whole were not something for which these students seemed to feel rewarded. Therefore, what they interpreted as important was not the inquiry process itself, but getting to some kind of endpoint (the final copy of the research) in the process.

Can it be argued that the routines themselves are what caused students to interpret the inquiry process as less important than the written report? Returning to Bernstein's (1975) notion that curriculum and evaluation are regulators of experience, one could argue that students' perception of the activities and their place in the overall routines regulated their perception of what counts and what they would be rewarded for, and they acted accordingly. The system was *designed* to provide a structure that would emphasize and reward ways of knowing, but students *negotiated and interpreted* it to emphasize or value product states. What issues might the Stanfords address to help them move closer to communicating their intended "message system" to the students? They might consider creating more tangible and visible rewards for aspects of the writing process that involve inquiry such as topic selection, drafting and revising. First, they could build activities into the research cycle that would make children's thinking processes more explicit. For instance, they could hold discussion groups that feature issues such as how children's thinking about a topic changed as they were writing, how a focus for their topic evolved, or how two students' topics substantively interrelate. Such discussions would be occasions for students to examine and share the work they devoted to drafting their reports and developing their understanding of a topic. Second, these teachers could give equal amounts of attention to giving feedback on drafting and on finished products. For example, they could hold writing conferences early in the drafting process (during topic selection or beginning stages of drafting) to discuss idea development with individuals or small groups. Taking the time to listen to students talk about their efforts during the early stages of writing communicates to students that efforts to clarify their understanding of their topic are important, and gives teachers the opportunity to show students how qualities of the finished product are linked to the earlier efforts to develop their understanding of the topic. Making the inquiry process more tangible and visible to students could change their perception of its relative importance in the research cycle.

Another area I examined that provides some clues to answering the question of how and why students interpreted the research cycle as they did is the relationship among students and teachers, which I will discuss in the following section.

Issues of Teacher-Student Relationships

It is often argued by researchers that writing tasks in classrooms should promote student ownership and shared responsibility (Applebee, 1986; Calkins, 1986; Rowland, 1986). If the writing process is truncated and students are not allowed to participate in the full spectrum of activities associated with genuine authorship (Moffett, 1979), students cannot reap the full benefits of writing as a means to develop thinking skills and the ability to monitor their own learning. However, control over the writing process is not easy to "give" (Greenleaf & Freedman, 1986; Michaels, Ulichney, & Watson-Gegeo, 1986). The typical nature of social relations and interaction in classrooms, with the teacher in the position of holder of knowledge and the students in the position as receivers, is a difficult cycle to break, and breaking such a cycle does not occur without resistance from students. In this section I define the pedagogical relationship, and discuss my own research on writing about American history to illustrate difficulties inherent in the pedagogical relationship that make writing to learn so complex.

Pedagogy as a Message System

In addition to curriculum and evaluation, pedagogy is a third message system that influences students' ways of seeing and interpreting the world (Bernstein, 1975). The frame, or relationship between teacher and student, includes the degree of control each has over content (including selection, organization, pacing and timing of the knowledge transmitted and received). A tight frame suggests more teacher control, while a loose frame suggests more student control over knowledge. I conceive of making decisions about the frame issue as another problem for teachers to solve in the writing-to-learn process, instead of as making an either/or choice between a tight or a loose frame. Thus, how students and teachers negotiate activities together in classrooms and the relative roles they take on in the learning process is another regulator of how students will develop knowledge and understanding of subject matter. The concept of frame is a useful one in thinking about writing to learn, because authorship entails selecting something to write about, organizing one's understanding of the topic, deciding how to go about developing ideas, and deciding when one is ready to share a piece of writing with the intended audience. The extent to which students have the opportunity to make such decisions is related to the "frame" between teacher and student, and has consequences for how students interact with subject matter knowledge. Now I return to my research on the American history unit, to examine the nature of the pedagogical relationship and consequences for learning opportunities.

A Guided Tour in Action

Mr. and Mrs. Stanford organized the history unit chronologically, and provided an array of choices within each time period that students could investigate further. For example, for their minimum reading requirement for the 1800s time period (15 selections), students could choose to read one or more selections on the Civil War (e.g., Harriet Tubman and the Underground Railroad, Abraham Lincoln, Robert E. Lee, Naval Actions in the Civil War, and the Gettysburg Address). Or they might choose instead to read about other topics in the 1800s (e.g., Alexander Graham Bell, Inventions, Mark Twain, The Industrial Revolution, The Homestead Act, and The Lewis and Clark Expedition). Within this overall structure of the subject matter, the Stanfords took on the role that is similar to a "tour guide." Their classroom environment was set up in a fashion similar to the way people sign up for guided tours of museums and historical sites to learn more about them than they might otherwise learn on their own. Students, therefore, entered into a relationship where they were willing to actively participate in the "guided tour" (the set of experiences that had been planned for them), at the pace at which it was planned, to take advantage of the learning experiences available. The teachers, as tour guides, were there to keep the pace moving, to offer new information and explanations, and to stimulate further inquiry into learning about the subject matter. In some ways this seems to change the typical rights and duties in the teacher-student relationship since in this case the students asked the questions and the teachers tried to answer them (or show students how to find out answers), instead of the usual situation where the teacher asks the questions and the students are to provide the correct answers (Mehan, 1979). Yet, in their role as tour guide, the teachers had a more detailed overall picture of the subject matter than the students. The teachers had an overall picture of the array of topics available, the amount of materials available for a given topic, and the amount of time they could spend at each "stop." The students, in the role of participant in the tour, were more or less counting on the teachers to make good selections, and make appropriate choices for stops along the way. While people often do not absorb all information or experiences on a tour, they get the flavor of the setting, the gist of the topic at hand, the opportunity to see where they need further inquiry. Then it is up to the people on the tour to follow up, at a later time, a topic that particularly interests them. It is this role relationship that the weekly research cycle suggested. How did this teacher-student relationship in the writing process shape learning opportunities?

I found that the students' interpretations of the writing-to-learn activities (topic selection for reading, and subsequent writing process) shaped the way they focused on new information as they encountered it. As they used the chronological framework to make sense of the subject matter and interpreted the guidelines for completing the steps of the research cycle, they filtered out other possible ways to make sense of or deepen their understanding of American history. While the writing process was intended to serve as a set of guided steps for expanding and developing students' knowledge, instead these steps tended to function to expand and develop it in very limited ways. A more detailed explanation of students' interpretations will illustrate these claims.

Mr. Stanford made reading topics available to students based on two main criteria: (1) what he thought students were interested in, and (2) what resources were available for children at appropriate reading levels. When I talked with students about why they chose the particular topic they read and wrote about, I discovered an array of reasons that included but went beyond Mr. Stanford's assumptions. The most common reasons were interest, or that students had some prior knowledge of or experience with learning about the topic. Following this in frequency were more practical reasons such as availability of resources, having to meet a deadline so something was chosen, and that the teacher recommended a selection. Thus, the way students interpreted their role relationship with their teacher (their rights and duties as students) influenced their actions as well as more intrinsic influences such as interest in the topic or prior knowledge of the topic. The students followed through on the unspoken agreement to participate in the tour Mr. Stanford set up for them. Choosing a topic is one aspect of the agreement they had to fulfill if the tour was to progress, and if they were to succeed within the reward structure that was set up in this classroom (e.g., follow the checklist and meet deadlines in a timely manner).

The role relationship that was manifested in the topic selection process is that Mr. Stanford maintained a tight frame over the topic selection, and therefore over the range of knowledge transmitted, while the students followed through on their obligations as learners and exercised the "freedom within limits" that Mr. Stanford intended to provide. They seemed conscious of the "limits" as they discussed their topic choices. Many seemed to fulfill their obligation by *finding* interest in reading and writing about a topic within the confines of the possible selections. Yet the skills required to make appropriate topic choices for further developing one's knowledge (e.g., determining one's knowledge level; one's ability to gain access to knowledge) were not specifically supported or developed in the writing process. I did not sense that some students were *starting with an interest* that they found resources (from the reading list) to satisfy, nor were they explicitly taught to pursue an unfamiliar topic, or one that they knew little about. Thus, I did not sense that they carefully examined the merits of their topic choice. If one measures these students' interpretations of the topic selection process against the notion of "full-fledged authoring" (Moffett, 1979), it becomes apparent that the way the topic selection was negotiated in this classroom could truncate part of the authoring process. The source of the problem does not lie in whether the frame was loose (choose anything you want to write about) or tight (choose from these topics). Instead, with either a focused or open-ended kind of choice, students may need instructional support as to how one goes about making an appropriate choice, given the purpose of using writing to develop and expand one's knowledge and understanding. If students are to develop ideas as authors that produce original, authentic expression of their ideas, trying to do so with a topic that students must *find* an interest in without instructional support, or one that is not carefully examined as an appropriate topic choice, may not lend itself to successfully do so. For example, students can be made aware that lack of genuine curiosity about the topic may lead to passive reading of and interpretation of material, and that it may encourage them to come to the reading and writing steps of the research cycle without much thinking about what they expect to read, or what they expect to find out. Moreover, students can learn to select topics that they have an adequate knowledge base on which to build and understand that some prior knowledge of the topic is required if the purpose for writing is to further develop understanding (Langer, 1985).

This example illustrates the complexities of trying to develop a role relationship with students that appropriately provides resources and guidance for pacing and timing, and still allows and provides support for exercising enough student autonomy so as not to truncate the writing to learn process. While Mr. Stanford intended to provide a rather open-ended array of reading choices to stimulate curiosity and help students figure out how their selected topic connected with others they read about, the students interpreted the research process more narrowly as a set of requirements to fulfill.

What alternatives might the Stanfords consider in developing the teacher-student relationship during the writing process to help students reach their intended purposes? First, students could be expected to take on more responsibility for their topic choices. Teaching students how to select and justify an appropriate topic for the purpose of developing knowledge and understanding might alleviate several problems. Through learning to carefully assess how appropriate a topic is for using writing as a tool to learn, students would learn to assess their current knowledge level and evaluate the extent to which they wish to develop their understanding before they undertake the complex writing process. These activities would require learning to clearly define purposes for reading and subsequent writing. Increased attention to the decision-making process would help students develop a broader view of the subject matter content as they repeatedly make choices over several research cycles and become more involved in the learning process. Second, students could define their audience for their research reports instead of writing for the teacher who presumably knows more about writing topics than students. This would provide occasions for students to learn to appropriately bring together their knowledge of topic, audience and language (Applebee, 1982) as genuine authors do (Moffett, 1979). Closely related to these alternatives in the teacher-student relationship is the nature of the guidance or support teachers provide to students to complete their writing. I examine this issue in the next section.

Scaffolding Issues: What to Support and How?

The tension between idea production (developing understanding of content) and text production (writing about the content in the appropriate form) is a major problem teachers face in figuring out how to provide instruction in writing to learn. Teachers not only need to understand how the two areas interact, but also need to decide *how much* and *what kind* of guidance and support to provide for both processes. In this section I define the term "scaffolding" and explain how it relates to providing guidance and support in the student-teacher relationship. I then return to my example from the American history unit to illustrate how students' interpretations of scaffolding for their research writing influenced their opportunities for knowledge development.

Scaffolding as Appropriate Support

I define "scaffolding" as the amount and type of support provided for the learner by the teacher. When teachers decide how much and what type of support to provide for learners it should be inversely related to the students' level of competence or ability to complete a task. For example, the more difficult it is for students to complete a task or achieve a goal, the more directive the teacher should be in guiding the process (Bruner, 1975; Wood, 1980). This notion of support is related to the notion of frame (discussed in the previous section) in that by providing support, teachers take at least some control over the situation. When teachers create any learning environment (by selecting activities available to students and by directing the discourse surrounding the learning activities) they inherently control to some degree several aspects of the experience: the scope of the curriculum, the quality and intensity of learnings available, and the breadth and depth of the curriculum (Barth, 1972; Michaels et al., 1986; Westbury, 1972). How appropriately teachers scoffold learning experiences for students will determine the quality and intensity of learnings available. By examining the nature of support provided during the writing process in the American history unit, I will identify difficulties the Stanfords faced in helping students manage the tension between idea development and appropriate use of written form.

How Scaffolding Shaped Topic Development

Mr. and Mrs. Stanford made decisions about how to support students' writing about their research topics based on what they saw as a need to help beginning writers select a focus for their writing. From their experience, beginning writers usually struggled with the question "What can I write?" and they intended to provide a way to help students make that decision. Therefore, they provided the following guide questions which students were to address in their research writing:

(a)   Who or what is your subject about?
(b)   When did it happen?
(c)   Why is it important?

The answers to questions (a) and (b) generally require recall of content found in the reading selection. The answer to question (c) may or may not be found directly in the reading, and would require the students to interpret, in light of other knowledge of the time period, the significance of the event. Requiring students to focus on content in this way was to serve two functions. It would help them recall what they read and help them place the factual knowledge in some kind of meaningful framework (the chronological framework in which the subject matter was organized). In essence, answering the guide questions served a "note-taking" function (Scardamalia & Bereiter, 1986) that would provide a basis for recall of information and comprehension of material. Mr. and Mrs. Stanford also intended it to serve a second function of providing a guide or outline for writing the composition that students would use as a framework for exploring and elaborating on their knowledge more fully (this is similar to the "text structures" Raphael and Englert discuss, this volume, pp. 105-151). They hoped students would internalize this framework and use it when they faced writing about other topics in the future. Thus, these teachers intended the guide questions to provide a scaffold or support for the process of developing their ideas (idea production) and for helping them organize and express their ideas in written form (text production).

When I discussed students' writing with them and tried to learn more about how they developed their ideas about their topic, I found they interpreted the guide questions more narrowly than the way their teachers intended. For example, they did not see the questions as a mere possibility of what to write about, but as *the content* that they should or must write about. When I examined their written products, I found them to be remarkably uniform. They each were a summary of the guide questions, exactly in the order in which the questions had originally been listed. One student's final copy research on the Star Spangled Banner illustrates the pattern (see Figure 1). The content of the piece follows the guide questions closely:

(a) Who or what is your subject for your research?

I am doing my research on the Star Spangled Banner.

(b) When did the event occur?

It was written in 1814.

(c) Why is it important?

Frances Scot Key wrote it because he was happy to see that the Americans did not give up.

I learned from my interview with Steve that he sometimes included the answer to a fourth question, which was to include "interesting facts." This seems to account for his final sentence, "Today it is our National Anthem."

This student's work is just one example of many I examined. In essence, the questions limited what the students paid attention to instead of providing support to broaden their knowledge base or their ability to critically appraise knowledge. The tight framing of subject matter content and selection (through available resources), organization (through the guide questions), and pacing and timing (through the direction of the weekly checklist with its deadlines) worked toward limiting students' focus on the subject matter knowledge that was available to them. One possible explanation for the students' interpretations is that they did not have a shared view of the overall experience with the teachers. Mr. and Mrs. Stanford had the "big picture" and their overall goals with which to interpret the purpose of the topic choices (provide guidelines and direction for students), the guide questions (gradually show students how to focus on reading and develop ideas in writing), the use of the checklist (teach them to take responsibility for their own learning). Unlike their teachers, the students experienced the activities without this "big picture" or knowledge of the teachers' overall goals. They interpreted the scaffolding quite literally, not as what they could do within the limits, but as what they should do.

What are some alternative ways the Stanfords might have considered implementing their guidance and support? Perhaps if the Stanfords had more clearly communicated their goals with students and had worked to develop shared goals, students would have taken more initiative to develop their knowledge and understanding. Second, as they were negotiated in this classroom, the teachers' intended scaffolding (guidelines that would gradually shift and change as the learners progressed) functioned more as a set of procedures that remained fixed over time in the way they were implemented and in the way they were interpreted. More flexible use of the routines might have improved the success of the support. For example, since the Stanfords wanted the students to internalize the guide questions over time, they might have gradually shifted the responsibility to the students, so that eventually the students would be responsible for developing their own questions and adapting them to the topic, their knowledge level, and their intended audience. It is important for teachers to adjust the amount of direction in relation to what students currently need.

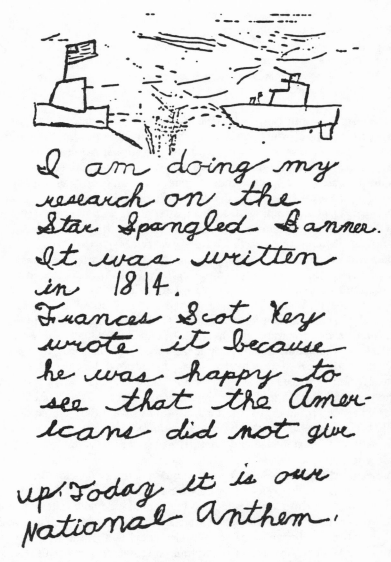

Figure 1. Steve's Research on the Star Spangled Banner

Another possible explanation for the students' interpretations is that the students simply answered the questions literally to reduce cognitive demands of the task and make it a manageable one (Bereiter & Scardamalia, 1985). Again, this relates to the problem teachers face of providing support for both idea production and text production in the writing process. Perhaps the Stanfords needed to provide more support for the students to develop and apply the appropriate thinking skills required to go beyond mere knowledge telling. For example, discussion groups or writing conferences could provide occasions for students to share and evaluate their efforts to understand their topic and appropriately communicate their understanding in written form. A final issue I will address in this section is the consideration of what children are capable of in writing to learn.

Addressing Issues of Developmental Limitations

A final problem teachers face in providing instruction for writing to learn is in addressing the extent to which children are able to effectively manage the tension between idea production and text production so that writing is profitable. I will briefly highlight questions of development that are pertinent to the issue of getting the most out of writing-to-learn activities. Then I will give a final example from my study of the American history unit to illustrate how one might view the interrelationship among activities within a unit of study to better understand what students can learn from their writing-to-learn efforts.

Questions of Student Capabilities

A recurrent topic in this chapter is developmental difficulties students face when they write to learn. One major task students face is learning to manage the tension between focusing on idea generation to produce the correct written form and understanding how the two areas interconnect to address a rhetorical problem. In addition to developing awareness of the need to balance the tension, children must learn specific strategies to cope with the demands inherent in writing about subject matter. An area that has not yet been considered in relation to students' developmental limitations is how writing activities may interconnect with other activities as students study subject matter. By conceiving of writing to learn as one of several experiences designed to learn about subject matter content, where students also read, discuss, do projects, ask questions, and many other activities, there may be ways to address developmental limitations that cannot be addressed solely within the writing-to-learn cycle. My final example from the American history unit will explore this possibility.

Writing to Learn as an Interrelated Cycle

To understand what students might learn from a particular activity, it is important to investigate how that activity fits with others that students complete, because learning activities are not experienced by students in isolation (Nespor, 1986; Rosaen, 1987b). From what I have described so far about the American history unit, it would appear that writing is viewed in this classroom as knowledge telling—answer the questions from the reading and show that you understand it. However, Mr. and Mrs. Stanford wanted students to participate in an overall investigative process of finding out how historical events relate to one another, in addition to producing finished products. They intended to use writing as a way to direct students' reading and help them develop their knowledge of key historical events. Likewise, the subject of "history" as a state of knowledge was subordinate to the process of figuring out how historical events fit together meaningfully. These teachers valued the process of finding out about historical events and figures as much as the finished knowledge state. Therefore, they understood that what they saw as a written product may not be the entire representation of how the student understood a topic. They provided other "avenues" during the American history unit for students to show that they were in touch with the investigative process (e.g., drawing, participation in group discussion or special event), and Mr. and Mrs. Stanford wanted to keep a more even emphasis in their reward structure on several aspects of the research process instead of just rewarding students for written products. The reading and writing activities were one of several means for developing a further understanding of how events interrelate. This *combined overall process* of reading, thinking about, discussing and writing and drawing about the topic was what these teachers thought would contribute to the students' developing historical knowledge (not just the knowledge reflected in a written product).

Because I learned from the teachers that they valued the interconnection among activities, I also investigated the students' responses to other activities, such as creating a drawing that illustrates the research, to understand more about what opportunities for knowledge development the entire unit offered to students. When I closely examined students' drawings and talked with them about their drawing and writing, I learned that they tended to go further than the focus questions (that they followed when they wrote) when they illustrated their research topic. For example, several students' drawings elaborated details they had written about (e.g., drawings of the action in a battle that was merely mentioned as a battle in the written text), or elaborated what they meant by certain terms used in the text (e.g., showing in pictorial form what it means to "discover" America). Others added information that went beyond addressing the three focus questions for writing (e.g., showing the overall mood of a ghost town through use of color and adding details about the weather). At times the use of the drawing seemed to help students express information or feelings they were not capable of putting into words (Dyson, 1983). Perhaps the children needed less support and therefore were more successful at using drawing as a tool. Yet I did not feel satisfied with that explanation for some of the older children whose drawings also elaborated the text.

When I looked closely at how both the writing and the drawing activities were structured, I found a possible explanation that provides an alternative explanation for the difference in the way students handled the two modes of expression within the same overall work structure. While the writing activity had focus questions that students interpreted as *the* content about which they should write, the drawing activity was optional (not a requirement on the checklist), and was open-ended (simply draw a picture about the research topic). Students were allowed to draw whatever they wanted, and were not asked to hand in a "rough copy" for someone else to judge its quality. They had more responsiblity for deciding what to draw, and for deciding whether the drawing was sufficient as a form of expression. Drawing, as it was structured in this context, was more closely an "avenue" for students to show they were "in touch" with the investigative process, whereas the writing activity was more of a requirement than an avenue as it was experienced by the students. As the frame or control over the activity loosened, the students changed the nature of their expression about their research topics. The looser frame, as students interpreted it, encouraged exploration of subject matter and more elaboration in areas of interest to the individual. The primary benefit of the looser frame was not that students could do whatever they wanted, but that for the purpose of idea generation, students perceived room within the task structure to explore and play around with ideas, which they did not perceive in the writing process. When they had the opportunity to set their own goals, and had the choice of whether or not to use this mode of expression at all, they seemed to work more toward the "intrinsic" rewards the Stanfords sought than they did with the writing required by the checklist. Thus, there may be occasions in teaching children to use the writing process for knowledge development when teachers decide that freedom of choice in use of details, level of details and mode of expression can be effective tools for idea generation.

In summary, the structure of the two activities contrasted in important ways, and as the two activities were negotiated, they resulted in different role relationships and different responsibilities on the part of students and teachers. One important consequence of this difference in role relationship was the way students experienced or interacted with the subject matter content. The drawing activity, as a tool for idea generation, helped students elaborate and develop new content while the writing activity (as it was structured, negotiated and interpreted) caused them to filter out elaborative details. A second important consequence was the way the drawing and writing activities *interacted* and *worked together* to complement students' idea development. The writing alone did not help students move beyond mere knowledge telling. However, *the writing paired with the drawing* provided an opportunity that moved closer to the direction of knowledge transformation that the Stanfords intended. As I continued to investigate the interconnection among learning activities in the unit, I discovered that the writing activity helped students gain knowledge that served as a basis for several other activities as well. These activities required students to explore and develop their understanding of the subject matter (e.g., a genealogy activity, a simulation of important battles in the Civil War). This discovery underscores the importance of evaluating the potential power of writing as it interacts with other forms of learning in the classroom over time. Understanding what students learn from a writing activity requires looking at the activity as it relates to a group of learning experiences and understanding the function the writing holds for students in the overall set of learning experiences (Rosaen, 1987b). Moreover, teachers can purposefully design activities to complement and build upon one another, so that writing to learn is not an isolated cycle in itself. There may be times when the writing process is part of a larger effort to learn and serves one smaller aspect of reaching toward learning goals. It does not have to be an "all or nothing" endeavor.

By designing their unit so there were close interconnections among several kinds of activities (e.g., writing, drawing, discussion, simulation games), the Stanfords found mutiple ways to help children develop and expand their understanding of American history instead of relying on the writing process as the only tool for development. They might have helped students become more aware of the cumulative nature of the unit's activities, and therefore helped them understand the "big picture" they had in mind. By making explicit ways in which the reading and writing provided a knowledge base for later activities, they could help students see the progressive nature of their developing understanding about a topic. By examining the history of their own knowledge development (e.g., through discussions or journal writing) students could become more aware of two aspects of the learning process. First, they could see the value in "reprocessing" information over time to develop deeper understandings with each experience (Scardamalia & Bereiter, 1986). Second, they could understand the value of monitoring their own learning and have a more tangible way of measuring ways in which self-regulatory behaviors (e.g., monitoring their own understanding; deciding which activities are most beneficial to understanding a topic) benefit the learning process. Such understanding allows students to take more responsibility for their own learning.

Learning from Teacher and Student Perspectives

These examples from classroom research illustrate several problems classroom teachers must try to solve when they implement writing-to-learn activities. The way the activities are designed in teachers' heads may not be the way they eventually are negotiated in the classroom setting (Nespor, 1985). For example, the way teachers conceive of their curriculum and how they intend to evaluate and reward learning experiences may change as students bring their own interpretations to the activities, so that students construct knowledge differently than teachers intend. Similarly, the teacher-student relationship develops in a complex social setting, and a range of influences shape how work is eventually interpreted and carried out. It is difficult for teachers to predict and take into account all influences on students' interpretations as they design writing activities. In addition, the nature of the support teachers provide for students to successfully use writing as a means to learn subject matter contributes to students' opportunities for knowledge development. If students interpret the support narrowly and literally, it may be that the support restricts rather than makes possible richer or more elaborate knowledge construction. Finally, because students' developmental limitations influence their capacity to use writing as a means to learn, teachers must take them into account when designing activities. Teachers can take advantage of the cumulative impact of a series of activities, of which writing may be one, instead of seeing writing as an isolated cycle in itself. This broader view of the interconnections among the writing process and other learning opportunities requires a complex understanding of how each learning activity contributes to students' knowledge development.

The examples in this section show how complex and difficult it is to try to implement writing-to-learn activities in the classroom, and highlight four problem areas teachers must address when they design and implement writing-to-learn activities: their conception of curriculum and evaluation of learning, the teacher-student relationship, the nature of scaffolding, and students' developmental limitations. These four areas were cast as "problem areas" in the classroom studied, but they should also be viewed as starting points for improving writing instruction. In the final section of this chapter, I offer some guidelines for classroom teachers to use as a framework for managing the complexities of teaching students to use writing as a means to understand subject matter.

ADDRESSING THE COMPLEXITIES OF WRITING TO LEARN

How can teachers provide writing activities that successfully help learners better understand subject matter and subsequently develop higher order thinking skills with which they can approach future learning situations? There is no easy answer to this question, and no answer that can address all classroom situations, but research has provided some fruitful starting points. We have learned from examining current instructional practices in writing that prescribing a "process approach" to writing is not enough (Applebee, 1986). Teaching students to effectively use writing to learn requires paying as much attention to helping students understand subject matter as is devoted to teaching students to learn to use the writing process itself. In addition, teachers need to help students understand how the two areas, content generation and generation of written text, are interconnected. In this section, I offer guidelines to classroom teachers interested in teaching students to use writing as a means to learn. These guidelines address four areas teachers need to take into consideration: (1) How are the subject matter and writing process interrelated? (2) How do writing-to-learn purposes apply to curriculum and evaluation? (3) What role relationship is required to achieve writing-to-learn purposes? (4) What is appropriate scaffolding to achieve the purposes? These guidelines are not intended to be steps to follow, but instead to be a set of principles that can be used as a framework for thinking about, designing, implementing, and evaluating effective writing-to-learn activities.

Explore Subject Matter and Writing Connections

One way to approach teaching students to use writing to learn is to stand back from traditional practices (e.g., assigning a research paper in social studies or a laboratory report in science; assuming writing does not lend itself to learning mathematics) and explore ways in which writing *could* connect with the subject matter to be taught. Teachers could explore how they assume the subject matter to be taught is organized, and how they might represent that subject matter to students through specific activities (Wilson & Shulman, 1987). This includes considering what kinds of thinking teachers want students to do about the subject matter. For example, do they want students to critically appraise the accuracy or worth of particular arguments in history? (For example, is the explanation that the cause of the Civil War was slavery adequate?) Do they want students to make links between the form of mathematical problems and their actual problem solving functions? (For example, I followed these steps in solving this problem correctly, but this answer is not telling me what I want to know). Do they want students to search for and find discrepancies in their own thinking about scientific phenomena? (For example, I thought plants needed water to grow, but the ones in the closet that were watered died. Why?) By identifying the kinds of thinking involved with learning and understanding subject matter, teachers then can explore ways in which the writing process might help students learn to develop and use such thinking. For example, they could consider whether the persuasive essay, or writing an explanation for the causes of the Civil War from two different perspectives, or writing a comparison and contrast essay, or writing a letter, or some other form of writing would best serve as an opportunity to engage students in thinking about the Civil War. Likewise, in the areas of math and science, teachers could consider whether a more personal form of writing such as a learning log, where students write a log to keep track of and explore their thinking (Calkins, 1986), or a more formal type of writing such as an explanatory essay might provide opportunities for students to engage in the desired thinking. In this way, learning to use the writing process functions as a form of meaningful learning in the content areas.

This does not necessarily mean teachers will have students do more writing. It may mean replacing less productive writing experiences with more productive ones. Consider how the Stanfords might have assessed students' interpretations of the research cycle mid-way through the 12-week unit. They might have decided that continued weekly expository writing would be less productive than using another written form to develop and expand knowledge of American history. For example, for these young children, a narrative form might have encouraged more elaborate development of details than the expository form that was expected. Or they might have decided to revise or eliminate parts of the cycle to more closely meet the current needs of students' knowledge development efforts. Perhaps one week's efforts could have focused exclusively on learning to make effective topic choices, instead of having students complete the entire cycle. Finally, teachers can explore how writing activities can serve other activities in a unit of study, so that they complement and build upon one another. The Stanfords intended to develop a cumulative effect during the course of the history unit, but also might have helped students understand how and why the interconnections among the activities (reading, writing, drawing, group activities) helped them understand history.

Thus, an initial exploration of the nature of the subject matter to be learned, the nature of the thinking required, and figuring out which kinds of writing activity provide rich opportunities for students to engage in certain kinds of thinking about particular subject matter can help replace less productive writing experiences with fruitful ones. Teachers can stretch their thinking about what is possible, and at the same time clarify for themselves what it is they want students to gain from the writing activity.

Explore Assumptions About Curriculum and Evaluation

Teachers often worry more about what students are learning (subject matter content knowledge) than about the overall message they communicate to students about their approach to learning subject matter. This may not mean they are unconcerned about the latter, but through their actions (e.g., giving tests that cover specific content knowledge, or only grading finished writing products) they may emphasize and reward "states of knowing" more than "ways of knowing." As the Stanfords' cases illustrate, it is usually not possible, or desirable, to make a choice between the two. Instead, teachers should examine their assumptions about curriculum (what is important to learn and why) and their evaluation practices (how they will know that students have learned and how they will reward learning) and clarify for themselves the extent to which there is room in their conception of curriculum for both kinds of knowing. If teachers are to help students develop and use higher order thinking skills when they make sense of subject matter, students need to learn specific subject matter content (states of knowledge) but they also need to learn how to think about the knowledge at higher levels than simply recall and comprehension (ways of knowing).

If teachers take on as a goal for their students that they will develop and use higher order thinking skills to interpret subject matter content, then writing-to-learn activities have a potential role in their classrooms. However, they need to closely examine their conception of curriculum and ways of defining what counts in their classroom to see if they are willing to include the writing process (as a "way of knowing") as something they will help foster and reward. This commitment must be there if students are to interpret the writing process (not just the finished product) as important and worthwhile (Applebee, 1986).

Explore the Teacher-Student Relationship

When they provide the opportunity for students to use writing to learn, teachers must explore a range of ways to develop the teacher-student relationship. The thought of this complex workload can be troublesome, and yet there are ways to allow the students to share the workload. Teachers who provide successful writing-to-learn activities take on the obligation to teach students to use the writing process to think as well as to teach students to understand and think about subject matter content. This obligation carries with it some requirements for the teacher-student relationship. Unlike the traditional approaches to writing in the content areas where the teacher assigns a topic, the form of the writing, and the deadlines, and the student's role is to comply, writing-to-learn activities suggest a shared responsibility and shared work load for developing and completing the work. For example, if teachers are to make it possible for students to be full-fledged authors (Moffett, 1979), they must set up a learning environment that allows students to define as well as solve problems (Applebee, 1986). As the Stanfords carefully crafted a learning environment in which they addressed the four instructional problems identified in this chapter, they took on several aspects of the workload of authorship that students might have been responsible for instead. For example, students could have taken a greater role in defining their audience, choosing the appropriate written form, and judging the quality of their writing. As authors, students need a working environment where they have some opportunities to make decisions about the mode of expression they will use to develop their thinking as well as choosing topics they will explore through writing (Rowland, 1986). Without such experiences, it is difficult for them to develop self-regulatory aspects of using writing as a means to learn (Scardamalia & Bereiter, 1986). In addition, if students see authorship as their responsibility, they are more likely to look for and find rewards for the full range of authorship activities. By exploring the nature of the relationship they negotiage with their students, teachers can better evaluate the merits of the writing-to-learn activities they design for their students.

Explore the Nature of Support Needed

Advice on how to structure writing-to-learn activities emphasizes the need for appropriate support so students can successfully complete the task. This includes providing support during the first phases of a writing task (beginning with topic or problem identification), on through the writing process where students will struggle with idea generation about subject matter content, and producing an appropriate finished product. Perhaps students could produce fewer finished products, and spend more time on composing. Teachers can initially slow down the writing process and concentrate on teaching students how to carry out each aspect of the composing process. More activities that focus on each aspect with more explicit discussion of how and why approaches to writing work will eventually allow students to become more independent writers. There will be a payoff to one's initial efforts to teach students how to use the writing process to help them think. In addition, students need support in managing the demands of text production (e.g., choosing the appropriate form, and producing the correct form.) Discussions, group writing conferences, self-help exercises (that direct students' attention to evaluating various aspects of their writing), and peer sharing sessions are ways to help students learn to manage this tension more effectively over time. Finally, teachers must provide ways for students to monitor and evaluate their own thinking process (about substance and form) so that they not only learn from that particular writing episode, but learn to improve their approach to using writing as a tool for learning subject matter. Teachers can provide occasions for students to take the time to reflect on the writing process (e.g., discussions, journal writing, writing conferences) and learn to make judgments about aspects of text or idea production such as when they need to get further information, when they need to change the written form to meet their writing purposes, or when they need to find out more about their intended audience. This is a complex set of requirements that needs careful examination, but the process is one that they can work on over a long period of time.

Teachers need to provide support (in the way it is designed and negotiated) that is *consistent with* decisions made about the nature of curriculum, the nature of the reward system, and the teacher-student relationship. As they address problems associated with teaching students to use writing to learn throughout the planning and teaching process, there are several questions teachers can ask themselves. For example, does the nature of interaction surrounding the writing activity emphasize and reward "ways of knowing" as well as "states of knowledge"? Do the writing activities allow students to experience the full range of authorship experiences? Do students interpret the activities in the desired ways, or do they place undue emphasis on products despite attempts at emphasizing the composing process? Does the support provided help students learn to think independently and beyond recall and comprehension, or does it oversimplify or truncate the composing process? Who takes responsibility for the overall quality of the piece (in both form and content)? Questions such as these can help teachers identify the extent to which the amount and quality of their support is appropriate to help students head toward desired goals.

A second way in which teachers can provide support for students is to design the writing activities in relation to surrounding learning activities and capitalize on interconnections. Students experience activities in a cumulative fashion, bringing their prior knowledge and understanding to each new experience, so that there is a growing and evolving interpretation of activities (Nespor, 1986; Rosaen, 1987b). How children come to understand the purpose of writing activities over time, within the broader context of their study of subject matter, should be made explicit and regularly examined throughout their instruction. It may be that certain difficulties with support provided for the writing cycle interrelate with difficulties in learning about the topic in other activities as well. Teachers and students can capitalize on "reprocessing" of ideas that takes place as students repeatedly encounter topics across activities (Scardamalia & Bereiter, 1986).

Making Tensions and Interconnections Work

Rather than deploring the complexity of taking on writing as a means to learn subject matter and as a means to develop higher order thinking skills, teachers can tackle it head on as a complex but powerful learning tool. Most teachers have students do some kind of writing about subject matter, even if it is at the level of sentence completion or writing definitions. It is incumbent on all teachers to think about and improve the quality of writing experiences they provide for students. Replacing less productive writing activities with challenging experiences that help students develop thinking skills and become more independent learners would be a tremendous payoff for time and effort spent. If educators are to help students learn to move beyond "knowledge telling" through writing, to helping them use writing as a means to develop higher order thinking and self-regulatory behavior, they must learn to understand the tensions they must manage and develop ways to make interconnections between writing and learning in the content areas work compatibly together.

NOTE

1. Pseudonyms are used throughout the study.

REFERENCES

Ammon, M.S., & Ammon, P.A. (1987). *Effects of content difficulty on performance of science writing tasks*. Paper presented at the Annual Meeting of the American Educational Research Association, Washington, DC.

Armento, B. (1986). Research on teaching social studies. In M. Wittrock (Ed.), *Handbook of research on teaching* (3rd ed.). New York: Macmillan.

Applebee, A.N. (1981). *Writing in the secondary school: English and the content areas*. Urbana, IL: National Council of Teachers of English.

Applebee, A.N. (1982). Writing and learning in school settings. In M. Nystrand (Ed.), *What writers know: The language, process, and structure of written discourse*. New York: Academic Press.

Applebee, A.N. (1984). Writing and reasoning. *Review of Educational Research, 54*(4), 577-596.

Applebee, A.N. (1986). Problems in process approaches: Toward a reconceptualization of process instruction. In A. Petrosky & D. Bartholomae (Eds.), *The eighty-fifth yearbook of the national society for the study of education* (Part II). Chicago: University of Chicago Press.

Barnes, D. (1969). Language in the secondary classroom. In D. Barnes, J. Britton, & H. Rosen (Eds.), *Language, the learner and the school*. Baltimore, MD: Penguin Books.

Barnes, D. (1979). *From communication to curriculum*. New York: Penguin Books.

Barth, R. (1972). *Open education and the American school*. New York: Agathon Press.

Bereiter, C. (1980). Development in writing. In L.W. Gregg & E.R. Steinberg (Eds.), *Cognitive processes in writing*. Hillsdale, NJ: Lawrence Erlbaum.

Bereiter, C., & Scardamalia, M. (1985). Cognitive coping strategies and the problem of "inert knowledge." In S.S. Chipman, J.W. Segal, & R. Glaser (Eds.), *Thinking and learning skills: Current research and open questions* (Vol. 2). Hillsdale, NJ: Lawrence Erlbaum.

Bernstein, B. (1975). *Class, codes, and control* (Vol. 3). London: Routledge & Kegan Paul.

Beyer, B.K. (1979, March). Pre-writing and rewriting to learn. *Social Education*, pp. 187-189.

Botvin, G.J., & Sutton-Smith, B. (1977). The development of structural complexity in children's fantasy narratives. *Developmental Psychology, 13*, 377-388.

Britton, J. Burgess, T., Martin, N., McLeod, A., & Rosen, H. (1975). *The development of writing abilities*. London: Macmillan Education.

Bruner, J.S. (1971). *The relevance of education*. New York: W.W. Norton.

Bruner, J.S. (1975). The ontogenesis of speech acts. *Journal of Child Language, 2*, 1-40.

Bruner, J.S. (1982). *The process of education*. Cambridge, MA: Harvard University Press. (Original work published 1960).

Burtis, P.J., Bereiter, C., Scardamalia, M., & Tetroe, J. (1983). The development of planning in writing. In G. Wells & B.M. Kroll (Eds.), *Explorations in the development of writing*. Chichester, England: John Wiley.

Calkins, L.M. (1983). *Lessons from a child*. Portsmouth, NH: Heinemann.

Calkins, L.M. (1986). *The art of teaching writing*. Portsmouth, NH: Heinemann.

Cazden, C. (1986). Classroom discourse. In M. Wittrock (Ed.), *Handbook of research on teaching* (3rd ed.). New York: MacMillan.

Chafe, W.L. (1977). Creativity in verbalization and its implications for the nature of stored knowledge. In R.O. Freedle (Ed.), *Discourse production and comprehension*. Norwood, NJ: Ablex.

Chi, M. (1985). Interactive roles of knowledge and strategies in development of organized sorting and recall. In S.S. Chipman, J.W. Segal, & R. Glaser (Eds.), *Thinking and learning skills: Current research and open questions* (Vol. 2). Hillsdale, NJ: Lawrence Erlbaum.

Collins, A., & Ginter. D. (1980). A framework for a cognitive theory of writing. In L.W. Gregg & E.R. Steinberg (Eds.), *Cognitive processes in writing*. Hillsdale, NJ: Lawrence Erlbaum.

de Beaugrande, R. (1984). *Text production: Toward a science of composition*. Norwood, NJ: Ablex.

Doyle, W. (1983). Academic work. *Review of Educational Research, 53*(2), 159-199.

Dyson, A.H. (1983). Research currents: Young children as composers. *Language Arts, 67*(7), 884-891.

Emig, J. (1977. Writing as a mode of learning. *College composition and communication, 28,* 122-128.

Emig, J. (1981). Non-magical thinking: Presenting writing developmentally in schools. In C.H. Frederickson & J. Dominic (Eds.), *Writing: The nature, development, and teaching of written communication, Vol. 2. Writing: Process, development and communication.* Hillsdale, NJ: Lawrence Erlbaum.

Flower, L., & Hayes, J. (1980a). The cognition of discovery: Defining a rhetorical problem. *College Composition and Communication, 31*(2), 21-32.

Flower, L., & Hayes, J. (1980b). The dynamics of composing: Making plans and juggling constraints. In L.W. Gregg & E.R. Steinberg (Eds.), *Cognitive processes in writing.* Hillsdale, NJ: Lawrence Erlbaum.

Giroux, H. (1979, March). Teaching content and thinking through writing. *Social Education* (pp. 190-193.

Graves, D.H. (1978). *Balance the basics: Let them write.* New York: Ford Foundation.

Greenleaf, C., & Freedman, S. (1986). *Preference analysis of a response episode: Getting to the cognitive content of classroom interactions.* Paper presented to the Annual Meeting of the American Educational Research Association, San Francisco, CA.

Gundlach, R.A. (1982). Children as writers: The beginnings of learning to write. In M. Nystrand (Ed.), *What writers know: The language, process, and structure of written discourse.* New York: Academic Press.

Hayes, J.R., & Flower, L.S. (1980). Writing as problem solving. *Visible Language, 14*(4), 388-399.

Langer, J. (1985). The effects of available information on responses to school writing tasks. *Research on the Teaching of English, 18*(1), 27-44.

Marshall, J.D. (1987). The effects of writing on students' understanding of literary texts. *Research in the Teaching of English, 21*(1), 30-63.

Mehan, H. (1979). "What time is it, Denise?": Asking known information questions in classroom discourse. *Theory Into Practice, 28*(4), 285-294.

Michaels, S. Ulichny, P., & Watson-Gegeo, K. (1986). *Writing conferences: Innovation or familiar routine?* Paper presented at the Annual Meeting of the American Educational Research Association, San Francisco, CA.

Moffett, J. (1979, December). Integrity in the teaching of writing. *Phi Delta Kappan,* pp. 276-279.

Mosenthal, P.B., Conley, M.W., Colella, A., & Davidson-Mosenthal, R. (1985). The influence of prior knowledge and teacher lesson structure on children's production of narratives. *The Elementary School Journal, 85*(5), 621-634.

Nespor, J. (1985). *Students' strategies for performing classroom work and tasks.* Paper presented at the Annual Meeting of the American Educational Research Association, Chicago, IL.

Nespor, J. (1986). Theoretical note: On students' experiences across the grade levels. *Anthropology and Education Quarterly, 17,* 203-216.

Newell, G.E. (1984). Learning from writing in two content areas: A case study/protocol analysis. *Research in the Teaching of English, 18*(3), 265-287.

Perrin, R. (1984). *Writing in the elementary classroom.* Paper presented at the Annual Meeting of the Indiana Teachers of Writing Conference, September, Indianapolis, IN.

Posner, G., Strike, K., Hewson, P., & Gertzog, W. (1982). Accommodation of a scientific conception: Toward a theory of conceptual change. *Science Education, 66*(2), 211-227.

Rosaen, C. (1987a). *Children as researchers: A descriptive study of intentions, interpretations, and social interaction in an elementary classroom.* Unpublished doctoral dissertation, Michigan State University, East Lansing.

Rosaen, C. (1987b). *Classroom structure and meaningful learning.* Paper presented at the Annual Meeting of the American Educational Research Association, Washington, DC.

Rowland, S. (1986). *The enquiring classroom: An introduction to children's learning.* New York: The Falmer Press.

Scardamalia, M. (1981). How children cope with the cognitive demands of writing. In C.H. Frederickson & J.F. Dominic (Eds.), *The nature, development, and teaching of written communication: Vol. 2. Writing: Process, development, and communication.* Hillsdale, NJ: Lawrence Erlbaum.

Scardamalia, M., & Bereiter, C. (1985). Fostering the development of self-regulation in children's knowledge processing. In S.S. Chipman, J.W. Segal, & R. Glaser (Eds.), *Thinking and learning skills: Current research and open questions* (Vol. 2). Hillsdale, NJ: Lawrence Erlbaum.

Scardamalia, M., & Bereiter, C. (1986). Research on written composition. In M. Wittrock (Ed.), *Handbook of research on teaching* (3rd ed.). New York: Macmillan.

Stein, N.L., & Trabasso, T. (1982). What's in a story: An approach to comprehension and instruction. In R. Glaser (Ed.), *Advances in instructional psychology.* Hillsdale, NJ: Lawrence Erlbaum.

Sunflower, C., & Crawford, L. (1985). *How frequently are elementary students writing?* Moorhead, MN: Moorhead State University. (ERIC Document Reproduction Service No. ED 272 895).

VanNostrand, A.D. (1979, March). Writing and the generation of knowledge. *Social Education,* pp. 178-180.

Ventre, R. (1979, March). Developmental writing: Social studies assignments. *Social Education,* pp. 181-183.

Vygotsky, L.C. (1962). *Thought and language.* Cambridge, MA: MIT Press.

Vygotsky, L.C. (1978). *Mind in Society.* Cambridge, MA: Harvard University Press.

Westbury, I. (1972). Conventional classrooms, "open" classrooms and the technology of teaching. *Journal of Curriculum Studies,* pp. 99-121.

Wilson, S., & Shulman, L. (1987). "150 different ways" of knowing: Representations of knowledge in teaching. In J. Calderhead (Ed.), *Exploring teacher thinking.* Sussex: Holt, Rinehart, & Winston.

Wittrock, M.C. (1977). *The human brain.* Englewood Cliffs, NJ: Prentice-Hall.

Wood, D.J. (1980). Teaching the young child: Some relationships between social interaction, language, and thought. In D.R. Olson (Ed.), *The social foundations of language and thought.* New York: Norton.

*   *   *

CROSS-TALK

Are there situations where tight framing or extensive scaffolding can contribute to genuine authorship? If so, what are your thoughts about when and how such situations occur? What do you see as the tradeoffs, in terms of student learning, between a tightly framed task such as answering the guide questions and a more loosely framed task like the student drawing? How, and to what extent, can those tradeoffs be avoided?

I think there is a definite role for both tight framing and extensive scaffolding in providing occasions for writing that help students learn to experience and manage genuine authorship. However, across the writing process, the frame must be fluid, flexible, and responsive to developing writers' learning needs. Of Calkins' four categories of teacher/student input discussed in the Florio-Ruane and Lensmire chapter (this volume, pp. 73-104), my recommendations fall in the fourth quadrant, high teacher and student input. Teachers do need to explicitly teach young writers to become aware of and use many aspects of the writing process, but they must do so in ways that allow students to share responsibility and control of the writing process. Addressing the problem of how much support to provide, and the nature of the support, requires standing back from each instructional instance and figuring out how it contributes to genuine authorship. Thus, the *selective* use of tightly framed activities (where the teacher has more control over the organization, selection, pacing, and timing of subject matter content) that are closely guided through instructional aids (such as giving students guide questions) must be *balanced against* careful consideration of the extent to which students are also given opportunities to make some of the same kinds of decisions (perhaps in other instances) themselves. Assigning students a topic or providing guide questions may be a valuable way to organize the instructional process to teach students how to evaluate the merits of a topic, or how to organize ideas in a written piece. Judgments about the merits of such activities must be weighed in terms of students' overall learning needs (e.g., How much do they know or understand about topic selection or organizing their ideas, and what do they need to learn about it?). Over time, as writers learn more about making appropriate topic choices, the nature of the support must shift in response to their emerging abilities. As discussed, the Stanfords began their writing instruction based on what they perceived to be students' current writing needs, but the nature of support was not adjusted in response to students' emerging abilities across the repeated writing cycles. The invariant use of the support structure contributed to students' narrow interpretations of the support.

If the frame for activities is flexible and responsive to developing writers' learning needs over time, "tradeoffs" can be minimized. Teaching students to use more tightly framed instructional aids such as guide questions, or think sheets (such as those discussed by Raphael and Englert, this volume, pp. 105-151) can be appropriate and helpful ways to support idea generation and text production by showing students one possible way to review their current understanding of a topic and organize it in a particular form. Yet limiting their instruction to the use of such supports runs the risk of students using them inflexibly and therefore reducing their use to "knowledge telling" instead of "knowledge transformation." This is where more loosely framed activities such as the drawing activity in the history unit can be used in a complementary way to help students learn to "play around" with ideas, to push their thinking, to explore other possible ways to discuss or emphasize their current thinking about a topic. For the Stanfords' students, the drawing activity seemed to be a more comfortable avenue for exploration and elaboration of their ideas. Pairing a required writing activity with an additional (but optional) avenue for further idea development resulted in more elaborate interaction with subject matter than just providing the required activity. Providing some elements of choice in the writing process is another way to create occasions for genuine authorship. Yet as classroom teachers and researchers well understand, setting up all activities as optional in a school context is unrealistic. The relationship between the students' idea development in each mode (writing and drawing) might have been addressed more specifically so the students could gain an awareness of the possible interconnections between the two processes. (Group reading and writing activities later in the unit also seemed to be a fruitful avenue for further exploration of ideas and is another way to frame activities that allow for increased student responsibility in the writing process, and could be important tool for idea generation.) Thus, both tightly framed and loosely framed activities can be used in concert to help students see ways to flexibly use supports provided, and to help them learn to make decisions about which supports are most useful in developing and expressing their understanding. By looking at the merits of each kind of activity, and promoting students' understanding of ways in which each type of activity might be helpful to them as authors, "tradeoffs" can be minimized.

Given that the curricular message in reading is not that students should be given opportunities to comprehend but, rather, that the reasoning processes should be taught *as they are to be applied* in the text to be read that day, can "text production" be taught as it is related to "idea production" associated with a specific writing-to-learn task? And, if so, would such a curricular format offer greater probability for accurate student interpretation of the curricular message?

Writing in the content areas shifts the instructional emphasis from focusing on producing written products to focusing on learning to use the writing process to explore and expand one's current understanding of subject matter. Yet, typically, written products will also be produced, so students also need support in learning to generate ideas as well as in learning to produce written text. Instruction in the writing process is similar to reading instruction, where the skills for writing are best taught in the context in which they are used. An important part of helping young writers learn to manage the interaction between idea and text production is to help them understand how the two areas interrelate. Thus, teaching students to generate ideas about which they will write is optimally done as part of a writing occasion, and not in isolation or as a separate activity that is later applied to a writing assignment. Similarly, learning to produce a particular written text is optimally learned in the context of the nature of the information to be communicated and the goals the writer has regarding knowledge development.

Much of the work of understanding and taking advantage of the interconnection between idea and text production takes place during planning and drafting phases of the writing process. Researchers on the writing process (e.g., Flower & Hayes, 1980; Scardamalia & Bereiter, 1986) argue that students need opportunities to progressively shape goals over time. Consider how a hypothetical content area writing task might provide for such opportunities. Once a student chooses a topic about which to write (e.g., photosynthesis) and identifies the audience for whom he will write (a study group with whom he works), he needs the opportunity to explore his knowledge of the topic as it relates to this particular rhetorical situation (e.g., "I can explain what happens during photosynthesis, but I still don't know the correct terms to use, and that is part of what I wanted to help my study group understand"). Support for this type of assessment might be in the form of a writing conference with the teacher, or a free-writing activity where the student writes what he knows and is asked to reflect on how his knowledge of the topic fits his intended purpose. At this point in the planning process, the writer has the opportunity to develop a knowledge development goal of matching his understanding of a process (he can provide a good explanation of photosynthesis) with new scientific terms (he wants to learn the scientific terms to use in his explanation). The teacher, or other members of his study group, can then help him identify resources that will be useful in finding the information he needs.

Once he feels comfortable with his knowledge level (as it relates to his writing purpose), he must also be supported in choosing a form of writing that serves his writing purpose (e.g., help his study group to understand photosynthesis and use scientific terms to describe the process). He might have assumed initially that he would use a standard expository form of writing such as writing an explanation, but the teacher could also help him explore other options that could also serve his purposes. For example, since he is trying to help the members of his group understand photosynthesis and help them learn the scientific terms, he could consider using an alternate form such as writing a dialogue between two students, which would enable him to interject questions at strategic points of his explanation to highlight and clarify possible areas of confusion. If he chose this alternate format, the teacher would also need to help him assess his knowledge and understanding of creating dialogue in the correct form, and he may conclude that he needs to learn to produce this kind of text before continuing with the writing process. Once he tries using the dialogue form, the teaching can help him decide whether this particular form is "working" for the purpose he intended. If not, he may decide to use a different form of writing. Once the piece is finished to the student's satisfaction, he can share it with his intended audience to decide on its success. When the entire process is finished, the teacher can help the student take a retrospective look at places in the process that were more or less productive for him in terms of helping him develop the knowledge he wanted to develop, and helping him produce a text that did (or did not) achieve his intended purposes.

As this example illustrates, the decisions about topic choice and development, choice of written form, and production of the written form progressively shape the written piece. The writing task is not fully defined and spelled out at the onset, yet the teacher does provide an overall framework and requirements within which the student can become aware of and learn to manage the interaction between idea and text production. By providing a writing occasion such as this one, the student has the opportunity to develop his capabilities in three areas: (a) his knowledge of the topic; (b) his writing knowledge and skill; and (c) his metacognitive knowledge of how to use the writing process for his intended purposes. At the same time, writing is used as an intricate part of the learning process as well as for genuine communicative processes.

If you were called into a district to serve as a consultant for the purpose of increasing classroom teachers' interest in and knowledge about writing-to-learn, what steps would you take?

Work in this area would need to take place over a long period of time (e.g., at least one school year), so that there would be time and opportunities for teachers to: examine their own practices; assess their own knowledge, skills, and attitudes; develop and try out some initial attempts at effecting change in their writing instruction; engage in dialogue with their colleagues and myself about relative successes with their attempts; continue to develop, try out and assess additional ideas.

I would start with a set of question that would guide my interaction with classroom teachers over time:

1. What is their current knowledge level of the writing process in general, and of content area writing in particular?
2. What is their current skill level at using their knowledge to develop effective writing-to-learn strategies?
3. To what extent are the teachers in "metacognitive control" (see Duffy & Roehler, this volume, pp. 1-33) of the complexities associated with implementing change in their instruction?
4. What are their attitudes about content area writing, and dispositions to develop and promote its use in the classroom?
5. Which aspects of improving their content area writing instruction are most interesting and challenging to them?

Given these five broad areas, I assume the teachers would fall somewhere on a continuum of "more" to "less" knowledge, skill, or disposition, and that my role would be to help them figure out ways to move closer to the "more" end of the continuum over time. I think it is important for the teachers to be involved in identifying and solving the problems of moving along the continuum, so they have ownership and an investment in the process.

Until I would have a better picture of the teachers' learning needs and desires, it is difficult to say what would come next. I think a general strategy that would be effective is to use the teachers' own writing as a starting point, and as a means of illustrating the complexities of the writing process. Understanding themselves better as learners could help guide their developing understanding of the instructional process required of their students, paticularly since some of the teachers may not consider themselves to be "mature" writers in the sense that they know or understand how to strategically use the writing process to promote knowledge development. Increasing their own knowledge and skill in this area might be one way to get inside the complexities of the teaching and learning process.

I think it would also be important to try to provide examples for inspiration and concrete ideas about instructional strategies and organizational patterns to try. Lucy Calkins' (1983) book *Lessons From A Child* is a vivid example of one child's writing development over time. It also gives a detailed picture of the nature of interaction surrounding the writing process. Examples such as this could serve as a common starting point for identifying problems and issues to be solved. This could lead to identifying further readings that are somewhat more concrete about how to design and implement appropriate writing instruction (e.g., Calkins' [1986] chapters on writing across the curriculum and content area writing in *The Art of Teaching Writing*). With readings such as these, I think it would be important to discuss ways in which the problems and issues raised compare and contrast with issues pertinent to this set of classroom teachers' instructional practices.

I would try to set up some working groups designed for the teachers to help each other develop their teaching across the year, and to identify ways in which I could be helpful to each group. These groups might be organized around common instructional issues (e.g., which teachers want to work on their knowledge about and skill in using particular writing strategies), or common areas of knowledge teachers want to develop as they try out new ideas in their classrooms (e.g., developing knowledge and understanding of modes of writing and how different modes might facilitate knowledge development in particular subject areas). These working groups would facilitate bringing out and building on knowledge, skills, and dispositions teachers already have (thus helping teachers realize what they already know and understand), as well as encouraging teachers to share their expertise. By finding ways for teachers to work together to identify and solve instructional problems, I think there is a greater chance that their improvement-oriented activities would continue after the initial support is no longer available.

Finally, I think it would be helpful to the teachers to encourage them to think of their initial phase of work (first year, or whatever) as "pilot work" targeted toward particular areas of their writing instruction that is crafted, tried out, and then evaluated for the desirability and plausibility of continuing or modifying. For example, a teacher might decide to target working on conducting different kinds of writing conferences. While she will need to look at how conferencing fits into her overall approach to instruction, she can take on improving this particular part of the writing process while leaving other areas of her instruction alone for the time being. Learning to teach writing well is a career goal, not a one-year project, but it is easy to lose sight of that when an instructional change is being focused on. Breaking down this career goal into manageable parts and helping teachers to see that it is acceptable to try new ideas without expecting complete success across every aspect of their instruction may make success more tangible and failure easier to take.

References to Cross-talk

Calkins, L.M. (1983). *Lessons from a child.* Portsmouth, NH: Heinemann.

Calkins, L.M. (1986). *The art of teaching writing.* Portsmouth, NH: Heinemann.

Flower, L., & Hayes, J. (1980). The cognition of discovery: Defining a rhetorical problem. *College Composition and Communication, 31*(2), 21-32.

Scardamalia, M., & Bereiter, C. (1986). Research on written composition. In M. Wittrock (Ed.), *Handbook of research on teaching* (3rd ed.). New York: Macmillan.

LEARNING MATHEMATICS
WITH UNDERSTANDING:
COGNITIVELY GUIDED INSTRUCTION

Elizabeth Fennema, Thomas P. Carpenter, and

Penelope L. Peterson

The consensus of a number of reports that have appeared in the last few years is that mathematics instruction is badly in need of reform (Conference Board of the Mathematical Sciences, 1984; National Science Board Commission on Precollege Education in Mathematics, Science, and Technology, 1983; Romberg, 1984). Cited as evidence for this belief are results of national surveys which show that although students perform reasonably well on low-level cognitive skills such as computation, many students have trouble with higher level cognitive skills involving understanding and problem solving (Carpenter, Matthews, Lindquist, & Silver, 1984). In addition, the relatively poor performance of American students when compared with the performance of students from other countries (Stevenson, Lee, & Stigler, 1986) has contributed to the belief that significant change needs to be made in the school mathematics curriculum.

Advances in Research on Teaching, Volume 1, pages 195-221.
Copyright © 1989 by JAI Press Inc.
All rights of reproduction in any form reserved.
ISBN: 0-89232-845-2

MATHEMATICS CURRICULUM AND UNDERSTANDING

A critical issue in the reform of the mathematics curriculum involves the emphasis on developing understanding. Recent reform movements can be characterized by their perspective on this issue. In the "new math" programs of the 1960s the emphasis was on mathematical structure and understanding, whereas the back-to-basics movement of the 1970s focused on teaching procedural skills. Current curricular recommendations as well as recent work in the psychology of children's thinking and problem solving and in research on teaching, are based on the proposition that the development of understanding and the teaching of procedural skills are not conflicting objectives; in fact, conceptual understanding and procedural skills are integrally related (Hiebert, 1986a; National Council of Teachers of Mathematics, 1987; Resnick & Ford, 1981; Romberg & Carpenter, 1986).

What does it mean to learn mathematics with understanding? This is an idea which has been written about for centuries, but it remains an elusive concept. Attempts to define understanding in mathematics over the last few decades have included the following: Thiele (1941, p. 48) stated that meaningful arithmetic is that "which helps children to appreciate and utilize the interrelationships in the number system." Van Engen (1953, p. 75) said that "the pupil who understands is in possession of the cause and effect relationships, the logical implications and the sequence of thought that unite two or more statements by means of the bonds of logic." More recently Hiebert (1986b) defined understanding as "the process of *creating* relationships between pieces of knowledge. Students understand something as they recognize how it relates to other things they already know" (p. 2)

The underlying theme in these definitions is that understanding involves establishing relationships between segments of knowledge. The definitions differ, however, in how they characterize those relationships. In the definitions of Thiele and Van Engen, relationships are based on the mathematical structure that is inherent in the content itself. On the other hand, for Hiebert, the critical consideration is the learner establishing relationships between the knowledge already possessed and the knowledge that he or she is acquiring.

Curriculum development movements over the last three decades reflect the distinctions in the different characterizations of understanding. During the 1960s, most of the new math school programs were based on the structure of mathematics and the interrelatedness of the important ideas of mathematics. There was little attempt to relate new ideas to the informal mathematics children brought with them to school. Mathematics was built up from primitive elements like sets and one-to-one correspondence, and even in the early grades the emphasis was on precise mathematical definitions rather than children's intuitive concepts. It was assumed that if mathematics was presented so that the interrelationships of mathematical ideas were logical, the result would be learning with understanding (Cambridge Conference on School Mathematics, 1963).

In the 1970s, some mathematics educators began to question whether a curriculum based solely on the structure of mathematics would result in instructional programs in which students learned mathematics with understanding. The research of Ausubel, Bruner, Gagné, Piaget, and others appeared to have implications for how mathematics should be taught, and a number of individuals began to suggest that knowledge about children's learning and development, as well as the structure of mathematics, should be considered when mathematics programs were developed (Shulman, 1970).

It is worth examining one curricular project that reflected those themes. *Developing Mathematical Processes* [*DMP*] (Romberg, Harvey, Moser, & Montgomery, 1974), while still organized around the structure of mathematics, also attempted to take into consideration how children learn mathematics. The content of instruction was carefully organized into learning hierarchies. The focus of instruction was on fundamental processes that children could use to solve mathematical problems. Instruction moved through different stages in representing mathematical ideas from concrete representations to symbols. Instruction was planned to be motivating for children, and learning activities were carefully designed to present important mathematical ideas in such a way that the children themselves might construct interrelationships among them.

Pedagogical concerns were specifically addressed in DMP. There were detailed directions for teaching, including pretests to give the teacher information about what topic the child was ready to learn, posttests which indicated whether the child had learned, and directions for how mathematical ideas should be sequenced for instruction. There was a management system planned to provide information for the teacher about what each child had learned, what the next step in the curriculum should be, and how children should be grouped for instruction. Large sets of manipulatives were included, and the instructional activities were specified for the teachers in great detail. In other words, there was an attempt to provide teachers with all the directions and aids they would need to make pedagogical decisions. In fact, the program was designed to make most of the important decisions for the teacher about the selection of content and how that content should be taught.

Unfortunately *DMP* was never implemented as the authors had planned. Stephens (1982) studied the implementation of *DMP* in schools and concluded that teachers who used the program became managers of an "efficient transfer of a body of subject matter to students" (p. 244) and, as such, subverted the major instructional objectives held by the authors. "DMP had, in effect, been presented to teachers as a complete mathematics curriculum, which they were to implement and manage" (p. 241). Teachers were "cast in the role of consumers of a prearranged mathematics curriculum" (p. 241) and were asked to assume a predetermined set of beliefs, purposes and values which had, in fact, been selected and articulated by the authors of *DMP*. Because the *DMP* authors' beliefs and objectives were not necessarily the teachers' beliefs and objectives, many of the teachers had a different agenda. Although they used most of the activities, they often altered them so that the underlying focus on developing understanding was lost.

DMP is still one of the most innovative mathematics programs available, and it made major contributions to further our knowledge of how instruction can be designed to build up children's understanding of mathematics. However, since the time that *DMP* was conceptualized and developed, we have learned a great deal about children's mathematical thinking, and we have developed alternative conceptions of teacher decision making.

CHILDREN'S MATHEMATICAL THINKING

Although the theories that were prevalent when *DMP* was being developed potentially addressed problems of learning mathematics and provided general guidelines for curriculum development, current research provides a much clearer picture of how children acquire specific mathematical concepts and procedures that are the focus of the mathematics curriculum (Romberg & Carpenter, 1986). A prominent feature of this research is the detailed analysis of the content being studied. The purpose of this analysis has not been simply to specify mathematical structure, but also to identify features that are related to the ways that children think about the content. A second prominent component of this work has been the focus on the processes that children use to solve specific problems within the specified mathematical domain. The research provides maps of how children move from relatively naive or intuitive knowledge within a domain to more sophisticated or more abstract knowledge. Each of these maps provides a framework that can be used to sequence and guide instruction (Case, 1983).

Consider, for example, the research on addition and subtraction which is guiding our work. Research has provided a highly structured, detailed analysis of the development of addition and subtraction concepts and skills as reflected in children's solutions of different types of word problems (for reviews of this research, see Carpenter, 1985; Carpenter & Moser, 1983; Riley, Greeno, & Heller, 1983). This research specifies a taxonomy of problem types and strategies used by children and provides explicit models of the major levels in the development of addition and subtraction concepts and skills.

The research is based on an analysis of addition and subtraction word problems which distinguishes between different classes of problems based upon semantic characteristics of the problems (Carpenter & Moser, 1983; Riley et al., 1983). These distinctions are illustrated by the problems in Table 1. Although all of the problems in Table 1 can be solved by solving the

Table 1. Classification of Word Problems

Problem Type	Result Unknown	Change Unknown	Start Unknown
Join	1. Connie had 5 marbles. Jim gave her 8 more marbles. How many does Connie have altogether?	2. Connie has 5 marbles. How many more marbles does she need to win to have 13 marbles altogether?	3. Connie had some marbles. Jim gave her 5 more marbles. Now she has 13 marbles. How many marbles did Connie have to start with?
Separate	4. Connie had 13 marbles. She gave 5 marbles to Jim. How many marbles does she have left?	5. Connie had 13 marbles. She gave some to Jim. Now she has 5 marbles left. How many marbles did Connie give to Jim?	6. Connie had some marbles. She gave 5 to Jim. Now she has 8 marbles left. How many marbles did Connie have to start with?
Combine	7. Connie has 5 red marbles and 8 blue marbles. How many marbles does she have?	8. Connie has 13 marbles. Five are red and the rest are blue. How many blue marbles does Connie have?	
Compare	9. Connie has 13 marbles. Jim has 5 marbles. How many more marbles does Connie have than Jim?	10. Jim has 5 marbles. Connie has 8 more than Jim. How many marbles does Connie have?	11. Connie has 13 marbles. She has 5 more marbles than Jim. How many marbles does Jim have?

199

mathematical sentences $5 + 8 = ?$ or $13 - 5 = ?$, each provides a distinct interpretation of addition and subtraction.

The Join and Separate problems in the first two rows of Table 1 involve two distinct types of action, whereas the Combine and Compare problems in the third and fourth rows describe static relationships. The Combine problems involve part-whole relationships within a set, and the Compare problems involve the comparison of two distinct sets. For each type of action or relation, distinct problems can be generated by varying which quantity is unknown, as is illustrated by the distinctions between problems within each row in Table 1. As can be seen from these examples, a number of semantically distinct problems can be generated by varying the structure of the problem, even though most of the same words appear in each problem.

These distinctions between problems are reflected in children's solutions. Most young children invent informal modeling and counting strategies for solving addition and subtraction problems that have a clear relationship to the structure of the problems (Carpenter & Moser, 1984). At the initial level of solving addition and subtraction problems, children are limited to solutions involving direct representations of the problem. They must use fingers or physical objects to represent each quantity in the problem, and they can represent only the specific action or relationship described in the problem. For example, to solve the second problem in Table 1, they construct a set of 5 objects, add more objects until there is a total of 13 objects, and count the number of objects added. To solve the fourth problem, they make a set of 13 objects, remove 5, and count the remaining objects. The ninth problem might be solved by matching two sets and counting the unmatched elements. Children at this level cannot solve problems like the sixth problem in Table 1, because the initial quantity is not known and, therefore, cannot be represented directly with objects.

Children's problem-solving strategies become increasingly abstract as direct modeling gives way to counting strategies like counting on and counting back. For example, to solve the second problem in Table 1, a child using a counting on strategy would recognize that it was unnecessary to construct the set of 5 objects, and instead would simply count on from 5 to 13, keeping track of the number of counts. The same child may solve the fourth problem by counting back from 13. Virtually all children use counting strategies before they learn number facts at a recall level.

Number facts are learned over an extended period of time during which some recall of number facts and counting are used concurrently. Children learn certain number combinations earlier than others. Before all the addition facts are completely committed to memory, many children use a small set of memorized facts to derive solutions for problems involving other number combinations. These solutions usually are based on doubles or numbers whose sum is 10. For example, to find $6 + 8 = ?$, a child might recognize that

6 + 6 = 12 and 6 + 8 is just 2 more than 12. Derived facts are not used just by a handful of bright students, but they play an important role in the learning of number facts for many children.

In summary, children's solution strategies to addition and subtraction problems become increasingly abstract. Initially they solve simple problems by directly modeling; they move on first to increasingly sophisticated counting strategies, to using derived facts, and finally, to recall of number facts. As solution strategies become more abstract, children become more flexible in their choice of strategies. Initially they can solve only problems that can be modeled directly. As they become more flexible, they learn to solve more difficult problems that cannot be easily modeled.

When children enter school almost all of them can solve simple problems by direct modeling, and many of them are using more advanced strategies. Even without explicit instruction, children discover the basic strategies described above, and even with instruction that emphasizes symbolic manipulation, children continue to rely on modeling and counting processes to solve problems.

This research documents the incredibly rich store of knowledge that children bring to instruction in one particular domain. If we accept Hiebert's characterization that understanding involves linking new knowledge to existing knowledge, instruction should be designed to build upon the knowledge that children have at different stages in the acquistion of particular concepts and procedures. This involves the identification of procedures that enable teachers to assess the knowledge children have so that appropriate instruction can be provided.

Specifically, instruction on early number concepts should be linked to the modeling and counting strategies described above. For a child to understand arithmetic, he or she should be able to relate the symbolic procedures learned in school to these intuitive modeling and counting problem-solving strategies. Too often children perceive their problem-solving strategies and the arithmetic they learn in school as separate, unrelated procedures. They solve their real problems using modeling and counting, and they use the procedures they learn in school to do the tasks in workbooks. If they do the school tasks incorrectly, they are not bothered by the discrepancy between the answer derived by symbolic manipulations and the answer to real problems found by counting or modeling (Cobb, 1988). To help children make this connection, mathematical symbols for addition and subtraction must be introduced as ways to represent the knowledge that children have already acquired. This gives the symbols meaning and helps to prevent arithmetic from being perceived as arbitrary manipulations of symbols that one performs only on school tasks.

AN ALTERNATIVE CONCEPTION OF
TEACHER DECISION MAKING

DMP attempted to prescribe teaching activities, assessment procedures, and instructional decisions for the teacher. An alternative conception of teaching portrays the teacher as a reflective professional making decisions about instruction, rather than as a technician delivering a product. Reviews of research on the teacher as a professional decision maker can be found in Clark and Peterson (1986) and Shavelson and Stern (1981). Clark and Peterson concluded that the research shows that thinking plays an important role in teaching. As thoughtful professionals, teachers have more in common with physicians and lawyers than they have in common with technicians. The research also shows that teachers plan for instruction in a rich variety of ways and that these plans have real consequences in the classroom. Furthermore, during interactive teaching, teachers are continually thinking and they report making decisions frequently—once every two minutes. Finally, teachers have theories and belief systems that influence their perceptions, plans, and actions in the classroom.

The research on teachers' thought processes substantiates the perspective that the teacher is a reflective, thoughtful individual. Moreover, the research documents that teaching is a complex and cognitively demanding human process. Teachers' beliefs, knowledge, judgments, thoughts, and decisions have a profound effect on the way that they teach as well as on students' learning in their classrooms. One can infer from this research that reform in mathematics instruction must actively address teachers' planning and decision making rather than attempting to provide a "teacher proof" curriculum.

TEACHERS' PEDAGOGICAL CONTENT KNOWLEDGE

There has been much concern with what teachers should know in order to make informed instructional decisions, and there is growing consensus that this should include what Shulman (1986) has defined as pedagogical content knowledge:

> the understanding of how particular topics, principles, strategies, and the like in specific subject areas are comprehended or typically misconstrued, are learned and likely to be forgotten. Such knowledge includes the categories within which similar problem types or conceptions can be classified (what are the ten most frequently encountered types of algebra word problems? least well-grasped grammatical constructions?), and the psychology of learning them. (p. 26)

Pedagogical content knowledge includes: (1) knowledge of the conceptual and procedural knowledge that students bring to the learning of a topic, (2) the misconceptions they may have developed, and (3) the stages of understanding that they are likely to pass through in moving from a state of having little understanding of the topic to mastery of it.

There is a high degree of consensus about children's cognitions in various addition and subtraction problems. Although there are minor variations in scholars' definitions of problem types and solution strategies, most would agree on the basic components described above. This knowledge provides a principled framework in which to study teachers' pedagogical content knowledge in a highly structured domain of mathematics. The Cognitively Guided Instruction project has done precisely that. We have been using this principled framework as a vehicle to study curriculum development in terms of teachers.

A NEW PARADIGM FOR CURRICULUM DEVELOPMENT

The Cognitively Guided Instruction Project (CGI) is an investigation of curriculum development, designed to increase learners' understanding by considering teachers, learners and mathematics. Using knowledge derived from the study of teaching and the study of children's cognitions, we have designed a model for curriculum development which is shown in Figure 1. As can be seen, the final component is children's understanding. This understanding is directly influenced by children's cognitions and behaviors, which are influenced by classroom instruction. More importantly from our point of view, however, this classroom instruction is determined by the decisions that teachers make which are directly influenced by teachers' knowledge and beliefs. In our research, we have been particularly concerned with teachers' knowledge and beliefs about students' learning and thinking processes (see Carpenter, Fennema, Peterson, & Carey, 1988; Peterson, Fennema, Carpenter, & Loef, 1989). The purpose of this chapter is to describe how knowledge about children's learning and thinking processes enables teachers to make decisions so that children learn mathematics with understanding. We will report briefly on two studies which support the belief that children can learn mathematics with understanding in classrooms where teachers have had access to knowledge about children's problem solving, have used this knowledge to assess their own children's thinking processes, and have based their instruction on it. Using these studies as a base, we then will describe in detail what it means to learn mathematics with understanding in a CGI classroom.

Cognitively Guided Instruction

The major tenets of CGI are: (1) Instruction must be based on what each learner knows, (2) Instruction should take into consideration how children's

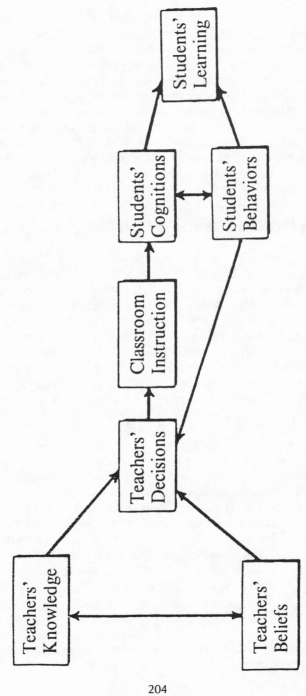

Figure 1. Model for Research and Curriculum Development

204

mathematical ideas develop naturally, and (3) Children must be mentally active as they learn mathematics. All children understand mathematics at some level. Before starting school, children have come to understand some basic mathematical ideas just by living in the world. When formal school instruction is based on these ideas that children bring with them to school, mathematics continues to be understandable. By continually basing instructional decisions on children's knowledge, teachers help children to learn that mathematics is not a magic set of activities, but is understandable and relevant.

Children's cognitions are the fulcrum of instructional decision making in a CGI classroom. All decisions about what and how to teach are dependent on what the child already knows and thinks. The pedagogical content knowledge available about addition and subtraction enables a teacher to be actively involved with young children's thinking in a way that has not been possible before. By knowing what each child is thinking and being able to predict some ways that the child's thinking will develop, teachers are able to plan instructional activities that keep the child mentally active and develop his/her mathematical knowledge in an accurate and comprehensive manner.

Research about Cognitively Guided Instruction

Is it possible for teachers to implement CGI and do children in such a classroom really learn mathematics with understanding? Two sets of data are available to help in answering these questions. One set of data comes from a study designed to investigate the effects of a workshop focused on giving teachers access to pedagogical content knowledge about addition and subtraction. The other data set was obtained by observations of the experimental CGI teachers and by case studies of six CGI teachers' classrooms.

For the experimental study of CGI (Carpenter, Fennema, Peterson, Chiang, & Loef, in press), 40 first-grade teachers were randomly assigned by school to an experimental or control group. The experimental (CGI) group participated in a four-week summer workshop in which they were given an opportunity to learn about children's cognitions in addition and subtraction. They were also given the time to plan their next year's mathematics program. During the following school year, children in both the CGI and control teachers' classrooms were pretested on mathematical computation and problem solving early in the year and posttested about 7 months later. Between the two tests, teachers and students were systematically observed during 16 mathematics periods by two observers in each classroom.

Several statistically significant differences between the mathematics programs of the CGI and control teachers were found. Control teachers spent twice as much time as did the CGI teachers focusing directly on the knowledge and use of simple computations using addition and subtraction number facts. CGI teachers spent significantly more time than did the control teachers having the children solve word problems, and listening to children explain the mental processes they used while solving word problems. CGI teachers also expected and accepted a larger variety of problem-solving strategies from their children than did the control teachers.

In spite of the larger amount of time spent on computation and number facts by control teachers and their classes, CGI teachers' classes did as well as did control teachers' classes on two standardized tests of computational skills. In addition, when interviewed, CGI teachers' children were actually able to recall number facts at a significantly higher level than did control teachers' children. Even more importantly, when compared to control teachers' classes, CGI teachers' classes showed significantly greater ability to solve complex addition and subtraction word problems. Children in CGI classes were also more confident of their ability to solve word problems than were children in control teachers' classes, perhaps reflecting their actual greater abilities at being able to solve such problems. (For a more complete discussion of CGI effects on student outcomes, see Carpenter et al. [in press].)

The tests that we used to measure learning indicated that lower-achieving CGI classes performed better than did lower-achieving control classes. On one standardized test of computational skills, and when solving simple Join and Separate result-unknown word problems, both the CGI and control groups' higher-achieving classes scored very high on the standardized computation tests and on the solution of simple Join and Separate problems. Thus, there was little room on these tests for differences to be found between higher-achieving classes in the way we measured learning. However, when lower-achieving classes did not "top out" on the computation and simple problem solving on tests, differences were found. It may well be that lower-achieving children particularly benefitted from CGI. They may have come from home environments where there were few experiences in solving problems and thus when given the opportunity in the CGI classrooms, their growth in problem solving was improved. It may also be true that we did not adequately measure what children in the higher-achieving classes knew. The restrictions placed upon us by our research design limited open-ended probing questions. During our observations, it was noted that many CGI children were solving problems which were more difficult than anything we had anticipated, so there is reason to believe that CGI children actually learned more than we know about.

The differences we found indicated to us that children in the CGI classes learned skills as well as did control children, but spent significantly less time drilling on these skills. On the most complex tasks that we measured, CGI children did significantly better.

Two of the basic tenets of CGI are that children should be involved in solving mathematical problems during much of their mathematics class and that instruction should be based on what children know. As far as was determined in this observational study, these CGI tenets were implemented. CGI teachers did spend considerably more time than did other teachers having children solve word problems in a variety of ways. Teachers spent more time listening to the children describe their mental processes as they solved problems. As a consequence, CGI teachers had more knowledge about their children's knowledge than did the control teachers (see Carpenter, Fennema, Peterson et al., in press). Thus, CGI teachers were able to base instruction on what children already knew.

In the year following the observational study, six classroom teachers were selected to participate in case studies of CGI classrooms (Carpenter, Fennema, Loef and Carey, in progress). These teachers were selected because of the wide variety of their teaching styles, experiences and beliefs about mathematics teaching. The purpose of the case studies was to understand how the individual teachers made decisions about mathematics instruction in their classrooms, to describe the common components of CGI classrooms, and to determine if children could learn mathematics with understanding in classrooms that appeared on the surface to be dramatically different. We also wanted to document what it meant for children to learn mathematics with understanding. From this study and from our observations of other CGI teachers, we have selected the vignettes which follow. These vignettes illustrate teachers instructing so that children learn with understanding. They are organized around two themes: (1) assessing children's cognitions, and (2) basing instruction on children's cognitions.

Assessing Cognitions

In order for a teacher to base instruction on children's cognitions, she/he must be able to assess children's thinking. CGI teachers found out what children knew about addition and subtraction by using the knowledge of problem types and solution strategies described above. This knowledge was used in various ways depending upon the teacher, the time of the year and the instructional objectives. Consider the following examples of teachers assessing children's knowledge near the beginning of the school year.

Ms. Bailey had her children sitting on a rug in front of her. She asked them to solve the following Join result-unknown problem: "Peg had four pennies and Jack gave her three more. How many did Peg have then?" Several children immediately began to use their fingers by holding up 4 fingers on one hand and three on another. One child touched his chin with each raised finger counting as he did so and then said "7." Another child just looked at her fingers and counted them and said "7." Some children watched the two who solved the problem and tried to mimic them while another child just said "7." The teacher asked a number of children how they solved the problem. The teacher then gave another Join result-unknown problem and a Separate result-unknown problem. She asked the children to solve the problems and mentally noted who could solve the problems, how they solved the problems, and who could not solve the problems. At the end of the period, she recorded her observations and planned to ask more of the same type of problems the next day. She also identified which children she knew nothing about, so that she could focus on them during the mathematics period the next day. She noted that several children were solving the simple problems easily and planned to ask some more complex problems to see if they could solve them.

Ms. Kelly used a somewhat different approach to assess her children's knowledge. She assessed 2-3 children per day on an individual basis while the rest of the children were working on activities which did not require her direct supervision. She had a fairly routinized set of procedures that she used to assess each child's knowledge. The first problem that she asked each child to solve was a Join change-unknown problem. Based on the solution of this problem, it was possible for Ms. Kelly to gain a great deal of information about each child's ability to solve the various types of addition and subtraction problems. If a child couldn't solve the Join change-unknown problem, it was safe to assume that the more difficult Start unknown and Compare problem types also couldn't be solved. If the Join change-unknown problems could be solved, it was safe to assume that the easier problems could be solved, and testing could continue with the more difficult problems. The following protocol illustrates Ms. Kelly's assessment of one child's problem solving ability.

> Ms. Kelly: "Robin picked 4 apples. Bob gave her some more apples. Now she has 9 apples. How many apples did Bob give her?" Susan counted out 4 blue chips and set them aside. Then she began to make a second group of yellow chips, counted on from 4, and stopped adding chips to the second set when she got to nine. Before responding, she checked her total by counting all the chips and then counting the yellow set and answered, "Five."
> Because Susan did not have trouble with a Join change-unknown problem, it was apparent that Susan would not have difficulty with the Join or Separate result-unknown problems. It was not known, however, whether she could solve more difficult start unknown problems or if she could use counting strategies when objects were not available, so problems that address these questions were given next. Susan was asked to solve a start unknown problem and given another problem to assess whether she could count on.

In the two examples given above, different strategies for assessing children's knowledge were illustrated. In the first, the assessment was informal and, continually ongoing. Whenever Ms. Bailey was teaching, she mentally noted what children could do and what they could not do. Her questions were embedded in her ongoing instruction. Ms. Kelly carried out a relatively formal assessment. She felt that she got better knowledge from focusing on each child individually. Both teachers, however, were basing their assessment on what is known about children's thinking in addition and subtraction.

Assessing each child's thinking and knowledge is an essential component of a CGI classroom. The assessment can be structured or unstructured or a combination of the two. However it is done, it should identify the processes that children use to solve problems. Children use a variety of strategies to solve the same problem. A child who solves a problem by directly modeling it with counters has very different knowledge and instructional needs than a child who solves the same problem by counting on or by using derived facts. The knowledge of problem types and solution strategies gained from the study of children's cognitions provides a framework for asking questions and understanding the responses made by children. It should also be pointed out that the major principle of assessing children, using a CGI framework, is to focus on the understanding demonstrated by the children as they solve problems. This focus is much broader than just listening to see if children obtain correct answers. Correct answers do not necessarily imply that children have mastered desired concepts or skills; neither do incorrect answers necessarily imply that a child does not understand a given problem. It is critical that a teacher understand the mental processes used by a child; these demonstrate whether or not that child understands.

This framework of addition and subtraction problems and children's cognitions about it has been derived from a substantial body of research. However, its power to give teachers insight into their children's knowledge has been demonstrated in real classrooms by real teachers. These teachers have been astonished by how much they are able to ascertain about their children's thinking and knowledge using that framework. Even teachers who have taught many years express amazement at how much their children know at the beginning of first grade and at how it is possible to understand children's thinking when using the framework as a basis of assessment. As one CGI teacher said: "I have always asked my children a lot of questions to find out what they know, but until now I never knew what questions to ask or what to listen for in their answers."

Basing Instruction on Children's Cognitions

The second major tenet of CGI is that instruction should be based on children's cognitions, and children generally should not be asked to do anything that does not have meaning for them. One way to ensure that children do activities with meaning is to sequence activities in a way that is consistent with the sequence in which concepts and skills naturally develop (Case, 1983). In other words, instruction should be sequenced to reflect major levels in the acquisition of a concept or skill; children should be guided to use some of the more productive strategies that are used by the most capable students; and they should be encouraged to grow in their ability to solve more complex problems. In order to do this, two basic emphases of CGI instruction have been identified: (1) early and continuing emphasis on word problems, and (2) structuring the learning environment so that children discover more advanced strategies to solve mathematical problems.

Early and Continuing Emphasis on Word Problems.   Traditional curriculum has been based on the assumption that computational skills must be learned before children are taught to solve even simple word problems. Word problems have often appeared only at the end of a unit, emphasizing the computational skills taught in the unit. Whatever value such exercises may have for practicing the computational skill, they do very little to ensure that children are working with understanding or to teach the higher cognitive skills like problem solving. For example, when children are taught that they are going to subtract the smaller number from the larger in each problem, and they are then asked to do a worksheet practicing that skill, they are being encouraged to perform rote computations and not to read carefully or to think about problems. The activity becomes one of understanding the teacher's instructions rather than understanding the mathematics. Thus, such exercises may actually contribute to the deterioration of mathematical understanding. Furthermore, many mathematics programs have provided only a limited exposure to different types of addition and subtraction problems. Research clearly shows that even before they receive formal instruction in addition and subtraction, children can solve a wide variety of addition and subtraction problems and can do so with understanding when they are allowed to model the problems with manipulatives or by using different counting strategies. Word problems are appropriate for introducing addition and subtraction and they not only should be integrated into the mathematics curriculum (Carpenter, Hiebert, & Moser, 1981) but should form the basis of it.

Most of the addition and subtraction curriculum of a CGI classroom is based on solving problems. Consider the following descriptions and vignettes from CGI classrooms.

Ms. Jackson, an experienced teacher, had about 20 children in her room. Although the children were officially in either first or second grade, it was impossible to distinguish them by the work they were doing. Sometimes small groups work with Ms. Jackson, and at other times she works with the entire group. Mathematics is incorporated throughout the day whenever a problem can be fitted in.

> In early October during the first few minutes of the day, Ms. Jackson asked how many children wanted hot lunches that day. Eighteen children raised their hands. Six children were going to eat cold lunches. Ms. Jackson asked "How many children are going to eat lunch here today?" By starting with 18 and counting on several children got the answer of 24. One child got out counters and counted out one set of 18 and another set of 6. He then counted all of them and said

24. Ms. Jackson then asked "How many more children are eating hot lunch than are eating cold lunch?" Several children counted back from 18 to 12. The child with the blocks matched 18 blocks with 6 blocks and counted the blocks left over. Ms. Jackson asked each child who volunteered to tell the rest of the class how he or she got the answer. She continued asking for different solutions until no one could think of a way to solve the problem that had not already been described. Throughout the day, when an opportunity which could involve addition and subtraction was seen, Ms. Jackson asked the children a question, permitted them to solve it in any way they wished, and then asked them to explain how they got the answer. Each of these problem-solving episodes took only a minute or two and fitted naturally into the flow of the day's activity.

While Ms. Jennings believed strongly that mathematics should be part of the entire school day, she also had a formal mathematics period. During that period, she asked children to solve problems she had written to reflect what the children knew. For example, when the class visited the school forest, the mathematics lessons for the next week reflected this visit. Ms. Jennings believed that her knowledge of the problem types enabled her to stretch the children's minds so she continually asked them to solve problems that were just slightly harder than those they had already solved. Either the size of the numbers was increased or the problem selected was a more difficult type. In this class, children continually talked to each other and argued about whether their way of solving a problem was different.

By about November two-thirds of Ms. Jennings' class was able to solve Compare problems. Some of these children were using numbers with sums less than 20 while others were using numbers with sums up to 100. Children were solving the problems mentally, or by using counters. At least once each day, Ms. Jennings gave the children a problem of a type which they had seldom encountered before (such as a problem with 4 addends or a problem with extraneous information).

About one third of the children in Ms. Jennings' class were having trouble with simple counting and numeral recognition. While most of their time was spent on counting activities, Ms. Jennings always spent some time asking them to solve very simple Join and Separate result-unknown problems.

Children in this classroom expected to be challenged in mathematics. They asked for and were given homework to be done with their parents. The children usually spent about 90 minutes per day actively involved in mathematics. Ms. Jennings didn't really know what her mathematics curriculum for the year would be. "It all depends on the kids. What they can learn will decide what I will teach."

Ms. Taylor could be characterized as an active mathematics teacher (Good, Grouws, & Ebmeier, 1983). Her classroom was well organized, she used total group instruction, children were on task most of the time, and she spent a fairly large proportion of class time on development, defined by Good and Grouws as "the process whereby a teacher facilitates the meaningful acquisition of an idea by a learner" (p. 206). As a CGI teacher, Ms. Taylor's development activities centered on problem solving. At the beginning of each mathematics class, her children gathered on the rug in front of her. The following interaction took place near the beginning of the school year:

> Ms. Taylor started the class by saying, "Today we are going to visit the Friendly Forest and the squirrels have been trick-or-treating. Flippy got 5 acorns and Licky got 3 acorns. How many acorns did they get altogether?" (A Part-part whole, whole-unknown problem.) She waited for a short time and when a number of hands were raised, she asked Bob for the answer, and he said "8 acorns."' Ms. Taylor asked him how he got the answer and he answered, "I said that Flippy's acorns were the fingers on one hand, and Licky's acorns were three fingers on my other hand. I counted them and got 8." Ms. Taylor asked if anyone solved the problem differently. Tia said, "I just knew that there were five fingers on one hand, and I counted 6,7,8, on the other hand." Ms. Taylor asked if anyone solved the problem another way. Ann responded that she used red blocks to show Flippy's acorns and blue blocks to show Licky's. Then she counted them all.
> Ms. Taylor asked if that was different than the way Bob solved the problem. A number of children talked about the two ways and decided that it was different in that Bob used fingers and Ann used blocks, but it was alike in that they counted to get the answer.
> Ms. Taylor continued to ask the children to solve Part-part whole and Join result-unknown problems (using sums less than 10) and to describe the mental processes they used. After about 15 minutes of this type of activity, half the children returned to their seats and did a worksheet where they were to write the answers to similar problems. Ms. Taylor worked with the other half of the class on the same type of problems using larger numbers (sums to 20). Children were encouraged to talk about their solutions, to use a variety of strategies and to listen to each other.

Ms. Taylor planned her entire first grade curriculum in addition and subtraction around the problem types and the Friendly Forest. To her, it was a lucky coincidence that there were 9 important problem types and nine months of school. She emphasized a problem type each month, although children were exposed to all problem types throughout the year. The theme of the Friendly Forest appeared limitless in enabling her to generate the various problems and she was able to modify the number size used depending on the development of various children in her classroom. While children in her class spent some time in drilling on number facts, most of the time was spent on actively solving various types of addition and subtraction problems. Near the end of the school year, Ms. Taylor found that many of her children could solve all types of addition and subtraction problems, could symbolize them, and knew their facts quite well. Because she wanted to continue to challenge them to solve problems, she introduced grouping and partitioning problems in the same way as she had worked with addition and subtraction problems.

In summary, word problems are the major organizing activity in CGI classrooms. The problems can be derived from the children's life or organized around a central theme. There can be an informal curriculum determined by what children can learn or a formal curriculum organized explicitly around the various problem types that children can solve. The classroom can be organized around total group instruction or around small groups. The critical component is that children are actively involved in solving problems of many types. They should demonstrate that these problems were solved with understanding by reporting their solution process.

Emphasizing the Development of More Mature Problem Solving Skills. As children progress through school, they should become increasingly able to utilize more sophisticated problem solving strategies and to solve more complex problems. Most young children enter school with the ability to solve simple addition and subtraction problems with sums less than 10 by directly modeling those problems with fingers or counters. Children should develop increasingly sophisticated solution strategies, learn to solve more complex problems, learn to use derived facts to eliminate the need for counting and finally use recall or computational procedures to solve most problems. At the same time, they should be developing the ability to use larger numbers, to symbolize the word problems directly and, eventually, to transform the direct symbolization of word problems into an addition or subtraction number sentence.

Although children come to school with a variety of strategies for solving problems by modeling and counting, they eventually need to learn the symbolic procedures that have been the traditional focus of the elementary school mathematics curriculum. In the past, instruction was organized to accomplish these goals by carefully determining the logical steps required and showing children how to do each step. Following this, children were asked to drill on each step until mastery was achieved. Using this approach, many children learned how to do the steps and developed adequate procedural knowledge (see Hiebert [1986a], for a discussion of procedural knowledge). However, many children did not develop adequate understanding and were unable to apply their procedural knowledge to either problem solving or the learning of new mathematical content (Hiebert, 1986b; Mack 1987).

Children do come to school with some understanding, as evidenced by their solving of simple addition and subtraction problems. Children also discover more mature strategies, such as simple counting strategies, by themselves (Carpenter & Moser, 1984; Groen & Resnick, 1977). In fact, many children's use of strategies appears to move naturally through a sequence: direct modeling, counting strategies, derived facts and recall of facts (Carpenter & Moser, 1983).

However, there is evidence that this movement through the sequence can be facilitated (Carpenter, Bebout, & Moser, 1985; Carpenter, Hiebert, &Moser, 1983; Secada, Fuson, & Hall, 1983; Steinberg, 1983; Thornton, Jones, & Toohey, 1983). Thus, the emphasis in a CGI classroom is to structure the learning environment in such a way that the child's progress to more mature mental functioning is facilitated.

The way to ensure that children advance to more mature strategies and problem types is to give them lots of opportunity to engage in problem solving. As children solve problems, teachers must be sensitive to what the child is doing, the ease with which the task is being done, and when the child is ready to be challenged to move on to more advanced thinking. Consider the following situations in which a CGI teacher used children's thinking and her knowledge of how that thinking might mature in making instructional decisions.

> Ms. Griffin had identified a group of children who counted on from the first number to solve Join result-unknown problems. They did this so easily that she decided that they were ready to move on. She gave them problems using numbers that were very different in size such as: Nathan had 2 pennies and Yolanda gave him 8 more. How many does Nathan have now? She asked the children to solve the problem, asked them how they solved it and asked them directly, "Wouldn't it have been easier to start counting at 8 rather than 2? Can anyone tell me how they would solve the problem starting at 8?" One child caught on immediately and demonstrated his solution by saying "8, 9, 10." Ms. Griffin continued to give problems in which one number was larger than the other and asked the children to identify the number at which they might start counting. Several children seemed to start with the larger number quite easily while others had more trouble. During the next few weeks Ms. Griffin continued to encourage the use of counting on from the larger but did not insist upon it.

Children within a classroom mature in the use of problem-solving skills differently. One of the most natural ways in which teachers encouraged movement to more mature strategies was to have children listen to other children talk about their problem solving strategies.

> Ms. Conrad used total group instruction most of the time. She had about 20 students in her class sitting at desks arranged in groups of three or four. In this lesson, children were given cups of valentine candy to use as counters. One at a time, Ms. Conrad read to her class word problems of different types and different number sizes. Each child solved each problem individually and raised his/her hand when the problem was completed. When most of the hands were in the air, Ms. Conrad called on one child to give the answer. She asked the child to explain how the answer was found. When the process of problem solution was explained, Ms. Conrad asked if anyone had solved the problem any other way. She continued to ask this question until no child indicated they had a

different solution. The processes described ranged from direct modeling, to counting on, to counting back, to derived facts. For a two-digit problem, one child gave a good explanation that indicated a good understanding of place value. When all of the problems had been solved, Ms. Conrad gave two more problems which had insufficient information to enable them to be solved. The children discussed why these problems could not be solved.

It was clear from observing the class that not every child was able to solve each problem. In addition, many children were using direct modeling while other children were using derived facts. However, the children had been taught to listen to each other and to think about other problem solutions.

Ms. Dean's class is also an example of children listening to other children's solution strategies.

Ms. Dean's class started immediately after lunch. As children came into the room, they went to sit on the rug around Ms. Dean. Those that wished went to the restroom or to get a drink of water. While the children on the rug were waiting, Ms. Dean asked such questions as "How many are here now? How many more need to come in before everyone is here?" When a child answered, Ms. Dean asked how she figured it out. Emphasis was always on "How did you figure that out?" "Is there another way to do it?"

It was evident that children used different strategies to solve the problems. In fact, some children did not appear to be able to solve this rather complex set of problems (often join change-unknown). However, the ones who related their solutions explained clearly, and the other children appeared to listen to them.

A major problem in the sequence of development of mature problem solutions is the use of symbols. Consider how Ms. Miller helped her children to develop their own understanding of the complex process of writing number sentences.

The children in Ms. Miller's class could solve Join result-unknown problems and Separate result-unknown problems quite well. Some children used direct modeling, some counting on, and a few, derived facts. Some children recalled facts with small numbers. No one used written symbols. Ms. Miller asked a small group to join her near the blackboard and asked them to solve a Join result-unknown problem. Ms. Miller then showed the children how that problem looked when represented by symbols and asked the children to explain the symbols. One of the children gave the following explanation for transferring what she did with her counters to the number sentence. "Numbers show the same things the counters show." Ms. Miller continued to have the children solve problems and to write the number sentences on the board. She always asked the children to relate how they had solved the problem to the number sentences.

Ms. Miller had observed her children and decided that this group was ready to move on to using symbols in conjunction with their more primitive problem-solving procedures. For the next several months, she carefully monitored their understanding of the relationships between strategies such as direct modeling and the writing of symbols. She never expected children to perform operations with symbols that they could not perform readily by direct modeling or counting strategies. However, she recognized that the most mature strategy involved symbols, so she continually pointed out the relationship of symbols to their less mature strategies. She believed that the children would eventually construct the relationship between symbols and other strategies and thus come to use the symbols with understanding.

Instruction should be designed to take into consideration children's cognitions and how they mature. While the examples given have been illustrative mainly of instruction in addition and subtraction, it should be pointed out that throughout kindergarten and first grade, addition and subtraction are the basis of the mathematics curriculum. While new content is added in the second grade, addition and subtraction are still emphasized. Thus, the defined pedagogical content knowledge is specifically appropriate for these early school years. Instruction in other content learning, even though children's cognitions in that area may not be as well-defined, can also be modeled on the addition and subtraction instruction. Consider the following illustration of a teacher taking into consideration children's cognitions both in assessing children's knowledge of place value and in planning instruction around what the children knew.

> Children in Ms. Jennings' class had been solving many kinds of story problems using addition and subtraction. They could write numerals up to about 100 but as yet had not discussed groups of 10s and ones. Ms. Jennings asked the children to solve this problem: "When we went to the school forest yesterday Juan collected 24 acorns and Betty collected 18 acorns. How many acorns did they bring back to our class?" The children solved this problem in a variety of ways. Ms. Jennings accepted their answers (which usually were 42) and said, "Can anyone tell me how many tens are in 42?" Maria answered, "4," and Ms. Jennings said, "How do you know?" Maria said, "Because I counted 10, 20, 30, 40" and she raised up a finger for each 10. "That means there are four tens."
>
> Ms. Jennings now knew that Maria knew about grouping by ten and had a process to determine how many tens are in a number. Maria did not appear to know that she could just look at the numeral "42" and ascertain that there were four tens because there was a "4" in the tens place. Over the next few days, Ms. Jennings continued to do informal assessment of the children's knowledge of grouping and recording tens as they continued to solve complex addition and subtraction problems. When all the children in the group appeared to understand grouping by tens, she began to work with two digit numerals in a variety of ways so that the children would learn how to record the tens and what the place values

of ten and one meant. When some children did not understand what a group of ten meant, Ms. Jennings gave them sets bigger than 11 to group by tens, and talked about how many tens there were and how many ones were left over.

CONCLUSIONS

We believe that mathematics must be learned with understanding, and we believe that the vignettes reported above are indicative of what it means for children to learn with understanding. Such understanding can be achieved in a variety of classrooms, being taught by teachers using a variety of styles. The critical component appears to be the teacher's pedagogical content knowledge. Such knowledge includes knowledge of mathematics, knowledge of instructional techniques, and knowledge of children's cognitions in specific subject areas. Teachers who had such knowledge demonstrated to us that they were able to structure their teaching environments so that children did learn with understanding.

It was clearly evident that children in the classrooms of the CGI case study teachers had learned with understanding. We interviewed children from each classroom near the end of the school year. While there was wide diversity in the ability of children to solve problems of various degrees of difficulty, we were amazed at how well the children evidenced understanding.

REFERENCES

Cambridge Conference on School Mathematics. (1963). *Goals for school mathematics: The report of the Cambridge Conference on School Mathematics.* Boston: Educational Sciences.

Carpenter, T.P. (1985). Learning to add and subtract: An exercise in problem solving. In E.A. Silver (Ed.), *Teaching and Learning mathematical problem solving: Multiple research perspectives* (pp. 17-40). Hillsdale, NJ: Erlbaum.

Carpenter, T.P., Bebout, H.C., & Moser, J.M. (1985). *The representation of basic addition and subtraction word problems.* Paper presented at the annual meeting of the American Educational Research Association, Chicago.

Carpenter, T.P., Fennema, E., Loef, M., & Carey, D. (in press). Asssessing children's thinking as the basis for teaching arithmetic: Six case studies.

Carpenter, T.P., Fennema, E., Peterson, P.L., & Carey, D.C. (1988). Teachers' pedagogical content knowledge of students' problem solving in elementary arithmetic. *Journal for Research in Mathematics Education, 19,* 385-401.

Carpenter, T.P., Fennema, E., Peterson, P.L., Chiang, C-P., & Loef, M. (in press): Using knowledge of children's mathematics thinking in classroom teaching: An experimental study. *American Educational Research Journal.*

Carpenter, T.P., Hiebert, J., & Moser, J.M. (1981). Problem structure and first grade children's initial solution processes for simple addition and subtraction problems. *Journal for Research in Mathematics Education, 12,* 27-39.

Carpenter, T.P., Hiebert, J., & Moser, J.M. (1983). The effect of instruction on children's solutions of addition and subtraction word problems. *Educational Studies in Mathematics, 14,* 55-72.

Carpenter, T.P., Matthews, W., Lindquist, M.M., & Silver, E.A. (1984). Achievement in mathematics: Results from the National Assessment. *Elementary School Journal, 84*(5), 485-495.

Carpenter, T.P., & Moser, J.M. (1983). The acquisition of addition and subtraction concepts. In R. Lesh, & M. Landau (Eds.), *Acquisition of mathematics concepts and processes.* New York: Academic Press.

Carpenter, T.P., & Moser, J.M. (1984). The acquisition of addition and subtraction concepts in grades one through three. *Journal for Research in Mathematics Education, 15*(3), 179-202.

Case, R. (1983). *Intellectual development: A systematic reinterpretation.* New York: Academic Press.

Clark, C.M., & Peterson, P.L. (1986). Teachers' thought processes. In M.C. Wittrock (Ed.), *Handbook of research on teaching* (3rd ed., pp. 255-296). New York: Macmillan.

Cobb, P. (1988). The tension between theories of learning and instruction in mathematics education. *Educational Psychologist, 23*(2), 87-103.

Conference Board of the Mathematical Sciences. (1984). *New goals for mathematical sciences education: The report of a conference.* Washington, DC: Author.

Good, T.L., Grouws, D.A., & Ebmeier, H. (1983). *Active mathematics teaching.* New York: Longman.

Groen, G.J., & Resnick, L.B. (1977). Can preschool children invent addition algorithms? *Journal of Educational Psychology, 69,* 645-652.

Hiebert, J. (Ed.). (1986a). *Conceptual and procedural knowledge: The case of mathematics.* Hillsdale, NJ: Erlbaum.

Hiebert, J. (1986b, October). *The relation between drill-and-practice and understanding in mathematics.* Paper prepared at the request of a Task Force of the Mathematical Sciences Education Board of the National Research Council.

Hiebert, J., & Wearne, D. (1988, May). *Methodologies for studying learning to inform teaching.* Paper prepared for the First Wisconsin Symposium for Research on Teaching and Learning Mathematics, sponsored by the Instruction/Learning Working Group of the National Center for Research in Mathematical Sciences Education, Madison, Wisconsin.

Mack, N.K. (1987). *Learning fractions with understanding: Eight clinical studies.* Unpublished Ph.D. dissertation, University of Wisconsin, Madison.

National Council of Teachers of Mathematics. (1987). *Curriculum and evaluation standards for school mathematics* (working draft). Reston, VA: Author.

National Science Board Commission on Precollege Education in Mathematics, Science and Technology. (1983). *Educating Americans for the 21st century: A plan of action for improving the mathematics, science and technology education for all American elementary and secondary students so that their achievement is the best in the world by 1995. A report to the American people and the National Science Board.* Washington, DC: National Science Foundation.

Peterson, P.L., Fennema, E., Carpenter, T.P. & Loef, M. (1989). Teachers' pedagogical content beliefs in mathematics. *Cognition and Instruction, 6,* 1-40.

Resnick, L.B., & Ford, W.W. (1981). *The psychology of mathematics for instruction.* Hillsdale, NJ: Lawrence Erlbaum.

Riley, M.S., Greeno, J.G., & Heller, J.I. (1983). Development of childrens' problem-solving ability in arithmetic. In H. Ginsburg (Ed.), *The development of mathematical thinking.* New York: Academic Press.

Romberg, T.A. (1984). *School mathematics: Options for the 1990's. Chairman's report of a conference.* Washington, DC: U.S. Government Printing Office.

Romberg, T.A., & Carpenter, T.P. (1986). Research on teaching and learning mathematics: Two disciplines of scientific inquiry. In M.C. Wittrock (Ed.), *Handbook of Research on Teaching* (3rd ed., pp. 850-873). New York: Macmillan.

Romberg, T.A., Harvey, J.G., Moser, J.M., & Montgomery, M.E. (1974). *Developing mathematical processes.* Chicago: Rand McNally.

Secada, W.G., Fuson, K.C., & Hall, J.W. (1983). The transition from counting all to counting on in addition. *Journal for Research in Mathematics Education, 14*, 47-57.

Shavelson, R.J., & Stern, P. (1981). Research on teachers' pedagogical thoughts, judgments, decisions, and behavior. *Review of Educational Research, 51*, 455-498.

Shulman, L.S. (1970). Psychology and mathematics education. In E. G. Begle (Ed.), *Mathematics education: The sixty-ninth yearbook of the National Society for the Study of Education* (pp. 23-71). Chicago: University of Chicago Press.

Shulman, L.S. (1986). Paradigms and research programs in the study of teaching: A contemporary perspective. In M.C. Wittrock (Ed.), *Handbook of research on teaching* (3rd ed., pp. 3-36). New York: Macmillan.

Steinberg, R.M. (1983). *Instruction in the use of derived facts strategies in addition and subtraction.* Unpublished Ph.D. dissertation, University of Wisconsin, Madison.

Stephens, W.M. (1982). *Mathematical knowledge and school work: A case study of the teaching of developing mathematical processes.* Unpublished Ph.D. dissertation, University of Wisconsin, Madison.

Stevenson, H.W., Lee, S., & Stigler, J.W. (1986). Mathematics achievement of Chinese, Japanese, and American children. *Science, 231*, 693-698.

Thiele, C.L. (1941). Arithmetic in the early grades from the point of view of interrelationships in the number systems. *Arithmetic in General Education: 16th yearbook.* Washington, DC: National Council of Teachers of Mathematics.

Thornton, C.A., Jones, G.A., & Toohey, M.A. (1983). A multidimensional approach to thinking strategies for remedial instruction in basic addition facts. *Journal for Research in Mathematics Education, 14*, 198-203.

Van Engen, H. (1953). The formation of concepts. In H.F. Fehr (Ed.), *The learning of mathematics: Its theory and practice. Twenty-first yearbook of the National Council of Teachers of Mathematics* (pp. 69-98). Washington, DC: National Council of Teachers of Mathematics.

*   *   *

CROSS-TALK

What are the similarities and differences between Cognitively Guided Instruction and the mathematics instruction which was described by Magdalene Lampert?

When comparing and contrasting Lampert's and our work, one should keep in mind that while her work is also theoretically grounded, our work is coming out of a more mature chain of inquiry. The addition and subtraction research which has been used to validate the CGI model has been accumulating for at least a decade. Hiebert and Wearne (in press) have suggested that without the knowledge derived from such a chain of inquiry, the CGI model may not be effective. Hiebert and Wearne's work is with decimals, as is Lampert's, so their position may have merit as one considers Lampert's work in relation to ours.

One major similarity between Lampert and us is that children's cognitions are one important basis (or fulcrum as was suggested in our chapter) of instructional decisions. Teachers plan, taking into consideration what their students already know; assessment to determine what knowledge the learner has is a vital part of both planning and instruction; and instruction is continually being adapted when new evidence is obtained about children's thinking. Vignettes are presented in our chapter illustrating teachers assessing children and planning instruction based on this assessment. Lampert reports altering her lesson plans on the spot as she discovers new knowledge or misconceptions that the children have.

Another important similarity between Lampert and CGI is the role of mathematics. While hers is a more structured approach which is heavily reliant on the abstract nature of mathematics, both of us base our instruction on an organized body of mathematics which forms the educational goals of the programs. In both programs mathematics is defined as being conceptual more than procedural. To gain this important conceptual knowledge, children are asked to think at high cognitive levels with interpretations of mathematics which are part of their lives. The emphasis is always on making the connections between the informal knowledge that children have with the formal knowledge of mathematics.

One important difference between Lampert's work and ours is the emphasis on the teacher. This difference may be due to the fact that the purpose of her work appears to be understanding how a single teacher, Lampert herself, can facilitate the learning of children, while the emphasis in our work has been on the education of teachers in order to determine the impact of their knowledge and beliefs on student learning. While this difference may be more semantic than real, there is almost an intuitive perception that Lampert as a teacher behaves in a very different way than do CGI teachers. Lampert appears to believe that it is the responsibility of the teacher to form the connection between the child's informal knowledge and the formal knowledge she wants them to obtain. We believe that children must form these connections themselves. The role of the teacher is to structure the learning environment so that the children become aware of and form the connections themselves. This does not mean that the teacher never tells children anything. In fact, in some cases the optimum way for children to become aware of the relationships between formal and informal knowledge is for the teacher to point them out. Because we believe that teachers interpret knowledge and make instructional decisions in relationships to their own beliefs, we are able to both accept and describe a large variety of teaching styles which are consistent with CGI. Lampert's work is unclear in how she anticipates it can or should impact teaching and teacher education. One could interpret her work to be very prescriptive of teacher behavior.

Lampert is more comprehensive in consideration of the total learning environment than we are. While we do not find her concern with social discourse in conflict with our work, we have not considered it. Social discourse adds an important dimension to descriptions of classrooms which CGI teachers consider as they make instructional decisions. We believe that teachers also consider many other dimensions as they make instructional decisions. Constraints imposed by the administration, physical surroundings, and the competing demands from other subject areas are a few dimensions which seem continually to be a part of instructional decision making. We have made the decision not to consider social discourse, or any of the other important dimensions because of the difficulty of studying more complex phenomena than we have. How does one study and then understand the totality of an educational environment? Can it be done? Are some considerations more important than others? Each researcher or research team makes such decisions as they plan for their work.

Is Cognitively Guided Instruction appropriate only for primary grades or is it a generic model that can be useful at all grade levels?

We do not *know,* but we *believe* that CGI is equally applicable to all grade levels. Learning mathematics with understanding should be the major goal of mathematics instruction at any age, and CGI is an attempt to ensure learners acquire that understanding. Treating teachers as professionals and helping them acquire knowledge that is useful in understanding learners' cognitions seems to be theoretically sound and supported by research evidence. However, some people question whether or not research has provided enough information about how learners think with more advanced ideas than addition and subtraction. Others question whether such a complete description of cognitions in other content is essential—or possible. The purpose of the Instruction/Learning group of The National Center for Research in Mathematical Sciences Education (a subset of the Wisconsin Center for Education Research) is to encourage research which investigates and/or modifies the CGI model for other grade levels and for different content. Perhaps within the next decade, we will have enough research to answer the question of the applicability of the CGI model to other areas.

What were some of the characteristics of teachers who failed to use CGI very well?

This is not a question that we addressed in our research, and we have only intuitive, informal knowledge about it. Certainly teachers implemented CGI to varying degrees. However, everyone but one teacher seems to have changed somewhat. In our original sample of 43 teachers and in about 20 teachers who have been educated by some of the original teachers, every teacher but one has reported to us that their instruction has changed since they acquired the knowledge of how children think about addition and subtraction. It appears to be very difficult for teachers not to take into consideration what children know, once it becomes apparent to them. While we have only informal knowledge ourselves about characteristics of teachers who were less successful CGI teachers than others, it does appear that teachers who had trouble planning instruction before CGI education still had trouble after CGI education. Teachers who had inadequate routines established in their classrooms before CGI had inadequate routines after the workshop. However, it appears that all teachers improved in their use of children's cognitions. It appears that most teachers' instruction changed. Both quality and quantity of this change varied.

Reference to Cross-talk

Hiebert, J., & Wearne, D. (1988). Instruction and cognitive change in mathematics. *Educational Psychologist, 23,* 105-117.

CHOOSING AND USING MATHEMATICAL TOOLS IN CLASSROOM DISCOURSE

Magdalene Lampert

INTRODUCTION

Learning new mathematical content in school involves learning to do certain operations and learning a language for talking about what you are doing. It involves learning new skills and, at the same time, giving meaning to operations and symbols as they are used. Students give meaning to the symbols and procedures that are used in the lessons they are taught whether or not the teacher makes it a conscious part of the instructional agenda (Barnes, 1976; Campbell, 1985; Cazden, 1986; Leinhardt & Putnam, 1987). It is possible, however, for the classroom teacher to guide the process of constructing meaning for mathematical symbols and operations so that what students are learning about mathematics is related to the central ideas in the discipline. In my experiments with this kind of mathematics teaching, I have engaged various representational tools to be used both by myself, for teaching, and by students, for doing and learning mathematics. The purpose of these tools is to connect mathematical operations and relationships with operations and relationships in domains that are familiar to students, like coins or rulers or rectangles.

Advances in Research on Teaching, Volume 1, pages 223-264.
ISBN: 0-89232-845-2

When students are able to reason about whether some operation or relationship makes sense in a familiar domain, they can be taught to make connections between what is familiar and the more abstract routines that pertain in the mathematical world of numbers and symbols. This connection makes it possible to shift the locus of authority in the classroom—*away from* the teacher as a judge and the textbook as a standard for judgment, and *toward* the teacher and students as inquirers who have the power to use mathematical tools to decide whether an answer or a procedure is reasonable. Students will not reason in mathematically appropriate ways about objects that have no meaning to them; in order for them to learn to reason about assertions involving such abstract symbols and operations as .000056 and $a^2 + b^3$, they need to connect these symbols and operations to a domain in which they are competent to "make sense." If such connections are not made, students must continue to check their work with the teacher or the textbook to find out whether what they are doing is mathematically correct.

The research on teaching to be described in this paper supports these assertions.[1] It began as an experiment to find out whether it was possible, in an ordinary classroom setting, to engage students in choosing and using representational tools to decide for themselves whether their answers to mathematics problems were right or wrong. Conducting this experiment has required an examination of what constitutes legitimate mathematical reasoning among mathematics learners, some fundamental reorganizations in the social organization of classroom discourse, and the invention of a curriculum of usable mathematical tools. It is this curriculum of tools, and the teaching and learning of fifth-grade students that resulted from its use, that will be the focus of this paper.

RESEARCH QUESTIONS AND METHOD

Can fifth-grade students be taught in ways that will engage them in the process of constructing reasonable warrants for the procedures they use to do mathematical problems? Can students become competent at using procedures to find solutions to problems, and at the same time consider those solutions as hypotheses until their reasonableness is adequately defended? Can this be done with the full range of students who attend ordinary public elementary schools? And if so, what does such teaching and learning look like in that setting? These are questions about the nature and practicability of mathematical pedagogy. They are directed toward understanding what it takes to teach students about doing mathematics in school.[2]

The method I have been using to examine my research questions is a case analysis: describing the mathematical tools that are engaged by teacher and students to make sense of symbols and operations in a particular set of school lessons. The case described in this paper is a set of lessons on comparing two numbers written as decimal fractions to decide which is larger or if they are equal. The lessons that are described took place during the regular 45-minute mathematics periods for which I am responsible five days per week in a fifth-grade classroom. They are representative of similar lessons taught during the school year on the multiplication and division of large numbers, finding percents, Cartesian graphing, equivalent fractions, and adding and subtracting numbers written as fractions.

The data I have collected on my teaching include: audio and video tapes of some lessons and written observations of most lessons; my own plans and anecdotal evaluations of all lessons; and students' written classwork and homework. I will use a portion of this data in this paper to describe my teaching and students' learning. The description and analysis will be at the level of reporting on the course of daily instruction over a two-week period, and it will focus on the interaction between children's reasoning about decimal numbers using various representational tools and my decisions about what and how to teach them.

The class to whom I taught these lessons was a group of 29 fifth graders. About a third of them speak English as a second language. Because of the neighborhood in which the school is located, they come from an unusually wide range of socioeconomic backgrounds. This is the only fifth-grade class in the school, so there is no "tracking." The students range in math skills from children who occasionally have difficulty doing subtraction with borrowing, to children who can do all four operations with whole numbers and addition and subtraction with fractions. Before these lessons took place, they received no formal instruction about decimal numbers.

REASONING ABOUT MATHEMATICS AS A TEACHING GOAL: CONCEPTUAL FRAMEWORKS

The primary "skill" objective of the introductory unit on decimal numbers in a typical fifth grade curriculum is that students be able to look at two different decimal numbers and decide which is larger or if the two numbers are equal. Students should be able to answer questions such as: How would you compare .099 and .2? Or 5.3 and 5.300? Or given a list of numbers written as decimals, they should be able to order them from smallest to largest. Usually, this is taught as an algorithm: "Add zeros after the digits to the right of the decimal point until the numbers you are comparing have the same number of decimal places. Now ignore the decimal point, and see which of the numbers is larger." When adults are asked to explain how they know that one decimal number is larger than or equal to another, this algorithm is probably what they will tell you. This is what it means to most people to "decide" which of two decimal numbers is larger. The question they answer is "How?" rather than "Why?" One need not know anything about what the numbers themselves are meant to represent in order to follow this procedure.

Mathematics

Although the use of this procedure represents some useful knowledge about how to compare decimals, it begs the question of how the user knows that the procedure can be relied on to correctly identify the larger quantity. Most often in school, this knowledge is based on a trust in the authority of the person who tells you to use the procedure: the teacher. The correct answer is ascertained through a combination of trust in authority, memory, and mechanical skill. These are not to be diminished as sources of useful knowledge, but they are *not* mathematics; it is not *mathematical knowledge* that confirms the truth of what you have done when you have used this procedure (Davis, 1983b; Polya, 1954). Students who learn to use procedures as described above as a strategy for finding answers to questions about numbers do not become independent doers of mathematics—unless they can also prove that the answer that has been obtained by this process is mathematically plausible.[3]

Comparing .099 and .2 by considering their *mathematical* relationship is quite a different process from following a set of mechanical rules for making a decision about which is larger. To determine what these numbers mean in relationship to one another, one must consider what the symbols represent, what it means for one decimal number to be larger than another, and the relationship between the quantities symbolized. In this example, .2 means two-tenths of a unit, while .099 means ninety-nine-thousandths of a unit. Ninety-nine-thousandths can be decomposed into ninety-thousandths and nine-thousandths, and ninety-thousandths indicates that same magnitude as nine-hundredths. But because there are *ten*-hundredths in *one*-tenth, and nine-thousandths does not even amount to one-hundredth, this quantity is less than two-tenths. This is true even though .099 breaks the unit up into many more pieces than .2; it is the size of the pieces that matters here. In order to come to the conclusion that .099 < .2, and know that one's conclusion is mathematically correct, this is the sort of thinking that is required.

Learning Psychology

This epistemological distinction between mathematical knowledge and mechanical knowledge about numerical procedures is similar to distinctions in kinds of learning and teaching made by cognitive scientists and philosophers of education. Greeno, Riley, and Gelman (1984), for example, distinguish between "procedural" and "conceptual" competence, and they use these concepts to analyze what children know that enables them to complete different sorts of counting tasks. They define procedural competence as an understanding of principles of action: knowing what to do and when to do t. Knowing that "adding zeroes" is the thing to do to make it possible to compare two decimal numbers is an example of this kind of competence. In contrast, conceptual competence is an understanding of the general principles in a domain, like knowing that place value is a determinant of the magnitude a number represents. It is more difficult to find manifestations of conceptual competence, however, because it is possible to understand principles without being able to articulate them. Greeno et al. propose three kinds of performance which, they argue, suggest that a learner has acquired conceptual competence: he generation of a new procedure or the modification of a known procedure hat is consistent with the principles of the domain, the capacity to evaluate one's own performance as correct or incorrect with respect to a principle, and performance that is systematically consistent with a principle. A combination of evidence of these various kinds can constitute a compelling argument that principles are understood significantly, but even if children have conceptual competence, there is no guarantee that they will always display it in their behavior (Gelman & Meck, 1986).

The most serious problem for instruction that follows from this work is that learners often do not have a propensity toward connecting their informally acquired conceptual knowledge with the use of the formal procedures taught n school; (Baroody & Ginsburg, 1986; Carpenter, 1985; Resnick & Omanson, 1987). In research specific to students' competence in interpreting and operating on decimal numbers, Hiebert and Wearne (1986) have identified three "sites" where such connections are often missing: in the student's initial interpretation of the written symbols (i.e., numbers with a decimal point), in the operations performed on such numbers, and in the judgment of whether the results of those operations are reasonable. Others have argued that the engagement of multiple systems of representation might help students to make these connections in the realm of rational numbers (Behr, Lesh, Post, & Silver, 1983).

When psychological research is considered in relation to appropriate objectives for school mathematics instruction, one can conclude that teaching ought to be rooted in the mathematical principles one seeks to have students understand, that teacher and students ought to engage multiple representations of those principles as they communicate about mathematical ideas, and that students ought to be given the opportunity to invent and modify procedures and to evaluate their own performance. It also argues for direct instruction about the connections among various interpretations of a mathematical relationship or operation.

Philosophy of Education

Educational philosophers distinguish between teaching that is instruction and teaching that is indoctrination (Green, 1971; Peters, 1967). Instruction is characterized as a "conversation" between teacher and learner involving both parties in the activities of giving reasons, weighing evidence, justifying, explaining, concluding, and the like. Indoctrination, in contrast, is an activity which aims at "inculcating the 'right answer' but not necessarily for the 'right reasons'" (Green, 1971, p. 31). The teacher who instructs has a different outcome in mind from the teacher who indoctrinates: his or her goal is to have students arrive at an answer on the basis of reasons that are appropriate to the discipline being taught.

This philosophical analysis of ends and means is useful for clarifying goals of mathematics instruction, although the conceptual distinction made between instruction and indoctrination is not so clear in the teaching practice that aims to achieve those goals. In practice—of both the teaching sort and the learning sort—one cannot so readily separate what is learned by indoctrination from what is learned by instruction. In fact, these two kinds of learning are found to serve one another in the acquisition of mathematical competence (Nesher, 1986; Resnick, in press). Furthermore, the teacher's authority has a part in enforcing students' reliance on reason rather than on mechanical procedures to arrive at their answers. What remains important, however, is the inclusion of learning to give reasons appropriate to the discipline in the teaching goals we hold for the subject of mathematics.

MATHEMATICAL PRINCIPLES AND STUDENT THINKING AS SOURCES OF CURRICULUM AND INSTRUCTION

All three conceptual frameworks—mathematical, psychological, and philosophical—require the teacher to reflect on the mathematical principles and mathematical forms of reasoning that underlie the competence she wishes her students to attain. Successful instruction also depends, however, on an assessment of what students might find diffcult about those principles and the employment of methods that will help them to confront those difficulties successfully. There has been very little research on the role that thinking about subject matter plays in teachers' decisions about what and how to teach, although this problem is currently of interest (Ball, 1988; Fennema, Carpenter, Peterson, Chiang, & Loef, 1988; Shulman, 1987). To argue that it is appropriate to base teaching decisions on principles of the discipline as well as other considerations requires some attention to how those principles come into play, both in planning lessons, and interactively during teaching. The focus here is not so much on understanding teacher knowledge use, however, as it is on the interplay between elements of the subject matter and the pedagogy of mathematics teaching.

As I planned my lessons on decimals, I related my knowledge about students and curriculum to what I knew about the concepts underlying the manipulation of numbers represented as decimal fractions, and this led me to focus on four mathematical principles: (1) the geometric progression of the base as you move from place to place in a number, (2) the relationship between the value of a digit and the value of the place it is in, (3) the "two-way" ratio between places, and (4) the bounded infinity of numbers between zero and one. Each of these concepts is involved in interpreting the quantity that is represented by a number written as a decimal fraction and, therefore, is used in deciding which of two numbers is larger.

Relating the Value of a Digit and the Value of the Place It Is In

This relationship is perhaps most clear, and easiest to talk about, when we restrict ourselves to different whole numbers built with the same digit and variable quantiites of zeroes, i.e., we can compare the orders of magnitude of numbers like 8, 80, 800, and 8000 just as we compare 1, 10, 100, and 1000. Comparisons among numbers are also relatively easy if we keep the quantity of zeroes in the number constant and vary the leading digit, because then we need only consider the counting order of the leading digits, e.g., comparing 2000 with 7000 is comparing 2.with 7. But when we compare a number like 89 with a number like 235, we are asking two different ordering questions at once: How many places are there, and what is the value of the digit in the leading place? It is useful to know that the answer to the first question may make the second question irrelevant, but there is a tendency to notice the digits first and their place value second because place value is to some extent "invisible."

This problematic invisibility of quantity in the place value system is exacerbated in the algorithms we use to find the products and quotients of large numbers. In learning to use arithmetic procedures, one is taught to "assume" the presence of zeroes in order to keep the numbers lined up correctly. Because these zeroes are sometimes "assumed" in the process of comparing or computing, the numbers that appear as one works through different parts of an algorithm do not look like the numbers that would match the quantities they actually represent. To get the final answer, one must follow the procedure carefully to recover the correct order of magnitude.

The number of places in any particular number in the algorithm can easily be lost sight of when one is working with these "assumed" zeroes. For example, consider the following procedures for doing multiplication and division where the work has been left unfinished:

$$
\begin{array}{r}
46 \\
\times\ 81 \\
\hline
46 \\
368 \\
\hline
\end{array}
\qquad\qquad
\begin{array}{r}
3 \\
19\ )\overline{6837} \\
57 \\
\hline
113 \\
\end{array}
$$

The threes here can mean 30, 300, or 3000, depending on where they are placed.[4] Their meaning is easily misunderstood because of the absence of assumed zeroes, particularly if one hesitates partway through a procedure. And in fact, there is a sense in which it is not helpful to think of the "3" at the end of 113 in the division example above as representing "30" because the next step is to figure out about how many times 19 "goes in to" 113.

It would not be surprising if these characteristics of arithmetic procedures had the effect of teaching students that place value was a strange mystery, or that taking account of it only gets in your way if the goal is getting this sort of computation done correctly. And these are the sorts of computations that dominate the curriculum that immediately precedes work on decimal numbers in most schools.

Additive Comparisons Versus Geometrical Progression, Or Why Place Value Is So Hard to Understand

One hundred is ten *times* ten, ten is ten *times* one, one is ten *times* one tenth— these relationships are the basis of place value in our number system. When we write 45.8, it means four tens, five ones, and eight-tenths. Even though "10", "1", and "1/10" do not appear anywhere in the number, it is the relationship among these quantities that gives the number symbols meaning. This meaning is often elusive in mathematics teaching and learning because we use the symbols and names of symbols to communicate about mathematical operations.

In order to understand place value in base ten, one must have a sense of the *common ratio* between ten and one, one hundred and ten, one thousand and one hundred, ten thousand and one thousand, and so on. The numbers 1, 10, 100, 1000, 10000, ... are the sort of series that mathematicians call a "geometric progression" because each is ten times more than the one before; the ratio between any adjacent pair is ten to one. In order to understand the meaning of the places in a decimal number, one must further extend this multiplicative notion to the idea that a tenth is ten times a hundredth, one hundredth is ten times a thousandth, and so on. One could also compare these pairs of numbers *additively*, by saying that one hundred is ninety *more than* ten, that one thousand is nine hundred *more than* one hundred, and so on, but this misses an essential feature of place value; one cannot get from these additive comparisons to the idea that one thousand is one hundred (10 x 10) times bigger than ten, ten thousand is one thousand (10 x 10 x 10) times bigger than ten, and so on.[5]

Comparing numbers that stand for two different magnitudes by asking "How many *more*?" seems to come to mind more readily than casting a relationship in terms of how many *times* a smaller number will fit into one that is larger. The first kind of comparison can be made by matching the members of each of the two groups and then "counting on" to see how many "extras" are in the larger group. For example, if one had seven cookies for nine children, one could count on past seven to find that there are two more children than cookies. This is an additive comparison. In contrast, the second kind of comparison requires using the smaller group over and over again as a measure, and keeping track of how many times one has used it. For example, one could compare a group of four children to a group of twenty cookies by "measuring out" four cookies, one to a child, over and over again (five times) until all the cookies were gone. It is possible to match one cookie with one child five times. What is being counted here is operations, not objects; it is not surprising that this is the more difficult of the two kinds of comparisons. The number obtained from counting *operations* signifies a *relationship* between two sets of objects, rather than the quantity of a set of objects. This is what is meant by a "ratio."

The "Two-way" Ratio That Exists Between Places

The relationship that exists between "places" in a number is made even more complex when we consider that the relationship between "places" can also be understood in terms of a ratio that is less than one; if ten is a group of ten ones, then one is *a tenth* of a group of ten, if a hundred is a group of ten tens, then ten is *one tenth* of a group of a hundred, and so on. Although it is based on the simple inverse relationship between multiplication and division—putting equal-sized groups together and taking them apart—this statement of the relationship between places in fractional terms does not follow easily from what students already know, at least in part because they have been taught very little about fractions. Yet to understand the way we speak about place value in decimal numbers, this fractional language for relating places must be familiar.

Bounded Infinity

Trying to figure out what is represented when a number is transformed by the "addition" of extra digits or zeroes to the right of the decimal point leads students directly into some complicated rational number concepts.[6] When they get to decimals "adding zeroes" suddenly does not matter, but they come to this part of the curriculum having usefully learned that if you "add a zero" to any whole number, it represents multiplying by ten, two zeroes, multiplying by one hundred, and so on. Even without a sense of the order of magnitude of the transformation, they know that the number with more zeroes on the end of it is bigger, just as they know that the magnitudes of 3489 and 993 can be compared by looking at which has more digits. "Adding digits" on to a whole number, whether zero or non-zero, always made the number bigger, except in the trivial case of adding zeroes in front of non-zero digits, as in transforming 893 to 00893.

With decimals, there are several other possibilties. What happens in the transformation from .893 to .893000 is quite different from what happens in the transformation from .893 to .000893, and .3489 is *not* bigger than .993, even though it has more digits. Students are also puzzled by the fact that putting more digits on to the right hand end of a decimal number *after* the decimal point makes the number larger, but never enough larger to make it equal to even *one* whole. So the conception that numbers get bigger by addition as they get longer, up to infinity, which students correctly derive from their work with whole numbers, now needs to be refined. "Adding digits" is no longer an operation equivalent to adding magnitude.

One might simply tell students that things do not work in the same way on the right side of the decimal point as they do on the left, but this distinction misses the most elegant feature of the place value numeration system and deprives students of the power that can be derived from understanding what whole number and decimal fraction place value have in common. The relationship among the places stays constant everywhere in the number, on both sides of the decimal point: in our base-ten system, every place is worth ten times the place to its right and one-tenth the place to its left. The placement of the decimal point between the "ones" place and the "tenths" place is mathematically insignificant. What *is* mathematically significant is that the largest digit that can be put in any place is a nine; a group of ten must be "carried" over into the place to the left, so the largest quantity that any one place can hold is nine-tenths of a unit in the place to its left. "Adding digits" on to the right hand end of a decimal number means adding "places" to the number that represent fractional parts of the unit in the place to their left; this maneuver thus always represents adding a quantity that is smaller than what would be needed to change the value of the places to the left.

What can these additional non-zero digits mean if they can be "tacked on" indefinitely and yet never make a decimal number big enough to get even as large as one whole? This is a question fifth graders are capable of wondering about if wonderment is encouraged in their learning of mathematics. When they are faced with trying to figure out what the digits to the right of the decimal point mean, they come up against another big but complicated mathematical idea: that there can be an infinity of numbers *between* zero and one. Putting zeroes between the decimal point and the non-zero digits moves the number closer to zero, but never gets it there; putting more digits on after the decimal point moves the decimal fraction closer to one, but never gets it there. These are operations which some fifth graders are disposed to perform, and they are curious about what these strings of digits might mean. What are you doing when you put more and more nines on the end of .99999999 ? And why does this string of digits never get as big as one whole if what you are doing is *adding* more and more to it? That the set of numbers between zero and one can be limitless seems to be in conflict with the idea of its being bounded; it is the principle of infinite divisibility, together with the way we use place value to count quantities and groups of quantities, that resolves this conflict in mathematics.

MATHEMATICAL CONTENT AND LESSON PLANNING: A PEDAGOGY FOR DEVELOPING MATHEMATICAL TOOLS

The decisions I made about what and how to teach during the unit on decimals were guided by these ideas about what sort of subject matter content could be engaged. I based my communication with students about these ideas on three representational tools that I believed would be more meaningful to them than the numerical symbols and English words we use to express mathematical relationships and operations in this domain: money, the number line, and pieces of a circle. My use of these tools in teaching was a dynamic creation based on a continuing assessment of what students would need to know to make them independent in the act of reasoning about relationships among numbers written as decimals. I planned the first lesson in some detail, and then taught it; after analysing what occurred during that lesson, I decided how I would proceed over the next several days. In this section I will describe the first lesson and the analysis of students' understanding that emerged from it. In this lesson, representational tools were used primarily for me to find out what my students already knew. In the next section I will describe the eight lessons that followed this initial analysis, in which I teach students to use representational tools to reason about numerical relationships. In the public discourse of the classroom, such reasoning occurs as argument among peers and between students and teacher. It is the ability to participate in such arguments that is the mark of mathematics learning.

Thinking About Where to Begin

I chose to begin my lessons on decimal numbers with the numerical representation of amounts of money and trading among different denominations of bills and coins so that my students could start to reason about the relationships among numbers written as decimals in a context that was universally familiar to them. Written amounts of money like $8.90 or $.89 have concrete referrents that can be called upon, actually or in the imagination, to check whether the relationships one asserts are sensible. Thus my students would be able to bring some of their own solid knowledge to the task of discussing the meaning of the decimal point right at the beginning of the unit. From the very beginning of this unit, then, they would be able to make judgments about the reasonability of their own assertions about mathematical relationships, the assertions of their peers, and the assertions of their teacher.

In order to focus on base ten relationships, I planned to ask the students to figure out the different amounts of ten dollar bills, one dollar bills, dimes, and pennies could be used to assemble particular amounts of money. In the domain of money, place value is transparently represented by different denominations of bills and coins.[7] Students would know that ten one-dollar bills could be traded for a ten-dollar bill, ten dimes for a dollar bill, and ten pennies for a dime. I would begin the first lesson by having them compile various combinations of these bills and coins, and explain why one combination could be traded for another without changing the value of the total amount of money.

By using coins and bills as a referrent for our early discussions, I was able to get students talking about ways in which 50 could be equal to 500, or 2 could be more than 99 (50 dimes = 500 pennies, 2 dollars is more than 99 cents), so that these sorts of comparisons would not seem strange when we applied them to the fractional units represented by decimal numbers. I also wanted to work in a medium where we could talk about fractional trading up and down the scale and not have the equivalents be a matter for deliberation: all fifth graders know the monetary equivalents, so it would not be so novel to talk about a dime as a tenth of a dollar; one can readily refer to a dollar as ten dimes. If we developed this way of speaking and relating quantities to number relationships in the domain of coins, the meaning of decimal equivalents and the terms we used to describe them would not need to hang entirely on abstractions like "one-tenth of one-tenth is one-hundredth."

Teaching the First Lesson:
Developing a Common Language for Talking About Numbers
Written as Decimals From What Students Already Understand

I began by writing $89.00, $8.90, and $.89 up on the blackboard, and asking students to discuss their relative values in terms of dollars, dimes and pennies. They spoke about $.89 as only part of a dollar, while they said that $8.90 meant eight whole dollars and most of another, and $89.00 meant eighty-nine whole dollars. I directed them to change each of these amounts entirely into dimes, and then into pennies, thereby reorienting the unit in our discussion from whole dollars to tenths of a dollar and again to hundredths of a dollar, while retaining the "power of ten" relationship (i.e., ratios of one to ten, one to one hundred, one to one thousand, and so on) among the different quantities of money. As they asserted equivalences using these different units, I asked them how they "knew" that certain quantities of coins or bills were worth the same amount of money, thereby eliciting their language for making sense of these "place value" type relationships. In order to make the comparisons among orders of magnitude even more concrete, I also asked students to speculate about what one could buy for each of these three amounts of money and we made separate "shopping lists" for each. I repeatedly used phrases such as "worth a hundred times more than" and "worth one tenth as much as" to refer to the amounts of money, the written symbols for money, and the objects students talked about being able to buy with given amounts of money. As the discussion progressed, students also began to use these phrases to compare values.

Then I ventured into different but still familar territory: I asked the class how what we had discussed could be extended to help us understand the relative value of larger amounts like $890.00, $8900.00, and so on, challenging them to find a general way to express the effect of "adding zeroes" between the decimal point and the non-zero digits to the *left* of the decimal point. I ascertained that several students could apply the language they had used in the earlier discussion to these larger numbers. The class was picking up a common language that would enable them to compare quantities in terms of place value, and they were able to relate the larger amounts to the smaller ones using the language of decimal fractions. At this point, I also asked the class to speculate on whether it made any difference to write "$890" or "$890.00", in order to begin to make the issue of zeroes on the right side of the decimal point part of the public conversation. Students referred to dollars or dimes or objects to assert that $890 and $890.00 were "the same."

In the next segment of the lesson, I asked the students to think about what $.089 might mean. Now we were moving away from familiar symbols and quantities, away from groups of familiar—albeit "fractional"—coins. I wanted to see what sort of an explanation might be invented out of the earlier conversation to give meaning to the non-zero digits on the right of the decimal point. In an attempt to explain $.089, one of the girls in the class observed, "Some countries have coins that are one tenth of a cent, so point-oh-eight-nine must be close to nine cents." The rest of the class agreed that this explanation of the meaning of $.089 made sense. It fit into the framework that had been established to relate the other, more familiar numbers with a meaningful referent. Then I wrote .0089 on the board to see whether this way of thinking in terms of coins that represented a fraction of a dollar might extend to even smaller decimal fractions.[8] I wondered if anyone would invent decimal coins of even smaller value to continue the progression, as the class to whom I had taught a similar lesson the year before had done. But before I even asked what .0089 could mean, someone raised his hand and said, "That's negative."

Another Representational Tool for Examining Student Thinking

What did he mean? How was I to interpret this assertion? Any discussion of negative numbers that had occurred so far in this school year had to do with temperature or with credits and debits in a bank account. When this student announced that .0089 was negative, we were very close to the end of our class period, but I was quite curious about what he and others might be thinking about the meaning of decimal place value. I quickly put a number line up on the board and labeled some points:

$$-100 \qquad\qquad\qquad 0 \qquad\qquad\qquad +100$$

I had not planned to use the number line as a representation in this lesson, but I brought it in here rather than continuing with the monetary representation because it is a mathematical tool that can be used to express *both* the relationship between whole and rational numbers, *and* the relationship between positive and negative numbers. It, therefore, seemed like an appropriate medium for getting my students to communicate something about what they were thinking about those relationships. As with the coins, I was giving students a tool with which they could examine the reasonability of mathematical assertions, making them less dependent on the teacher to judge their "answers" right or wrong.

Because we were switching to a new medium for representing numbers, I went back again to more familiar conceptual territory. I began by writing the number 89 on the board and asked where it would go on the number line, so that everyone could get his or her bearings in the new representational medium before trying to find a place on the number line for .0089. Someone suggested 89 should "go between zero and a hundred, closer to the hundred." When I asked for her reasons, she said: "Because it's almost 90, and 90 is almost to one hundred." She was using the order of natural numbers, counting by tens to support her answer; the ratio between 10 and 100 was the basis for her decision. Then we did 8.9, and that was located by another student "between zero and ten." He explained his placement by saying that he thought of dividing the distance between 0 and 100 in half, then the half closer to zero into fifths, and placing the number just a little to the left of the point where ten would be; again the place value ratio came into play. These explanations referred the "proof" of whether the student's assertion was correct to the realm of mathematical discourse, rather than having them rely on my authority to judge them right or wrong.

When I put .89 up on the board and asked where it should go on the number line, a student volunteered: "It would be between 0 and 1," and explained that it was "closer to 1 because it was close to a dollar." She had switched back to coins as a medium for making sense of the order of these numbers, which is not surprising since we had moved from whole numbers to the less familiar decimal fractions. She was transferring what she knew about a ten-to-one relationship in one domain to a representation of that relationship in a different symbol system, suggesting that she had some understanding of the concept of decimal place value.

Next I asked the class where .089 should go on the number line, and there was some disagreement. The argument that ensued provided some evidence that students were approaching decimal numbers as a part of mathematics that was supposed to have meaning, but that they were not yet certain what that meaning might be. First someone said that .089 should go "behind the zero." When I asked for more precise directions he said "to the left of the 0." I pointed to a spot a little to the left of the zero, with a questioning look on my face, and someone else said, again referring back to the earlier representation: "No, it's near 8 cents, and that's more than nothing." I asked the student who had made the first comment what he thought about that, and he said, "Yeah, if you think about it that way, I guess she's right. It should be just a little to the right of the zero." Putting the monetary representation together with the number line led this student to revise his initial idea that .089 should go to the left (on the "negative" side) of the zero on the number line. The rest of the class concurred that this placement, just a little to the right of zero, made sense. The reference to coins had enabled them to make a judgment about the reasonableness of their assertions.

There was no mention in this part of the discussion of "negative" numbers. By this time, we had gone several minutes past the end of math period and I was on the verge of making the class late for lunch, but I was very curious to know what the students would do with .0089 on the number line because of the earlier assertion that this number was negative. I was quite intrigued by the fact that the presence of the number line on the board had evoked the speculation that .089 might "go to the left of zero," when everyone had earlier agreed that it meant "a little less than 9 cents." This was evidence for the fragility of their understanding—they could not yet move easily back and forth from one representational system to another.

Several students had disengaged from the lesson at this point, and were putting away their notebooks, but I decided to continue the discussion for a moment. A few students who were still attending asserted unanimously that .0089 was "definintely negative" and should go "a tiny bit" to the *left* of the zero on the number line. I put a dot there to represent their assertion, and said I would be very interested in continuing our discussion over the next few days, and that I wanted to find out why they thought .0089 was "negative." Other students who were attending seemed puzzled, and still others were shaking their heads in disagreement. The class went off to lunch, and I went off to figure out what to do next.

Should my first priority in the second lesson be simply to tell these students that decimals are definitely *not* negative numbers? My wish to present mathematics as a subject in which legitimate conclusions are based on reasoning, rather than on acquiescing to teacherly authority, led me away from that approach. I wanted to enable the students themselves to question their own assertions and test their reasonability within a mathematical framework.

I believed that in order to get them to do this, I needed to figure out how whatever they were thinking about decimals might be seen to make sense, rather than proceeding as if they were simply on the wrong track. And I thought what they needed to learn was more ways of thinking about the meaning of the symbols we use to write decimal numbers before they could figure out whether their assertions about those numbers made sense.

I did not interpret the students' assertions as a statement that they believed that decimal numbers were the mathematical equivalent of negative numbers; I did not think that what they meant by "negative' in this situation was what mathematicians mean by negative. They were expressing *something* about what a number like .0089 meant to them, but what was it? From one perspective, my use of money relationships as a representation for the place value relationships in decimal numbers could be seen as the cause of their conclusion that .0089 was negative. Because this numerical symbol cannot easily be related to familiar coins, the students might have interpreted it as a symbol for "less than nothing." But from another perspective, the representation functioned to raise a question in their minds; because there was a disagreement in the class about the meaning of .0089, this problem and its resolution *belonged to the students*. This is a rare and valuable turn of events in the school classroom, where most problems belong to teachers or textbooks.

Conjectures About Students' Thinking As Part of the Lesson Planning Process

If students are to develop independence in making mathematical sense of the work with numbers they are expected to do in school, they need to be considered as meaning-makers rather than as mistake-makers. Their attempts to figure out what it could mean for a number to get smaller and smaller and smaller had landed them in something of a minefield: negative numbers. My job was to help them get out of it with some understanding of decimal numbers.

What did it mean to these students to put a number like .0089 "to the left of the zero" on the number line? How widespread through the class was the idea that .0089 was "negative"? Why did their sense that decimal numbers were fractions become more fragile as more zeroes appeared between the decimal point and the non-zero digits? To what extent was their thinking attributable to the limitations of the monetary system as a representation of decimal numbers smaller than .01? What did they *mean* when they said the number was "negative"? There are no readily available concrete things for a fifth grader to associate with .0089; perhaps they reasoned that .089 should be on the positive side of the number line because it could be associated with "more than 8 cents," while smaller decimal numbers belonged on "the left side of zero" on the number line and so should be called "negative". It could be that they were not making a distinction between numbers that are less than *zero* and numbers that are less than *one*. They have not had much opportunity to associate either negative numbers or fractions with anything that would give them a concrete meaning, so they might think that either a fraction or a negative number could mean "not something" or "less than nothing". As we proceeded from talking about the relationships among $.89, $8.90, and $89.00 to constructing a meaning for $.089, and .0089, there may have been a confusion between a number becoming smaller by taking something away from it (subtraction), which is the more familiar operation, and making a number smaller by taking a fractional part of it (division). If getting smaller is associated with the action of "taking away" it would be reasonable to conclude that at some point, one would get to "nothing" or even "less than nothing."

Their uncertainty about fractions may have been compounded by the symbols that are used for decimals and the symbolization of negative numbers on the number line. The "line of symmetry" on the *number line* is at zero, while the line of symmetry for naming the places in a *number* goes through the "units" or "ones" place. The decimal point itself is between the "ones" and the "tenths" place (see Figure 1). Of course, the negative numbers are on the *left* side of zero on the number line, while the decimal fractions are on the *right* side of the decimal point. But this directional opposition could be less influential than the idea that the decimal point or the units place was "the dividing line" between positive and negative numbers. *Zero*, after all, is used in two different ways: to mark the divide between positive and negative numbers on the number line and to "hold places" between the decimal point and the non-zero digits in a decimal number. One could thus interpret the zeroes in decimal numbers as separating the positive part of the number from the negative (e.g., interpreting 46 in 46.032, as positive and 32 as negative), especially if one's sense of what these numbers might mean is quite fragile to begin with.

In addition to these difficulties related to mathematical symbols, I thought about characteristics of classroom instruction that might explain what my students were thinking. The teacher *writes* on the blackboard with her back to students and *talks* facing them, making it easy to misuse the directions "left" and "right." It may have been that the student told me to put the point for .089 "behind the zero" and "a little to the *right* of the zero" on the number line, and as I turned around to do it, I put the point to the left instead of to the right, having focused on the word "behind." If the students saw me do this, it could have confused their already fragile understanding of the way the number line is used to represent fractions and negative numbers. It may also have been that the students' assertions had little to do with a misunderstanding, but could be attributed to their thinking that learning about negative numbers was a prestigious thing to do in fifth grade. They may have turned the conversation to negative numbers, once they got an opening to do so, because they were anxious to get on with learning higher mathematics.

My conjectures about how fifth-grade students think about decimals and negative numbers have become more refined as I have continued to observe

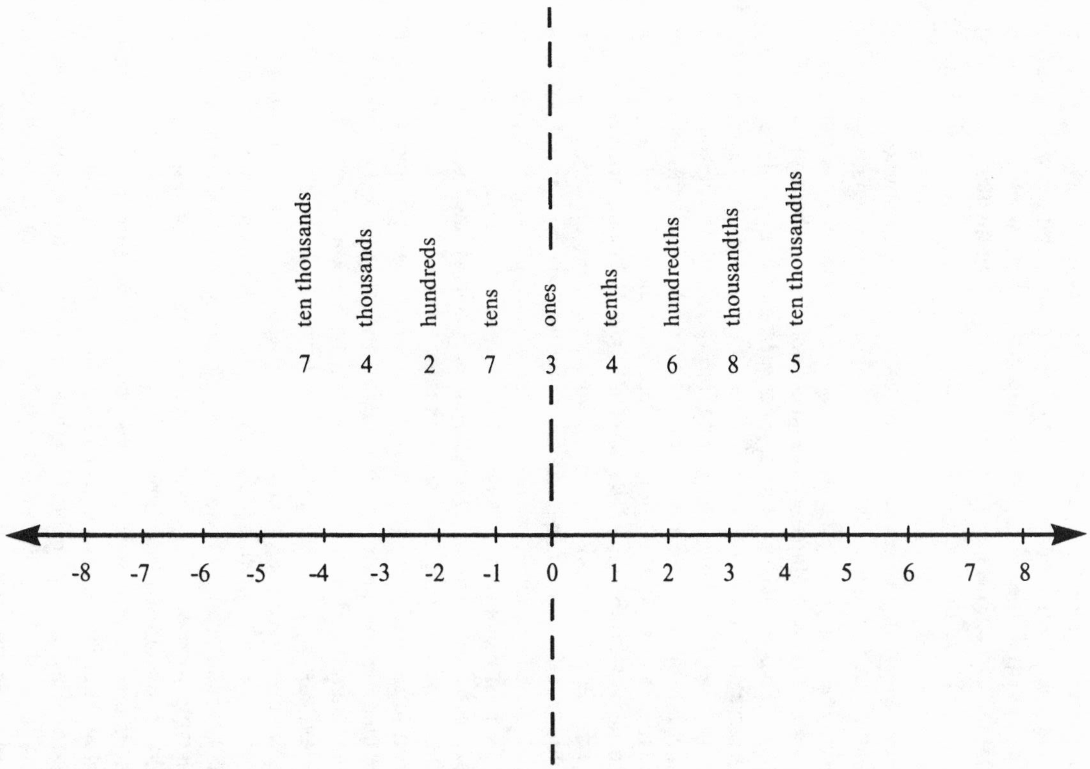

ten thousandths 5
thousandths 8
hundredths 6
tenths 4
ones 3
tens 7
hundreds 2
thousands 4
ten thousands 7

8 7 6 5 4 3 2 1 0 -1 -2 -3 -4 -5 -6 -7 -8

Figure 1. Contrasting Symmetrics

their activities in different contexts and as I have analyzed the mathematical concepts involved in the ordering of decimal numbers. But these were the ideas I recorded in my plan book at the time the lesson occurred. These conjectures led me to find representations of decimal fractions that would focus students' thinking on the idea that a quantity could get smaller and smaller by base ten orders of magnitude, and yet never become nothing or less than nothing. I wanted to show them pictures that could be connected with the conventional names of the decimal places to indicate that those were names for "something," not "nothing" or "less than nothing."

Choosing Representations That Are Responsive to Students' Thinking

I decided to present two new representations of decimal numbers to the class and to emphasize the relationship between them, as well as making connections between these new representations and the number line. One representation I planned to teach was picturing decimal numbers between zero and one as fractional parts of a circle; I would also teach the class to name the "decimal places" in a mirror image of the whole number place value names, with the unit as the mirror (see Figure 1). The simpler way to name decimal numbers is to begin with "point" and then read off the digits in the fraction (as in "point-oh-oh-seven-four" for .0074), but this language makes no connection with the meaning of the place where each digit is located. To relate parts of a circle with decimal place names, the "unit place" is associated with one whole circle, and the digit in the units place indicates how many whole circles are under consideration. The numbers to the left of the units place indicate groups of whole circles in multiples of ten, one hundred, and so on. The numbers to the right of the units place tell both how many pieces to divide the unit circle into (also multiples of ten, one hundred, and so forth), and how many of those pieces are under consideration. The *names* of the decimal places, i.e., "tenths," "hundredths," "thousandths," and so on are a point of connection between the place values in decimal numbers and their representation as fractional parts of a circular region.

In choosing these modes of representation, I also anticipated another one of the difficulties that students encounter in comparing numbers written as decimals: how can a number like ".57" mean *both* fifty-seven hundredths and five-tenths and seven-hundredths? For students who do not have a firm knowledge of how fractions can be equivalent, this decomposition and recomposition is not at all obvious in the manipulation of numerical symbols (i.e., .5 = .50 because 5/10 = 50/100), and their prior work with whole numbers does not give them much flexibility with taking numbers apart in different ways to consider the relationships among their component parts. But moving back and forth between these two interpretations is useful in deciding, for example, whether .57 represents a quantity that is larger or smaller than the quantity

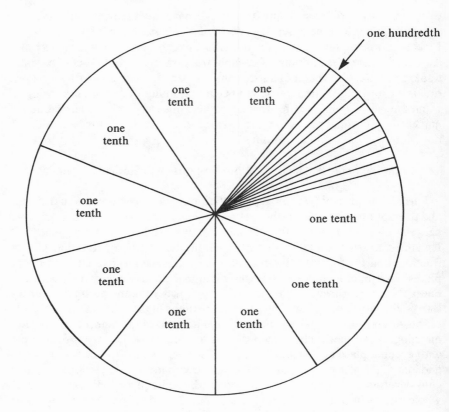

Figure 2.   Decimals as Fractions of a Circular Region

represented by .6. Relating the names of the places with a visual representation of the relationship between tenths and hundredths would give students a way to talk about different fractional names for the same quantity.

   In addition to their lack of experience with decomposing numbers and regrouping them in various ways, there is another problem which leads to students' misunderstanding the magnitude of decimal numbers which the "fractions of a circle" representation helps to address. When one talks of .564 as 5 tenths, 6 hundredths and 4 thousandths, it is not obvious to students that 6 hundredths is a much smaller quantity than 5 tenths. The relationships among relatively large whole numbers like 6 hundre*ds* and 5 te*ns* can be hung easily onto concrete quantities; it is clear to a fifth grader that 50 units of something is not as much as even *one* hundred. But when one comes to fractions, there is an ambiguity in the language which cannot be resolved without some connection to the meaning of the words we use to talk about fractions: although ten is *smaller* than a hundred, a tenth is *larger* than a hundredth (see Figure 2). And moreover, it takes ten hundredths to make only one tenth. When one talks of a hundredth or a thousandth, it would not be surprising if what students think is: "that's a big number," and in one sense, this is the right thing to think— it means dividing a unit up into many pieces. But each piece, indicated by "one thousandth" is actually quite small in relation to the unit. In a circle, the hundredths are necessarily skinnier slices, and the thousandths skinnier yet, and the smaller pieces seem to be inside the larger pieces. There are some problems, both pedagogical and mathematical, with using slices of a circle to represent fractions, but at the time, this tool seemed to meet the needs of the lessons I wanted to teach.

TEACHING AND LEARNING WITH MATHEMATICAL TOOLS: THE PROGRESSION FROM USING TO CHOOSING IN EIGHT LESSONS

The lessons to be described in this section are about teaching students *how to use* representational tools and then teaching them *to choose to use* those tools to reason about comparisons among numbers written as decimals. I taught students visual, verbal, and symbolic representations for decimal fractions, and what the connections were among them, and then they practiced using these representations in homework and written classwork, in the way one might practice using a hammer by banging a nail into a scrap of wood. This sort of practice in carpentry is prior to using a hammer to build a bookcase, just as practice with making a visual representation of .57 is prior to using that visual representation to support the argument that .57 is smaller than .9. As a teacher of carpentry might demonstrate the use of a hammer in building a bookcase concurrently with having students begin to use hammers on scraps of wood in order to give the student a sense of purpose for his or her practice, so too did I demonstrate the use of the tools students were learning about in making decisions about the magnitude of decimal numbers. There was a progression of teaching goals in this series of lessons from getting students to practice with using the tools for the purpose of becoming familiar with the tools themselves, to getting them to choose to use them to solve decimal comparison problems, and on to getting them to adapt and invent tools of their own. In this way, the aim of increasing students' capacities to make independent mathematical judgments was interwoven with the aim of their becoming competent at comparing numbers written as decimals.

Multiple Representations

The content of the next lesson in this series was a collection of bits and pieces relating decimals to other, more familiar topics and continuing with some of the themes of the lesson the day before. I proposed an imaginary coin that would be worth one-tenth of a cent, and we did some trading exercises relating that coin to quantities of real coins and paper money. I gave the class a list of numbers to order on the basis of place value (50, .05, 500, 5, 5000, 5, .5), and once the list was ordered, we discussed what smaller and smaller numbers in this series would look like. This exercise provided exposure to the names of both the whole number and the deicmal places. I drew a number line on the board, marking off zero and one, and we constructed the placement of one-tenth, two-tenths, and so on up to nine-tenths, by dividing up the line segment between zero and one into ten equal pieces. Finally, we did the same sort of dividing up and labeling for ten equal regions of a circle.

Each of these parts of the lesson was about a representation of the relationships among the digits in a number with a decimal point. In the interactions of this lesson, I learned more about where the fragilities were in my students' understanding. Although .5 was unanimously associated with five-tenths and this quantity was located half way between zero and one whole, some students associated .3 with one third. With accurate representations of the common fractions 1/3 and 3/10 on the number line and in the circle, some questions were raised about this association, and a larger point about how the number to the right of the decimal point is to be interpreted in relation to fractions was elaborated. Another problem was raised as we counted by tenths: should ten tenths be written as .10? or as 1.0? Portraying ten tenths on the circle and on the number line resolved this question: if it is a whole, it must be written as 1.0. The representations were chosen by the teacher as the appropriate tools for solving these problems, but they were used by students to answer *their* mathematical questions. Their conflicts were resolved in their thinking, not by teacher fiat.

Learning Place Value As Fractional Parts of Fractional Parts

In the next lesson, I expanded from the representation of tenths on the circle to the representation of hundredths. Several students were able to explain, each in his or her own words, that you could get a hundred equal pieces in the circle if you cut each tenth up into ten pieces. At the blackboard, I went through the tedious business of actually dividing a large circle into one hundred slices by this process. The class counted the tiny slices: one hundredth, two hundredths, three hundredths, and so on; as I divided each tenth into ten hundredths. I noted the equivalences of ten hundredths with each tenth after counting each ten pieces and wrote them in numerical symbols: $10/100 = 1/10$, $20/100 = 2/10$, $30/100 = 3/10$, $40/100 = 4/10$, and so on.

With all of these equations on the board, I asked different students to talk about the patterns they could observe. Then I wrote and read the decimal notations for the same divisions, asserting that the second place to the right of the decimal point was called the "hundredths" place, and listening to students' ideas about why it might be called that. Using a different color of chalk, I labeled the hundredths pieces as we counted again—same words, different symbols: .01 ("one-hundredth"), .02, .03, .04, .05, .06, .07, .08, .09, *.10* = *.1* ("ten-hundredths equals one-tenth"), .11 ("eleven-hundredths"), .12. 13., and so on, all the way up to .99, and then, *1.00* ("one-hundred-hundredths"), at which point one student said, "*That's* why it's called the hundredths place," and several others concurred.

These remarks, together with the work I saw students doing several days later, counting slices as they puzzled over questions like "Which is bigger, .19 or .4?" confirmed my sense that this seemingly dull counting and labeling exercise would make fractional pieces of a circle and the names of the decimal places part of the students' repertoire of tools for making sense of the numerical relationships that underlie the concept of place value. The very monotony of counting out one hundred hundredths had the power to convey their magnitude in relation to one tenth and one whole. Students practiced trading between tenths and hundredths using the language of pieces of the circle, and then I asked what *thousandths* might look like, as fractions written with a numerator and denominator, as decimal numbers, and as slices of a circle. Several students were able to extend the representation appropriately in all of these domains and others were anxious to discuss their ideas for "drawing" ten-thousandths, millionths, and even billionths. Their enthusiasm was a dramatic expression of their sense of the relationship between making more and more pieces, and of the pieces becoming tinier and tinier as the number of pieces got larger, as well as of the base ten relationship among these pieces. There was no mention of decimal numbers "becoming negative" as they represented tinier and tinier pieces of the circle.

The "pieces of a circle" representation embodied all of the mathematical principles that I had wanted to address in this unit: it gave a picture of the place value relationships in decimal numbers that would enable students to appreciate the "two-way" ratio between places, with an emphasis on the fractional parts of fractional parts. Because hundredths were "inside" of tenths, and more than nine of them would fill up the space, students were able to talk about more and more pieces that were also smaller and smaller. The whole circle was one unit, and no piece was zero; small pieces, no matter how small, were more than "nothing." The circumference of the circle functioned as a sort of lasso that kept all of those pieces in an appropriate relation to one another and to one whole unit. It gave some meaning to the infinity of numbers between zero and one, although this continued to be an idea for students to wonder about. The representational tool I had chosen worked successfully to give the students a basis on which to judge by themselves whether their assertions made mathematical sense, and it functioned as a medium for me to communicate with them about the subject matter.

Practice With a New Representational Tool

In the next class there was more practice with representing quantities of tenths and hundredths on the circle and reading numbers with decimal parts. Using the circle representation, we did whole group verbal and individual written practice with changing back and forth between groups of tenths and groups of hundredths: How many hundredths would three-tenths be? Eight-tenths? How many tenths would you get out of 48-hundredths? And how many hundredths left over? I showed the class how numbers like .32 would look on the circle, and illustrated the equality between "three-tenths plus two-hundredths" and "thirty-two hundredths" by counting up the hundredths slices that were within the tenths. They practiced individually with prepared circles on worksheets that were already divided into tenths, coloring in regions to represent numbers like .6, .65, .13, .8, .88, and so on.

Why *is* nine tenths and five hundredths the same thing as ninety five hundredths? When that question came up during this class discussion, one student said "Because you just add zeroes to both parts of nine-tenths and you get ninety-hundredths, and you add that to five hundredths." He knew the *procedure* for producing equivalent fractions, and there were four or five others in the class who could also do this. I represented what he said on the blackboard as:

$$\frac{9}{10} = \frac{90}{100}$$

But when I asked for volunteers in the class to *explain* what was happening when you "added zeroes" to the numerator and denominator of a fraction, no one had anything to say. Even those who knew it was a valid procedure did not have any way of explaining what it meant. This gave me some clues as to what students needed: a more solid connection between operations on numbers and operations on pieces of the circle.

Teaching Students How to Use Representational Tools
To Solve Mathematical Problems

After three classes in which we practiced with the pieces of a circle representation, I put the numbers 7.4, 7.40, and 7.48 up on the blackboard and asked if anyone could explain which was bigger and why. I was more interested in building students' confidence in their use of representational tools to reason about these comparisons at this point than in testing their ability to make more difficult comparisons, so I began with a problem in which the numbers do not suggest alternative interpretations. (An example of a more complex kind of comparison problem would be to ask students to figure out whether 2.9 was larger or smaller than 2.09; here the number symbols put more stress on students' fragile knowledge because 209 > 29.)

The boy who spoke first gave a very articulate explanation of the claim that 7.48 was biggest. He said it was because "Seven-point-four-eight has eight hundredths pieces colored in in addition to seven wholes and four-tenths, which they both have." That was an elegant explanation using the terms of the referent I had been working to teach. In a student's language, the "pieces of a circle" referent was being used to figure out the meaning of two decimal numbers to see how they might compare. But how much of this sort of comprehension was there in the class?

In order to find out more precisely what other members of the class would do with this problem, I then asked how anyone might compare 7.40 with 7.4. I took a poll: "Raise your hand if you think 7.40 is bigger. If you think 7.4 is bigger. If you think they are both the same." Several students thought 7.40 was bigger, none thought 7.4 was bigger, and a few thought they were the same. I then asked for some explanations of these two assertions in terms of parts of the circle, and called on some students who had been quiet over the last few classes to explain their choices so that my assessment would not be based only on the contributions of the more verbally aggressive students. I was taking a more passive role now in producing the representation; I wanted to see what the students would construct to picture the relationship among these numbers. The students who spoke agreed that you needed seven whole circles for the seven part, and that you would also need some parts of another circle. One student suggested that the parts would be found by dividing the circle into *seven* pieces, another that the circle might be divided into *four* pieces, and another thought maybe it should be *ten* pieces.

How would we decide? Instead of telling them which was the correct interpretation of ".4" on the circle, I wrote .4 = 4/10 on the board, saying "Point-four equals four-tenths" and one of the students, connecting these symbols with the circle pieces, said, "Oh yeah, it's ten pieces with four colored in." She still needed the trigger of the number *written as a conventional fraction* to be certain about that, even though we had also been naming ".4" as "four-tenths." Her assertion of the connection between the decimal fraction .4 and the four parts of a circle divided into ten equal pieces served to refute the other interpretations; I did not say anything else about them myself but made a picture of both 7.4 and 7.40 on the board. Then I took a poll of the whole class again, writing the relationships on the board: "How many people think 7.4 > 7.40?" No one. "How many people think 7.4 = 7.40?" A few. "How many people think 7.4 < 7.40?" Fewer, tentatively. Those who claimed that the two numbers were equal said it was because they "had the same amount shaded in." Those who thought 7.40 might be larger said it was because "it has more pieces." These students also perceived that the amount shaded in for four-tenths is the same as the amount shaded in for forty-hundredths, but the meaning of "equal" in their minds was not "same amount shaded in." Again, we came up against a mathematical convention, not a question of understanding. I told the class that in mathematics, one way to think about equal fractions is that they stand for the same amount out of the whole, no matter how many pieces the whole is divided into. I used an even more concrete referent—pizza—to emphasize that four-tenths slices and forty-hundredths slices would give you the same amount to eat, even though the tiny pieces would be messier.

Teaching Students When To Use Representational Tools To Solve Mathematical Problems

I concluded from the results of a homework assignment after this lesson that the capacity to figure out effective ways of comparing different kinds of decimal numbers was widely distributed in the class, albeit unevenly. The errors students made were in the sorts of comparisons that are symbolically most difficult. I thought everyone would benefit from the opportunity to listen to their peers make arguments about why one decimal number was larger than or smaller than another. So I began the next class by putting this list of decimal numbers on the board and saying that we were going to put these numbers in order, from smallest to largest.

$$1$$
$$8.88$$
$$.6$$
$$3.2$$
$$.04$$
$$0$$
$$.999$$

These were not the same numbers as those on the homework assignment, but ordering them posed the same sorts of problems. I included both zero and one on the list thinking that this would result in an implicit "lesson" about where decimal fractions that were less than one would stand in order in relation to "nothing."

First I picked a pair of numbers from the list and wrote them in a different place on the blackboard: .6 and 3.2. The following dialogue illustrates the ways in which students talked about the referent in their arguments for the reasonability of their assertions:

T: Which of these [.6 or 3.2] is bigger?
S₁: Three point two, because it has a whole number part.
T: [writing these on the board] Now what about .6 and .04?
S₂: Point six is bigger because tenths are bigger pieces, and there are more of them, anyway.

So I put a partial ordered list on the board:

.04
.6
3.2

The next student to volunteer placed .999 after .6 saying: "Because point-oh-four has *no* big pieces, point-six comes next, not point-nine-nine-nine." Several other students picked up her reference to the tenths as "big pieces" and expanded on it, calling the hundredths "little pieces" and the thousandths "really little pieces" as they gave further explanations about why one decimal number was larger than another in constructing an ordered list.

Ordering Decimals and Knowing Why:
A Public Mathematical Discourse Among Students and Teacher

In the next lesson, I presented more ambiguous ordering problems, to give students practice with using the "pieces of a circle" representation to figure out more of the sort of problems on which they had made errors in the homework assignment. I constructed a set of eight ordering problems and put them on the board at the beginning of the class. Students were directed to put <, >, or = in the circles between the numbers.

5.19 ◯ 5.218   .8 ◯ .65
5.3 ◯ 5.19   .087 ◯ .8
2.31 ◯ 2.5   7.65 ◯ 7.8
2.31 ◯ 2.047   7.087 ◯ 7.8

The question of what kind of quantities decimal numbers might represent was on the table, and figuring out an answer to that question was interwoven with the task of deciding which of two decimal numbers is larger. Being able to make that decision in a way that could be supported with a reasonable argument would require students to resolve questions about the meaning of zero after the decimal point, about how the relative size of a fractional part was related to the number of parts in determining magnitude, and about the relationship among the digits to the right of the decimal point. Class discussions and individual conversations informed me that they now had many conflicting ideas about these matters, and the work of learning would entail resolving those conflicts. We were at a critical point in this series of lessons; the interaction that occurred now was a test of whether the students had learned to think things through on their own.

This class could be seen as an exercise in the *social construction* of mathematical truth. Students would have the opportunity to build upon one another's ideas and the challenge of explaining themselves to their peers and their teacher. This group activity was preliminary to their working independently on ordering problems. I have included considerable detail about the content of the group discussion in this lesson here so that the reader can share in my assessment of what the class had learned up to this point, both about how to compare decimal numbers and about the use of representational tools to reason about those comparisons. The reporting of this sort of "group" data is unusual in the field of research on teaching and learning. It is a dynamic aggregate that represents the outcomes and activities of teaching and learning in the classroom.

The routine I had established meant that students came in from recess and started to work on whatever problems I put on the board at the beginning of class, writing in their notebooks, and doing it independently. The students were aware of my expectations for this part of the class. They also knew that the work they did during this time was going to be discussed at some point during the day's lesson. By introducing these problems at the beginning of the class, I was setting the stage in which we could move back and forth between individual thinking and writing, and group discussion.

I began the class discussion, not with the problems on the board, but with a more abstract question. I asked the class what they thought about the assertion: "A decimal number is bigger if it has more numbers after the decimal point." My purpose was to see how far the students had come in resolving the conceptual conflicts associated with decimal place value, and whether they had a meaning structure that they would *choose to use* to make appropriate judgments about the magnitude of decimal numbers. By confronting them with a belief they had held in earlier class discussions, I was challenging them to argue in some more general way about whether it was true or false.

Several students voiced the opinion that it was *more likely* that the number with more digits after the decimal point would be bigger but that it was not always true. I then put an ordering problem on the board in which one of the numbers not only had more digits after the decimal point, but had larger digits as well:

$$1.1 \quad \bigcirc \quad .999$$

The first student to volunteer an opinion about which was larger explained her thinking using fractional pieces of the circle, but in a way I would not have expected. She said that 1.1 was larger because it *needed* nine "tenths pieces" to make *two* wholes. She did not know how many fractional pieces to add to .999, she said, "but even so, it would only have *one* whole." The "pieces of a circle" tool had worked for her as a counter to seeing only the number and size of the digits as relevant—because she had a way to give meaning to the digits, she was able to reason the comparison through correctly. She also manipulated the tool in a way that was different enough from what I had taught her that gave evidence that she understood the concept of decimal place value.

The next student to speak said, "What if you put more nines on the end of it?" He was still holding on to the possibility that more digits, especially nines, might make the number on the right larger. But he was offering a speculation rather than an assertion, suggesting that he was open to alternative ideas. So now we had on the board:

$$1.1 \quad \bigcirc \quad .999999$$

I asked the class what they thought, and one student said that "It's getting farther away from one whole." I wondered what the "it" was that she was referring to, and to find out more and engage a representational tool that would help thinking and communication, I said, "Let's think about money again. We could say .9 (point-nine) is nine-tenths of a dollar, nine dimes, or ninety cents. We could also write it this way: .90. Now how would you compare that with .99?" The following discussion fragment illustrates teacher and student use of the "coins" representation of decimal numbers as a tool to reason about this puzzle.

T: How would you compare .99 with .90?
S_1: Nine-nine cents is more than ninety cents.
T: Which is closer to one whole dollar?
S_2: I'm not sure, but it seems like .999 might be *past* a dollar.
S_3: Ninety-nine cents is closer to a dollar than ninety cents, because it is only one cent away.
T: So if you put nines on to the end of a decimal number, does it get bigger or smaller?
S_4: The units you are adding get smaller.
T: But what about the number as a whole?
S_5: The amount you are adding gets tinier, but the number is getting a little bigger.
T: So if I keep adding on to the end of .9999999 (point nine nine nine nine nine nine nine) will it ever get to one?
S_5: No. You would always need one more added to the last part.
T: Do you mean adding one whole?
S_5: No, adding one of *those* parts.

Further discussion clarified that "those parts" meant the fractional part represented by the digit at the farthest right-hand end of the number. One student created the image of a "chain raction" to describe what would happen to the number of you added *one* of "those parts" instead of putting on another digit, i.e.,

$$
\begin{array}{r}
.99999999 \\
+ .00000001 \\
\hline
\end{array}
$$

These students were actively engaged in figuring out the meaning of decimal place value. Some of them returned to me over the next several days with ideas about the "chain reaction" and its relationship to the bounded infinity between zero and one. They seemed to be using some relationship among the money representation, pieces of a circle, and numerical symbols to reason about their questions.

At this point I turned to the ordering problems I had put on the board at the beginning of class. The first student to volunteer said that 5.19 was less than 5.218. I asked him why he thought that made sense. He said: "They both have five wholes, so you look at the decimal part to see which is larger. Two-hundred-and-eighteen-thousandths is more than one-fifth. Nineteen-hundredths is less than one-fifth. So five and nineteen-hundredths is smaller." He was using equivalent fractions, a mathematical system which he knows more about than other members of the class, to make sense of fractions written as decimals. I did not think many students in this class had the facility with fractions that this student did, and I wanted to illustrate that there were many ways to figure out any one problem, so I asked whether anyone had a different idea or a different explanation of the same inequality. Another student said, "I agree that 5.218 is larger. All you have to do is look at the first number after the decimal point, because those are the bigger pieces." I reminded him and the class that those pieces were called "tenths" and said that this student had a theory that "the tenths are what really matters when you are comparing decimals." Then I asked, pressing on in an area where their thinking about decimal numbers had earlier broken down, "But what about the *nine* next to the one tenth in 5.19? Doesn't that make a difference?" Another student said, "No. You need ten of those to make a tenth, and there are only nine." I drew a circle on the board and divided it up to illustrate what he was saying about .19 for the whole class. I engaged the less verbal members in the class to direct me in the activity of symbolization, picturing, reading, and writing the numbers .01, .02, .03, up to .09. "Now how do we write *ten* hundredths?" "Point-one-oh." "And why can we also call that *one* tenth?" Our discussion here referred to the illustration of fractional parts of the circle for explanations. In elaborating the student's explanation I was able to involve others in a low-risk contribution to the discussion and give them practice using the "pieces of a circle" tool to support the comparison of .19 with .2. The result of this was that some of them volunteered more complicated contributions later in the discussion.

The next problem was: "Which is bigger 5.3 or 5.19?" The student who answered this one said "Five-point-three is bigger because it has three big pieces. That's the same as *thirty* little pieces, and that's bigger than nineteen." I did not draw anything to illustrate her answer, but I assumed she was referring to tenths and hundredths. I decided not to fuss about the imprecision of terms like "big" and "little" because these seemed like a bridge between the system of place value in decimal numbers and the students' ways of making sense. Those ways of making sense would become less and less fragile over the next few days, and then it might be appropriate to try to impose higher standards of precision.

"Which is bigger 2.31 or 2.5?" The answer to this problem was explained by a reference to our conversation about the first problem on the list. The student who answered used the language and thinking of one of his peers to conclude that 2.5 was larger, but along the way, he expressed the ambiguity of his thinking and the fragility of his conclusion. He said, "It's like in the second one where the tenths are bigger. Two-point-three-one has three-tenths and one-hundredth, but two-point-five *only* has five-tenths." The use of the word "only" here alerted me to the possibility that this student might still be thinking that five tenths was in some sense less than thirty-one hundredths because five is less than thirty-one. This led me to illustrate the fractional part of this problem using parts of circles. At each step of the illustration, I called on the student who had answered to tell me how to show that part of the number, hoping that the activity would give him a firmer idea of which number was larger. When we finished the illustration, the class was over for that day.

Finding Out More About Individual Students' Use of Tools to Reason Mathematically

The next lesson was organized so that I could spend time talking with individual students while they worked individually on decimal comparison problems. This would give me a better idea of what those who had not taken leadership roles in large group discussions were able to do and explain. I passed out the worksheets so that students would be working on something different from the person next to them most of the time.

What did I learn from watching and interviewing? All of the students had learned to choose to use the representation of decimals as fractions of a circle to give the places to the right of the decimal point some meaning. In some cases, however, even with this tool, their knowledge was fragile and could be thrown off by long strings of digits after the decimal point and by zeroes between the decimal point and the non-zero digits. All students used the language that they had heard from their peers to explain what they were doing. They did not seem to refer to *bigger* and *smaller* pieces of the circle to solve ordering problems when there were long strings of digits, but instead they talked about the relationship between numbers being "closer" or "further away from" the decimal point and whether there were smaller or larger "pieces" being indicated. This strategy is interesting because it seems to be a combination of algorithmic knowledge and understanding. All of the students I interviewed could tell me that it was most important to pay attention to the tenths, because they were the "biggest pieces." They were more or less articulate about the relationship of the smaller pieces to the tenths and to one another, and they had a physical image of groups of the smaller pieces being able to "fit inside" one-tenth. They spoke easily about tenths, hundredths, and thousandths, and they knew where these places were in the numbers. A few students had actually drawn circles on their papers and divided them into pieces, and all students were able to do that when I asked them to explain an ordering to me. No student used the number line as a tool in ordering the lists of decimals.

Whole Group Consolidation:
Using and Choosing Mathematical Tools
To Make Decisions About Decimal Numbers

In the last class in this series, I returned to the list of comparison problems I had put up on the board two days earlier for discussion.

5.19 ◯ 5.218		.8 ◯ .65
5.3 ◯ 5.19		.087 ◯ .8
2.31 ◯ 2.5		7.65 ◯ 7.8
2.31 ◯ 2.047		7.087 ◯ 7.8

Students had by now written down and in some cases revised their decisions about which in each pair of numbers was larger. I called upon them to explain their "answers" to me and the class, taking up where we had left off earlier with the fourth problem.

The first student who spoke used the "pieces of a circle" representation and the same sort of "completion" strategy that had been used by another student a few days before. She said that 2.31 was greater than 2.047 "because you have to add more to two-point-oh-four-seven to get to the next whole." The next problem was solved using the number line as a referent: "Point-eight is bigger because point-six-five comes between point-six and point-seven on the line." Another of the problems was an occasion for a student to express a strategy he had invented for himself, by analogy with his current vocabulary work. He said he did these problems like "alphabetical order"—if the two numbers in the first place after the decimal point are the same, you look at the next two numbers, and if those are the same, you look at the next pair, and so on.

This class marked the end of the unit on comparing decimal numbers. From here we went on to adding and subtracting numbers written as decimals, beginning with problems like: "Add two-hundredths to all of the numbers in this list; 7.432, .666, 39.087, .4, 56, 4.0987, 23.00004." The referrents that had been developed in the unit described here continued to be called on by both students and teacher to reason about the results of various computations and to support the development of meaningful procedures.

MATHEMATIC TEACHING AND MATHEMATICS LEARNING: WHAT DO WE KNOW?

This saga of teaching my fifth-grade students to choose to use representational tools to solve comparison problems with decimal numbers is an example of what Zarinnia, Lamon, and Romberg (1987) call the "epistemic teaching of school mathematics," in that it is congruent with notions of what it means to know mathematics. These authors point out five significant themes in current research on "learning mathematics for long-term understanding" that have implications for this kind of mathematics teaching: deriving mathematical structures from problem situations, multiple representation, dialogue, diagnostic teaching, and devolution and dissimilarity. In the lessons that I have described, each of these themes is illustrated from the perspective of the classroom teacher. The problem addressed in the learning research is how novices come to assign meaning to the notations we use to indicate mathematical entities and operations, without losing the power of mathematical abstraction that these notations embody. This is the kind of mathematics learning that gives students the ability to reason independently about their answers and procedures in school. My teaching experiments illustrate what this sort of learning might look like in a school classroom in relation to a familiar topic in the curriculum.

Research on mathematics learning suggests that one way to work toward the goal of having students assign appropriate meaning to mathematical symbols is to create instructional situations in which *learners are involved with a phenomenon that feels problematic to them,* so that the mathematical modeling of the phenomenon is used in a context where a problem arises whose solution *matters.* This is often accomplished by engaging students in working on a real-world problem whose solution they come to care about (Lesh, 1985) like buying supplies for a class project, or by having students come to identify with a character in a dramatic story who uses mathematics to solve a problem (Bransford, Hasselbring, Barron, Littlefield, & Goin, 1987; Lampert, 1985).

In my classes on decimals, there was no such real-world connection, but the creation of a representation for decimal place value did become an issue of concern to my students because of their disagreement about whether decimal numbers were "negative." They became engaged in trying to resolve this issue, and the mathematical tools they learned to use served the resolution.

Another trend in research on mathematics learning suggests that *multiple representations of a concept* contribute to long term understanding and knowledge use. Multiple representations are at the intersection of mathematical and cognitive ideals; the creation of mathematics itself depends on capturing structures with symbols and using those symbols to move among structures of different types (Hademard, 1945; Kaput, 1985; Vergnaud, 1983). The process of moving among representational systems that have a common structure occurred in my classroom as my students used pieces of a circle to confirm their reasoning about fractional coins; as they used coins to make sense of the names of the decimal places; as they used these names to fit together the pieces of a circle with numerical symbols for decimal numbers. Using these multiple representations, they not only solved common ordering problems, but they raised new mathematical questions for themselves about such profound ideas as infinity and limits.

From the perspective of classroom teaching, it is interesting that this research on individual learning has recently been complemented by significant attention to the social processes involved in creating mathematical meaning. This work emphasizes *dialogue*—between teacher and students, and among students themselves—as a replacement for the traditional "teacher tells, students listen" routine in mathematics classrooms. Drawing heavily on the currently popular work of Vygotsky (1962), but repeating themes that were developed earlier in the social psychology of G.H. Mead (1934), researchers in this tradition assert that students come to understand through a process of interaction with more sophisticated knowers in the solution of a problem (Collins, Brown, & Newman, 1987; Schoenfeld, 1987). Meaning is created in social discourse, and the standard is set by the most expert member of the group; social conflict creates the need for cognitive resolution (Bell, Pratt, & Purdy, 1986; Brown & Campione, 1987; Palincsar, 1986). In the class discussions I have reported here about decimal numbers, my teaching task was to provide some language and some visual representations. These were modified and took on meaning in their use by students in interaction with me and with one another. They resolved conflicts by calling on mathematically legitimate representations to support their arguments, and through this activity, they learned both about mathematics and about doing mathematics.

A fourth trend in research on coming to know mathematics supports the practice of *diagnostic teaching,* i.e., teaching that is based on a continuing assessment of what students can do and what they understand about what they are doing (Carpenter, Fennema, Peterson, Chiang, & Loef, 1988; Davis, 1983a;

Lampert, 1988b). This approach contrasts to the more management-oriented way of thinking about assessment in terms of pre-tests and post-tests with teaching happening in between. One cannot get a very rich picture of what a student understands from a simple paper and pencil test of mathematical skills (Erlwanger, 1975; Ginsburg, 1977). The sort of dynamic interaction between what students do in any particular lesson and the tools the teacher uses to improve their skills and knowledge that is described in the above series of lessons involves a more complex sort of diagnosis, and results in teaching that is targeted to students' cognitive and social needs. Learning is not simply measured by a "terminal test" because knowledge is considered to be something more than the ability to answer questions correctly.

Finally, these lessons illustrate the current learning research theme of *collaboration among diverse participants* in the process of learning how to solve a problem. New knowledge is constructed as a joint venture in the class rather than as a communication from teacher to students. This kind of teaching and learning has been monitored most closely in classrooms where students interact in pairs with computers to learn mathematics (Kaput, 1985), but other more general studies report that collaboration and engagement in the learning process are closely related (Freudenthal, 1978; Whitney, 1985; von Glasersfeld, 1983) and that knowledge is more likely to be used in collaborative problem solving efforts (Resnick, in press; Schoenfeld, 1986).

Although it seems clear from the research on learning that the sort of mathematics teaching that is described here could result in students becoming independent and empowererd doers of mathematics, there are significant problems involved in making this sort of teaching practical and widespread in schools. One kind of problem has to do with the social structure of the typical classroom and to what extent it can be altered to accommodate students and teachers arguing about mathematical assertions. The size of the typical class group, the schedule of the school day and year, the age-grouping that determines a class and other features of the way we organize learning in schools can make this sort of activity problematic (Cuban, 1984; Doyle, 1985; Doyle & Carter, 1984; Lampert, 1988b; Sarason, 1971). Another problem is figuring out what teachers need to know to do this sort of teaching and how to educate them to do it (Ball, 1987; Ball & McDiarmid, 1987; Lampert, 1988a). But taking up questions of policy, teacher education, and school organization seem subsequent to answering questions about what is possible and what this sort of teaching might look like.

ACKNOWLEDGMENTS

The author would like to acknowledge the helpful comments of Deborah Ball, Jere Brophy, Lauren Resnick, Margaret Buchmann, Robert Floden, Ralph Putnam, and

David K. Cohen on earlier drafts of this paper and the collaboration of Thom Dye in the work of recording teaching and learning activities. The research reported herein was supported by the Spencer Foundation through a grant from the National Academy of Education.

NOTES

1. See Schoenfeld (in press) for further evidence supporting these assertions, drawn from high school geometry and college math classrooms.

2. I refer to the process of figuring out whether one's answers and procedures are mathematically legitimate as "doing mathematics"; the tools that fifth graders use in this process will be different from the tools mathematicians use, but there are essential similarities in the process (Balacheff, 1987; Bell, 1976).

3. See Balacheff (1987) for an analysis of what "proof" might mean in the mathematics classroom.

4. Roman numerals provide a contrast: in CXXVIII, the symbol for one unit (I) *looks different* from the symbol for one ten (X) or one hundred (C).

5. It is the propensity to think in terms of an additive rather than a geometric relationship between numbers that leads many adults into shock when they are brought to the realization that there are a *thousand* millions in a billion. We know a billion is more than a million, but how much more it is often comes as a surprise. The linguistic distinction between "a thousand more" and "a thousand times more" is not powerful enough to convey the order of magnitude of differences, and once we get beyond a hundred, it is difficult to imagine comparing these groups of quantities concretely (see Davis & Hersch, 1986; Hofstadter, 1985; see also Dienes, 1960, for an explanation of the mathematical concept of place value).

6. "Adding" digits to the right of the decimal place is a classroom colloquialism that probably contributes to students' ambiguous conceptualization of what is happening as numbers get longer to the right of the decimal point. On these grounds, one could argue that such imprecise language should be banished from instructional settings. But it is also necessary to talk about mathematics in a way that is not entirely foreign if students are going to believe they actually have a chance of figuring out what it is all about. The word "add" has two meanings, one is the common sense in which it means something like "put," as in adding flour to a bowl of milk; the other is the mathematical sense, meaning to join two disjoint sets and count the total members of the new set. In the latter sense, one would not "add" six tenths and five hundredths and get a total of eleven; in the more common sense, however, one could "put" five hundredths next to six-tenths and get sixty five hundredths. If the process of adding a digit is not clarified, it is difficult to be clear about whether it can result in turning decimal fractions into numbers greater than or equal to one. A possible solution to this problem is to represent the distinction concurrently in a medium other than the English language or number symbols, such as in a drawing or on the number line.

The use of this ambiguous term is further confused by the casual use of the word "number" when one means "digit." Perhaps what ought to happen in the classroom is that students come to see a *need* for the more precise language of mathematics. It does not seem to work to impose it.

7. In the American system, the decimal point in the written symbols for quantities of money can be seen to separate amounts of paper money from amounts of coins. As with the physical representations of any mathematical idea, this concrete meaning of the decimal point can actually limit one's appreciation of the structure of number if one never gets beyond it, but it seemed like a good place to begin to extend students' ideas about the relationships among places in whole numbers into the realm of fractions.

8. I stopped using the dollar sign in front of these numbers without making a conscious decision to do so. The possible consequences of this action will be discussed below.

REFERENCES

Balacheff, N. (1987). Processus de preuve et situations de validation [Processes of proof and approaches to validation]. *Educational Studies in Mathematics, 18,* 147-176.

Ball, D. (1988). Unlearning to teach mathematics. *For the Learning of Mathematics, 8*(1), 40-48.

Ball, D., & McDiarmid, G.W. (1987). *Keeping track of teacher learning.* Unpublished paper, National Center for Research on Teacher Education, East Lansing, MI.

Barnes, D. (1976). *From communication to curriculum.* London: Penguin.

Baroody, A.J., & Ginsburg, H.P. (1986). The relationship between initial meaningful and mechanical knowledge of arithmetic. In J. Hiebert (Ed.), *Conceptual and procedural knowledge: The case of mathematics.* Hillsdale, NJ: Lawrence Erlbaum.

Behr, M.J., Lesh, R., Post, T.R., & Silver, E.A. (1983). Rational number concepts. In R. Lesh & M. Landau (Eds.), *Acquisition of mathematical concepts and processes* (pp. 91-126). New York: Academic Press.

Bell, A.W. (1976). A study of pupils' proof explanations in mathematical situations. *Educational Studies in Mathematics, 7,* 23-40.

Bell, A.W., Pratt, K., & Purdy, D. (1986). *Teaching by conflict discussion–A comparative experiment.* Nottingham: Shell Centre for Mathematical Education, University of Nottingham.

Bransford, J., Hasselbring, T., Barron, B., Littlefield, J., & Goin, L. (1987). The use of macro-contexts to facilitate mathematical thinking. In R. Charles and E. Silver (Eds.), *Teaching and evaluating mathematical problem solving* (pp. 125-147). Hillsdale, NJ: Erlbaum.

Brown, A., & Campione, J. (1987). On the importance of knowing what you are doing: Metacognition and mathematics. In R. Charles and E. Silver (Eds.), *Teaching and evaluating mathematical problem solving* (pp. 93-114). Hillsdale, NJ: Erlbaum.

Campbell, D. (1985). *Teaching elementary mathematics as discourse.* Paper presented at the annual meeting of the American Educational Research Association, Chicago, Illinois.

Carpenter, T.P. (1985). Learning to add and subtract: An exercise in mathematical problem solving. In E.A. Silver (Ed.), *Teaching and learning mathematical problem solving: Multiple research perspectives* (pp. 17-40). Hillsdale, NJ: Erlbaum.

Carpenter, T., Fennema, E., Peterson, P.L., Chiang, C.-P., & Loef, M. (1988, May). *Using knowledge of children's mathematical thinking in classroom teaching: An experimental study.* Paper presented at American Educational Research Association, New Orleans, LA.

Cazden, C. (1968). Classroom discourse. In M.C. Wittrock (Ed.), *Handbook of research on teaching* (3rd ed., pp. 432-463). New York: Macmillan.

Collins, A., Brown, J.S., & Newman, S.E. (1987). *Cognitive apprenticeship: Teaching the craft of reading, writing, and mathematics* (Technical Report 6459). Cambridge, MA: BBN Laboratories Incorporated.

Cuban, L. (1984). Policy and research dilemmas in the teaching of reasoning: Unplanned designs. *Review of Educational Research, 54*(4), 655-681.

Davis, P.J., & Hersch, R. (1986). *Descartes' dream: The world according to mathematics.* San Diego: Harcourt Brace Jovanovich.

Davis, R.B. (1983a). Diagnosis and evaluation in mathematics instruction: Making contact with students' mental representations. In D.C. Smith (Ed.), *Essential knowledge for beginning educators* (pp. 101-111). Washington, DC: American Association of Colleges for Teacher Education.

Davis, R.B. (1983b). *Learning mathematics: The cognitive science approach to mathematics education*. Norwood, NJ: Ablex.

Dienes, Z.P. (1960). *Building up mathematics*. New York: Hutchinson.

Doyle, W. (1985). *Content representation in teachers' definitions of academic work*. Austin: Research and Development Center for Teacher Education, University of Texas at Austin.

Doyle, W., & Carter, K. (1984). Academic tasks in classrooms. *Curriculum Inquiry, 14*, 129-149.

Erlwanger, S.H. (1975). Case studies of children's conceptions of mathematics (Part 1). *Journal of Children's Mathematical Behavior, 1*, 7-26.

Fennema, E., Carpenter, T.P., & Peterson, P.L. (1986). *Teachers' decision making and cognitively guided instruction: A new paradigm for curriculum development*. Paper presented to the Seventh Annual Psychology of Mathematics Education Conference, London, England.

Freudenthal, H. (1978). *Weeding and sowing: Preface to a science of mathematics education*. Boston: Reidel.

Gelman, R., & Meck, E. (1986). The notion of principle: The case of counting. In J. Hiebert (Ed.), *Conceptual and procedural knowledge: The case of mathematics* (pp. 29-57). Hillsdale, NJ: Erlbaum.

Ginsburg, H.A. (1977). *Children's arithmetic: The learning process*. New York, Van Nostrand.

Green, T. (1971). *The activities of teaching*. New York: McGraw Hill.

Greeno, J., Riley, M., & Gelman, R. (1984). Conceptual competence in children's counting. *Cognitive Psychology, 16*, 94-143.

Hademard, J. (1945). *An essay on the psychology of invention in the mathematical field*. Princeton, NJ: Princeton University Press.

Hiebert, J., & Wearne, D. (1986). Procedures over concepts: The acquisition of decimal number knowledge. In J. Hiebert (Ed.), *Conceptual and procedural knowledge: The case of mathematics* (pp. 199-223). Hillsdale, NJ: Erlbaum.

Hofstadter, D.R. (1985). *Metamagical themas: Questing for the essence of mind and pattern*. Toronto: Bantam Books.

Kaput, J.J. (1985). *Multiplicative word problems and intensive quantities: An integrated software response* (Technical report 85-19). Cambridge, MA: Harvard University, Educational Technology Center.

Lakatos, I. (1976). *Proofs and refutations. The logic of mathematical discovery*. Cambridge: Cambridge University Press.

Lampert, M. (1985). Mathematics learning in context: The Voyage of the Mimi. *The Journal of Mathematical Behavior, 4*(2), 157-168.

Lampert, M. (1988). *Teachers' thinking about students' thinking about geometry: The effects of new teaching tools* (Technical Report TR88-1). Cambridge, MA: Harvard University, Educational Technology Center.

Lampert, M. (in press). *Reinterpreting mathematics: An experiment in teacher education* (Technical Report). East Lansing: Michigan State University, National Center for Research on Teacher Education.

Leinhardt, G., & Putnam, R.T. (1987). The skill of learning from classroom lessons. *American Educational Research Journal, 24*, 557-587.

Lesh, R. (1985). Conceptual analysis of mathematical ideas and problem solving processes. In L. Streefland (Ed.), *Procedings of the Ninth International Conference for the Psychology of Mathematics Education* (Vol. 2, pp. 73-97). Utrecht, The Netherlands: University of Utrecht, Research Group on Mathematics Education and Educational Computer Center, Subfaculty of Mathematics.

Mead, G.H. (1934). *Mind, self, and society*. (Charles W. Morris, Ed.). Chicago: University of Chicago Press.

Nesher, P. (1986). Are mathematical understanding and algorithmic performance related? *For the Learning of Mathematics, 6*(3), 2-9.

Palincsar, A.S. (1986). The role of dialogue in providing scaffolded instruction. *Educational Psychologist, 21*(1, 2), 73-98.

Peters, R.S. (1967). *Ethics and education.* Atlanta: Scott Foresman.

Polya, G. (1954). *Mathematics and plausible reasoning. Volume 1: Introduction and analogy in mathematics.* Princeton, NJ: Princeton University Press.

Putnam, R.T., & Leinhardt, G. (1986). *Curriculum scripts and the adjustment of content in mathematics lessons.* Paper presented at the annual meeting of the American Educational Research Association, San Francisco.

Resnick, L.B. (in press). Constructing knowledge in school. In L.S. Liben & D.H. Feldman (Eds.), *Development and learning: Conflict or congruence?* Hillsdale, NJ: Erlbaum.

Resnick, L.B., & Omanson, S.F. (1987). Learning to understand arithmetic. In R. Glaser (Ed.), *Advances in instructional psychology* (Vol. 3). Hillsdale, NJ: Erlbaum.

Sarason, S. (1971). *The culture of school and the problem of change.* New York: Allyn and Bacon.

Schoenfeld, A. (1987). Confessions of an accidental theorist. *For the Learning of Mathematics, 7*(1), 30-38.

Schoenfeld, A. (in press). On mathematics as sense-making: An informal attack on the unfortunate divorce of formal and informal mathematics. In D.N. Perkins, J. Segal, & J. Voss (Eds.), *Informal reasoning and education.* Hillsdale, NJ: Erlbaum.

Shulman, L.S. (1987). Knowledge and teaching: Foundations of a new reform. *Harvard Educational Review, 57,* 1-22.

Vergnaud, G. (1983). Multiplicative structures. In R. Lesh & M. Landau (Eds.), *Acquisition of mathematical concepts and processes* (pp. 127-168). New York: Academic Press.

von Glasersfeld, E. (1983). Learning as a constructive activity. In J.C. Bergeron & N. Herskovics (Eds.), *Proceedings of the Fifth Annual Meeting, North America Chapter of the International Group for the Psychology of Mathematics Education* (Vol. 1, pp. 41-69). Montreal: Universite de Montreal, Faculte des Sciences de l'Education.

Vygotsky, L.S. (1962). *Thought and language.* Cambridge, MA: MIT Press.

Whitney, H. (1985). Taking responsibility in school mathematics education. In L. Streefland (Ed.), *Proceedings of the Ninth International Conference for the Psychology of Mathematics Education* (Vol. 2, pp. 123-141). Utrecht, The Netherlands: University of Utrecht, Research Group on Mathematics Education and Educational Computer Center, Subfaculty of Mathematics.

Zarrinnia, E.A., Lamon, S.J., & Romberg, T.A. (1987, March). *Epistemic teaching of social mathematics.* Program Report 87-3. School Mathematics Mointoring Center, University of Wisconsin School of Education, Madison.

*   *   *

CROSS-TALK

What is the distinction between approaches to teaching that focus on *content* and those that focus on *process*?

In mathematics, truth is established and new knowledge is acquired through a process of mathematical reasoning. The purpose of the representational tools which I used to teach the lessons described was to enable students to do such mathematical reasoning to arrive at their answers. If they could "prove" to themselves and to one another that one decimal number was larger than another by reference to the meaning of those numbers, then they would be "self-regulated" in the sense that they would not need to ask the teacher or check with the answer book to see if their answers were correct. This is learning in the school classroom about processes that are used in the discipline of mathematics. It is not learning to be self-regulated, except in the sense that mathematics is a discipline in which deductive proof is an acceptable kind of argument. It *is* learning content in the sense that it is learning how mathematics is done. What the students are expected to know at the end of the lessons is *how to figure out* whether one decimal number is larger than another using mathematical strategies rather than mechanical ones, and *how to know whether the answer is correct* using mathematical warrants rather than asking the teacher. The content is the process and the process is the content.

What is the conflict between the authoritative role of the teacher and the devolution of intellectual authority to students?

This conflict is one that teachers (in school and out) have recognized for a long time; it is coming to the fore again because of currently popular cognitive theories of learning which cast the learner as a "constructor" of knowledge, but it is also familiar in the dialogues of Plato, the ruminations of Rousseau, and the writings of Dewey. The teacher who has subject matter expertise, a responsibility for heading classroom discourse in a publicly agreed on direction, and the job of managing the social arrangements in a large group of learners who are compelled to be present cannot turn over the agenda to students. The teacher chooses both the subject matter to be studied and the modes of representation that will be used to communicate that subject matter to students. At the same time, the agenda for learning belongs to each individual learner, and each makes his or her own meaning out of whatever the teacher presents.

In the lessons I have described, I attempted to manage this fundamental teaching dilemma by taking on the job of enabling students to construct legitimate mathematical meaning for the numerical and relational symbols in their world. They *did* not, and I would speculate that they *would* not, choose to undertake such an endeavor independently. I was teaching them both how to make mathematical meaning and that it is important and intellectually satisfying to do so, hopefully engendering their commitment to the activity of meaning making in the process. But the symbols and relationships which were the focus of this activity are given by the culture in which we (teacher and students) live. As a competent adult in that culture, I was making a judgment about what I should exercise my authority about. Being able to compare decimal numbers is a piece of mathematical knowledge that underlies both theory and applications, and if students are to go on to participate in the use of mathematics as adults, they need to be able to do that.

As for making decisions about which representations would best support students' understanding, I have no doubt that I did not make the ideal decisions, considered from each learner's point of view, and thus that I in some sense "rode roughshod" over their attempts to understand. But I also have confidence that I did the best that I could, short of an individual tutorial relationship with each member of the class. My choices were based on knowing fifth graders, knowing the particular difficulties these fifth graders were having with the content, and knowing the content well enough to design representations of its most salient features.

Which brings me to the next issue.

How could one learn to teach mathematics the way you do? What would it take for a teacher to teach like you have described? What knowledge would be required? And how could it be learned? What do you think are the prospects for ordinary teachers without specialized mathematical training to teach in ways that are generally similar to what you have described?

My response to these questions is speculative, but based on my work as a teacher educator and teacher advisor over the past fifteen years. The issue that is raised here is an extremely complex one, asking nothing less than "What should be the 'ideal' relationship among: people who understand and work in and with disciplinary knowledge; people who design curriculum; people who design instructional processes; teachers; and learners of a discipline who are not yet of an age to choose their life's work?"

For the sake of promoting a continuing conversation about this question, I would submit that in order to teach mathematics the way I do, someone would need to learn mathematics, learn the pedagogical implications of the sort of discipline mathematics is, and learn how to act on that knowledge in a classroom full of learners who are compelled to be present. Of mathematics, one would need to know the meaning of the basic operations and relationships in and among numbers, shapes, and measurements; and the nature of mathematical argument, i.e., how truth is established in the discipline. Of pedagogy, one would need to be able to move around in the mathematical territory where the topic of a lesson might reside, and do that moving around in response to students' assertions, questions, and confusions; at each "stop" along the way, one would need to refer to or invent a store of representations of key ideas, also in response to students; and one would need to know some routines for conducting group activities in ways that were both safe for all participants and productive of mathematical learning.

And I would submit further that the "how to" knowledge (as contrasted with mathematical and pedagogical knowledge) necessary for such teaching might most appropriately be acquired by watching poeople who do it, talking with them about what has occurred in a particular lesson, having someone who does it watch your teaching, and conferring about that as well. Here I clearly take a stand for the art and craft view of teaching and learning to teach. I do not mean to imply that "scientific" knowledge is not useful to teachers. Rather I am making a statement about the sort of institutional relationships that might exist for delivering that knowledge to novices. I should think it would make some difference if scientific knowledge about learning and teaching for understanding were delivered by someone who has used it and found it useful. This method of conveying usable or practiceable knowledge is found in many professions from pure mathematics to cabinetmaking. It does not deny the usefulness of scientific knowledge produced by researchers to being productive in these fields, but it puts such knowledge in a different perspective.

My exploratory research suggests that one can teach children to understand mathematics without identifying isolated strategies and teaching them the strategies *apart from* reasoning and argument about some element of the discipline, like whether one decimal number is smaller than, larger than, or equal to another. Research is yet to be done that will establish empirically whether understanding mathematics is a useful kind of knowledge for teachers to have; such research would be difficult to conduct, at least in part because preservice and inservice education as they now stand are rarely organized to enable teachers to study the subject matter they will be teaching at a level that would support understanding. It is easy to teach strategies within the institutional arrangements that now exist in teacher education; we should not let this ease lower our expectations of what could occur if those institutional arrangements were different. My argument about what teachers need to know *about mathematics* to teach mathematics for understanding is rhetorical: it seems difficult to imagine that someone could teach mathematics for understanding without understanding the mathematics they are attemping to teach.

In response to the question about whether "ordinary teachers without specialized mathematical training" can learn to teach in ways that are similar to what is described in my chapter, I would say that the understanding of decimal numbers, place value, ratio and proportion, number symbols and representations that underlies this teaching is not understanding that would be acquired during "specialized mathematical training." This understanding can, and might I say should, be acquired in elementary school. As for knowledge about how truth is established in the discipline, it could be acquired in secondary school if the course in geometry were taught as if understanding (rather than memorizing) proofs was the goal of instruction. With this sort of "lower" education as a foundation for professional education in teaching, teacher education could focus on providing novices with knowledge about how to represent their understanding to learners.

An alternative to teachers acquiring understanding of the subject matter they are supposed to teach, and one that is embraced by several of the programs described in this volume, is to have designers of curriculum and instruction distill "strategies" from their analyses of expertise in a discipline, and deliver those to practitioners in preservice and inservice education. This approach is more economical, to be sure. There are two reasons why I hesitate to embrace this approach. One is the many hours I have spent observing teachers who can mimic the strategies they are taught, but come nowhere close to communicating to students the character of the disciplinary context (e.g., the writing process) from which those strategies were distilled. The other is that the research that has been done on the effectiveness of such strategies has been done with failing readers, beginning primary school students, and poor writers. Even if such strategies can get teachers to be successful at having students understand and be self-directed at this level, I wonder if the same kinds of strategies can be carried over to having students understand ratio and proportion, or algebra, or the novel, or to enabling them to write analytic prose of the sort that academics depend on for communication? If "experts" at these endeavors are queried, I wonder if such a clear list of enabling strategies would emerge from an attempt to understand how they do their work.

TEACHING FOR MEANINGFUL AND SELF-REGULATED LEARNING OF SCIENCE

Charles W. Anderson and Kathleen J. Roth

Teacher: *Do you understand?*
Student: *Yes.*

Exchanges like this take place many times in science classrooms. We have noticed that students almost always answer "Yes" when asked if they understand; yet the students' reassurances generally do not end our uncertainty about the state of their knowledge. "Understanding" of science is an elusive concept; it can mean different things to different people.

We, therefore, begin this paper with an exploration of the nature of scientific understanding in in-school and out-of-school contexts. The second section of the chapter focuses on the learning of science, reporting on our investigations of how students come to achieve understanding and the circumstances that facilitate their success. Finally, we discuss our investigations of science classroom teaching, reporting what we have learned and what we still have to learn about teaching for scientific understanding.

Advances in Research on Teaching, Volume 1, pages 265-309.
ISBN: 0-89232-845-2

UNDERSTANDING SCIENCE

Our work is based on a set of theories and beliefs about the nature of student understanding. Our analysis of scientific understanding has two components. One focuses on the *functions* or uses of scientific knowledge: The activities that successful learners of science are prepared to engage in. The other component of our analysis focuses on the *structure* of scientific knowledge: The interconnections that successful learners of science are able to make among scientific knowledge, other realms of knowledge, and their own personal understanding of the world.

This dual analysis draws on two different research traditions, each of which provides insights into the nature of scientific understanding. The functional analysis draws on research in fields such as linguistics, anthropology, and social constructivist psychology (cf. Resnick, 1987; Rogoff & Lave, 1984; Toulmin, 1972; Vygotsky, 1962). This analysis focuses on knowledge as it is embodied in observable forms such as tools and text, and in people's speech and behavior in social contexts. The structural analysis draws on research on misconceptions and conceptual change in science learning (cf. Anderson & Smith, 1987; West & Pines, 1985). Research in these traditions has shown how our conceptual and procedural knowledge is organized into complex systems that have multiple levels of meaning. Thus each analysis captures something of what we mean by "understanding."

A Functional Analysis of Scientific Understanding

What do people *do* with scientific knowledge? Inside classrooms, the answer to this question is often quite simple: They answer questions, usually recall questions. They may answer these questions in class "discussions," from the textbook, or on tests. In classrooms where the activity of answering recall questions plays a dominant role, this activity often becomes the basis for students' operational definitions of scientific understanding. Students who say that they "understand" a topic or a chapter often mean that they are prepared to answer recall questions about it; in their experience, this is the sole or primary function of scientific knowledge.

Outside of school classrooms, however, people use scientific knowledge to engage in a wide variety of activities that are generally more complex, more useful, and more under the control of the actors than the question-answering that predominates in school classrooms. We have found it useful to think of the activities of scientifically literate people in terms of four general categories: description, explanation, prediction, and control of real-world systems or events. These classes of activities are described below.[1]

- *Description.* Scientific knowledge is often used for purposes that are essentially descriptive in nature: Providing names for things, measuring them, classifying them, or describing them. The ability to provide precise and accurate names, descriptions, or measurements of natural systems or phenomena is one characteristic of a scientifically literate adult.
- *Explanation.* Toulmin (1961, 1972) emphasized explanation as a primary goal of science. We acquire scientific knowledge and develop theories because we want to explain how the world around us works. Thus a scientifically literate person should be able to use scientific knowledge to explain natural phenomena. Explanation is the function of scientific knowledge that has been emphasized most heavily in our work and other "misconceptions" research, most of which can be viewed as investigating the nature of good explanations and the knowledge necessary to produce them (cf. Hesse & Anderson, 1988; West & Pines, 1985).
- *Prediction.* The ability to generate accurate predictions is a key test of the validity of a scientific theory as well as an important use of scientific knowledge. Thus, scientifically literate adults often use their scientific knowledge to generate predictions about future observations or events.
- *Control.* Control of natural systems and phenomena is more a function of technology than of science per se. Scientific knowledge, however, plays an essential role in the development and use of technology, and many of the justifications for teaching science in our schools concern the development of technological competence and knowledge essential for making decisions about technological issues among workers and citizens.

When Are These Activities "Scientific?"

Even people who know little or nothing about science are capable of describing, explaining, making predictions, and controlling the world around them. Thus scientific knowledge is not necessary for these activities. However, scientific knowledge enables its possessors to engage in these activities in ways that are in several respects different from and arguably "better" than the attempts of those who lack scientific knowledge.

Scientific knowledge provides us with a wide array of conceptual and technological tools. People who use these tools—the language, theories, and instruments of science—are capable of describing, explaining, making predictions about, or controlling the world with a precision, a power, and a depth of understanding that would be impossible otherwise. Furthermore, the tools of science provide their possessors with access to the community of scientists and to the knowledge and power that community possesses. There is no clear line of demarcation between "scientific" and "unscientific" description, explanation, prediction, and control. People engage in these activities scientifically to the extent that they use the conceptual and technological tools of science to increase the power and precision of their performance.

These thoughts suggest a view of the science curriculum in which students develop a progressively deeper understanding of science by using scientific knowledge to engage in these activities. Children enter school already describing, explaining, predicting, and trying to control the world around them, although often in ways that lack power and precision. We would like to see school science focus on increasing the power and precision with which children engage in these important activities, rather than on developing students' abilities to recall scientific facts.

In the early elementary grades, this may sometimes mean that school science is not recognizably "scientific." Young children who have not fully mastered the conceptual and technological tools provided by our common cultural heritage (for example, color names or simple measurement techniques) may need to develop these tools before acquiring specialized scientific knowledge. However, as the children's descriptions, explanations, predictions, and strategies for controlling the world around them become more sophisticated, and as they encounter a wider range of phenomena, they need to use an increasingly wide range of scientific concepts and theories. Those concepts and theories will be meaningful to the students if they can use them successfully to describe, predict, explain, and control the world.

Functions of Scientific Knowledge In the Classroom

Most of our research studies during the last seven years have involved observation and analysis of the activities of teachers and students in science classrooms; the results of that research are reported in a series of papers. A number of those papers report case studies of individual teachers and their students (Anderson, Belt, Gamalski, & Greminger, 1987; Eaton, Anderson, & Smith, 1984; Hollon & Anderson, 1987; Roth, 1984, 1987; Roth, Anderson, & Smith, 1987; Singer, Anderson & Smith, 1983; Smith & Anderson, 1984; Smith & Sendelbach, 1982). Other papers report quantitative frequencies of various types of teacher behavior (Anderson & Smith, 1983; Blakeslee, Anderson, & Smith, 1987). Although a wide variety of analytical systems and categories were used in developing those reports, the research in toto warrants several generalizations about the activities of teachers and students in science classrooms.

The most important of these generalizations is that in our naturalistic observations (that is, observations of classrooms where we have not intervened), we have rarely seen teaching that engaged students in using scientific knowledge in the ways that scientifically literate adults do. Students in most classrooms are *not* practicing scientific description, explanation, prediction, and control. Instead, we have seen a variety of instructional patterns, each of which is inadequate in some crucial respect.

Many teachers, for example, teach students about the conceptual tools of science—facts, words, and theories—but do not teach students how to use those tools. In these classrooms, students are generally exposed to large numbers of facts and vocabulary words, tested for recall, and moved on to the next topic (cf. Eaton et al., 1984; Hollon & Anderson, 1987). The facts and vocabulary words are considered to be "understood" when students can provide or recognize definitions of them. These facts are rarely used for the purposes of describing, explaining, predicting, or controlling the real world.

This instructional pattern is sometimes justified, implicitly or explicitly, by the assertion that students need to learn "basic facts" before moving on to "higher-order thinking." Teachers argue that they can expose students to these facts and concepts early on, but that students will develop meaningful understandings of these ideas only later, when they are capable of abstract thinking.

A functional analysis of scientific reasoning reveals that this is an empty rationalization. In fact, children begin to engage in the activities labeled as "higher-order thinking"—description, explanation, prediction, and control of the world around them—*before* they learn to memorize facts and reproduce them on demand. In fact, students who are made to memorize and reproduce facts are practicing an activity that has little in common with meaningful uses of scientific knowledge.

Although the instructional pattern described above is a common one, it is generally recognized by professional educators as inadequate. In most of our research we have focused not on obviously inadequate instructional practices, but on the practices of skilled, experienced teachers who are thoughtful in their planning and teaching (cf. Anderson et al., 1987; Hollon & Anderson, 1987; Roth, 1984, 1987; Singer et al., 1983; Smith & Anderson, 1984). Even these teachers often fail to do all that is necessary to help their students acquire a full functional understanding of science.

A common instructional pattern in the classrooms of skilled and experienced science teachers is one in which the *teacher* engages in description, explanation, and prediction (less commonly control) during lectures and discussions, but not the students. The students witness the teacher's performance and often participate in it in a limited way, providing important words or bits of information as requested by the teacher. However, they do not practice the activities independently. Thus, in these classrooms the students are exposed to coherent models of scientific description, explanation, and prediction, but, as in the fact-oriented classrooms, students practice primarily the activity of producing small bits of information on demand.

Our research indicates that under these circumstances a few students are able to rehearse spontaneously the activities that the teacher engages in and to monitor their own performance, thus successfully engaging in the activities themselves. For these students the pattern of instruction described above is sufficient to produce a functional understanding of science. Most students, however, seem to master only the simpler and more limited repertoire of activities that they practice themselves, not the more complex and meaningful activities modeled by the teacher.

Thus, a functional analysis of scientific understanding provides both insight into students' scientific cognition and a useful conceptual tool for analyzing curriculum and instruction in science classrooms.

A Structural Analysis of Scientific Understanding

In this section we have developed a functional criterion for scientific understanding: Briefly, *understanding consists of the ability to use scientific knowledge to describe, explain, predict, and control the world around us.* By itself, however, this criterion does not provide an adequate basis for analyzing the teaching and learning of science because it says little about the organizational or structural characteristics of the knowledge that is used to perform these activities. Those structural characteristics are discussed below.

In discussing the *structure* of scientific knowledge we use the terms structure and function in a way analogous to the biological usage of those terms.[2] Like biological systems, systems of scientific knowledge are highly structured or organized, but not in the static, simplistic way that the term "structure" connotes for some people (e.g., Phillips, 1986). We view the structures of scientific knowledge as the same as biological structures, as dynamic and constantly changing. Systems of scientific knowledge are also like biological systems in that multiple structures or patterns of organization exist within a single system. It is difficult to discuss "the" structure of scientific knowledge not because it lacks structure, but because it is highly structured in so many different ways.

Systems of scientific knowledge and biological systems are also analogous in that structure and function are inextricably intertwined. For example, it makes no sense to think of biological functions (such as breathing) without considering the structures (such as lungs) that perform those functions. Conversely, biological structures cannot be understood without reference to the functions that they perform. Similarly, we cannot analyze functions of scientific knowledge such as description and explanation without reference to the conceptual structures that make those activities possible. Neither can we understand the conceptual structures without reference to the functions or activities for which they are used.

Structural Characteristics of Scientific Understanding

All our research on the teaching and learning of science has included analysis of structural characteristics of students' knowledge. In particular, we have compared structural characteristics of the knowledge of students who have achieved greater or lesser degrees of understanding of a variety of scientific topics, including respiration and photosynthesis (Anderson, Roth, Hollon, & Blakeslee, 1987; Anderson, Sheldon, & DuBay, 1986; Roth & Anderson, 1987; Roth, Smith, & Anderson, 1983), light and vision (Anderson & Smith, 1987; Eaton, Harding, & Anderson, 1986), ecological matter cycling (Smith & Anderson, 1986), chemical reactions (Hesse & Anderson, 1988), evolution by natural selection (Bishop & Anderson, 1986), and the kinetic molecular theory (Berkheimer, Anderson, Lee, & Blakeslee, in press; Eichinger & Lee, 1988). We have often presented the findings of these studies in tables such as Table 1. Our research in this respect is part of a tradition of research on naive conceptions of scientific topics (cf. Driver, Guesne, & Tiberghien, 1985; West & Pines, 1985).

We have not attempted, in Table 1 or in our other research, to develop models that provide complete or general descriptions of students' knowledge of a scientific topic such as photosynthesis. Rather, we have attempted to summarize some of the most salient differences between the thinking of students (in this case middle school students) who have achieved a satisfactory understanding of the process of photosynthesis and the thinking of students who have not achieved such understanding (for a more complete analysis, see Roth & Anderson, 1987).

Although topic-specific analyses like the one summarized in Table 1 should play a necessary role in the development of science curriculum and instruction, it is also possible to make some general statements about how students understand different scientific concepts. The "goal conceptions" column in Table 1 depicts some key elements of a deep and powerful understanding of photosynthesis at the middle school level. This understanding has at least two characteristics that generalize to the understanding of other topics at other levels, and that are often lacking in students' understanding of science concepts.

First, the goal conceptions listed in Table 1, are integrated into a complex network of scientific concepts that are useful for the important functions of science. Many students "learn" science by memorizing large amounts of information in simple, list-like forms. While these list-like structures are useful for some limited purposes (such as answering recall questions), they are of little use for the more complex functions of description, explanation, prediction, and control. Any one of these complex functions requires the integration of multiple concepts; conversely, any given concept can be used for multiple functions. Scientific understanding, in other words, requires extensive conceptual integration and an ability to work out the complex relationships between structure and function.

Table 1. Student Versus Scientific Conceptions Related to Photosynthesis

Issue	Scientific Conception	Student Conception
1. Plants' source of food	Plants make their own food internally using carbon dioxide, water, and sun in a process called photosynthesis.	Plants take in their food from the outside environment.
2. Germinating plants' source of food	Plants store extra food made during photosynthesis in the cotyledon of seeds. This is the initial food for germinating plants.	The seed is one of many sources of food for growing plant.
3. Function of light for plants	Plants need sunlight to make food.	Plants need sun to live, grow, be green. (No notion of energy being absorbed, needed, or changed.)
4. Importance of photosynthesis for plants	Photosynthesis is plants' *only* source of food.	Plants have *multiple* sources of food. Photosynthesis is not important to plants—it is something they do for the benefit of people/animals.

Second, students who achieve a rich understanding of a scientific topic have successfully integrated accurate scientific knowledge with their own personal knowledge of the world. Many students fail to do this; they view scientific knowledge as separate and distinct from their personal knowledge. They perceive scientific knowledge as being about objects that are too small, too distant, too abstract, or too unusual to be part of the everyday world; such as atoms, quasars, momentum, or strange chemicals. Thus science becomes, for these students, a list of strange and obscure facts rather than a system of conceptual tools for understanding the world around them. In contrast, successful learners of science develop clear conceptual linkages between scientific conceptions and their "common sense" understandings. The two fit together into a single integrated understanding of the world.

Students also fail to see the connections between personal and scientific knowledge because their personal understandings are often different from, and sometimes incompatible with, scientific understandings of the world. The elucidation of students' "alternative frameworks" (also labeled misconceptions, naive conceptions, and so forth) has been a major research focus in our own work and in the work of many others (cf. Driver & Erickson, 1983; Osborne & Freyberg, 1985; West & Pines, 1985). The general picture that emerges from this research is one that shows students almost always entering instruction with ways of understanding that are substantially different from scientific understanding, as shown in Table 1. Thus learning science, for most students, involves a complex process of *conceptual change.*

Structural Characteristics of Knowledge in Science Classrooms

The above discussion of characteristics of scientific understanding suggests a second set of criteria by which science classroom teaching can be evaluated: To what extent does science teaching help students to develop knowledge that has the structural characteristics of scientific understanding?

Our observational studies of science classrooms suggest that most teachers are especially concerned about helping students develop knowledge that is faithful to scientific conceptions, and that they generally find ways to make sure that the information presented to students is scientifically accurate. Even teachers who know very little science manage to accomplish this by depending heavily on textbooks and films (which are generally scientifically accurate) as sources of information for students, rather than trying to present it themselves.

However, scientific knowledge is typically presented to students without concern for integrating that knowledge with students' personal knowledge and without the rich conceptual coherence needed to make the knowledge useful in explaining real-world phenomena. For example, some teachers present scientific information in a list-like form, with little conceptual awareness of or interest in students' personal knowledge. Thus they present science to students as a collection of facts and skills that are isolated from each other and from students' personal knowledge of the world (e.g., Mr. Armstrong in Hollon & Anderson, 1987).

Other teachers present scientific information in a manner that is highly integrated conceptually and that demonstrates considerable awareness and understanding of their students' prior knowledge (e.g., Mr. Barnes in Roth, 1987). Even in these classrooms, however, students are rarely asked to speak or write about relationships among concepts, uses of scientific knowledge, or relationships between scientific knowledge and their personal knowledge. Thus, the teacher displays well-integrated knowledge to students, but students are not actively engaged in constructing such knowledge themselves.

Mr. Barnes was typical of many of those teachers in that he was aware that his students generally were not achieving a full understanding of the knowledge that he presented. He felt that his teaching practices were justified, however, for several reasons. First, he was not sure that most of his students were capable of achieving a conceptually integrated, functional understanding. He also saw a conflict between his desire to present a full and accurate picture of science and the slow and confusing process of working through students' imperfect expressions of their own ideas. Mr. Barnes resolved these dilemmas by presenting his students with a coherent and complete picture of science, but expecting from them a much less fully integrated understanding. Our research suggests that other resolutions to Mr. Barnes' dilemma are possible.

Summary: The Nature of Scientific Understanding

We began this chapter with a puzzle: Why do so many students claim to "understand" scientific topics in situations where it seems to us that they do not? The discussion in this section suggests at least a partial solution to that puzzle. The students, we believe, are often answering honestly, and in a way that is consistent with the nature of school science as they have experienced it. In most classrooms the primary function of scientific knowledge (for the students if not for the teacher) is to answer recall questions. Students can often succeed in this task by memorizing simple lists of words and facts. In this task environment, it is not surprising that many students define "understanding" in terms of their ability to reduce knowledge of a scientific topic to a list of facts that can be memorized.

A look at how science is used in the real world, however, suggests that scientifically literate adults need a form of scientific understanding that is much more complex and difficult to achieve. In particular, we suggest that students' science learning can be considered progress toward full scientific literacy only if it meets two criteria. The first of these is functional: *Students should develop knowledge that is useful for the essential functions of describing, explaining, predicting, and controlling the world around us.* The second criterion is structural: *Students should develop knowledge that is conceptually coherent and integrated with their personal knowledge of the world,* as well as being scientifically accurate. Although these criteria seem reasonable and straightforward, they are rarely achieved in typical science classrooms.

This chapter began with a discussion of the nature of scientific understanding because of the important, although hidden, role that implicit definitions of understanding often play in science classrooms. They affect not only students' answers to questions about their understanding, but also the entire process of learning, in ways that are examined in the next section.

LEARNING SCIENCE

This section is devoted primarily to discussing the results of a single study (Roth, 1985, 1987), in which we analyzed the strategies that different students used to learn science and the nature of the learning that resulted. The study provided critical insights about ways in which students' learning goals and strategies were influenced by the nature of academic tasks embedded in their textbooks, and, in turn, ways in which students' learning goals and strategies influenced (and often constrained) the kinds of scientific understanding they developed.

The study investigated student learning from science text. Nineteen middle school students were divided into three groups using a stratified random sampling procedure, so that each group consisted of students reading above, below, and at grade level. Students in each group took a pretest that assessed their understanding of photosynthesis. They then read about photosynthesis over a three-day period. Each day, the students read a section of text and answered in writing any questions posed by the text, then met with a researcher for a clinical interview. The clinical interviews had two parts, one eliciting students' recall of the text and their strategies for learning from the text, and the other probing students' explanations about how plants get their food. After the three days of reading, students took a posttest that was identical to the pretest.

Each group read a different text chapter about photosynthesis. The three texts were similar in length (about 3400 words, or 20 pages each) and in reading level (grade levels of 5 to 6 according to the Fry readability formula). They were also matched with regard to content coverage. Two of the text passages were excerpted from standard commercial textbooks: *Concepts in Science* (Brandwein et al., 1981), and *Modern Science* (Smith, Blecha, & Pless, 1974). The third group read an experimental text that incorporated a variety of features designed to enhance conceptual change learning (Roth, 1985).

The results of the study are summarized in Table 2. The experimental text was obviously more successful than the commercial texts in promoting learning of the scientific conceptions listed in Table 1 (and of other scientific conceptions). The most important results of this study, however, lie not in the posttest results, but in the knowledge gained about how different students approached the task of learning science from these school texts and about the role that the students' learning goals played in their reading of the text. These results are summarized in the column of Table 2 labeled "Reading Strategy."

The choice of reading strategy was the primary determinant of success on the posttest (see Table 2). Students who used Reading Strategy 5, conceptual change sense-making, were successful on the posttest regardless of the text that they were using; students who used other reading strategies were not. In the remainder of this section, we describe the kinds of conceptual change that these students needed to undergo in order to develop well-structured and functional understandings of photosynthesis. Descriptions of the successes and failures of different learning strategies in achieving this kind of understanding are then provided.

Table 2. Learning Outcomes

Text	Student	Dominant Learning Strategy	Reading Level	Plants make food, do not take it in	Learning of Goal Concepts		
					Need light to make food	Get food only by making it	Get food from seeds at first
Experimental	Daryl	5	3.4	+	+	+	−
	Evalina	5	5.6	+	+	+	+
	Allison	mixed	7.6	−	+	−	+
	Doug	5	8.1	+	+	+	+
	Vera	5	8.6	+	+	+	+
	James	5	11.3	+	+	+	+
	Sheila	5	PHS	+	+	+	+
Concepts in Science	Jill	2	4.0	*	*	*	NA
	Maria	1	4.0	−	−	−	NA
	Myra	3	6.0	−	−	−	NA
	Phil	4	6.0	−	+	−	NA
	Deborah	4	10.0	−	+	−	NA
	Parker	4	PHS	−	−	−	NA
Modern Science	Linda	1	4.5	−	−	−	−
	Tracey	1	5.6	−	−	−	−
	Danny	3	7.1	−	+	−	−
	Sally	4	8.4	−	+	−	−
	Kevin	4	12.6	−	+	−	+
	Susan	5	12.6	+	+	+	+

Key to Learning of Food Concepts: + = understood the concept
                                      − = did not understand the concept
                                      NA = not addressed in this text
                                      * = did not take posttest

Key to Learning Strategies: 1. Procedural display based on prior knowledge
                               2. Procedural display based on big words
                               3. Learning lists of facts
                               4. Egocentric sense-making
                               5. Conceptual change sense-making

276

Understanding Photosynthesis: The Need for Conceptual Change

What does it mean to understand photosynthesis? What conceptual change do students need to undergo to develop such understandings?

Most middle school teachers would like students to understand that photosynthesis is the process by which green plants make their own food, using carbon dioxide, water, and light energy. In special chlorophyll-containing cells in their leaves, plants transform carbon dioxide and water taken in from the environment into *food* (specifically glucose), which is needed for growth and life processes. Because photosynthesis is virtually the only food-making process available to living things, animals as well as plants are dependent on photosynthesis for their food.

The pretest revealed that all 19 students began the study with beliefs more like those in the "naive conceptions" column of Table 1 than like those in the "goal conceptions" column. These results did not surprise us; we knew from previous research that most students begin the study of photosynthesis with some deeply held, although largely unexamined, beliefs about how organisms obtain and use food in ways that are somehow analogous to those of the organisms they are most familiar with: Human beings.

Middle school students begin the study of photosynthesis already knowing a great deal about food, especially food for people, and they bring these associations to bear on their interpretations of explanations about how plants make their own food. Below are listed several beliefs about food that students commonly hold:

1. Food is something that you consume or eat; so it is taken in from the outside environment.
2. There are many different kinds of food.
3. Food gives you energy.
4. Food helps you grow.
5. Food is necessary for life.

These beliefs about food are not entirely wrong. The last three beliefs listed are all essentially correct, and the third belief—that food supplies energy— identifies the key element in most scientific definitions of food (i.e., that food contains organic materials which provide chemical potential energy for metabolism).[3] However, the implicit analogy between plants and people leads students to assume that, like people, plants must take in food from their environment in many different forms. These beliefs are incorrect. Green plants have a unique ability to make energy-containing food out of non-energy containing matter that they take in from their environment. In the process, they transform light energy from the sun into chemical potential energy stored in food and available for use by plants and animals. The matter that plants take in (carbon dioxide, water, and soil minerals) is not food in this sense.

To understand photosynthesis, students must go through a complex process of conceptual change. They must abandon their assumptions about the metabolic similarities between plants and humans and restructure their thinking about the nature of food. In this restructuring process, they must learn that the first two beliefs about food do not generalize from humans to plants while allowing the third belief to take on a new importance and meaning. This belief needs to be clarified, expanded, and given new prominence. Without this involved process of restructuring and integration of personal knowledge with scientific knowledge, students cannot be successful in using knowledge about photosynthesis to make reasonable predictions and explanations of real-world phenomena. One student who succeeded in working her way through this conceptual change process was Evalina.

Conceptual Change Sense-making: Successful Science Learning

Evalina's Learning

Like all of the students in the study, Evalina began with the everyday beliefs about food described above. On the pretest, she identified water as one of plants' main foods. She also described plants as having multiple kinds of food that they take in from the environment: Water, sunlight, air, fertilizer, and soil. She had no idea that plants make their own food and defined food as what organisms need "to live." As she read the experimental text and participated in the interviews, Evalina came to see her ways of thinking about food for plants as problematic. After reading on Day 1 about the distinction between energy-containing food and non-energy-containing matter, for example, Evalina recognized that her belief that water is a critical food for plants was worth questioning:

> I: So where does the plant get its food then?
> E: Where does the plant get its food? I don't know. From the water. I think from the water.
> I: Do you think food for plants is the same as food for animals?
> E: Well, some animals they drink water . . . and plants, they drink water, too.
> I: Okay. So that's food for plants and animals? It's the same?
> E: (Pause). Water isn't food. I learned that much! (laughs). If water isn't food then what is the, what kinds of food is it for the plant? But I know that my mother, she gives water to her plants. . . . And animals have water, too. I'm sure they do. I don't know.

After the third day of reading, Evalina had resolved this conflict between her personal views and scientific views, and she had begun using her newly structured knowledge to make predictions and explanations of phenomena. For example, when asked what would happen if a box covered a plant so that only one leaf could get light, she gave the following answer:

> I think that the ones that's under the box, it would start to die because it needs some light down on it to help it make food. And the one that's probably out in the light, it would probably help feed the plant that's under the box, because if the food is going down the stem like that, it probably would extend to some of the other leaves. But if it didn't, then those under the box, they probably wouldn't live that long, and the one's that out, it would.

Evalina's written answers to questions on the posttest reveal similar changes in the nature of her understanding:

Q: Describe what *food* is for plants.
E: Plants make thier [sic] own food from water, sunlight, and air.
Q: Joan planted two bean seeds in good soil and watered them. When the plants were still very small, she put one plant in the sunlight and one plant in the dark.

   T or F   If the cotyledons are cut off, then the plant in the light will stop growing. Explain your answer.

E: False.   Because plants can make thier [sic] own food by air, water, and light.

These answers reveal that Evalina understood photosynthesis not just in the narrow sense of being able to answer recall questions about what she read, but in the deeper sense as discussed above. Whereas her explanations and predictions on the pretest were based on her personal knowledge (which was incorrect in several important respects), on the posttest she successfully used scientific knowledge to explain and make predictions about the world. In making these explanations and predictions, Evalina integrated information about food, water, sunlight, air, transport of materials within plants, and other issues. Clearly, Evalina had successfully worked through a process of conceptual change; she had used scientific knowledge to change her personal ideas about how plants live and get their food.

Evalina's responses to interview questions after Days 1 and 2 reveal a good deal about how this process of conceptual change took place. These interviews show Evalina consistently trying to use scientific knowledge to explain and make predictions about the world. Often, she found the process difficult and confusing, as she encountered areas where her knowledge was incomplete or where there were conflicts between what the text said and her personal knowledge. For example, in the exchange described above, Evalina struggles with the issue of whether water should be considered food for plants. As she tried to explain how plants and animals get food, she ran into problems that made her aware of the need to restructure her personal ways of thinking about food for plants. At first, she ignored the new definition of food that she had memorized from the text and relied only on her personal beliefs. However, as the text continued simultaneously to remind her of the new definition and to engage her in explaining how plants and animals get food, Evalina confronted the need to change her personal beliefs.

Although the interviewers avoided giving the students scientific information, the reexamination of the text and of her own thinking prompted by the interviews sometimes played an important role in advancing Evalina's understanding.[4] For example, on Day 2, in response to one of the text's questions, she had written the following explanation of the results of an experiment in which grass plants in the dark died while the ones in the light lived:

> Because in the dark the plant couldn't breathe I think. And in the sunshine it did.

In the interview Evalina changed this incorrect explanation to one that appropriately used the goal conceptions:

> E: Because they need light so they can grow and help make their food. When they're in the dark, they don't have enough sunlight to help them make their food . . . I think my answer is wrong.
> I: You said they couldn't breathe.
> E: Yeah.
> I: What do you think now?
> E: I think they didn't have enough food in the dark, I *know* they didn't have enough food because they need the light to help them make the food. . . .

In summary, Evalina's learning was a complex, intellectually active process of conceptual change, in which she substantially restructured her understanding of how plants get food as she repeatedly attempted to use her developing understanding to describe, predict, and explain how plants get their food. She found this process difficult and frustrating at times, but she was rewarded through the achievement of a deeper and more satisfying understanding of how plants work. The process was social in nature;[5] it was driven by Evalina's interaction with the text through reading and writing and by her spoken interactions with the interviewer. It was driven by a sense-making goal. She was engaged in a series of problems that seemed real to her: Is my mother feeding the plants when she waters them? If not, then how are they getting their food? With careful support from the experimental text, she was able to pursue meaningful answers to these real-life questions rather than to memorize definitions and equations remote from personal experience.

Conceptual Change Learning In Other Students

The characteristics of Evalina's learning summarized above were shared by the other six students who successfully used the conceptual change learning strategy. As Table 2 indicates, the experimental text clearly helped Evalina and the other students to engage in the appropriate learning strategies and to use them successfully. Some of the characteristics of the experimental text that were responsible for their success are discussed in the section on teaching, below.

The commercial texts obviously provided much less support for conceptual change learning than the experimental text. Nevertheless, one of the 12 students reading the commercial texts, Susan, learned in a way that in most respects paralleled Evalina's learning. Like Evalina, Susan consistently tried to use information from the text to describe and explain plant life processes, monitored the success of her efforts, and worked her way through a process of conceptual restructuring when necessary. The key difference between Evalina and Susan, of course, is that Susan was able to use these learning strategies without explicit prompting and support from the text.[6]

The pattern of results seen in this study has generally been replicated in our studies of learning in classroom contexts (Blakeslee et al., 1987; Eaton et al., 1984; Hesse & Anderson, 1988; Roth, 1984; see also Table 3). Standard classroom teaching is normally about as effective as the commercial texts in this study: A small portion of the students (generally 0-20%), like Susan, spontaneously use conceptual change learning strategies. A much larger portion of the students (generally in the 40-80% range), like Evalina, successfully use conceptual change learning strategies when supported by appropriate materials and teaching methods. When such support is lacking, most students use learning strategies resembling those of the less successful students in the Roth study. Some of the characteristics of their learning strategies and goals are discussed below.

Other Learning Strategies: Settling for Less

The majority of the students in the study, including 11 of the 12 students reading the two commercial texts, did not use conceptual change learning strategies and did not experience significant conceptual change. In this respect they were typical of most students in the conventional science classrooms that we have studied.

These students, however, *felt* successful. They all said that they "understood" the texts that they were reading, and they all succeeded in answering correctly some or all of the questions posed in those texts. In this section we describe how these students were able to succeed in school tasks without changing their misconceptions, and we consider ways in which their learning goals and performance are consistent with the conceptions of scientific understanding that are implicit in the texts that they were reading and in many classroom contexts.

Strategies 1 and 2: Avoiding Learning

The least successful students pursued strategies that enabled them to accomplish some school tasks without actually learning anything at all. The goal driving their reading of the text was not sense-making but completion of school tasks.

Maria, for example, used Strategy 1: Procedural display based on prior knowledge. When she read a section of the *Concepts of Science* text that used milk as an example of how all foods can ultimately be traced back to green plants, the food producers, Maria announced that "most of this stuff I already knew," and that this was the easiest section to understand. "It was about milk." When probed, she expanded her summary of the "text": "It's just about milk . . . how we get our milk from cows." She never made any connection between milk and plants. This is typical of her pattern of reading to find familiar ideas, ignoring the rest of the text, and relying on prior knowledge to fill in the details.

The students using this strategy answered questions posed in the text by using their personal knowledge rather than text knowledge. For example, Maria came up with the right answer to the following question by using her personal knowledge about vegetarians, but without considering plants' role in producing food:

Question: All the food we eat can be traced finally back to the
            (a)   green plants
            (b)   cows

Maria: Correctly picked "a" and explained: I don't know . . . I just circled green plants because everybody eats . . . not everybody eats cows but *everybody* eats green plants.

Students who relied on Strategy 2 also managed to accomplish school tasks without actually learning, but in a different way. In answering text-posed questions, they simply looked for a "big" word in the question, located that word in the text, and copied the word along with words surrounding it in the text. These copied words may or may not have sensibly answered the question, but the students were satisfied just to have an answer. Frequently, this strategy produced answers that would be acceptable to most teachers.

When these students were asked interview questions about real-world plants, they relied totally on their personal knowledge. No relationship was seen between the text and this personal knowledge. Thus, Tracey (who alternated between Strategies 1 and 2) recalled the book being about "chlorophyll" and "photosynthesis," but these words were never mentioned when she was asked about how a particular plant gets its food.

Although the students who relied on Strategies 1 and 2 were not even learning science in the limited sense of being able to answer recall questions, it is interesting to note how often they were successful in answering the questions posed in the two commercial texts. In fact, no knowledge from the texts was needed to answer many of the questions. We do not believe that the authors of these textbooks were incapable of formulating questions that would better assess student understanding. Rather, it seems to us that the easy questions are an intentional characteristic of the texts. The inclusion of more difficult questions would make it obvious that many students did not understand what they had read. This, in turn, would make both students and teachers uncomfortable. Texts that make teachers uncomfortable do not sell well. The questions in science textbooks, therefore, are often written in ways that faciliate *procedural display* (the correct answering of questions so that instruction can proceed; cf. Bloome & Argumedo, 1983) rather than to check student understanding or to aid student learning.

The middle school students using Strategies 1 and 2 found ways of meeting the demand for procedural display without actually learning the intended content. The structure of the texts conveyed the impression that understanding science was a fairly straightforward process. The texts did not encourage students to confront conflicts between personal and scientific knowledge, and the questions posed in them did not engage students in using new knowledge to construct explanations and predictions of real-world phenomena. Thus, students' strategies of ignoring the text or picking out only big words were successful in completing the school tasks, while falling far short of enabling meaningful scientific understanding.

Strategy 3: Learning Lists of Facts and Definitions

The better readers had higher goals for their learning than just finishing assigned work, and they relied on reading strategies that did in fact lead to some learning. Students who relied on Strategy 3, however, learned in a way that was more consistent with the restricted definition of scientific understanding that is implicit in many science classrooms and in the two commercial texts than with the fuller conception of scientific understanding developed in the first section of this chapter.

While students using Strategy 2 tended to recall single words which they listed without reference to any meaning, students using Strategy 3 often had fairly accurate and complete recalls of explicit text materials. They might recall, for example, that "plants make their food" and that "chlorophyll is what makes the leaves green." However, they remembered ideas in no particular conceptual order, they placed equal emphasis on trivial details and on main points, and they did not link facts together to develop an overall picture of the main ideas. They had poorly structured scientific knowledge that was not useful in developing improved explanations of the world and that remained separate from their personal knowledge. For example, Myra read in the *Concepts in Science* text about an experiment that described how bubbles of oxygen formed on water plants when the sun was shining but did not form in the dark. In the recall portion of her interview she was able to remember many details about the experiment:

> She had some fish and she had some plants in there and one day she was looking at them and a bubble came out of one of the plants. And she started experimenting a little, and she noticed they were giving off oxygen. . . . They asked us what we think about is she trying—is it oxygen, they asked us what we thought. I put one time it did and one time it didn't. . . . They said the first time it wasn't sunny all the time. The first time it was out for 1 week and every day it was sunny.

However, when the interviewer asked Myra about whether the girl doing the experiment had made a conclusion about the role of the sun in oxygen production, Myra said simply, "no." Although she remembered a lot of details, she missed the critical reason that the experiment was included in the text.

Like students using Strategies 1 and 2, students using this strategy answered questions about real plants without making reference to any of the facts they had read about in the text and included in their recall. Like students who relied on Strategies 1 and 2, students using Strategy 3 generally stated that they had "understood" what they read. In fact they had satisfied the criteria for understanding that prevail in typical school contexts. They had not only met the needs for procedural display by successfully answering the questions in the text, but also learned enough facts to do well on recall tests like those that predominate in many science classrooms.

At the same time, however, they had failed to learn anything of value. The facts that they had learned did not help them describe, explain, predict, or control the world, were not conceptually coherent, and were viewed by the students as separate from their personal knowledge of the world. Is it surprising that apparently successful students such as these come to view science as useless and boring?

Strategy 4: Egocentric Sense-making

The best readers of the commercial texts (except for Susan) relied on a strategy that led to a form of knowledge that had many of the characteristics of true scientific understanding as well as meeting the demands of procedural display and factual recall. They developed an understanding of the text that was functional, conceptually coherent, and integrated with their personal knowledge of the world. However, they did this without giving up all of their misconceptions about food for plants. They were able to reconcile their personal beliefs with the information in the texts because they distorted the meaning of the text in subtle but important ways. Smith (1987) refers to this process as egocentric sense-making.

Kevin was one student who relied on Strategy 4. Like Susan, Kevin was an eighth grader reading at a 12.9 grade level. Like Susan, Kevin read the *Modern Science* text and was able to recall what he read with considerable depth and accuracy of detail. Here, for example, is his recall of how the text described the process of photosynthesis on Day 2:

> Well, the leaves, in the green plants, they have little chloroplasts which inside that have chlorophyll. When the sun shines in it does photosynthesis. Which changes, well it doesn't really change, but the plant has certain chemicals that change the sunlight. . . . Well, they have certain chemicals that the sunlight changes into sugars which is energy for the plant. And it runs up and down the stem.

Kevin was unlike Susan, however, in that he did not fully recognize the conflict between the text's definition of food and his personal understanding of food and plants. For example, the following exchange also occurred in Kevin's interview on Day 2:

> I: Could you summarize where does the plant get its food?
> K: Whew, from *lots* of places. From the soil for one, for the minerals and water, and from the air for oxygen. The sunlight for sun and it would change chemicals to sugars. It sort of makes its own food and gets food from the ground. And from the air.

On Day 2, Kevin was asked to reread and comment on the following passage from the *Modern Science* text. Note that the fourth and fifth sentences directly contradict Kevin's views about the definition of food and the nature of food for plants:

> *Production of food.* As do all other green plants, flowering plants produce their own food. How do they do this?
>
> Flowering plants, as you know, take in water and certain materials from the soil. They also take in carbon dioxide from the air. But these materials are not food. No animal, for example, can get energy from them or use them to make the protoplasm of its body. What do flowering plants do to these things to change them into food?

In Kevin's commentary on the passage, he seemed to make some minor adjustments in his ideas about the nature of food for plants. He did not notice that the paragraph explicitly contradicted his beliefs that water and minerals are food for plants:

> I was wrong about oxygen being food. It's not food. It just helps plants live.

This episode is one of many that demonstrate the power of naive conceptions as interpretive frameworks. Like the students who relied on Strategies 1, 2, and 3, Kevin had become committed to his conceptions through years of personal experience, internalization of linguistic patterns, and the development of sensible, but unexamined, analogies and generalizations. Unlike those students, Kevin succeeded in fitting both his prior knowledge and his new knowledge from the text into a conceptually coherent framework. He greatly simplified this task by ignoring a few sentences that did not fit into his developing framework. Seeing Kevin's difficulties helps one to appreciate the magnitude of Susan's accomplishment. Rather than ignoring those awkward sentences, she was able to recognize them as signaling the need for a substantial restructuring of her own thinking.

In fact, Kevin never changed his beliefs. His list of types of food for plants on the posttest was essentially the same as the one he gave in the interview on Day 2; even oxygen was once again included. Not surprisingly, Kevin perceived the text as having little to offer beyond a few details to add to what he already knew about plants:

Day 2
K: This is mostly the same (as what I did before) except for a little more detail.

Day 3
I: Was there anything you didn't understand?
K: No, not really. Because much of this is sort of like a review for me with more detail.

Although they differed in the exact nature of the misconceptions that they retained, the other students who used Strategy 4 shared with Kevin a general pattern of learning: Like Kevin, they developed a coherent, integrated understanding of the text that subtly distorted its meaning. These subtle distortions enabled them to assimilate information from the text into their personal knowledge without going through the difficult process of conceptual change. They were able to answer the questions posed by the text accurately and in detail, and they believed that they understood the text thoroughly. Like Kevin, they perceived the text as helping them to add details to their personal knowledge, but not as being particularly new or difficult. Students like these obviously are capable of developing much richer forms of scientific understanding, but in present school contexts this is not occurring.

Discussion of Learning Science

We have described a variety of strategies that students use in trying to learn science. One of those strategies, the conceptual change strategy, leads to the functional and conceptually coherent understanding that we described as desirable in the first section of this paper. This strategy demands a great deal of effort from students. They must keep trying to use scientific knowledge to describe, explain, predict, or control the world, and they must seek to reconcile new knowledge with their own prior knowledge. They must monitor their success, and they must be prepared to sometimes fail and have to try again. The strategy is difficult for students, but it is also potentially rewarding, for it leads to a deeper and richer understanding of the world.

In contrast, the students relying on other learning strategies did not work as hard, did not learn as much, and were not aware that they were missing any important ideas. They were all successful at least in satisfying demands for procedural display, and they all believed that they understood what they had read. However, their goals and strategies failed to help them develop understandings that met two important criteria for understanding science: (a) functional usefulness of the knowledge they developed, and (b) integration of personal and scientific knowledge.

These findings clearly raise a question: How can we help more students to see their understanding of science as problematic and to engage in the difficult but rewarding process of conceptual change learning? This question is addressed in the next section.

TEACHING SCIENCE

In the first two sections of this chapter we developed views of scientific understanding and of science learning that contrast sharply with those which prevail implicitly in most science classrooms. In this section we describe some of our attempts to develop teaching strategies, teaching materials, and classroom environments where conceptual change learning is encouraged and supported.

The task of teaching effectively for conceptual change is a complex and multifaceted one. As Linda Anderson (this volume, pp. 311-343) argues, classrooms in which successful teaching for conceptual change occurs differ from typical science classrooms along a number of dimensions, including the nature of academic goals and academic tasks, teacher and student roles, and the social environment of the classroom. Furthermore, change is not easy along any of these dimensions. Science textbooks and other materials, management and curricular demands imposed by school environments, and teachers' beliefs about science teaching and learning all mitigate against the development of classroom environments that promote conceptual change learning.

In our research and practice we have attempted to help teachers work within these constraints to promote conceptual change sense-making. We have worked on this goal in two ways. First, we have developed programs of preservice and inservice teacher education. Some of these efforts are discussed in our chapter in the second volume of this series (Hollon, Anderson, & Roth, in preparation). Second, we have developed teaching materials like the experimental text described above (Anderson & Smith, 1983; Berkheimer et al., in press; Roth & Anderson, 1987). In addition to text materials, the teaching materials we have developed include overhead transparencies, laboratory activities, handouts and worksheets, and diagnostic tests, as well as teachers' guides explaining how the materials are intended to facilitate conceptual change learning and how they can be used. Because they were designed to be used by teachers with little or no special training, they do not include activities that demand extensive preparation time, expensive technology, or unconventional forms of classroom organization.

The results of studies providing evaluative information about the effectiveness of teachers' use of these materials are summarized in Table 3.[7] In general, these studies indicate that, even within the limits imposed by the nature of conventional classrooms, the materials that we have developed do make a difference. Although there is plenty of room for improvement, the experimental materials help teachers and students to interact in ways that encourage and facilitate conceptual change learning.

What have we learned from these studies about how conceptual change sense-making can be encouraged and supported? Two general features characterize both the materials we have developed and the practice of the most effective teachers we have observed. First, there is a curricular commitment to teaching for understanding rather than to covering a wide range of content superficially. This narrowing and deepening of the curriculum enables teachers to focus students' attention on sense-making rather than on memorization of long lists of facts and terms. Second, there is a recognition that teaching for conceptual change understanding is a complicated process involving different kinds of work with students at different points in time. Thus, there is a need for an array of teaching strategies that can be used flexibly in response to students' needs. However, these strategies share an important characteristic: They all engage students in conceptual change sense-making, involving them in actively struggling with ideas rather than simply witnessing the teacher's performance. Using Collins, Brown, and Newman's terms (in press), we would characterize successful conceptual change teaching as a process of "cognitive apprenticeship" in the use of scientific knowledge to describe, explain, predict, and control the world around us.

In the remainder of this section we discuss the classroom curricular and teaching practices that we found especially helpful in promoting conceptual change learning. To illustrate these teaching strategies, we will describe ways

Table 3. Results of Studies Comparing Student Learning In Classrooms Using Commercial versus Conceptual Change Materials

Topic and Grade Level	Reference	Number of Classrooms Per Group		Percentage of Students Understanding Goal Conceptions*	
		Expt.	Control	Commercial Materials	Experimental Materials
Light and vision (fifth grade)	Anderson and Smith (1984, 1986)	6	5	18	58
Photosynthesis (fifth grade)	Roth (1984, 1985)	1	1	5	57
Photosynthesis (middle school)	Smith and Andeson (1987)	8	5	28	60
Respiration (middle school)	Smith and Anderson (1987)	4	9	12	23.5

Note: * Percentages are averaged across several important conceptions in each case.

in which our curriculum materials and the practices of several classroom teachers were successful in helping many fifth and seventh grade students develop well-structured and useful understandings of the concept of photosynthesis and food for plants.

Curricular Characteristics: Teaching for Understanding

It is not possible to understand science in the sense described above if science is conceived of as a list of facts, formulas, terms, and definitions. Nor can students understand ideas that they find too complex or technical to integrate with their personal knowledge of the world. Much of our work has therefore focused on the development of curricular goals and academic tasks that are both worth engaging in and accessible to students.

Developing curricular goals and tasks that have these characteristics is a difficult, complex, and time-consuming process. It is essentially an engineering process, a search for tasks and goals that satisfy multiple constraints imposed by the nature of students' prior knowledge, the topic being studied, the nature of school classrooms, and our beliefs about the nature of scientific understanding.

Academic Goals and Tasks in Teaching Materials

The developing of goals and tasks that work within these multiple constraints is the single most time-consuming aspect of our curriculum development work and perhaps also the single most important. We have generally sought to develop treatments of topics that omit much of the technical vocabulary and detail of typical textbook treatments of a topic without sacrificing too much explanatory power.

For example, our materials on photosynthesis (Roth, 1985; Roth & Anderson, 1987) omit many ideas that are present in most middle school textbooks. They do not present a formula for the chemical reactions of photosynthesis, do not discuss the role of chlorophyll, and do not identify the sequences of chemical photosynthesis. This may at first glance appear to be a "watered-down" curriculum. However, the purpose of these materials is to help students develop a rich and meaningful understanding of some basic ideas about plant metabolism. We have tried to accomplish this by embedding these ideas in an academic task structure that encourages students to develop understandings that integrate personal and scientific knowledge appropriately and that are useful in describing, explaining, predicting, or controlling the world.

Rather than emphasizing technical details and vocabulary, the photosynthesis materials are developed around the central conception of "food" for plants: What is "food" for plants and how is that food similar and different from food for people and animals? The unit begins by asking students for their personal definition of food and of food for plants and by posing a problem. Students then read a discussion of different ways of defining food that leads to a scientific definition of food as energy-containing matter. The materials introduce the idea that different matter taken into organisms can serve different functions, and the importance of energy-containing food for both plants and animals is emphasized. This explanation is followed by questions which give students a chance to use this new definition of food to explain everyday phenomena. For example, students are asked whether water, juice, and vitamin pills would be considered food for people using the scientific definition of food as supplying energy: Can you live on water and vitamin pills alone? Why or why not?

Throughout the unit, students are asked to use this definition of food to analyze experimental observations of plants, to think about similarities and differences between plants and animals, to distinguish between materials taken into plants and materials made by plants during photosynthesis, and to distinguish between energy-containing and non-energy-containing materials that people consume. Thus, students are supported in making connections between their own ideas and scientific concepts, and they are engaged in using these newly structured conceptions to make predictions and to develop more satisfying explanations of everyday phenomena that are very familiar to them. This support is spread over a series of lessons, giving students repeated opportunities to integrate this new definition of food into their everyday ways of thinking about food.

Academic Goals and Tasks in Science Classrooms

One reason that we have paid so much attention to the development of academic goals and tasks in our curriculum development efforts is that teaching materials generally have a much larger influence on the academic goals and tasks in science classrooms than on the other dimensions of classroom life discussed by L. Anderson (this volume, pp. 311-343): Teacher roles, student roles, and the social environment. The goals and tasks embedded in these materials, however, are substantially different from those in most science textbooks and science classrooms, and not all teachers respond to them in the same way.

Some teachers, like Ms. Copeland (Hollon & Anderson, 1987), find the goals and tasks in our materials identical to or compatible with their own. Ms. Copeland, like other teachers in this group, realized that the goals she shared with our materials set her (and our materials) apart from many other science teachers:

Teachers who lecture, then have it spit back at you. . . . They see themselves as dispensers of information . . . their whole expectation of "to know" is a lot different. If the kid can spit it back at you on the test on Monday, then he knows it—NO! I don't think he knows it at all. . . .

Ms. Copeland and other teachers like her used our materials easily and flexibly, using them as tools to accomplish our shared purposes. Sometimes these teachers modified the goals and tasks in our materials, but in ways that were generally sensitive to the rationale and purpose for their development. These teachers invariably responded positively to our materials, seeing them as tools that relieved them of the burden of struggling to use or modify texts and other materials that were incompatible with their own teaching goals.

Many teachers, however, were not as comfortable as Ms. Copeland with the goals and tasks in our materials. Mr. Armstrong, for instance, who viewed science as essentially a list of facts to be learned, had trouble seeing the purpose of all the extra stuff that we inserted between facts:

[Y]ou could take every other paragraph or two paragraphs and end up with what you could teach the kids or maybe one sentence of it that was important, so why deal with the rest?

For this age group, you have to eliminate as much of the garbage as you can and get down to nothing but the facts. You aren't going to keep their attention long enough to do much else . . . you are just going to confuse the kids.

Despite his belief that our materials were repetitious, Mr. Armstrong was used to depending on prepared curriculum materials, so he did not attempt to modify the goals and tasks incorporated in them. Mr. Barnes, on the other hand (Hollon & Anderson, 1987; Roth, 1987), had a deep and rich understanding of the nature of science. He felt the materials were "watered-down," and he added content to beef them up. For example, on the first two days of the photosynthesis unit, he explained the following ideas, none of which was mentioned in the photosynthesis materials: Molecular structure of chlorophyll, compounds, carbon atoms, atomic arrangement of carbon dioxide and water molecules, sucrose, transpiration, palisade cells, spongy cells, chloroplasts, auxins, hormones, tropisms, positive phototropism, hardening, adaptations, temperate zone, atomic energy, stomata, fats, oils, starches, fibers, proteins, carbohydrates.

Although we empathize with Mr. Barnes' desire to share with his students the full richness of scientific knowledge, our research has convinced us that the effect of including many additional facts, no matter how interesting and relevant, is often to lose focus on the students' own reasoning and understanding. Science presented in this way is so remote from students' experience that it is difficult for students to integrate with their personal knowledge.

Instruction for Meaningful Understanding

Appropriate academic goals and tasks are necessary but not sufficient to promote meaningful understanding of science. Most students also require the support of well designed instruction. Ideally, this instruction should take the form of scaffolded dialogue (cf. Palincsar & Brown, this volume, pp. 35-71) and academic work (cf. Doyle, 1983) in a learning community: A community in which teacher and students are working together to develop and use scientific knowledge. In this section we discuss some of the key characteristics of learning communities that promote scientific understanding. In the classrooms operating most successfully as scientific learning communities, we generally see at least three kinds of activities occurring: Establishing problems that engage students in scientific thinking, modeling and coaching through scaffolded tasks and dialogue, and student work that leads to independent use of scientific knowledge and integration with other scientific knowledge. Each of these activities is discussed below.

Establishing Problems That Engage Students in Scientific Thinking

As described above, students who are confronted with scientific knowledge often are not aware that the scientific knowledge is useful for any purpose that is real to them, or that it is "about" anything that is familiar to them. In addition, teachers are often unfamiliar with their students' reasoning about topics that they are preparing to teach. For these reasons, it is important that instruction begin with teachers asking students questions that elicit their reasoning about the topics that they will be studying and *listening* to what they say. This process activates prior student knowledge and helps make them aware of its limitations, serves an important diagnostic function for the teacher, and engages teacher and students ind ialogue about commonly understood issues.

The questions or problems that work best for this purpose tend to focus on objects and ideas that are familiar to the students, and on the scientific functions of description, explanation, prediction, and control. In the experimental photosynthesis text materials, for example, students were asked at the outset to: (a) write about how plants get food, (b) write about what kind of food plants use, and (c) draw arrows (on a diagram of a plant) to show how food moves in a plant.

The students' responses to those instructions played an important diagnostic role for the teacher: The Teacher's guide contained information about common student responses and the reasoning that led to those responses. However, those responses also played a critical role for the students, helping them to articulate their ideas and to realize that their study of science is related to things they already know about the world. Throughout the photosynthesis unit, students revisited these questions in order to change their responses to them as they developed new understandings. At the end of the unit, the same questions were posed to students again, and students were instructed to reread what they had written at the beginning of the unit and to write about how their ideas had changed.

The more successful science teachers that we have watched, including Ms. Copeland, used instructions such as these to pose problems that engaged students in active discussion. They listened to students' ideas, sometimes helping them to see points of disagreement or inconsistencies in their thinking, but not telling them initially the "correct" scientific answers to their questions.

This is not easy for many teachers. It reverses teacher and student roles in classrooms where the teacher normally talks while students listen. In addition, coping with the diversity of student ideas that emerge in such a discussion is a major intellectual challenge, demanding a deep understanding of both scientific content and student thinking. Thus while Ms. Copeland began her teaching of the photosynthesis unit with an hour-long debate about the nature of food for humans and plants, successfully engaging students in a problem, Mr. Barnes began the photosynthesis unit by presenting a filmstrip which described photosynthesis in some detail. He stopped the filmstrip frequently to give mini-lectures elaborating points made in the filmstrip. Thus he did not first establish a problem and elicit students' ideas about the problem. Rather, he started by presenting scientists' explanations about photosynthesis before his students were fully engaged in the problem that photosynthesis "solves."

Modeling and Coaching Through Scaffolded Tasks and Dialogue

If appropriate problems are established at the beginning of a unit, students will soon see that although they do have important knowledge and beliefs about these problems, they cannot solve them adequately without additional knowledge. At this point the teacher and students can enter into what Palincsar and Brown (this volume, pp. 35-71) refer to as scaffolded dialogue, in which students encounter and use new scientific ideas. The ways in which those new ideas are encountered and used, however, are of critical importance.

Our research suggests that students should encounter new ideas in contexts where both the usefulness of those ideas for solving important problems and the relation of those ideas to their own personal knowledge are apparent to them. This implies that modeling, in which the teacher (or text) shows how scientific knowledge can be used to solve a problem, is generally a more appropriate way to present new ideas than traditional lecturing. It also implies that teachers should be very specific about how scientific ideas connect or conflict with ideas that the students have expressed.

No matter how well scientific ideas are presented, however, students cannot understand them in the way that we have described without themselves using the ideas to describe, explain, predict, or control the world around them.

Students often need extensive support in their initial attempts to use new ideas. Scaffolding of tasks so that the demands on students are simplified and clarified is one way of providing such support. Teachers can also support their students by fostering classroom dialogue in which they and their students listen carefully to each other and respond to each other, sometimes critically but in ways that reflect serious and respectful attention to the ideas of the speaker. At their best, such dialogues provide a content where teachers can coach students or students can coach each other as they use new ideas, providing them with the necessary support to engage socially in problem-solving processes that they are not ready to carry out independently. The feedback that students receive is also essential to the process of knowledge restructuring, as they learn precisely how their personal beliefs conflict and connect with scientific knowledge.

We have tried to incorporate opportunities for scaffolded dialgoue and tasks into the materials we have developed in a variety of ways. Some of these involve reading and writing tasks; others involve discussions of student responses to questions posed in the text, in laboratory activities, or on overhead transparencies. In the photosynthesis materials, for example, students are asked at several different points to answer sets of questions that require them to make predictions and explanations about plants. In one such set of questions, the student text scaffolds that task by reminding students of key ideas about what is and is not food for plants. Students are instructed to refer to this list of key ideas as they write answers to the questions. In another section, students are asked to explain the differences between how plants get their food and how people get their food. To scaffold this task, the text provides a chart to encourage students to consider a series of critical issues that need to be considered and integrated in order to develop a well-structured explanation:

How many sources of food?	What is their food?	Where do they get their food?	How do they get their food?	When can they get/make their food?

HUMANS

PLANTS

The Nature of Dialogue in Science Classrooms

As might be expected, not all teachers were comfortable and successful in holding discussions that were scaffolded dialogues rather than teacher monologues with students filling in the blanks. One teacher who did so successfully was Ms. Copeland (Hollon & Anderson, 1987, pp. 9-10).

Ms. Copeland began the second lesson of the photosynthesis unit with a short review of the previous day's lesson concerning the nature of food for plants and the definition of food as energy-containing matter. Staci, who had argued vehemently the day before that water was food for plants, commented:

> Now I'm convinced. The people I polled say you need food and water to survive. . . . I asked my dad and he said food has to have calories so I believe that.

After discussing the role of water, Ms. Copeland posed several questions about how plants obtain food. By now, most of the students had become silent and appeared puzzled by the questions. Ms. Copeland said that things "like plant food and food sticks make it *sound* like a plant reaches out and munches food."

At this point, Ms. Copeland told students to write down their thoughts about how plants get food and how food moves in a plant. She then asked students to talk about how food moves in plants. Several students described food entering through the roots of the plant, from carbon dioxide in the air, and from water in the soil. She wrote on the blackboard "How Plants Get Food," and listed students' responses. The list included "water from the soil, carbon dioxide from the air, soil, sunlight, rain, other plants, roots and leaves," and "themselves."

> T: Look at at the list up there. If they get it from the soil, is it like there's little "Big Macs" in there?
> S_5: It's minerals and nutrients. . . .
> T: Do minerals supply energy?
> S_2: Yeah . . . things like potato peels in the soil give it minerals.
> T: Do plants *make* the food or are minerals the food? Do minerals supply energy?
> S_6: Sometimes. . . .
> T: Does that mean "just on some days"? Anybody think more on that one?
> S_7: If they supply energy, they'd be food, right? But wouldn't that be the same as saying water is food?
> T: How many calories in minerals? Is food for plants the same as food for people? If that were true, all you'd have to do is give them minerals. . . .

After discussing each item on the list, Ms. Copeland asked if any of the items were really food for plants. A few individuals insisted that some were while others made comments like, "I'm confused . . . where are we?" One student volunteered, "All that stuff just *helps* the plant make its food." Ms. Copeland repeated the statement, emphasizing the words "help" and "make," then repeated the original question about the plant:

T: Where does it get its food?
S: (several call out) They make it!

The above dialogue illustrates several features of scaffolded dialogue that are critical to the development of scientific understanding. First, the dialogue centered on a question that was both scientifically significant and "real" to the students: Explaining how plants get their food. In addition, Ms. Copeland listened to her students and took their ideas seriously without accepting them uncritically. She helped the students think about whether or not their ideas were consistent with other aspects of their own personal knowledge and the scientific definition of food to which they had been introduced. As a result, students were helped to restructure their understanding of food and to begin using their new scientific ideas. In the research we have done to date the successful dialogues we have observed have been largely teacher-student exchanges like this one. We are interested in understanding the extent to which student-student dialogues can result in appropriate knowledge restructuring.

In contrast with Ms. Copeland, when Mr. Barnes tried to use a similar strategy on the second day of his photosynthesis unit, he found himself slipping into a form of dialogue that more closely resembled the teacher-centered "discussions" to which he and his students were accustomed (Roth, 1987, pp. 38-41).

T: How do you think plants get their food?
S: From the soil, minerals and fertilizers.
T: Minerals from the soil she says. Let's list some of these on the board.
S: From the roots and the soil.
S: From the air.
S: From sunlight.

In contrast with Ms. Copeland, Mr. Barnes slipped into a knowledge-telling strategy as he addressed each of the students' suggestions which he had listed on the board:

T: Let's go back to what we talked about yesterday. We said, we gave a definition for food. What was the definition for food?
S: Energy? Anything you can eat that is energy?
T: All right. In talking about food for ourselves, we say it's the things that we eat but it's to obtain energy for life processes. [Writes on board: Food: Materials that contain energy to help living live and grow.] That's close . . . on p. 2 they gave a definition (he reads it aloud). . . . So that's pretty close to a scientific definition of food.

S: You left "things" out.
T: Yes. We could say "organisms." If a plant is a living thing . . . is a plant a living thing?
S: [several nod yes]
T: Sure, we all understand that plants are living things. If a plant is a living thing, then it has to use some food for energy. What they want you to struggle with is where do they get food from. All too often we're brainwashed—the stuff we get from the store is labelled "plant food." That does help plants grow but does it contain energy?
S: [very quietly] No.
T: It's hard to visualize whether it does contain energy. It does seem to help plants grow. But it's like vitamins. . . . We came to this conclusion yesterday, didn't we? That vitamins don't give us energy but do help us live and grow. It's the same situation with plant food, the stuff we buy at the store. It's improperly labelled. They're fertilizers that help the plant grow but they don't contain energy. [Points to "minerals" on the students' list on the board.] Minerals from the soil are fertilizer types of stuff but there's not really energy in minerals you get from the soil. [Points to "air" on the list on the board.] The air does contain things that plants use but they really don't contain energy. Yesterday we saw a filmstrip. Anybody remember where did all the energy come from that plants were using?

In this lesson sequence, Mr. Barnes took about one minute to construct explanations to contradict each of the students' ideas, and then he moved on to explain photosynthesis. Although he did elicit students' ideas, he did not support students in working through their ideas and restructuring their understandings of food for plants. Because he did not engage students in constructing and puzzling through that understanding themselves, eliciting students' thinking was an empty rather than a critical teaching move.

Independent Student Work and Use of Ideas in Other Contexts

Participation in scaffolded tasks and dialogue helps students to develop and use scientific knowledge, but such dialogues and tasks cannot and should not last forever. If students are to use scientific knowledge outside of the classroom context, the support must be gradually faded out, until students are working independently. Thus independent practice activities also play an important role in successful science instruction.

There are several essential qualities in independent student work that promote conceptual change. First, the work should involve students in tasks where they use scientific knowledge for meaningful purposes, as opposed to reproducing words or applying algorithms on demand. Second, independent practice is useful only for students who have achieved a basic understanding of the ideas they are expected to use through participation in scaffolded dialogue or tasks.

Furthermore, the process of learning about a science topic or concept should not be bounded by a given unit of instruction. Truly powerful ideas are useful in other contexts and are connected with other ideas. For example, the ideas about photosynthesis discussed above play an essential role in explaining not only plant structure and function, but also energy flow and matter cycling in ecosystems: They are intimately connected with understandings of cellular respiration, and thus of the functioning of animals' respiratory, digestive, and circulatory systems, and so forth. Students do not always see even connections that seem quite obvious to scientifically literate adults, so teachers must help students to make those connections and use their scientific knowledge in other contexts.

Although we are convinced of the importance of those activities that build connections between units, we have little research evidence to support our convictions; our research to date has focused on the teaching of individual units. One of us (Roth) is about to begin a year-long longitudinal study in which the process of building those connections and their effects on student learning over time will be a primary topic of investigation.

Facilitating Self-Regulated Learning in Science

In our description of conceptual change teaching strategies, we have emphasized the critical role of the teacher in scaffolding and coaching student thinking. But an important goal of science instruction is to help students learn how to learn science independently. This is clearly possible for some students. In the Roth study of textbook reading, for example, Susan used a conceptual change learning strategy to make sense of photosynthesis as she read from a traditional science textbook. Similarly, Table 3 shows that some students achieve meaningful scientific understanding in classrooms taught by traditional methods. How can we help more students be like Susan? What would it take for a struggling student like Evalina to be able to use a conceptual change learning strategy without the support of scaffolded dialogues or specially constructed curriculum materials?

Although we lack a fully developed answer to these questions, we presently view self-regulation of meaningful science learning as conceptually rather than strategically driven. From this perspective, Susan's success in undergoing conceptual change without a lot of support depends more on her understanding of what it means to make sense of science concepts than on her knowledge of specific learning strategies. Susan differed from other students reading the commercial texts in two respects. First, she had a goal of developing coherent and useful scientific knowledge; she adhered to this goal even when it was not fully supported by the text. Second, she was exceptionally sensitive to conflicts between the information in the text and her own personal knowledge and she resolved those conflicts in ways that enabled her to develop an accurate construction of the meaning of the text.

This analysis of science learning is similar to Gelman and Meck's (1986) view of children's developing mathematical knowledge. They argue that young children develop conceptions of what good counting is like before they master actual counting procedures. As children attempt to execute counting procedures, they evaluate their success in light of their conceptions of good counting. Similarly, Susan and other successful conceptual change learners were searching for interpretations of the text that fit within the constraints imposed by their conceptions of scientific understanding and their interpretations of the content of the texts.

From this perspective, what would be the best way to help students become self-regulated learners of science? This is a question that we plan to investigate in future studies in which we will look at students' learning over longer periods of time than a 3-6 week unit. However, we feel that most students will need to begin with the kinds of heavily scaffolded instruction described in this chapter. Our analysis of students' learning strategies from text and of a pilot study in which Roth attempted to teach students to use the strategies in Palincsar and Brown's reciprocal teaching model suggests that explicit teaching of conceptual change learning strategies will be meaningless for students until they have first internalized a conception of a meaningful scientific understanding.

In the reciprocal teaching trial, for example, students learned to make predictions of text, to ask clarification questions, and to summarize the text as they read. Without a conceptual change learning goal, however, the students used the strategies to predict trivia, to summarize details, and to clarify big words. In fact, they often came up with "clarification" questions that they could answer easily; they did not feel confused because their interpretation of the text was satisfactory according to their conceptions of scientific understanding. Thus, students learned the names for particular learning strategies that should promote self-regulated learning, but they used the strategies in ways that did not foster the development of meaningful understandings. Even with more extensive training in the summarizing and clarifying strategies, students are unlikely to succeed in using these strategies effectively until they develop a robust conception of what it means to make sense in science.

In contrast with students trained to clarify, summarize, and predict, Evalina and the other students in our studies who succeeded in making sense of photosynthesis and food for plants in meaningful ways (with the support of special curriculum materials and/or teachers who use conceptual change teaching strategies effectively) could not name the learning strategies they used, but they had taken a more important first step toward self-regulated learning. They had begun the challenging work of developing an internal model or goal of meaningful learning by making personal sense of a particular science concept. Evalina was caught up in a problem that genuinely puzzled her, and in resolving this problem she used a variety of effective learning strategies. For example, she asked *meaningful* clarification questions as she read the experimental text. She did not ask these questions because she was asked to find something that puzzled her, but because she was pursuing a resolution to her problem. By the end of the photosynthesis unit, she recognized that her ways of thinking about food for plants had changed and that her new explanations were more satisfying to her. Now Evalina has a sense of what it feels like to puzzle and to work through that puzzle, which represents a critical beginning in the process of developing a conception of the nature of meaningful science learning. We propose that it will take numerous successes in working through such conceptual changes to enable Evalina to change her learning goals in science. As such a shift in her learning goals occurs, explicit identification and instruction about particular learning strategies may prove helpful to her.

CONCLUSION

In this paper, we drew from our studies of classroom teaching and learning to illustrate how science teaching can foster different kinds of science learning. In our research, we have attempted to improve the quality of student understanding in science classrooms by developing teaching materials and strategies that support conceptual change teaching and learning. These efforts have led to some significant successes; teachers using our materials have been able to significantly improve the understanding of their students in typical elementary and middle school classrooms. Their students have developed understandings that are well-structured and functional. While these student understandings may not include a great deal of technical vocabulary and factual detail, they represent students' success in integrating their personal knowledge with scientific knowledge in ways that enable them to use science concepts to explain in more personally satisfying ways the world they live in.

Although we are pleased with these successes, we are far from satisfied. The programs that we have developed so far are limited in both their practical usefulness and their long-term potential. Their practical usefulness is limited by factors such as those discussed by Linda Anderson (this volume, pp. 311-343). In particular, the full implementation of conceptual change teaching demands substantial changes in role relationships between teachers and students and the social environments of classrooms. In addition, the use of conceptual change teaching methods demands the development of a considerable knowledge base about science and about children's scientific cognition, both in individual teachers and in the profession as a whole. It also requires a curriculum emphasis on depth over breadth, and such an emphasis is not supported by current science teaching materials or by state and district curriculum guidelines.

Even in ideal conditions, however, the materials and techniques we have developed remain limited tools. We know relatively little about how conceptual change teaching strategies foster important long-term goals such as promoting self-regulated learning and helping students build conceptual understandings across topics or units of instruction. Even more important, we have generally failed to help a significant portion of the students in most classrooms develop meaningful scientific understanding. One teacher cannot successfully conduct individual dialogues with 25 students, but a substantial number of students in every class need such individual attention. We still have, in other words, many questions left to answer as we continue to investigate, and try to improve, learning in science classrooms.

ACKNOWLEDGMENTS

This work is sponsored in part by the Institute for Research on Teaching, College of Education, Michigan State University. The Institute for Research on Teaching is funded from a variety of federal, state, and private sources including the United States Department of Education and Michigan State University. The opinions expressed in this publication do not necessarily reflect the position, policy, or endorsement of the funding agencies.

The work reported in this chapter is the product not only of our efforts, but also of many other colleagues, students, and teachers who worked on the research projects leading to this chapter. In particular, we acknowledge the contributions of Edward L. Smith, Robert Hollon, Theron Blakeslee, Beth Bishop, Lucille Singer, and Janet Eaton.

NOTES

1. The activities that we discuss as functions of science have some resemblance to the activities commonly labeled as "science processes" in the science education literature. Science processes, such as our functions of science, represent an attempt to understand what science is by analyzing what scientists do. However, analyses that lead to lists of science processes are generally limited in two important respects.

First, analyses of science processes tend to focus on research, especially experimental research, as the primary activity that scientists engage in. We feel that this presents a very limited and inaccurate picture of the total scientific enterprise. The primary activities of most practicing scientists are not the discovery of new knowledge, but the application of existing knowledge— in teaching, in technology, in policy decisions, and so forth. This characterization is even more true for the science-related activities of adults who are not practicing scientists.

The second limitation of most analyses of science processes is that they are conceived of as skills ("science process skills") that are at least partially separate from conceptual scientific knowledge. We view the functions of science as ways in which conceptual knowledge is used, not as separate skills (cf. Millar & Driver, 1987).

2. Note also that the distinction between structure and function is *not* equivalent to the distinction between content and process, or conceptual and procedural knowledge. Structure refers to *all* knowledge (conceptual, procedural, metacognitive, and so forth), and function refers to the *tasks* or actions that students use their knowledge to accomplish.

We assert that all meaningful scientific knowledge has certain structural and functional characteristics. For example, all scientific knowledge is useful for describing, explaining, predicting, or controlling some aspect of the world. This does not preclude the possibility that scientific knowledge may also have many other functions as well.

3. Not all biologists would agree that food can be characterized in scientific terms. However, the definition that we offer is consistent with the usage of the word in phrases such as "food chains" and "food webs," which are inevitably characterized as beginning with plants as producers (of food). In teaching about photosynthesis, it is important to deal with definitions of food because that word, unlike more scientifically precise terms such as glucose, is richly embedded in students' personal knowledge.

4. It is interesting to note the overlap between the activities of the interview and the activities of reciprocal teaching (cf. Palincsar& Brown, this volume, pp. 35-71). The interviews required students to engage in two important activities of reciprocal teaching: summarizing and clarifying. In addition, the interviews required students to apply information in the text to the description and explanation of plants and their functions. Although these activities aided learning by the successful students, they were not sufficient to assure successful learning; 11 of the 12 students reading the commercial texts did not change most of their misconceptions.

5. The social nature of Evalina's learning can be contrasted with the image of scientists as learning primarily through direct observation and experimentation in the natural world. Although positivistic ideas about the role of observation and experimentation in the development of scientific knowledge are no longer generally accepted by historians and philosophers of science (cf. Kuhn, 1970; Mayr, 1982; Toulmin, 1972), they are often retained in "hands-on" or "inquiry" approaches to science teaching. The experimental text used by Evalina was developed in response to the failure of a "hands-on" program to help students understand photosynthesis (Roth, 1984).

Although we believe that observation and experiment play an essential role in science learning and have included laboratory activities in most of our teaching materials, our investigations of science teaching and learning have focused more on learning through social interactions (i.e., reading, writing, listening, and speaking) than on learning through observation and experiment. In this respect our work is closer to a Vygotskian (Vygotsky, 1962, 1978; Wertsch, 1985) than to a Piagetian orientation. Given the importance of observation and experimentation in scientific thinking, we find that in general there is a remarkable dearth of philosophically and psychologically sound research on their role in science teaching and learning.

6. Except for the general observation that students who succeed in conceptual change learning in ordinary classrooms are generally inquisitive and academically successful, we have little information about the personal characteristics that predispose students to successful conceptual change learning (see also Eaton et al., 1984; Smith & Lott, 1983).

7. We do not consider the numbers in Table 3 to be particularly meaningful, because they summarize disparate results across a variety of conceptions. They do provide crude indications, though, of the "amount of conceptual change learning" that occurred in classrooms using different types of materials. The references include more detailed reports of the analyses.

REFERENCES

Anderson, C.W., Belt, B.L., Gamalski, J.M., & Greminger, J. (1987). A social constructivist analysis of science classroom teaching. In J. Novak (Ed.), *Proceedings of the second international seminar on misconceptions and educational strategies in science and mathematics* (Vol. 1). Ithaca, NY: Cornell University.

Anderson, C.W., Roth, K.J., Hollon, R.E., & Blakeslee, T.D. (1987). *The power cell: Teacher's guide to respiration* (Occasional Paper No. 115). East Lansing: Michigan State University, Institute for Research on Teaching.

Anderson, C.W., Sheldon, T.H., & DuBay, J. (1986). *The effects of instruction on college nonmajors' conceptions of respiration and photosynthesis* (Research Series No. 164). East Lansing: Michigan State University, Institute for Research on Teaching.

Anderson, C.W., & Smith, E.L. (1983, April). *Teacher behavior associated with conceptual learning in science.* Paper presented at the annual meeting of the American Educational Research Association, Montreal, Canada.

Anderson, C.W., & Smith, E.L. (1987). *Children's conceptions of light and color: Developing the concept of unseen rays* (Research Series No. 166). East Lansing: Michigan State University, Institute for Research on Teaching.

Anderson, C.W., & Smith, E.L. (1987). Teaching Science. In Virginia Koehler (Ed.), *The educator's handbook: A research perspective.* New York: Longman.

Berkheimer, G.D., Anderson, C.W., Lee, O., & Blakeslee, T.D. (in press). *Matter and molecules teacher's guide: Activity book* (Occasional Paper No. 122). East Lansing: Michigan State University, Institute for Research on Teaching.

Bishop, B.A., & Anderson, C.W. (1986). *Evolution by natural selection: A teaching module* (Occasional Paper No. 91). East Lansing: Michigan State University, Institute for Research on Teaching.

Blakeslee, T.D., Anderson, C.W., & Smith, E.L. (1987, April). *Teaching strategies associated with conceptual change learning in science.* Paper presented at the annual meeting of the American Educational Research Association, Washington, DC.

Bloome, D., & Argumedo, B. (1983, April). *Procedural display and classroom instruction at the middle school level: Another look at academic engaged time.* Paper presented at the annual meeting of the American Educational Research Association, Montreal, Canada.

Brandwein, P.F., Cooper, E.K., Blackwood, P.E., Cottom-Winslow, N., Giddings, M.G., Romero, F., & Carin, A.A. (1980). *Concepts in science.* New York: Harcourt, Brace, Jovanovich.

Collins, A., Brown, J.S., & Newman, S.E. (1989). Cognitive apprenticeship, teaching the craft of reading, writing, and mathematics. In L.B. Resnick (Ed.), *Knowing and learning: Essays in honor of Robert Glaser* (pp. 453-494). Hillsdale, NJ: Erlbaum.

Doyle, W. (1983). Academic work. *Review of Educational Research, 53*(2), 159-200.

Driver, R., & Erickson, G. (1983). Theories-in-action: Some theoretical and empirical issues in the study of students' conceptual frameworks in science. *Studies in Science Education, 10,* 37-60.

Driver, R., Guesne, E., & Tiberghien, A. (1985). *Children's ideas in science.* Philadelphia, PA: Open University Press.

Eaton, J.F., Anderson, C.W., & Smith, E.L. (1984). Student preconceptions interfere with learning: Case studies of fifth-grade students. *Elementary School Journal,* 365-379.

Eaton, J.F., Harding, T., & Anderson, C.W. (1986). *Light: A teaching module* (Occasional Paper No. 92). East Lansing: Michigan State University, Institute for Research on Teaching.

Eichinger, D.C., & Lee, O. (1988, April). *Student conceptions of the kinetic molecular theory.* Paper presented at the annual meeting of the National Association for Research on Science Teaching, Lake Ozark, MO.

Hesse, J.J., & Anderson, C.W. (1988, April). *Students' conceptions of chemical change.* Paper presented at the annual meeting of the American Educational Research Association, New Orleans, LA.

Hollon, R.E., & Anderson, C.W. (1987, April). *Teachers' beliefs about students' learning processes in science: Self-reinforcing belief systems.* Paper presented at the annual meeting of the American Educational Research Association, Washington, DC.

Hollon, R.E., Anderson, C.W., & Roth, K.J. (in preparation). Teachers' conceptions of science teaching and learning. In J. Brophy (Ed.), *Advances in research on teaching: Vol. 2. Teachers' knowledge of subject matter as it relates to their eaching practice.* Greenwich, CT: JAI Press.

Kuhn, T. (1970). *The structure of scientific revolutions* (2nd ed.). Chicago, IL: University of Chicago Press.

Mayr, E. (1982). *The growth of biological thought.* Cambridge, MA: Belknap.

Millar, R., & Driver, R. (1987). Beyond processes. *Studies in Science Education, 14,* 33-62.

Osborne, R.J., & Freyberg, P. (1985). *Learning in science: The implications of children's science.* Portsmouth, NH: Heinemann.

Phillips, D.C. (1986). *The conceptual minefield of "structure."* Paper presented at the annual meeting of the American Educational Research Association, San Francisco, CA.

Resnick, L.B. (1987). Learning in school and out. *Educational Researcher, 16*(9), 13-20.

Rogoff, B., & Lave, J. (Eds.). (1984). *Everyday cognition.* Cambridge, MA: Harvard University Press.

Roth, K.J. (1984). Using classroom observations to improve science teaching and curriculum materials. In C.W. Anderson (Ed.), *Observing science classrooms: Perspectives from research and practice* (1984 yearbook of the Association for the Education of Teachers in Science) (pp. 77-102). Columbus, OH: ERIC/SMEAC.

Roth, K.J. (1985). *The effects of science texts on students' misconceptions about food for plants.* Unpublished Ph.D. dissertation, Michigan State University.

Roth, K.J. (1987, April). *Helping science teachers change: The critical role of teachers' knowledge about science and science learning.* Paper presented at the annual meeting of the American Educational Research Association, Washington, DC.

Roth, K.J., & Anderson, C.W. (1987). *The power plant: Teacher's guide to photosynthesis* (Occasional Paper No. 112). East Lansing: Michigan State University, Institute for Research on Teaching.

Roth, K.J., Anderson, C.W., & Smith, E.L. (1987). Curriculum materials, teacher talk, and student learning: Case studies of fifth grade science teaching. *Journal of Curriculum Studies, 19,* 527-548.

Roth, K.J., Smith, E.L., & Anderson, C.W. (1983, April). *Students' conceptions of photosynthesis and food for plants.* Paper presented at the annual meeting of the American Educational Research Association, Montreal, Canada.

Slinger, L.A., Anderson, C.W., & Smith, E.L. (1983). *Studying light in the fifth grade: A case study of text-based science teaching* (Research Series No. 129). East Lansing: Michigan State University, Institute for Research on Teaching.

Smith, A.H., Blecha, M.K., & Pless, H. (1974). *Modern science, level six.* River Forest, IL: Laidlaw Brothers.

Smith, E.L. (1987, July). *What besides misconceptions needs to change in conceptual change learning?* Paper presented at the Second International Seminar on Misconceptions and Educational Strategies in Science and Mathematics, Cornell University, Ithaca, NY.

Smith, E.L., & Anderson, C.W. (1984). Plants as producers: A case study of elementary school science teaching. *Journal of Research in Science Teaching, 21*(7), 685-695.

Smith, E.L., & Anderson, C.W. (1986, April). *Middle school students' conceptions of matter cycling in ecosystems.* Paper presented at the annual meeting of the National Association for Research in Science Teaching, San Francisco, CA.

Smith, E.L., & Lott, G.W. (1983). Teaching for conceptual change: Ways of going wrong. In H. Heim & J. Novak (Eds.), *Proceedings of the international seminar on student misconceptions in science and mathematics.* Ithaca, NY: Cornell University.

Smith, E.L., & Sendelbach, N.B. (1982). The program, the plans, and the activities of the classroom: The demands of activity-based science. In J. Olson (Ed.), *Innovation in the science curriculum: Classroom knowledge and curriculum change.* London: Croom-Helm.

Toulmin, S. (1961). *Foresight and understanding.* London: The Anchor Press, Ltd.

Toulmin, S. (1972). *Human understanding.* Princeton, NJ: Princeton University Press.

Vygotsky, L.S. (1962). *Thought and language.* Cambridge, MA: MIT Press.

Vygotsky, L.S. (1978). *Mind in society.* Cambridge, MA: Harvard University Press.
Wertsch, J. (1985). *Vygotsky and the social formation of mind.* Cambridge, MA: Harvard
    University Press.
West, L.H.T., & Pines, A.L. (Eds.). (1985). *Cognitive structure and conceptual change.* Orlando,
    FL: Academic Press.

*   *   *

CROSS-TALK

Are meaningful understanding and self-regulation distinctly different goals that should be approached by teachers in very different ways, or do we create artificial dichotomies by thinking of understanding and self-regulation as separate goals?

Although meaningful understanding and self-regulation are not the same, we do not believe that they can be taught entirely separately. The experience of learning with understanding is a necessary but not sufficient condition for self-regulation of that process. The students using Strategies 3 and 4 (pages 283-286) were, in a sense, self-regulated learners of science, but the "science" that they learned was not the full, rich understanding that we believe students to need. We believe that for these students the first step toward self-regulation of the development of true scientific understanding should be a learning experience like Evalina's, in which they successfully experience conceptual change learning with extensive support. We believe (without supporting evidence) that with a carefully regulated succession of such experiences, some of that support could be withdrawn. Students would become more successful self-regulated learners as they began to hold some of the goals and to engage spontaneously in some of the activities described on pages 287-299 of this chapter.

What are ways that reciprocal teaching (or, more generally, dialogue about comprehension processes) can become part of teaching for conceptual change?

The characteristics of scientific understanding described in the first part of the paper suggest two comprehension processes that we feel are essential to meaningful learning. The first of these might be labelled *applying:* Using scientific knowledge to describe, explain, predict, and/or control the real world. The second could be labelled integrating: Working out the relationships between prior knowledge and new scientific knowledge. Conceptual change learning can occur only if students engage successfully in these processes, and many of the teaching strategies described in this chapter are essentially ways of assuring that this happens.

Explicit labeling and discussion of these processes clearly is not essential for the development of scientific understanding; we have not done so in our curriculum materials. Such labeling and dialogues about these processes may, however, be useful in helping students become self-regulated learners of science. In our college classes, we have found that by adding these activities to the reciprocal teaching activities of summarizing, questioning, and clarifying, we were able to produce a useful guide for journal writing and class discussions.

What is your position on the relative influence of teachers and text on student learning? Are you saying that instructional improvement should emphasize primarily the production of better text or the production of better teachers? What is the conflict between wanting to help teachers by simplifying the work they need to do and the essentially non-simple tasks of understanding science and understanding science teaching?

Our emphasis on curriculum development is due primarily to the fact that we are preparing a paper about teachers' knowledge for the second volume of this series (Hollon, Anderson, & Roth, in preparation). It does not reflect a belief that textbooks are somehow more important than teachers.

We do believe, however, that the improvement of textbooks and other teaching materials must play an essential role in the long-term improvement of science teaching. Textbooks and other curriculum materials are the tools that teachers must use, and our present tools are woefully inadequate. Trying to teach for scientific understanding with most current textbooks is rather like trying to perform surgery with a wooden spoon. In fact, much of our teaching in science methods courses is devoted to helping prospective teachers learn to transform the curriculum materials they are given into something minimally adequate for teaching for understanding. Our contention is that this is a waste of time. Should surgeons' training include courses in how to make scalpels?

Furthermore, our research indicates that although few teachers are successful in teaching for understanding with present text materials, a significant number of experienced teachers (although by no means all) have developed the knowledge and skills they need to support conceptual change learning in their students. We have seen very few teachers who have the knowledge, time, and energy needed to transform curriculum materials *and* teach for conceptual change. Thus we feel that current commercial materials make conceptual change teaching extensively and unnecessarily complex. Trying to ease some of the hurdles created by inadequate tools is a reasonable and effective strategy for improving teaching.

It may be useful to distinguish between two different ways of simplifying teachers' work: It is possible to make life easier for teachers by implicitly or explicitly lowering expectations, or by giving them access to better tools. Many teaching materials take the former approach, and they deserve the criticism they receive. In the long run, however, the latter kind of simplification is essential to progress in the field. Teachers will find the time, energy, and mental "space" to think about the issues discussed in this chapter only if we can find ways of reducing the levels of social and cognitive complexity inherent in teaching for conceptual change to a manageable level.

In the long run, it is reasonable to believe that improved teaching tools could help to transform teachers' work in ways analogous to the changes in navigators' work described by Resnick (1987). As Resnick suggests, building more knowledge into the tools that people use both changes the nature of their work and makes possible a level of performance that is impossible with more primitive tools. Progress in teaching, as in other fields, involves mutually supporting changes in practitioners' knowledge and the tools that they use.

Are you advocating that the conceptual change approach and the criteria of description, explanation, prediction, and control of real world systems or events in selecting content for inclusion should be primary guiding principles for science instruction at all levels, or at some point would one phase this out and phase in more encyclopedic courses of the kind now taught at the advanced high school level and the college level?

Rich scientific understanding at *all* levels has the structural and functional characteristics described in the first section of this chapter, and rich scientific understanding should be the goal of teaching at all levels. This does not necessarily mean that the same teaching strategies should be used at all levels. Students who have become self-regulated learners in the sense described above, for example, could achieve understanding with far less coaching and scaffolding than we advocate in this chapter. Unfortunately, it has been our observation that many students survive in upper-level science courses by developing sophisticated forms of Strategy 3 (memorizing facts). Didactic teaching that gives students few opportunities to use scientific knowledge or to integrate it with personal knowledge encourages the use of this strategy.

What kind of social environment and corresponding teacher-student role relationships are necessary to make scaffolded dialogue possible? How can teachers, who may well value this model but not be very adept at it, learn to engage in this instruction?

Most of our answers to these questions (in as much as we have answers) must await our paper in the second volume of this series. We wish to point out here, however, that to take students' ideas seriously without accepting them uncritically is both an intellectually and a socially demanding task. Intellectually, teachers must both understand what is reasonable about student responses from a student perspective (even those that are stumbling or incomplete) *and* what is problematic about them from a scientific perspective. Socially, they must respond to their students in ways that communicate their appreciation of both the reasonableness and the problems with the students' statements.

In addition, they must engender social norms in the classroom that encourage students to treat each other in similar ways. This does not mean that all points of view should be treated as equally acceptable. The goal in teaching for conceptual change is for all students to understand the conclusions and modes of reasoning accepted by the scientific community, understanding that they are socially valuable and intellectually powerful even if they are not the immutable "truth."

Our teachers' guides are designed to help teachers deal with at least the intellectual demands of supporting scaffolded dialogue. For each question posed in the student materials, the teachers' guide (a) explains how students are likely to answer and the reasoning that underlies those answers, and (b) contrasts typical student answers with acceptable scientific answers. In some cases, the teacher's guide also suggests how the teacher could respond to common incorrect answers. Teachers generally respond to these portions of the teacher's guide very positively and report reading them carefully.

References to Cross-talk

Hollon, R.E., Anderson, C.W., & Roth, K.J. (in preparation). Teachers' conceptions of science teaching and learning. In J. Broph (Ed.), *Advances in research on teaching: Vol. 2. Teachers' knowledge of subject matter as it relates to their teaching practice.* Greenwich, CT: JAI Press.

Resnick, L.B. (1987). Learning in school and out. *Educational Researcher, 16*(9), 13-20.

IMPLEMENTING INSTRUCTIONAL PROGRAMS TO PROMOTE MEANINGFUL, SELF-REGULATED LEARNING

Linda M. Anderson

The other papers in this book describe recent developments in instruction in specific subject-matter areas. Five papers specifically describe instructional programs that were the basis of experimental intervention studies carried out in classrooms: science;[1] math;[2] reading;[3] writing;[4] and reading.[5] This paper is an analysis of several issues concerning the implementation of these five programs in classrooms.

The results reported for experimental studies of these five programs and others like them (e.g., Paris & Jacobs, 1984; Scardamalia & Bereiter, 1985; Schoenfeld, 1985) are promising. It is tempting to conclude that instructional applications of cognitive science herald important reforms in schools toward development of "higher order thinking skills" by more students.

However, as the developers of these programs probably would be the first to point out, there is more to promoting change in classrooms than the design of a theoretically sound program of instruction. The process of developing and implementing such programs requires an understanding of classroom

Advances in Research on Teaching, Volume 1, pages 311-343.
Copyright © 1989 by JAI Press Inc.
All rights of reproduction in any form reserved.
ISBN: 0-89232-845-2

environments and how teachers and students operate within them. The main point of this paper is to use the five programs as examples of efforts to promote higher-order learning through the development of subject-specific curricula and/or teaching methods.

More specifically, it is proposed in this paper that classrooms and teachers differ along five dimensions that determine the environment within which instruction takes place. These differences among classrooms and teachers exist *before* instructional programs are introduced, and they have implications for how instructional programs are implemented and what effects these programs have on student learning. The five dimensions are defined below in terms of two contrasting poles:

1. *The academic goals of schooling.* The academic goals that drive instruction can range from recall of facts and context-specific application of skills to the development of "expertise" that is demonstrated through strategic and flexible (i.e., decontextualized) use of knowledge.

2. *Teachers' instructional roles.* Teachers (and students and administrators) may view teachers' most important role as conveying information to students or as mediating learning as it is constructed by students.

3. *Students' roles in promoting their own learning.* Corresponding to the teachers' instructional roles are various perceptions of the roles played by students, ranging from that of receptor of information to be applied directly to practice activities to that of an active constructor of meaningful cognitive networks that are used during problem solving in a self-regulated manner.

4. *The nature of academic tasks.* Tasks may be viewed as sites for application of algorithmic procedures to problems with single correct answers, or they may be viewed as situations that require students to define and represent problems and transform existing knowledge into one of many possible solutions.

5. *The social environment as the context for individual learning.* Social environments may present conditions in which failure has social consequences, the source of cognitive regulation is external to the student, and other students are viewed as hindrances to learning. On the other hand, social environments may present conditions in which failure is accepted as a part of learning, self-regulation of cognition is valued more than other-regulation, and other students are viewed as resources for learning.

It is argued in this paper that these five dimensions can be used to describe the basic underlying premises of teachers' belief systems, classroom norms (as perceived by both teachers and students), and instructional programs. Teachers and classrooms vary along each of these dimensions, although placement on any dimension is probably correlated with the other dimensions. (For example, perceptions of teacher and student roles are likely to be related to one's academic goals.) Although there is variance among teachers and classrooms, descriptive studies (to be cited in the following sections) suggest that many, if not most, classrooms could be placed at one end of all five dimensions: the first pole previously presented for each dimension, representing a "traditional," basic-skills, direct-instruction approach to schooling.

In contrast to teachers and classrooms, each of the experimental instructional programs discussed in this book (and others like them) are based on premises that reflect the latter pole of each dimension, the opposite of the pattern found for many classrooms. In fact, many of the program developers would probably argue that they developed their models of instruction precisely to serve as an alternative to existing patterns of instruction that seemed to inhibit the development of higher order thinking.

Thus, a situation exists in which several promising programs have been developed, are being studied, and will (presumably) be made available to schools in the future, if they are not already being disseminated. These programs are based on fundamentally different premises than most classrooms. Thus, there is likely to be some incongruence between the instructional programs and many of the classrooms in which they are to be implemented.

The remainder of the chapter describes the nature of possible incongruence for each of the five dimensions. For each dimension, the features of the instructional programs are described first. Then, the likely variation of teachers and classrooms along that dimension is described, and the implications of incongruence between programs, teachers, and classrooms are discussed. Finally, some recommendations for staff developers, curriculum developers, and researchers are offered.

DIMENSION 1:
ACADEMIC GOALS OF SCHOOLING

Features of Instructional Programs

The instructional programs have been described in this volume as promoting meaningful understanding and/or self-regulated learning. The first goal applies most clearly to the science and math programs (see Anderson & Roth; Fennema, Carpenter & Peterson), while the second goal most fits the reading and writing programs (see Duffy & Roehler; Englert & Raphael; Palincsar & Brown). However, these are not disparate goals; the five instructional programs have in common the underlying premise that the primary academic purpose of schooling is the acquisition of expertise in problem sovling in many specific domains.

Although the term "expertise" sometimes connotes a rare quality, held only by a few adults in society, the term is used differently here, in that expertise is viewed more as a style of cognitive response to problems than as are absolute status conferred by society on a select few. This characterization of expertise could be applied as well to an 8-year-old who is solving a second-grade math problem as to a nuclear physicist who is pondering the workings of atoms, if their problem solving performance shared certain characteristics.

Expertise has been studied extensively in the past decade. Expertise is domain-specific; that is, expertise in one area (e.g., reading expository text) does not necessarily correlate with expertise in another area (e.g., map use). Within a given domain, experts' knowledge has been described as having more coherent, complex organization than the knowledge of that domain held by novices (the term used to describe someone whose performance is not expert-like). Furthermore, experts access their knowledge easily and efficiently when solving problems. An expert in a particular domain of knowledge approaches problems by first identifying the nature of a task, determining what knowledge is most relevant, and then accessing and transforming this knowledge in order to resolve a problem or carry out a task (Bransford, Kitsch, & Franks, 1977; Chi, Glaser, & Rees, 1982; Glaser, 1984).

In order to develop expertise in a particular domain (e.g., elementary mathematical operations), learners must acquire and construct coherent networks of knowledge, and they must develop the self-regulatory mechanisms that allow them to analyze situations and determine what knowledge to access and how to use it. In accord with this view, each of the instructional programs attempts to develop some aspect of expertise.

For example, Anderson and Roth describe a science curriculum whose purpose is to effect substantial changes in learners' cognitive structures regarding natural phenomena: from "naive," unscientific conceptions toward more scientifically defensible conceptions. Such conceptual change enables the learner to function more like an expert on scientific problems of describing, explaining, predicting, and controlling natural phenomena. The expert-like performance is more likely when conceptual change has occurred because (presumably) the learner's knowledge base is reorganized into a network that is especially appropriate for solving scientific problems of describing, explaining, predicting, and controlling. This network features certain key propositions, such as "Light is reflected by objects", and those key propositions are connected to other propositions by means of causal, associational, conditional, and sequential relationships (e.g., "We see when our eyes detect light that is reflected by objects.") The instructional program was designed to help teachers help students to understand how certain propositional knowledge can be used to solve scientific problems. Thus, the program focuses on one component of the development of expertise—the organization of knowledge that is accessed during problem solving.

The goals of the math program described by Fennema et al. are similar to those of the science program. In the math program, the goal for student learning is mathematical understanding, and this is also defined in terms of the relationships between segments of knowledge. A child who understands math would be able to comprehend the mathematical relationships inherent in a problem and its solution, and would not be limited to rote application of algorithms. A student can only become expert in the solution of mathematical problems when both conceptual and procedural knowledge are accessible and can be used flexibly.

The reading and writing programs contrast to the math and science programs in that they emphasize a different aspect of expertise: self-regulation of cognition during problem solving. Duffy and Roehler have developed a program to aid teachers to teach students that reading is a strategic activity, and that the purpose of learning specific strategies is to use them flexibly in "real reading", not just in basal readers and workbooks. They emphasize that teachers should model for students how fluent (i.e., expert) readers consider problems in text as they encounter them, and select from among the strategies that they have available. Thus, the aspect of expert performance emphasized in this instructional program is the definition of the problem and the search for appropriate knowledge (in this case, strategic knowledge) to bring to bear on the problem.

Similarly, the methods of Reciprocal Teaching by Palincsar and Brown highlight the ways that expert readers foster and monitor their own comprehension, which can be construed as a continuous problem-solving activity during reading. The goal of the Reciprocal Teaching Program is to help readers learn to recognize and define problems of reading, to monitor their own comprehension by means of questioning themselves and summarizing, and to access their background knowledge to aid them in predicting and clarifying text. All of these activities are aspects of expert performance.

Englert and Raphael developed a program for teaching expository writing. This program fosters development of expertise in two ways. First, there is restructuring of students' knowledge about text through instruction in text structures and their purposes. Thus, when writing, students have not only their own background knowledge to draw on when composing, but they also have text structure knowledge to use when making decisions about how to organize their thoughts on paper. The program also emphasizes a second feature of expert writing: self-regulation of the cognitive processes of planning, composing, and revising. One aim of the program is to aid students in the internalization of guiding questions that will trigger expert performance (e.g., "Who is my audience?") In particular, the program encourages the development of a perspective on writing as "knowledge-transformation" as opposed to "knowledge-telling" (Scardamalia & Bereiter, 1986). Knowledge-telling results when students write all that they know about a topic without imposing any organization on their knowledge to aid the comprehension of a reader. Knowledge transformation involves the imposition of a framework on one's knowledge to help the reader understand one's purpose and to provide the reader with necessary background knowledge. Knowledge transformation during writing is a good example of the kind of performance that characterizes expert problem-solvers (Bereiter & Scardamalia, 1986).

Instructional practices recommended by the programs are derived from theoretical assumptions about the nature of expertise. For example, all of the instructional programs reflect a concern with the conceptual links between bits of information that are formed by learners, because expertise cannot develop on the basis of facts and skills learned in isolation from one another. Thus, there is an emphasis on "how," "why," and "when" questions and explanations by both teachers and students in all of the programs. Because expertise requires that learners access and transform their knowledge in a flexible manner, the programs each recommend that teachers provide experiences in which students carry out self-regulated (although perhaps guided) searches of knowledge and its application to problems that are incompletely defined. These and other recommended practices are discussed in later sections of this paper.

Features of Teachers and Classrooms

Thus, the experimental instructional programs are grounded in their developers' perspectives that the goal of academic learning in schools is the development of expertise in several domains. How congruent are these perspectives and the perspectives of the teachers and students who "receive" the programs? Available descriptive data suggest that, in many classrooms, academic goals are perceived as something very different from the development of expertise as it was described in the preceding section.

Perhaps the most prevalent alternative to the expertise goal is a "fact and skill acquisition" goal, in which students learn much content, but the links among the separate components are not emphasized, and evaluation of learning requires only the demonstration of the skills or facts per se, not their application to a problem whose representation is uncertain. (For example, students learn addition facts, and then demonstrate their knowledge on a test with computational problems already expressed as addition; such a task does not reveal anything about students' knowledge of mathematical relationships or students' capacities to define and represent a problem requiring addition.)

Recent descriptions of schooling have decried the passive approach to knowledge taken in many schools (Goodlad, 1984; Sirotnik, 1983). This concern is reflected in results of recent administrations of the National Assessment of Educational Progress (1983) measures, on which American students perform poorly for items requiring "higher order" thinking, or application of their knowledge to problem situations. However, test results are not as discouraging for questions requiring rote recall of a fact or skill, suggesting that schools are accomplishing goals of teaching facts and skills.

Studies of instruction in specific subject-matter areas support these conclusions. Anderson and Smith (1987) surveyed science education and reported that "meaningful learning in science courses is usually limited to a small minority of students. The students who are 'good in science' understand while all the rest memorize" (p. 87). Similarly, studies of math teaching and learning often report that an emphasis on form and procedures dominates over conceptual understanding (Hiebert, 1986).

An analysis of the resulting learning is offered by Davis (1986), who describes how students become dependent on textbook patterns in order to access the mathematical knowledge needed to solve a problem. He reports that students' knowledge may be context-bound and not accessible for problems that do not conform to textbook patterns. Davis (1986) argues that such context-bound knowledge results from an instructional emphasis on mathematics as written symbols that are manipulated according to a set of rules, with the goals of learning math defined in these terms (i.e., learning the precise rules and applying them only to written symbols).

Curricula and instructional practices in reading and writing have received a great deal of analysis, with similar conclusions reached about the goals that apparently drive the instruction. Duffy, Roehler et al. found in a series of studies of elementary reading teachers that basal readers drive instruction, and the result is an emphasis on reading skills learned in isolation from purposeful reading of text (Duffy & McIntyre, 1982; Duffy, Roehler et al., 1987). This conclusion has also been reached by others in the reading field (Anderson, Osborn, & Tierney, 1984).

A similar case is noted by Applebee (1981) for writing instruction. He characterized writing instruction as focusing on isolated skills with very few opportunities for students to engage in extended writing that requires planning and revision.

These findings do not mean that no teachers hold the development of expertise as their primary academic goal. However, these findings do suggest that there are other academic goals in place in classrooms. It is not the case that fact and skill learning have no place in the development of expertise; however, there is a distinction between facts and skills learned for their own sake and facts and skills learned as part of an integrated cognitive network that is used to solve problems. The examples offered above suggest that the problem with much current instruction is that learning of facts and skills in isolation is too often the terminal goal of instruction, not a means to the end of understanding.

Teachers' goals for academic learning influence their instructional decisions, in part by influencing perceptions about what kind of information should be sought from students in order to plan further instruction (i.e., information is valuable if it helps one make goal-related decisions). Teachers whose goal is to promote the development of expertise will attend to particular cues from students such as the students' explanations of connections between ideas or the students' apparent awareness of the demands of a problem. Such a teacher will, in fact, instruct so as to solicit these cues, because progress toward the goal cannot be judged without them. (The paper by Lampert [this volume, pp. 223-264] describes this kind of teaching within elementary math.) In contrast, teachers who see fact and skill acquisition as terminal goals for instruction will solicit and attend to other cues from students, such as the correctness of answers.

DIMENSION 2:
PERCEPTIONS OF TEACHERS' INSTRUCTIONAL ROLES

Features of Instructional Programs

The instructional programs described here focus only on teachers' *instructional* roles, not their socializing or management roles. Within that instructional role, the programs deemphasize teachers' roles as providers of information (e.g., through direct instruction about facts and skills) and instead emphasize teachers' roles as *mediators* of student learning about strategies and about conceptual networks. This mediational role is enacted through interactions with students and through provision of tasks that engage students in problem solving.

Within these programs, what does it mean to be a mediator? Mediation by a teacher helps a child see conceptual connections between new ideas or skills and other ideas on situations. However, teachers do not simply supply the information that they assume will make a connection; instead, they continue interacting with the child to gain evidence that the child's understanding is appropriate.

Feuerstein (cited in Brainin, 1985) suggested four components of instructional mediation, all of which are reflected to some extent in the instructional programs: the *expression of intentionality* through explicitness about purpose and prediction of what will occur and how events relate to the instructional purpose; exploration and *assignment of meaning to stimuli*, interpreting events for a child in a meaningful manner; *relating those meanings to a larger sphere of significance*, and thus showing what individual problems and solutions have in common with one another; and *providing opportunities for new understanding to be applied*. In all of these ways, teachers help students to make conceptual connections and to see how new learning applies in a variety of contexts.

According to some theories (Vygotsky, 1978; Wertsch, 1985), mediation is most effective during social interactions surrounding problem-solving; through these mediated interactions, learners internalize self-regulatory capacities. The five instructional programs emphasize such problem-centered social interactions, during which the teacher and student(s) jointly work to reach solutions.

The term usually used to describe mediation by the teacher during joint problem solving is *scaffolding*, defined as "a process that enables a child or novice to solve a problem, carry out a task, or achieve a goal which would be beyond his unassisted efforts" (Wood, Bruner, & Ross, 1976, p. 90). Palincsar (1986) describes scaffolded instruction as beginning with the selection of a learning task that is just barely within the learner's capabilities, within what Vygotsky (1978) called the "zone of proximal development". Scaffolded instruction proceeds by means of task simplification by the teacher along with highlighting of critical features of the task, in order to help the learner organize information from the experience for future efforts (in which, presumably, less support will be necessary). Simplification and highlighting of relevant cues may involve teacher modeling, questioning, and explaining, but exactly what is done depends on the student's performance. Gradually, there is shifting of the responsibility for doing the cognitive work from the teacher to the student.

Collins, Brown, and Newman (1989) also offer a description of mediated, scaffolded instruction that aids the development of expertise. They compare this kind of teaching to a "cognitive apprenticeship" in which learners become part of an expert culture and learn from the modeling and coaching of their mentors (in this case, the mentors are more accomplished readers, writers, mathematicians, and natural and social scientists).

Palincsar (1986) points out that teacher-student dialogue is essential to scaffolded instruction. Because instruction must be flexible and sensitive to students' emerging understandings, there is a limit to how much instruction can be planned in advance and relegated to independent student reading and completion of assignments.

Each of the instructional programs portrays teachers' roles largely in terms of their frequent and extensive dialogues with students about content and its applications to various problems, with the teacher serving as mediator and scaffolder, providing the cues and prompts that help students make necessary conceptual linkages (sometimes through questions, in a Socratic manner, and sometimes through direct explanations).

For example, Anderson and Roth and their colleagues created science curricula that emphasize ways that teachers can help students replace naive preconceptions with more scientific conceptions. The curriculum provides a series of application questions to be posed during class discussion, and suggests ways that the teacher can engage students in problems of description, explanation, and prediction instead of simply providing facts to be memorized.

Teachers in their studies learned how and when to respond to students' answers in different ways (e.g., to probe, to explain, to coach, to model). Thus, dialogue, explication of conceptual links, and scaffolding are all elements of this program.

Similarly, in the Fennema et al. program, the teachers in the CGI (Cognitively Guided Instruction) group were less likely than the non-CGI teachers to focus on rules for computations and number facts, and instead spent more time talking with students about word problems and listening to students explain their reasoning, recognizing that different students might have different strategies for the same problem. The case studies presented in the Fennema et al. chapter portray teachers who engaged in dialogue with students about problems, sometimes offering suggestions but primarily serving as mediators and helping students see new connections between ideas.

Duffy and Roehler emphasize the importance of teacher explicitness about how and when strategies can help accomplish reading goals. Explicit instruction occurs in a group setting and is followed by interaction with students, in which the teacher offers guided assistance and probing for student understanding until students can perform without extensive scaffolding. In their instructional program, they highlight the role of purpose-setting for students (or, in Feuerstein's terms, expressing intentionality). They argue that students need to be told explicitly how new reading strategies will help them do "real reading", so that skills are not practiced only in the context of the basal reader. Thus, the teacher is portrayed as a critical mediator between the content and the students.

Palincsar and Brown developed Reciprocal Teaching around the principles of scaffolded instruction. The teacher is not primarily a presenter of new content, except in the very beginning of the program when students learn the procedures associated with the method. Instead, the teacher is first a cognitive model, and then provides cognitive support as the students engage in the problems of comprehending text. This program is a clear example of scaffolding during problem solving; the teacher mediates the students' developing understanding of how to approach the problem by alternately modeling, coaching, and then fading prompts as students become more capable.

Englert and Raphael encouraged their teachers to model the cognitive processes used by expert writers, and then to coach students through the writing process, gradually withdrawing support as students begin to internalize the questions that expert writers ask themselves. In this program, students also use "think-sheets" as a form of scaffolding to be used when the teacher is not immediately available. On the think-sheets, each step in the writing process corresponds to a color-coded sheet on which are listed the questions that expert writers answer as they think through their writing problems (e.g., "Why am I writing this? What's my purpose?").

Thus, each of the programs incorporates a similar perspective on the mediational role of teachers. Through scaffolded instruction during dialogue about problems, they ensure that students recognize purposes, make appropriate conceptual connections in their understanding of new content, select and use strategies to accomplish their goals, and learn to apply content flexibly across several contexts.

Features of Teachers and Classrooms

How congruent is this perspective about teachers' roles with current instructional practices? Available evidence suggests that it is not very congruent, in that the role of mediator, scaffolder, and dialogue participant is not the predominant instructional role enacted by most teachers.

Palincsar (1986) notes that descriptive studies of classrooms reveal little dialogue that fits her definition. To be dialogue, the teachers' comments must respond to student comments and questions. What happens in many classrooms, instead, is that teacher-student interaction consists of questions with specific correct answers which are not discussed in depth. Teachers often do not respond to student answers substantively or probe the students' understanding.

Two descriptive studies provide examples of lack of teacher mediation during task assignment. Anderson, Brubaker, Alleman-Brooks, and Duffy (1985) found that reading seatwork assignments to first graders were usually presented without any reminders about purposes or about strategies. Brophy, Rohrkemper, Rashid, and Goldberger (1983) found that sixth-grade teachers tended to present assignments as procedures, without placing the work into context of what was being learned and why it was important. Such data suggest that some teachers do not see themselves as mediators of instruction, but rather as presenters of content and as orchestrators of activities that bring students in contact with that content.

When teachers do not readily identify with the goals of expertise development and the role of mediator, and yet are asked to implement one of the instructional programs, they adapt the program to fit with more familiar goals and instructional roles. That is, they change the recommended curriculum and instructional practices to more closely resemble fact and skill transmittal from the teacher to the student.

Some good examples of this kind of adaptation are available from analyses of dialogues from the instructional programs (Duffy, Roehler, & Rackliffe, 1986; Palincsar, 1986; Raphael, Englert, & Anderson, 1987). In these analyses, researchers noted differences among teachers in the quality of their dialogues. All teachers were involved in staff development efforts encouraging dialogue in which student thinking is probed and scaffolding provided by the teacher as necessary. However, some teachers in each study created dialogues that were more like traditional recitation patterns in which the teacher posed questions that required short answers that could be deemed correct or incorrect, and the teacher directly taught all new information, rather than modeling or teaching through guided practice and scaffolding.

It is not clear from these three studies why the teachers used a recitation model rather than a mediational model. One possible reason is that the teachers did not agree with the underlying premises of the mediational model. Teachers, like anyone else, are likely to be uncomfortable with new procedures that do not "make sense" and that do not appear to move one toward one's goals. In such a situation, one is likely to revert to familiar (and personally sensible) patterns of action. (See Duffy & Roehler [1986] for further discussion of difficulties faced by their teachers in adoption of the instructional program.)

Work by Olson (1983) sheds light on one source of difficulty in implementing a new instructional approach. He studied British teachers who were implementing a new science curriculum that required teachers allow students to experiment, hypothesize, and problem-solve in order to learn science content. Although the mediational role of the teacher in this endeavor was not made explicit, it was implicit in the curriculum; teachers were somehow supposed to create conditions in which they could guide students to the desired scientific knowledge without actually telling them the answers.

Olson approached the study of eight teachers using this program with a great deal of sympathy for the teachers' perspective. One of his opening statements is appropriate for the current chapter: "People outside of schools constantly seek to influence what those inside do and fail. Why do they fail? They fail, I think, because outsiders do not understand what teachers are trying to do. As a consequence a gap exists; what one group means to say, the other does not understand" (Olson, 1983, p. 17).

Olson determined that his teachers held what he called "theories of influence" that determined their perceptions of their roles. They defined their most pressing academic goals as preparation of the students for external examinations requiring fact and skill knowledge. Accordingly, the teachers had a great need for a syllabus—a written list of what facts and skills should be taught—and this figured prominently in their pedagogical theories.

Olson analyzed the language used by the teachers and concluded that their implicit theories of influence were an important source of terms. For example, they talked about their goals in terms of "getting the facts in," "hammering ideas," being a "fount of widsom," and "putting right" the students' misunderstandings. He used this analysis of language to understand why the teachers resisted and even "sabotaged" the place of student problem solving in the curriculum:

> Rather than using a language whose terms are developed from a theory of mental events, teachers used a language whose terms were given meaning by their theories of classroom

influence; That is, theories about authority and the nature of their efficacy....The language they used to describe how they saw the low-influence role (required in order to run problem-solving activities) captures the sense of their withdrawal and illustrates, by default, their theories of influence: 'uninvolved,' 'hovering,' 'checking off,' 'technician,' 'observer,' 'referee,' 'in the background.' *Doing problem-solving was translated as losing influence.* (Olson, 1983, p. 22).

Similarly, Johnston (1987) also analyzed British teachers' implementation of a science curriculum that required them to adopt a mediational role. Her findings are congruent with Olson's study. She reports a case study of a teacher who ran a lesson in which the curriculum developers intended that students present their own conclusions after an experiment, but the teacher ended up dominating the discussion (preventing a true dialogue) and presenting the "correct" explanations. The teacher was pleased with the outcome of the lesson, because he had met his own objectives for covering the content within the time allotted. The teacher offered this explanation of the teacher's role in such a lesson:

> Let *them* put forward their ideas, then my job is to 'pull the threads together,' fill in the missing bits, put it all in the correct order and tell them what the answer is. My job as a teacher is, after all, to help them succeed (pass exams). Johnston, 1987, p. 35)

These findings help to explain the different styles of dialogue observed by Duffy et al. (1986), Palincsar (1986), and Raphael et al. (1987). If teachers' theories of influence are strong, they will interpret advice in terms of those theories. In this case, a mediated dialogue may appear to mean nothing more than asking many questions so that students offer their ideas, but ending with the teacher giving the "correct" answer.

Although the designers of instructional programs believe that the teacher has a great deal of influence on student learning, they recommend that influence should be enacted in a form that is not familiar to most teachers. Therefore, the mediational role may be viewed by many teachers as risky, putting the teacher in jeopardy of losing control of the class and having nothing to show for the lesson. It is little wonder that teachers who perceive the programs in this way implement them in a manner that makes teacher control more obvious.

DIMENSION 3:
THE NATURE OF LEARNING AND STUDENTS' ROLES IN LEARNING

Features of Instructional Programs

Related closely to teachers' definitions of their instructional roles are their beliefs about the nature of learning and about students' participation in their own learning. These beliefs, in turn, are tied to beliefs about the goals of academic learning in schools. The five instructional programs share certain underlying beliefs about the nature of learning and students' roles that are not necessarily shared by all teachers and students.

As described for Dimension 1, the instructional programs each promote the development of some aspect of domain-specific expertise. Underlying this goal is a two-part view of expertise: it is a function of (1) the knowledge base (and its organization) and (2) the capabilities inherent in an individual's executive control system, especially knowledge of one's own cognitive processes and how to regulate their use (or metacognition). Executive control allows the individual to analyze the demands of a task, strategically search for relevant knowledge, and select and execute strategies for problem solution.

How do the instructional programs assume that these components of expertise develop? Acquisition of the knowledge base is explained by means of a constructivist theory in which individuals hold unique prior knowledge (organized into schemata) into which they assimilate new information when possible. When new information does not "fit" into existing schemata, then accommodation occurs, and schemata are reorganized. These processes can not be forced by an outsider; the learner is the constructor, although others, serving as mediators, can influence the ways that learners organize and reorganize their knowledge. (The basis of such theories has been expressed by many, with Piaget as perhaps the best known example [for subject-specific examples, see Anderson & Pearson, 1984; Posner, Strike, Hewson, & Gertzog, 1982; Romberg & Carpenter, 1986]).

The instructional programs assume that executive control, like knowledge acquisition, is also influenced through interactions with the environment, especially with individuals who exhibit more expertise and who model, coach, and sometimes directly teach how to approach problems strategically (Collins et al., 1989; Wertsch, 1985). The acquisition of executive control (and its underlying knowledge base of cognitive and metacognitive strategies) is not accomplished automatically through mere exposure to instruction about strategies; learners must actively make sense of the information themselves, integrating it into their existing schemata or modifying those schemata.

In each of the instructional programs, the language used to describe student learning reflects this view of students' roles. For example, in the work of Anderson and Roth student learning is described as "conceptual change," meaning that students' topic-specific conceptions undergo major restructuring.

In the math study by Fennema et al., the beliefs about student learning are clearly evident. The basis for the program is earlier research on ways that childern construct understandings of mathematics in the absence of formal instruction. Within this program, a basic instructional principle is that decisions about what and how to teach depend on each child's knowledge and thinking about math.

Duffy and Roehler describe students "restructuring" their understandings of how to read. Palinscar and Brown describe students developing metacognitive control, and portray instructional dialogues as opportunities for students to gradually internalize the questions that direct them in controlling their own cognition. Englert and Raphael also emphasize the students' construction of an understanding of the process of writing and the development of metacognitive control by internalization of guiding questions.

In each case, students play the central role in attaining the academic goals. Learning is accomplished essentially by the student with guidance from the teacher. Unless the teacher can stimulate mental activity that results in student construction of new knowledge, the teacher cannot effect learning. This view of students' roles as constructors of their own learning does *not* mean that teachers do not influence learning, although the instructional role of mediator may be interpreted by teachers as lacking influence when teachers do not hold a constructivist view of learning.

Features of Teachers and Classrooms

How does a constructivist view of learning compare to views held by many teachers and students in classrooms where such instructional programs might be implemented? Descriptive studies suggest that there is a range among teachers in their theories about student learning. Bussis, Chittendon, and Amarel (1976) interviewed 60 teachers who were teaching in open classrooms that were based on a "child-centered" constructivist approach to learning. They found differences among the teachers in the centrality of the belief that children are primary resources for instruction (meaning that they bring important knowledge that affects the outcomes of instruction) as opposed to a view that centers on children coming to instruction with deficits in their knowledge that should be remedied by the teacher. Bussis et al. also found that teachers who held the "child as resource" view were more likely to engage in "phenomenological inquiry," or attempts to learn from dialogue with the child how the child was understanding the world. Such "phenomenological inquiry" is a characteristic of the mediated dialogues advocated by the instructional programs. These data reported by Bussis et al. suggest that teachers' theories of child learning will affect how willingly they enter into such dialogue.

Hollon and Anderson (1987) also found a range of teacher beliefs about the nature of learning and reasons that students fail to learn, and these beliefs were related to teachers' instructional practice, particularly their use of class discussions that were mediated dialogues. They categorized 13 teachers into three groups according to their views of learning: Conceptual Development (learning occurs when students change their schemata that explain the world); Content Understanding (learning involves acquisition of new ideas or knowledge, but this learning does not require reconstruction of schemata); and

Fact Acquisition (no clear theories about student learning; failure to learn is attributed to student characteristics).

Peterson, Fennema, Carpenter, and Loef (1987) measured teachers' beliefs about how students learned and should be taught mathematics. (This study preceded the work reported by Fennema et al.) Peterson et al. (1987) found that there was a range of beliefs; while some teachers recognized the constructive role played by the child, other teachers did not. They also found that the students of the teachers with more "cognitively based" beliefs achieved more on problem solving measures than the students of teachers who were less "cognitively based".

Clift, Ghatala, and Naus (1987) surveyed 37 elementary and secondary teachers about their awareness of cognitive strategies and frequency of strategy instruction. Such a survey reveals something about the place in teachers' thinking of one component of executive control. Clift et al. (1987) found, to their surprise, that many of the teachers said that they taught strategies regularly. However, when they followed the questionnaire with in-depth interviews with ten of the teachers, they learned that the teachers viewed strategy instruction as directly teaching or modeling procedures, but did not include any metacognitive components of strategy use—deciding *when, why,* and *how* to control use of strategies. The metacognitive components are essential if the learner is to become self-regulated in the use of strategies. Otherwise, strategy instruction becomes another form of content delivery from the teacher to the students, who learn strategies as specific skills to be used when given specific cues. Thus, the teachers (at least those who were interviewed) did not reveal a theory of learning that featured the active, controlling learner as the central player in strategic thinking.

These studies suggest that there is a range of teachers' beliefs about student learning, with some teachers much closer than others to the perspective on learning and learners that is represented in the instructional programs. It is reasonable that teachers who hold a different set of beliefs about student learning would have a difficult time adopting the mediator role advocated by the instructional programs. As revealed in the quote given earlier from Johnston's (1987) case study, some teachers may simply have more faith in the knowledge that they can deliver to students than they do in any knowledge constructed by students, especially if they assume that the teacher's knowledge, as delivered, will be encoded by students in that form. Although teachers may hold beliefs that student participation, practice, concrete experiences, and other student activities are important, they may view activities as a way of getting the knowledge into the students, without concern for how it is interpreted once inside their heads.

If one adheres to a constructivist theory of learning and understanding, then it is also important to examine the role played by *students' beliefs* about the academic goals of schooling, teachers' roles, and students' roles. Students' beliefs in these areas may be at odds with the premises of the instructional programs. When at odds, student resistance to the programs may prove to be a strong obstacle to implementation, even when the teacher's beliefs and goals are congruent with the program.

Bereiter and Scardamalia (1985) address this issue by describing students' "cognitive coping strategies." They expressed concerns with the prevalence of "inert knowledge" as described by Whitehead (1929): knowledge that can be expressed under specific conditions (such as school tasks) but that is not usable in other forms. They believe that this form of knowledge is prevalent in schools, and as a result, students learn to survive by developing cognitive coping strategies that allow them to succeed with school tasks. One example of a coping strategy is the knowledge-telling strategy for school writing, which contrasts to the knowledge-transforming strategies of expert writers. (Knowledge-telling is essentially a dumping of information until there are no more ideas left to express; knowledge-transforming is a more strategic selection and organization of ideas for a particular goal and audience.) These coping strategies are so entrenched, argue Bereiter and Scardamalia, that they threaten to override instructional programs designed to promote expertise. That is, students will assimilate the new information into their familiar, comfortable ways of defining the demands of school tasks and responding to them.

Similarly, Doyle (1983) has argued that students come to define classroom experiences in terms of accountability systems, and as a result, students resist assignments designed to promote higher-order learning when those assignments combine risk of failure with ambiguity about how to succeed. Doyle suggests that students will attempt to negotiate with teachers to simplify demands of "higher-order" tasks.

Thus, students may resist teachers' efforts to accomplish new academic goals that are incongruent with the students' understanding of how school is supposed to be run. Given that students are the critical constructors of their own new understandings, based in large part on the beliefs and knowledge they bring with them to instruction, it is folly to ignore the importance of students' schemata for understanding classroom events.

If the instructional programs are to take seriously their own premise that students are the primary constructors of meaningful understanding and self-regulation, then they must apply that premise to the task of helping teachers help students redefine what is reasonable and appropriate when doing academic work in schools. In order to create conditions in which the instructional programs will take root, teachers need to attend to students' beliefs and coping strategies. For example, Lampert (1987) describes some problems encountered by teachers who wish to incorporate student thinking into the teaching of math. One of the tasks of the teacher is to redefine authority away from the teacher and text and toward the students, which requires teaching the students how to demonstrate that authority (e.g., teaching them how to explain their own thinking).

A related recommendation is made by Borkowski, Weyhing, & Turner (1986) who suggest that it is not enough to teach students how and when to use strategies; students must also become convinced that strategic thinking will promote success on important tasks. That is, students must learn to attribute success to strategic planning and monitoring, and failure to the lack of strategies. Without these associated attributions, students are not likely to actively construct an understanding of how strategies can aid performance.

DIMENSION 4:
ACADEMIC TASKS

Closely related to questions about students' understanding of schooling is the issue of what kinds of tasks are presented to students and for what purposes. Tasks are any activities associated with academic instruction that are engaged in by students, usually at the teacher's behest, for purposes of acquiring and/ or using knowledge, skills, or strategies. Tasks are considered by some as a fundamental unit for analyzing classroom events (Blumenfeld, Mergendollar, & Swarthout, 1987; Doyle, 1983).

Features of Instructional Programs

Tasks form the basis for the accountability system in the classroom, so that they typically serve dual purposes: students both learn from tasks and are evaluated for their performance on tasks. Within the instructional programs described here, tasks explicitly fulfill only one of these purposes, that of helping students learn. In the instructional programs, the recommended tasks are not presented as the basis for formal evaluation. (In fact, the programs are silent on the issue of how students should be formally evaluated, although this is a pervasive feature of schooling in the eyes of most teachers and students.)

Tasks fulfill instructional purposes in these programs because they create contexts within which teachers may assess students' understanding and provide scaffolding to guide their thinking. In order to accomplish this, tasks in the programs are characterized by the following features.

- *Tasks are problems to be solved, not stimuli for the recall of specific information.* Scardamalia and Bereiter (1985) characterize appropriate tasks as "compositional", with "emergent goals." This means that one's goals change as the problem's demands become clearer. Examples of compositional tasks include planning a trip, constructing a scientific theory, and writing an essay. As such, these tasks provide opportunities for the application of expertise, which requires definition of the problem or goal, along with its resolution.

- *Questions have many "correct" responses.* Although some responses to questions are better than others, there are not typically single correct answers. Even when a specific answer is desired, the students' explanations of their thinking (which can vary) are as valued as the answers.
- *The difficulty of any task can be adjusted on the spot.* Because the tasks often occur within group dialogue (rather than as isolated independent work), the teacher provides scaffolding to adjust the difficulty of the demands made on individual students. In this way, tasks may become increasingly complex as students acquire expertise.

These features characterize most, if not all, of the tasks in the five experimental instructional programs. In Anderson and Roth, a critical task for students is the explanation of natural phenomena while participating in a class discussion in which the teacher models and mediates the use of scientific concepts to explain the "real-life" occurrences. For example, an overhead transparency shows a boy standing behind a wall which separates him from a car. The question is posed: Why can't the boy see the car? Students are to answer in terms of what they have learned about how light waves reflect off objects in a straight line.

In the program by Fennema et al., the nature of mathematics tasks is critical. Rather than presenting computational problems to students, where the operation is specified and there are no clear links to concrete situations, teachers are encouraged to provide students with word problems that engage them with the task of defining what is needed to solve the problem.

In the Duffy and Roehler program, students engage in verbal analysis of reading problems in a group. Their explanations of their thinking are probed; short answers of how to read the word are not acceptable without some explication. Because this program was studied in classrooms where basal reader programs were also in use, students still engaged in more traditional seatwork tasks (e.g., reading workbooks) when they left the group. In this case, Duffy and Roehler emphasize the importance of the teacher placing seatwork tasks into a purposeful context, relating them to the content of the lesson that day.

In Palincsar and Brown's Reciprocal Teaching model, the only task required of students is their explicit demonstration of the four strategies for fostering and monitoring their own comprehension. There are no single correct answers, and the teacher is present to respond with scaffolding as necessary.

In the Englert and Raphael program, the students' task is to write expository text, using the "think-sheets" to help them make decisions about what to write, why, for whom, and with what organization. After the initial draft, students engage in peer editing and revision, again using think-sheets as scaffolding to guide them through. Teachers may assist with copy-editing or other editing, but the program discourages teachers from using the students' writing as a basis for formal evaluation.

Features of Teachers and Classrooms

How do the tasks in the experimental instructional programs compare to typical tasks in many classrooms? Available evidence suggests that they are very different, and this discrepancy may have serious implications for implementation of the programs, considering how strongly many students feel about the imposition of ambiguity in tasks and the need to know what exactly is expected of them (Doyle, 1983).

Many of the sources cited for other dimensions (especially for the nature of academic goals) provide evidence for the nature of tasks in many classrooms (Anderson et al., 1985; Applebee, 1981; Blumenfeld et al., 1987; Davis, 1986; Doyle, 1983; Durkin, 1984; Goodlad, 1984). Tasks are frequently characterized by demands for knowledge reproduction—rote recall of facts or skills—without the need for students to consider purposes of goals of the task. Many tasks are performed by students working on their own, so that the tasks do not provide an opportunity for interaction during problem solving, the mechanism through which the instructional programs assume that students develop executive control. Many classroom tasks may be completed through reliance on cues that are extraneous to the content being learned, so that a student could determine the correct answers on one task, and yet not be able to access the same knowledge for a task that appeared in a different format.

Bereiter and Scardamalia (1985) suggest that many of these characteristics of school tasks create ideal conditions in which context-bound, "inert knowledge" is useful and helps students meet the immediate demands of task completion. They define "inert knowledge" as propositional knowledge that can be expressed but not used, citing Whitehead (1929) who believed that the central problem of education was to prevent inert knowledge, which could arise from school demands of a certain nature.

Bereiter and Scardamalia (1985) say that common features of classroom tasks that reinforce the use of inert knowledge include: testing only on content taught in a course in the form that it was taught; presenting test items in the order given in the course (helping those who store knowledge episodically, not meaningfully); teaching concepts in hierarchically ordered fashion and expecting students to learn in this manner (which means that descriptor-driven recall will suffice, and there is no need for students to engage in goal-directed memory searches); and assigning topics for writing that 'turn students on' but that provide for a ready flow of spontaneously recalled content, not goal-directed accessing and transforming of one's knowledge.

The disparity between typical classroom tasks and the tasks that accompany the instructional programs means that teachers must help students redefine how "new" kinds of tasks fit into the accountability system of the classroom. In particular, teachers need to be sensitive to students' needs to feel less risk with highly ambiguous tasks, given that most of the programs' tasks are ambiguous for students, in that the path to the desired response is not clear. In his recent work, Doyle (1986) has studied ways that teachers reduce risk when creating tasks that require "higher-order thinking." It would be worthwhile to learn more about ways that teachers engage students with such tasks—how they hold students accountable for serious participation without imposing too great a sense of risk, especially for the lower achievers. These are issues that have not been addressed in the materials for teachers that were produced with the instructional programs, but the success or failure of a program in a particular classroom might depend upon these issues.

DIMENSION 5:
THE SOCIAL ENVIRONMENT AS THE CONTEXT
FOR INDIVIDUAL LEARNING

The final way in which classrooms and instructional programs may be incongruent is in the role ascribed to the social environment as the context for individual learning. A distinguishing feature of classrooms has always been their blending of social and individual roles and demands (Jackson, 1968; Lortie, 1975).

Features of Instructional Programs

The instructional programs seldom focus explicitly on the social environment of the classroom beyond the designation of group settings for dialogue. What is left implicit are assumptions about the nature of the larger social context of the classroom—the context within which specific group lessons and dialogues are carried out. At least three social conditions are implicitly necessary for successful implementation of the instructional programs.

First, because the development of expertise in problem solving may require ambiguity and some initial failure, it must take place in an environment in which failure on academic tasks does not entail too high a cost for individuals. If students are subject to either teacher or peer criticism for failure, they are less likely to become fully involved in problem-solving efforts and more likely to "save face" through lack of effort (Covington, 1984).

Second, because development of expertise in problem-solving requires the development of self-regulation, the instructional programs assume an environment in which independent decision-making is valued. When students normally work in an atmosphere where the teacher is the only authority and decision maker, then it will be difficult to slip into a self-regulating mode for some lessons, much less to transfer that self-regulation to other tasks.

Third, the instructional programs are grounded in part in a theory of learning that emphasizes the role of social interactions in the development of expertise.

This means that individuals learn best when they are listening to and discussing with others the problems that they are learning to solve. Thus, the programs assume a social environment in which students value one another's contributions and know how to talk with one another about their thinking while problem solving. Other students are cognitive resources, not impediments to learning or competitors.

Within the Anderson and Roth program, these conditions would have to be met in order for the recommended type of class discussion to take place. In these discussions, the teacher poses questions about physical phenomena, and students discuss the merits of each other's explanations. Ideally, all students participate at some point, even given the almost necessary condition that some of the explanations offered will be insufficient. In fact, one of the basic conditions of conceptual change learning is that individuals become dissatisfied with their own misconceptions, and see the advantages of scientific conceptions as alternative explanations (Posner et al., 1982). In order for this to occur, students must accept the risk of failure that comes from grappling publicly with ambiguous problems. At the same time, they must learn that other students are as likely to contribute to the "correct" understanding as is the teacher, and all students will benefit from the group's efforts.

Similarly, within the Duffy and Roehler and the Palincsar and Brown programs, instruction takes place through group discussions in which students must offer their explanations of the strategy and/or content of the reading selection. If the teacher is gradually increasing the level of demand as individuals become more expert, then students will regularly encounter some difficulty. (If they did not, the teacher would not be able to diagnose their needs for adjustments of the scaffolding). Especially within Reciprocal Teaching, the students learn to rely on one another as they take on the role of teacher.

In the math program described by Fennema et al., students discuss word problems in groups with the teacher and on their own with one another. The case studies presented in the chapter reveal a great deal of interaction among the students as they grapple with math programs and construct solutions together.

In Englert and Raphael's writing program students not only discuss writing strategies when teachers make instructional presentations, they also read and critique one another's work, in order to gain a sense of what is needed to adjust writing for a particular audience. Hopefully, students learn that this is an inevitable feature of good writing. One never becomes "good enough" to forego editing and revision; writing remains a social activity that requires that one risk hearing the honest opinion of a reader. One's peers, therefore, are invaluable resources for improving one's writing.

Thus, successful implementation of each of the five programs requires a social environment that is characterized by low cost for initial failure, opportunities for self-regulation, and valuing of peers as a source of knowledge.

Features of Teachers and Classrooms

How do the social requirements of the instructional programs compare to the range of conditions of real classrooms? As with the other dimensions, evidence from descriptive studies of classrooms suggests that there are differences among classrooms, and that in many classrooms, conditions are incongruent with the premises of the instructional programs.

Classrooms vary in the meaning of failure. In some classrooms, students are very aware of an achievement hierarchy, and base their own self-evaluations on their place in the hierarchy (Marshall & Weinstein, 1984; Weinstein, 1983). Self-evaluations then figure in the students' thinking about the role of personal effort (and perhaps about the usefulness of a strategy, such as might be taught in one of the instructional programs) and about the probability of embarrassment or rewards should they decide to participate in a group problem-solving session. Some classrooms are based on norms that learning is valued for its own sake, with mistakes an integral part of learning, but other classrooms do not exemplify this view (Marshall, 1987). As Doyle (1983) has pointed out, students tend to want to minimize ambiguity and risk under any circumstances, and in some classrooms, this orientation may be fostered to an extreme degree when risks of failure are too high.

Classrooms also vary in the extent to which self-reliance and self-regulation are encouraged. Anderson, Stevens, Prawat, and Nickerson (1988) studied 24 elementary classrooms and found that they varied widely in the extent to which students' independence and responsibility were encouraged and developed. In classrooms where students were judged to be more self-regulating and where students revealed desirable self-perceptions (i.e., self-confidence and perceived internal control), the teachers had provided much information about the standards and about how, why, and when to invoke those standards. The teachers also provided the students with many opportunities to regulate their own behavior (e.g., expectations and procedures were in place for students to initiate their assigned housekeeping jobs or to turn work in without explicit teacher direction). Through the information and opportunities provided, the teachers served as mediators for the students' learning about how to function in that particular classroom environment. In other classrooms, in contrast, teachers revealed more authoritarian stances and made most of the decisions about what was done when and by whom in the classroom. In these classrooms, students did not appear to be as self-regulating, and their self-perceptions were less positive. When instructional programs are introduced into classrooms where self-regulation is not promoted and valued in general, then the demands on the students to engage in problem definition and explanations of their thinking will be especially difficult.

Classrooms also differ in the extent to which the peer group is considered a resource for learning, as opposed to an impediment. In many classrooms, students spend up to 70% of their instructional time with seatwork. Classrooms may differ with regard to the degree of helpful interactions allowed during seatwork time, but the ground rules usually remain that individuals must complete the assignment independently. That is, the result should show individual thinking, not group effort. In some classrooms, there is beginning to be more of an emphasis on cooperative groups, although many of these use peer cooperation for the purpose of accomplishing individual work (Slavin, 1984). A cooperative team that functions to get everyone passesd on a set of multiplication fact tests represents a different meaning of cooperation than that required by the instructional programs.

The programs instead require that students learn to listen to one another talk about their thinking, not just answers or procedures. This requires a sensitivity to and valuing of one another's thinking both for its own sake and for its contribution to the understanding of others. This means more than mutual cooperation toward a common goal; it means development of a "theory of mind" that recognizes that individual knowledge is at least in part the result of social construction. From the point of view of the instructional programs, the teacher should be fairly explicit in articulating this theory and in modeling this attitude for the students. However, little available evidence suggests that this perspective is common in classrooms, which have a much more individualistic focus in their underlying "theories of mind".

Thus, descriptive data suggest that the social environment of many classrooms would not provide the conditions necessary for optimal implementation of the instructional programs.

CONCLUSIONS

Teachers' beliefs about their roles and goals and the classroom environments that they create vary along the same dimensions that define the basic premises of the instructional programs discussed in this book. As described in the preceding sections, when the instructional programs are introduced into classrooms with incongruent premises, teachers and students will interpret and adapt the programs in light of their existing beliefs.

If teachers (or students) believe that the primary goal of schooling is the acquisition of specific facts and skills to be evaluated through performance on traditional school tasks and tests, and if they believe that this goal is advanced primarily through direct instruction by the teacher and solitary practice on school tasks by students, then the instructional programs will not make much sense to them. Implementation in such circumstances will be superficial, at best. Dialogues become direct explanations or times when students talk but little learning occurs. Engagement with tasks drops because of uncertainty about how tasks fit into the accountability system, with either resulting management problems or (more likely) adaptation of the tasks by the teacher to make them more congruent with the rest of classroom life.

Such interpretations and adaptations are not blameworthy. Teachers face an incredibly complex task and are not different from anyone else in an ambiguous situation that presents high costs for failure: they make sense of the situation and define their problem space using the knowledge and beliefs available. Within that space, they make decisions and design actions that efficiently allocate available resources to accomplish their most important goals.

Given the sensibility of teachers' responses, what might curriculum developers and staff developers consider if they hope to promote meaningful implementation of instructional programs like the ones described in this book? For one thing, they need to consider that, from the perspective of many teachers, there is no need for such programs. Therefore, if programs are to influence instructional practice, a case must be made that is convincing to teachers that alternatives to present practices exist and are worth trying. Clearly, one way to influence teachers' beliefs is through preservice teacher preparation, where there may be greater opportunities to influence basic premises about the nature of teaching, learning, and classrooms. However, this does not address the needs of staff developers working with experienced teachers.

One way that teachers might begin to rethink their goals and roles is through further development of their own content knowledge. It is difficult to teach for flexible expertise if one's own content knowledge is not flexible. Unfortunately, many sources portray a large number of practicing teachers as having less content knowledge than is needed for the kind of teaching required in the instructional programs (e.g., Anderson & Smith, 1987; Carpenter, Fennema, Peterson, & Carey, 1987; Lanier, 1986; McDiarmid, Ball, & Anderson, 1989; Shulman, 1987). If teachers do not hold rich conceptual conceptions of the content they teach, then they are unlikely to hold as an academic goal the construction of such conceptions by students. Thus, increased subject matter knowledge might be one mechanism for promoting change in teachers' perceptions of goals and associated roles. (The next volume in this series addresses issues surrounding the study and advancement of teachers' content knowledge.)

However, increased subject matter knowledge is no guarantee that teachers' underlying premises about instruction will change. Instead, staff and curriculum developers should pay explicit attention to these premises and spend time on discussion of them. For example, in the Fennema et al. math program, the workshop for teachers focused on how students learned math, not just on how to teach math. In any program, initial interactions with teachers might focus on discussions of their own theories of learning and how instruction affects it, or how the social environments of classrooms vary and what teachers notice about the effects.

However, discussion alone does not accomplish conceptual change. As recommended in the instructional programs, significant learning often results from a mediational approach to instruction in which two or more people engage in the defiintion and solution of meaningful problems. Thus, part of staff development must be dialogue about meaningful problems of teaching. A discussion of the full implications of this assertion for staff development is beyond the scope of this paper. Instead, what is proposed are several sites for dialogue with and among teachers about instructional programs and the ways that they do and do not fit into existing classroom practices.

These sites for dialogue represent aspects of practice that have not typically been addressed by the instructional programs, but that represent critical aspects of classroom life for teachers or students. Within dialogue, staff developers and teachers serve as mediators for one another, as they grapple with the problem of adapting an instructional program and a particular classroom simultaneously so that resulting practice is coherent and satisfactory to the teacher.

Sites for Dialogue about Classrooms and Instructional Programs

Curriculum and staff developers tend to think about the programs as intact packages that may be applied to many classrooms, and there are many principles that do apply generally (such as the importance of teacher-student dialogue about problems). However, teachers (including teachers whose beliefs are congruent with the instructional programs) must think about their particular classroom and group of students, and consider how to "fine-tune" the program to fit their particular situation. It is this consideration of the particular case that provides the sites for dialogues about how an instructional program fits with the rest of the academic curriculum and the classroom social system.

First, teachers and staff developers may consider how the program fits with *other content objectives*, particularly objectives determined by external mandates (which tend to be facts and skills that may be measured on achievement tests). Most of the instructional programs described here do not address the complete curriculum for a subject area in a particular grade. For example, the writing program of Englert and Raphael focuses on composition of expository text, and does not address questions of, for example, how to teach punctuation rules or grammar. Thus, the writing program addressed only a small portion of the writing curriculum, the rest of which was determined by a combination of textbooks and teacher-developed materials. What happens if teachers present writing as the development of expertise on some days, but as the learning of arbitrary rules on other days? Unless the teacher can help students see the connections between what is learned about writing in different lessons, then students are not likely to integrate any new knowledge, and thus would not develop the highly organized, flexible knowledge base necessary for true expertise. Instead, they might learn to demonstrate new knowledge of the writing process or rules of grammar when given specific cues about what is desired, but would not necessarily integrate the two.

Reconciling two seemingly different aspects of learning about a content area is not easy, and teachers deserve support as they grapple with the problem in their particular classrooms. None of the instructional programs claim that "lower order" or procedural learning is not worthwhile. On the contrary, some are explicit about the importance of procedural knowledge, but see it developing in tandem with conceptual understanding (Fennema et al.; Hiebert, 1986). Considering that researchers of learning are still uncertain about exactly how these two aspects of learning are related, it seeems reasonable that teachers need opportunities to think about how to reconcile apparent discrepancies in their academic goals.

A second site for dialogue about program implementation is the *intersection of instructional roles with other roles*, such as socialization of students' personal and social development and management of classroom activities. Teachers do much more than instruct about content. Sometimes other role demands seem to conflict with instructional demands, so that the teacher is continually adjusting actions to meet multiple goals (Lampert, 1985). The instructional programs cannot be implemented without becoming part of the teacher's orchestration of various roles, and this means that sometimes the instructional role prescribed by the program is compromised. For example, teachers must allocate their time among students. However, an instructional model that relies on teacher scaffolding during public discussion of problems makes tremendous demands on the teacher's and students' time. Is all instructional time to be spent in dialogue? What is the right blend of dialogue and independent practice and peer work? How might students be arranged in order to help one another during problem solving? Far from trivial, such management concerns represent fundamental decisions that can determine how successfully a program can be implemented.

A third site for dialogue is how the tasks associated with the instructional program fit within the *accountability system* of a classroom. In particular, how can teachers hold students accountable for engagement with "higher-order" tasks that have no single criterion for completeness or accuracy? This will be especially important early in the implementation of an instructional program, when students will try to interpret task demands in light of past expectations, which will probably lead to negotiations to reduce ambiguity (e.g., "How many pages does it have to be?"). Part of establishing the accountability system for such tasks will be teaching students about how they are different from past work, why they are important, and how to learn to evaluate their own efforts at problem-solving. Teachers need support when trying to accomplish this, because they may be working against several years of ingrained coping strategies in the students.

As instructional programs are developed, research on their effects on student learning will continue to be important. However, there should be an equally significant and complementary focus on research about the process of implementation. Such research can inform teachers and staff developers about conditions under which the programs work best. Each of the sites for dialogue is a possible site for research about ways that teachers adapt programs and their classrooms. Similarly, the five dimensions can serve as a framework for examining the implementation of future instructional programs.

One purpose of this chapter has been to inject a note of caution into the discussion of the instructional programs that are based on recent developments in cognitive science. These programs hold much promise for helping to achieve some much-needed reforms in education, especially in working with students who have traditionally failed to thrive in our public schools. However, that promise will not be realized unless the cognitive science base is joined by an informed perspective on the realities of teaching and learning in classrooms.

NOTES

1. See, in this volume, C.W. Anderson and K.J. Roth's paper, "Teaching for Meaningfuul and Self-regulated Learning of Science" (pp. 265-309).

2. See, in this volume, E. Fennema, T.P. Carpenter, and P.L. Peterson's paper, "Learning Mathematics with Understanding: Cognitively Guided Instruction" (pp. 195-221).

3. See, in this volume, G.G. Duffy and L.R. Roehler's paper, "The Tension Between Information-giving and Mediation: Perspectives on Instructional Explanation and Teacher Change" (pp. 1-33).

4. See, in this volume, C.S. Englert and T.E. Raphael's paper, "Developing Successful Writers Through Cognitive Strategy Instruction" (pp. 105-151).

5. See, in this volume, A.S. Palincsar and A.L. Brown's paper, "Classroom Dialogues to Promote Self-regulated Comprehension" (pp. 35-71).

REFERENCES

Anderson, C.W., & Smith, E.L. (1987). Teaching science. In V. Richardson-Koehler (Ed.), *Educator's handbook: A research perspective.* New York: Longman.

Anderson, L., Brubaker, N., Alleman-Brooks, J., & Duffy, G. (1985). A qualitative study of seatwork in first-grade classrooms. *Elementary School Journal, 86,* 123-140.

Anderson, L., Stevens, D., Prawat, R., & Nickerson, J. (1988). Classroom task environments and students' task-related beliefs. *Elementary School Journal, 88,* 281-296.

Anderson, R., & Pearson, P.D. (1984). A schema-theoretic view of basic processes in reading comprehension. In P.D. Pearson (Ed.), *Handbook of reading research.* New York: Longman.

Anderson, R., Osborn, J., & Tierney, R. (Eds.) (1984). *Learning to read in American schools: Basal readers and content texts.* Hillsdale, NJ: Erlbaum.

Applebee, A. (1981). *Writing in the secondary school: English and the content areas.* Urbana, IL: National Council of Teachers of English.

Bereiter, C. & Scardamalia, M. (1985). Cognitive coping strategies and the problem of "inert knowledge." In S. Chipman, J. Segal, & R. Glaser (Eds.), *Thinking and learning skills: Vol 2. Current research and open questions.* Hillsdale, NJ: Erlbaum.

Blumenfeld, P.C., Mergendoller, J.R., & Swarthout, D.W. (1987). Task as a heuristic for understanding student learning and motivation. *Journal of Curriculum Studies, 19,* 135-148.

Borkowski, J., Weyhing, R., & Turner, L. (1986). Attributional retraining and the teaching of strategies. *Exceptional Children, 53,* 130-137.

Brainin, S. (1985). Mediating learning: Pedagogical issues in the improvement of cognitive functioning. In E.W. Gordon (Ed.), *Review of research in education* (Vol. 12). Washington, DC: American Educational Research Association.

Bransford, J., Kitsch, K., & Franks, J. (1977). Schooling and the facilitation of knowing. In R. Anderson, R. Spiro, & W. Montague (Eds.), *Schooling and the acquisition of knowledge.* Hillsdale, NJ: Erlbaum.

Brophy, J., Rohrkemper, M., Rashid, H., & Goldberger, M. (1983). Relationships between teachers' presentations of classroom tasks and students' engagement in those tasks. *Journal of Educational Psychology, 75,* 544-552.

Bussis, A., Chittendon, F., & Amarel, M. (1976). *Beyond surface curriculum.* Boulder, CO: Westview Press.

Carpenter, T., Fennema, E., Peterson, P., & Carey, D. (1987, April). *Teachers' pedagogical content knowledge in mathematics.* Paper presented at the annual meeting of the American Educational Research Association, Washington, D.C.

Chi, M., Glaser, R., & Rees, E. (1982). Expertise in problem solving. In R. Sternberg (Ed.), *Advances in the psychology of human intelligence* (Vol. 1). Hillsdale, NJ: Erlbaum.

Clift, R., Ghatala, E., & Naus, M. (1987, April). *Exploring teachers' knowledge of strategic study activity.* Paper presented at the annual meeting of the American Educational Research Association, Washington, D.C.

Collins, A., Brown, J., & Newman, S. (1989). Cognitive apprenticeship: Teaching the craft of reading, writing and mathematics. In L. Resnick (Ed.), *Knowing and learning: Essays in honor of Robert Glaser.* Hillsdale, NJ: Erlbaum.

Covington, M.B. (1984). The self-worth theory of achievement motivation: Findings and implications. *Elementary School Journal, 85,* 5-20.

Davis, R. (1986). Conceptual and procedural knowledge in mathematics: A summary analysis. In J. Hiebert (Ed.), *Conceptual and procedural knowledge: The case of mathematics.* Hillsdale, NJ: Erlbaum.

Doyle, W. .(1983). Academic work. *Review of Educational Research, 53,* 159-199.

Doyle, W. (1986). Content representation in teachers' definitions of academic work. *Journal of Curriculum Studies, 18,* 365-379.

Duffy, G., & McIntyre, L. (1982). A naturalistic study of instructional assistance in primary grade reading. *Elementary School Journal, 83,* 15-23.

Duffy, G., & Roehler, L. (1986). Constraints on teacher change. *Journal of Teacher Education, 37,* 55-58.

Duffy, G., Roehler, L., & Rackliffe, G. (1986). How teachers' instructional talk influences students' understanding of lesson content. *Elementary School Journal, 87,* 3-16.

Duffy, G., Roehler, L., Sivan, E., Rackliffe, G., Book, C., Meloth, M., Vavrus, L., Wesselman, R., Putnam, J., & Bassiri, D. (1987). The effects of explaining the mental processing associated with using reading strategies on the awareness and achievement of low group third graders. *Reading Research Quarterly, 22,* 347-368.

Durkin, D. (1984). Do basal manuals teach reading comprehension? In R.C. Anderson, J. Osborn, & R.J. Tierney (Eds.), *Learning to read in American schools: Basal readers and content texts.* Hillsdale, NJ: Erlbaum.

Glaser, R. (1984). Education and thinking: The role of knowledge. *American Psychologist, 39,* 93-104.

Goodlad, J.I. (1984). *A place called school.* New York: McGraw-Hill.

Hiebert, J. (Ed.). (1986). *Conceptual and procedural knowledge: The case for mathematics.* Hillsdale, NJ: Erlbaum.

Hollon, R., & Anderson, C. (1987, April). *Teachers' beliefs about students' learning processes in science: Self-reinforcing belief systems.* Paper presented at the annual meeting of the American Educational Research Association, Washington, D.C.

Jackson, P. (1968). *Life in classrooms.* New York: Holt, Rinehart, and Winston.

Johnston, K. (1987, July). *Changing teachers' conceptions of teaching and learning.* Paper presented at the British Educational Research Association Conference on Teachers' Professional Learning, University of Lancaster, U.K.

Lampert, M. (1985). How do teachers manage to teach? *Harvard Educational Review, 55,* 178-194.

Lampert, M. (1987, April). *Attending to students' thinking in math classes.* Paper presented at the annual meeting of the American Educational Research Association, Washington, D.C.

Lanier, J. (1986). Research on teacher education. In M. Wittrock (Ed.), *Handbook of research on teaching* (3rd ed.) New York: Macmillan.

Lortie, D. (1975). *Schoolteacher: A sociological study.* Chicago: University of Chicago Press.

Marshall, H. (1987). Motivational strategies of three fifth-grade teachers. *Elementary School Journal, 88,* 135-150.

Marshall, H., & Weinstein, R.S. (1984). Classroom factors affecting students' self-evaluations: An interactional model. *Review of Educational Research, 54,* 301-325.

McDiarmid, G.W., Ball, D., & Anderson, C. (1989). Why staying one chapter ahead doesn't really work: Subject-specific pedagogy. In M. Reynolds (Ed.), *The knowledge base for the beginning teacher.* New York: Pergamon Press.

National Assessment of Educational Progress (1983). *Reading, science, and mathematical trends: A closer look.* Denver: Education Commission of the States.

Olson, J. (1983). Guide writing as advice giving: Learning the classroom language. *Journal of Curriculum Studies, 15,* 17-26.

Palincsar, A. (1986). The role of dialogue in providing scaffolded instruction. *Educational Psychologist, 21,* 73-98.

Paris, S., & Jacobs, J. (1984). The benefits of informed instruction for children's reading awareness and comprehension skils. *Child Development, 55,* 2083-2093.

Peterson, P., Fennema, E., Carpenter, T., & Loef, M. (1987, April). *Teachers' pedagogical content beliefs in mathematics.* Paper presented at the annual meeting of the American Educational Research Association, Washington, D.C.

Posner, G.J., Strike, K.A., Hewson, P.W., & Gertzog, W.A. (1982). Accommodation of a scientific conception: Toward a theory of conceptual change. *Science Education, 66,* 211-228.

Raphael, T., Englert, C., & Anderson, L. (1987, December). *What is effective instructional talk? A comparison of two writing lessons.* Paper presented at the annual meeting of the National Reading Conference, St. Petersburg, Florida.

Romberg, T., & Carpenter, T. (1986). Research on teaching and learning mathematics: Two disciplines of scientific inquiry. In M.C. Wittrock (Ed.), *Handbook of research on teaching* (3rd ed.). New York: Macmillan.

Scardamalia, M., & Bereiter, C. (1985). Fostering the development of self-regulation in children's knowledge processing. In S. Chipman, W. Segal & R. Glaser (Eds.), *Thinking and learning skills: Vol. 2. Research and open questions.* Hillsdale, NJ: Erlbaum.

Scardamalia, M., & Bereiter, C. (1986). Research on written composition. In M. Wittrock (Ed.), *Handbook of research on teaching* (3rd ed.). New York: Macmillan.

Schoenfeld, A. (1985). *Mathematical problem solving.* New York: Academic Press.

Shulman, L. (1987). Knowledge and teaching: Foundations of the new reform. *Harvard Educational Review, 57*, 1-22.

Sirotnik, K.A. (1983). What you see is what you get. *Harvard Educational Review, 54*, 16-32.

Slavin, R. (1984). Students motivating students to excel: Cooperative incentives, cooperative tasks, and student achievement. *Elementary School Journal, 84*, 53-63.

Vygotsky, L.S. (1978). *Mind in society: The development of higher psychological processes.* (M. Cole, V. John-Steiner, S. Scribner, & E. Souberman, Eds. & Trans.). Cambridge: Harvard University Press.

Weinstein, R. (1983). Student perceptions of schooling. *Elementary School Journal, 83*, 288-312.

Wertsch, J. (1985). *Vygotsky and the social formation of mind.* Cambridge, MA: Harvard University Press.

Whitehead, A. (1929). *The aims of education.* New York: Macmillan.

Wood, D.J., Bruner, J.S., & Ross, G. (1987). The role of tutoring in problem-solving. *Journal of Child Psychology and Psychiatry, 17*, 89-100.

*   *   *

CROSS-TALK

How do factors external to the classroom affect implementation of instructional programs? What kinds of external support might teachers need when implementing those programs, and what kinds of constraints are imposed by the larger social-political milieu in which teaching occurs?

When I defined the five dimensions along which instructional programs and classrooms might be placed, I did not talk about *why* most classrooms are characterized in certain ways. I think that the reason that most classrooms, teachers, and students reflect particular views of teaching and learning (that are different from the views offered by the other authors in this volume) is that broader social and political forces have shaped and continue to maintain those views. While it is easier to attempt to make changes in a few classrooms than it is to make changes in an entire educational system, we can not ignore the impact of the larger context on individual teachers and classrooms.

In particular, I can think of two kinds of policies made at the district level that help account for prevalent instructional patterns and that impose constraints on teachers who wish to implement the kind of instructional program described in this book. First, teachers often must attend to curriculum mandates that define what content should be covered at what grade level (and, in too many cases, what materials should be used to cover that content and what skills tests should be passed to demonstrate learning). District-wide curriculum mandates imply a belief that knowledge exists outside of children's heads and should be placed into their heads in a regular, uniform manner. This is a prime example of incongruence with the premises underlying the instructional programs.

If a teacher is bound to meet district requirements for content coverage and test results, it may be very difficult to give sufficient time and attention to an instructional program designed to promote individual students' meaningful understanding of what may appear (to district administrators) to be a small amount of content. When districts are unwilling to release teachers from such requirements in order to try a new approach to teaching, then staff developers must assist teachers by moving slowly with changes and engaging in problem-solving with teachers about ways to "cover" the required content by teaching it in ways that are more likely to promote higher-order learning.

Class size is a second policy area that may impose constraints on the implementation of new instructional programs like those described here. The teacher-student dialogue that is the centerpiece of these programs is labor-intensive. Many prevalent classroom practices, such as large group recitations and lots of time spent doing routine seatwork, are, in spite of their instructional limitations, ways of coping with large classes. Replacing these instructional formats with more small groups for dialogues is not easy without administrative support for instructional aides and/or sufficient materials and technology to support purposeful independent work by students.

Can the belief systems that you see as dichotomous be made compatible enough to result in coherent classroom practices? Do you see teachers' work as management of seemingly contradictory beliefs, rather than posing absolute choices between two belief systems?

I am not sure how teachers might manage the contradictions inherent in the two poles of each continuum, if by that you mean accepting both as equally valid as the basis of long-range goals. In the cases of teachers whose practices reflect the principles of the instructional programs (such as the example offered in Lampert's chapter about her math teaching), it does not seem to me that the teachers are managing two conflicting belief systems. It seems instead that the teachers have based long-range goals and general views of teaching on the same premises that support the instructional programs, although their specific actions may not always appear to reflect these views. For example, all teachers, even those most devoted to constructivist views of learning, sometimes tell students correct answers without engaging in a scaffolded dialogue. This action may appear to contradict certain instructional theories, but it may make sense at the moment because of factors like time pressures, external curriculum constraints, or students' personal needs. However, teachers whose beliefs are congruent with the premises of the instructional programs are not likely to provide answers in place of dialogue all or even most of the time, because such an imbalance would impede progress toward their long-range goals for students' learning. If this is the kind of management of contradictions that you mean, then I agree that we, as researchers and program or staff developers, need to recognize that some dilemmas never go away, and none of us would be able to "teach the program" 100% of the time.

What is your prediction about the fate of the key ideas and methods of these programs? Will they become standard practice in most classrooms, or abandoned as overly ambitious or impractical?

I think the practices advocated in these programs (not the specific programs themselves, which will continue to develop and change) could become widespread, but that will only happen if there are widespread changes both in teacher education and in the teaching profession and educational bureaucracy. Teacher education can help teachers prepare to teach from the constructivist perspective, but only if it focuses on each teacher's development of personally-held theories about learning, learners, and instruction. Currently, many teacher education courses can be characterized in the same way that my chapter characterized many K-12 classrooms: goals are limited to specific skills and facts; students are treated as if they should absorb the information offered by the teacher educator; tasks do not always represent real problems of teaching and, when they do, they are not the basis for scaffolded dialogue; and the social context of teacher education does not foster willingness to risk, self-regulation, or recognition that one's peers contribute to one's developing knowledge about teaching. Unless this pattern is changed, then teacher education will not support the higher-order learning that is required to develop teaching expertise.

However, even significant reform in teacher education will not provide a sufficient base for widespread changes in teaching practice unless there are corresponding changes in teachers' professional status, especially in their autonomy to determine curriculum within their own classrooms. As I noted in an earlier response, the premise underlying many district-level curriculum mandates is that content can be predetermined and that teachers should be held accountable for conveying that content. As long as teachers are not given some authority to make decisions about how to present what content, based on what they know about the content, about their students, and about the nature of meaningful learning and self-regulation, then the kind of instruction described here cannot become widespread.

CONCLUSION:

TOWARD A THEORY OF TEACHING

Jere Brophy

Each of the lines of work represented in this volume has made important contributions to the scholarly literature on teaching in a particular subject matter area. In addition, because the different contributors share common views about learning and teaching, many aspects of their work are comparable and thus potentially cumulative in their contribution to our knowledge about good teaching. In particular, all of the contributors share a theory of learning informed by the information processing approach to human cognition, with its view of knowledge development as requiring the learner's own schema construction accomplished through active information processing and sense-making efforts. This view of learning implies a corresponding view of teaching that emphasizes not only the ultimate learning goals to be accomplished, but the particulars of the students' current knowledge and of the information processing and conceptual change that will be required to enable the students to reach the intended learning goals. By noting the common elements that the different investigators have stressed as they explored what was involved in effectively teaching particular subject matter content, one can begin to identify components for a model or theory describing good subject matter teaching.

Advances in Research on Teaching, Volume 1, pages 345-355.
Copyright © 1989 by JAI Press Inc.
All rights of reproduction in any form reserved.
ISBN: 0-89232-845-2

Linda Anderson identified and discussed five such common elements: (1) instructional goals emphasize developing student expertise within an application-oriented context and with emphasis on conceptual understanding of content and self-regulated application of skills; (2) the teacher's role is not just to present information but also to scaffold and respond to students' learning efforts; (3) the students' role is not just to absorb or copy input but to actively make sense and construct meaning; (4) activities and assignments feature tasks that call for problem solving or critical thinking, not just memory or reproduction; and (5) the teacher works to create a social environment in the classroom that could be described as a learning community featuring discourse or dialogue designed to promote understanding. I concur with this list and suggest the following elaborations and additions.

First, it is helpful if both teachers and students come to see instruction as designed to empower students with knowledge and skills that they will find useful both inside and outside of the classroom. To accomplish this, it will be necessary to consider students' motivation as well their cognition, and in particular to stimulate their motivation to learn the content or skills to be taught (Brophy, 1987; Good & Brophy, 1987). It will also be necessary to ensure that the learning will be accessible for application when needed, which implies that students have been encouraged both to integrate the new learning with relevant prior knowledge and to apply it within a range of problem solving or decision making situations (Prawat, 1988). Presumably there are good reasons why students are required to learn particular content; learning should progress more smoothly if students are made aware of these reasons and keep them in mind as they engage in activities and assignments.

The research described here also raises curricular issues. Teaching for meaningful understanding and self-regulated learning takes time, which means that teachers will have to sacrifice breadth of coverage in order to allow time for depth of development of particular topics. Efficiency can be accomplished by structuring curricula around powerful concepts and generalizations drawn from the academic disciplines and by integrating instruction across areas and using curricular content as the focus for application of basic skills (as suggested by Rosaen and others in this volume). Still, there are limits on what can be accomplished within the available time, so that teachers who want to emphasize meaningful understanding and self-regulated learning will have to drop significant content coverage in addition to teaching the content they do cover more thoroughly. This is difficult because there are constant pressures for infusion of new content into the curriculum and because teachers are resistant to dropping content that they have been teaching (Floden, Porter, Schmidt, Freeman, & Schwille, 1981).

Several papers implied that isolated skills practice is one good candidate for reduction in emphasis, especially practice of part skills that occurs outside the context of application to whole tasks. In fact, if findings like those reported by Fennema, Carpenter, and Peterson should also be obtained in other subject matter areas, they would imply, within limits, that practice of part skills that occurs in the context of meaningful reading for understanding, writing for communication, or using content in problem solving or other higher order application contexts can produce as much or more skill mastery as greater amounts of time spent in isolated part skills practice. A related point is that students appear to need to develop understanding of the purposes and rationales for scientific experiments more than they need to spend a great deal of time working through all of the procedures involved in such experiments.

Several papers also underscored the importance of looking more to students' existing knowledge or beliefs about a topic (including those developed informally as well as those learned previously in school) than to content organization schemes favored by the disciplines in deciding what to teach at which grade levels and how to represent the content to the students. The importance of linking the new learning to students' existing knowledge is stressed by all of the authors, and several also imply that formal learning is made easier for students if topics are introduced in the order in which they are likely to be learned informally. Most authors treated students' current knowledge as a resource and starting place for teachers, but Anderson and Roth's work serves as a reminder that students may also possess misconceptions that will need to be corrected.

Several authors touched on the need to identify good examples, metaphors, or analogies for representing content to students in ways that are both valid (i.e., they accurately reflect networks of knowledge developed by the disciplines from which the content is drawn) and meaningful to the students (i.e., relatable to their exisiting knowledge, especially to what Piaget has called operative knowledge that is anchored in concrete experience). Several authors also stressed the value of multiple representations of content, most notably Lampert in her discussion of the reasons why money, number line, and parts of a circle were all needed as ways to represent the mathematical content she was teaching at various points in the development of the students' knowledge.

All the authors emphasized the importance of attention to higher order thinking processes and metacognition. However, in contrast to the frequently-taken approach of teaching these processes as generic skills, they favor teaching them as they occur naturally within the applications aspects of teaching content for meaningful understanding and self-regulated learning. The implication here is that, within the context established by the overall goals of instruction, planning starts with the content to be taught (and follows through to include problem solving, critical thinking, decision making, and other higher order applications of that content), rather than starting with a list of higher order thinking skills or metacognitive strategies to be taught and then searching for content that might provide an appropriate context for application.

A related point implied by several authors is that higher order thinking is involved in the process of achieving conceptual understanding of content. Because comprehension is near the bottom of the hierarchy in the Bloom, Englehart, Furst, Hill, and Krathwohl (1956) taxonomy of cognitive objectives (knowledge, comprehension, application, analysis, synthesis, and evaluation), teaching for understanding of concepts, generalizations, or principles is often viewed as a low-level cognitive objective. Several lines of work represented in this volume imply that teaching for conceptual understanding is actually a higher level objective, or alternatively, that students will have to engage in application, analysis, synthesis, and evaluation in the process of achieving a reasonably complete understanding of a concept, so that the very notion of separating and classifying learning objectives breaks down when one is confronted with the kind of integrated instruction involved in teaching for meaningful understanding.

Even while stressing the importance of active student information processing controlled through metacognitive awareness, most authors also reaffirmed the importance of explicit explanation and other aspects of direct instruction by the teacher. Duffy and Roehler stressed that such explicit instruction needs to occur not only during presentations and demonstrations given at the beginnings of lessons, but throughout lessons and follow-up activities in the form of responsive elaboration keyed to students' comments, questions, and mistakes. All the authors who touched on skills instruction spoke of the importance of teaching skills as tools to be used strategically to solve problems or accomplish some purpose, and not merely as algorithms to be practiced to automaticity. They favored conducting such skills instruction within a content application context and with attention to its cognitive and metacognitive components, and they emphasized that such instruction should focus not only on procedural knowledge but also on related propositional and conditional knowledge.

Several authors stressed the value of cognitive modeling (thinking aloud while demonstrating) for teaching skills as strategies. This is one of the most important, but as yet least publicized and appreciated, contributions of the cognitive orientation to our understanding of effective teaching. Not only is cognitive modeling well-suited to the idea of teaching skills within the context of application of content, it also provides a more direct and powerful method of communicating the key elements of these skills to students, compared to traditional methods. Strategy modeling that includes first-person language verbalization of the self-talk that guides behavior provides students with an integrated, within-context demonstration of how to approach and solve a problem. This is easier for them to retain and use than information presented in third-person language or even instructions presented in second-person language that must first be internalized and then translated into first-person language that can be used to guide behavior. Thus, cognitive modeling allows learners to focus directly on the processes to be learned, with minimum strain on their cognitive capacities. Palincsar and Brown have designed reciprocal teaching so that students are exposed to modeling not only by the teacher, but by their peers as well.

Finally, all the authors stated or implied the need for methods of evaluating student learning that go far beyond the familiar multiple-choice recognition items by probing students' understanding of and ability to apply what they are supposed to be learning. Often this requires extended interviews, complex assignments, or other opportunities for students to present their ideas at length in their own words or to integrate and apply their knowledge in the process of creating a substantial product (composition, research report, and so forth). A larger implication here is that there should be alignment among the intended learning goals, the content selected for focus, the methods selected for teaching the content (including the ways that the content is represented to the students, the nature of the teacher-student discourse, and the kinds of activities and assignments that are scheduled), and the methods selected for evaluating student learning. If the learning goals include meaningful understanding and self-regulated learning, then content, method, and evaluation choices should follow accordingly.

These elements of good teaching implied by the work described in this volume appear to be not only compatible but mutually supportive, and thus to constitute key elements in a model or theory of effective teaching of academic content. Furthermore, they fit well with the implications of scholarly work on other aspects of good teaching. For example, research on effective classroom management (reviewed in Brophy [1983] and Doyle [1986]) suggests that teachers need to approach classroom management in terms of establishing a productive learning environment (not just maintaining order), and that they need to be clear in communicating not only their behavioral expectations and desired daily routines but the reasons for them, so that the students can internalize these rationales and regulate their own behavior for the most part. Similarly, reviews of scholarly work on motivation in the classroom (Brophy, 1987; Good & Brophy, 1987) suggest the need for strategies for developing students' motivation to learn (i.e., their disposition to engage in academic activities with the intention of getting the intended knowledge or skill benefits from them). Thus, common elements in the findings described in this volume not only constitute the beginnings of a theory of good teaching of academic content, but also combine well with other work to form the beginnings of more general theorizing about effective classroom teaching.

UNRESOLVED ISSUES AND NEEDED RESEARCH

These are just beginnings, of course. Even the teaching concepts and associated principles (conceptual change teaching, responsive elaboration, and so on) featured in the lines of work represented in this volume have so far been applied to just a few topics at a few grade levels. Ultimately, we will need much more specific information about all major topics at all grade levels. Ideally, the teachers' manuals of the future will be much more detailed than they are now and will include not only information about goal selection and suggestions concerning instruction and evaluation of learning, but also information about students' likely knowledge and beliefs (including misconceptions) that will need to be taken into account. Outlines of model lessons (or better yet, examples on videotape) would be desirable too, because strategic teaching for meaningful understanding and self-regulated learning is a complex task calling for orchestration of a variety of knowledge and skills, so that teachers are likely to need modeling, coaching, and other forms of scaffolding to assist them as they develop expertise at it.

Even with assistance from such scaffolding, however, it seems clear that teachers will need considerable specialized knowledge if they are to be consistently effective in teaching for meaningful understanding and self-regulated learning. Shulman (1986) has referred to this specialized knowledge as pedagogical content knowledge and has argued that it includes three elements: (a) knowledge of the subject matter, (b) knowledge of the students (especially their current knowledge and beliefs about the subject matter), and (c) knowledge of effective ways to represent the subject matter to these students through well-chosen examples, analogies, or metaphors. Research has begun to accumulate on the ways in which teachers' professional pedagogical knowledge develops and changes with experience and on the relationship between teachers' knowledge and beliefs about teaching particular subject matter and the ways that they teach it in the classroom. These topics will be the focus of the second volume in this series (see Brophy, in press).

My emphasis so far has been on commonalities, but there also are some interesting contrasts in the chapters. These include the degree to which the emphasis is on knowledge versus skills, the degree of structuring or scaffolding favored, the degree to which there is emphasis on presentations or demonstrations made at the beginnings of lessons in addition to responsive elaboration or other instruction that occurs later during teacher-student discourse, the degree to which it is assumed that instruction is predictable and thus can be planned in detail, the degree to which students' ideas are treated as foundations to build on versus as misconceptions to be corrected, the whole class versus a small group as the setting for instruction, and the degree to which the investigators have proceeded by using theory to develop and then test models of good teaching versus by developing such models inductively by identifying dimensions on which expert teachers differ from less effective teachers.

Most of these contrasts appear to be mere differences rather than direct contradictions. Often they are connected with subject matter differences in relative emphasis on knowledge versus skills or in the degree to which scholarly literature has accumulated about teaching in the subject matter area that supports theoretical derivation of models of good teaching. Most of the more direct disagreements surround two related issues: (a) the degree to which teachers should consistently structure and guide students' learning efforts according to previously established instructional goals versus adapting as they go along to pursue other goals deemed worthwhile because of student interest or misconceptions that emerge during teacher-student discourse, and (b) the degree to which teachers should provide a great deal of explanation and scaffolding assistance (at least in the early stages of instruction) versus providing students with only as much advance information as they need to get started in problem solving or other application efforts (so that most instruction occurs in the form of feedback or responsive elaboration during discourse surrounding these activities).

There also are differences in the degree to which instruction in strategic skills application emphasizes conscious decision making and other metacognitive awareness components vs. smooth, error-free, successful performance. My sense is that differences here depend on the stage in the development of student expertise that the investigators were concentrating on. Presumably, all would agree that students should understand skills and know when and why to apply them, not just how to apply them when cued to do so. This implies detailed instruction in cognitive strategies and related metacognitive control mechanisms, with more emphasis on the conceptual understanding of skill applications than on efficiency of performance. Smooth application that included efficient use of algorithms and short cuts would be desired eventually, but even then, because students had developed expertise in using these methods consciously, they would retain the capacity to monitor their performance, diagnose the reasons for difficulties, and shift strategies when necessary.

The idea that teaching tactics evolve as one progresses from introduction of entirely new content to student self-regulated learning in the content area appears to explain some of the other differences between chapters as well. In particular, authors concerned with introducing content that is new to the students tended to emphasize the role of teacher explanation and modeling, whereas authors who focused more on applications and self-regulated learning tended to say much less about expository instruction and instead to emphasize the teacher's role in supplying discourse or assignments that would enable students to analyze and synthesize what they had been learning or to apply it in problem solving contexts.

Certain issues raised by the research described in the present volume were already mentioned in the previous section (how to represent content effectively with students, how to decide what to drop in order to make time to go into greater depth on fewer topics). A related issue is the need for criteria for identifying the content to be taught at particular grade levels and, in particular, for phrasing the key concepts or generalizations that curriculum strands will be built around. Lists of fundamental concepts have been developed for each of the various academic disciplines. These are helpful in pointing the way toward powerful, integrative ideas, but by themselves they provide no guidance concerning which aspects of the vast network of theories, generalizations, concepts, and facts that have been developed around these ideas should be taught at a particular grade level, let alone how this content should be represented to students and linked to their current ideas and prior experience.

Prawat (1988) suggests that the key ideas in curriculum units and lessons ordinarily should be middle range generalizations that express relationships between concepts, as opposed to the individual concepts themselves (too molecular) and to general theories or systems (too molar). In geography, for example, the notion that there are relationships between the characteristics of a geographical area and the customs of the people who live in that area is a fundamental concept, but phrased in that form it is too general and abstract to be ideal as the key concept in an elementary grades social studies lesson. At the other extreme, particular facts (Eskimos used ice to build igloos, plains Indians used animal skins to build teepees, and so forth) or concepts (shelter, living quarters) lack meaningful integration. Learning is likely to be more meaningful if built around middle-range generalizations such as "the kind of shelter that people need depends on the climate of the region in which they live" and "the raw materials used in constructing living quarters will depend on the natural resources abundant in the region."

Related issues concern how far to go in teaching for conceptual understanting. The frequently-made observation that current curricula merely mention a great many things without developing systematic knowledge about them indicates the need to reduce breadth of coverage and increase depth of development of the topics that are covered, but somewhere there is a line between thorough instruction and overkill. Given that there are more worthwhile things to teach them time to teach them, it seems clear that even teaching for meaningful understanding implies optimizing rather than maximizing instruction on any particular topic. Lampert struggled with this issue at the level of trying to decide whether it was worth pursuing students' mistaken ideas through extended dialogue (rather than supplying a brief corrective explanation and then moving on with the intended lesson), and most authors at least implied recognition of the need to accept compromises by limiting both the breadth and depth of their planned coverage of particular topics and by accepting something less than total mastery by all students of the key concepts emphasized in the instruction. I sense, however, that none of the authors has yet come to grips with the fact that there are limits to the degree to which one can sacrifice breadth for depth and the fact that pressures to move on keep building the longer one stays with a given topic.

There are also parallel issues concerning how far to go in seeking to promote self-regulated learning. It seems clear that schools currently place too much emphasis on isolated subskill practice and not enough on whole-task applications. But again, how much is too much (or more specifically, too much in view of what is being sacrificed so that more time can be spent on applications of already-covered topics)?

The authors have made important contributions to our understandings of the kinds of teacher-student discourse that occur when one attempts to teach for meaningful understanding and self-regulated learning. Much more needs to be discovered, however, concerning the different forms of discourse that are appropriate to different instructional goals, the changes in teacher role and tactics that should occur as student expertise develops, and when and how to probe, give feedback, pursue a wrong idea or side issue, or introduce elaboration. For example, the concept of responsive elaboration strikes me as a powerful one that should be applicable to all kinds of teaching. To date, however, our notions about what constitutes responsive elaboration come from Duffy and Roehler's work on the teaching of reading comprehension, which emphasizes skills instruction (procedural and conditional knowledge). The concept of responsive elaboration appears to apply just as well to lessons in literature or social studies that emphasize propositional knowledge, but its concrete implementation probably would differ (e.g., instead of continuously focusing on understanding and application of the same basic strategy guidelines, the discourse would proceed by probing the limits of the concept or generalization under discussion, relating it to other concepts, discussing examples and nonexamples, and in other ways building up a network of knowledge surrounding the concept and probing its implications).

There is also a need for much more information about the purposes for which activities and assignments would be used in different subject matter areas, the nature of the activities and assignments that would be suitable for accomplishing these purposes at different grade levels, how they should be presented to the students, and how student work should be monitored and evaluated. The very notion of teaching for self-regulated learning implies the importance of assignments that afford students opportunities to integrate and apply what they are learning, but not much is said either here or in other classroom research about how assignments should be designed and implemented to accomplish particular purposes. Some guidelines about desirable features of assignments are provided by Rosaen and by Florio-Ruane and Lensmire, and the paper by Englert and Raphael illustrated ways in which scaffolding can be used to help students to cope with challenging tasks. These and contributions by others such as Bennett and Desforges (1988), Doyle (1983), and Osborn (1984), however, are just beginnings in what ultimately must become a much larger scholarly literature on classroom activities and assignments.

Certain topics are well represented in this volume, but others are addressed only lightly if at all, and the latter provide clues to needed research. For example, much was said about instructing students in the strategic use of skills and the understanding of processes, but not much was said about building up networks of propositional knowledge of the kind emphasized, for example, in social studies classes. At the moment, we can only speculate about the degree to which concepts such as conceptual change teaching, reciprocal teaching, responsive elaboration, or scaffolding of assignments would apply to teaching about topics such as the American Declaration of Independence or the U.S. Constitution at various grade levels.

The work represented here, like most research on teaching, addresses the elementary and middle school grades but not the secondary grades. Research is needed on the degree to which these findings would apply at secondary and post-secondary levels of education and on potential differences in the ways that particular approaches would be implemented at different grade levels where they do apply.

The lines of work reported here all have been driven at least in part by ideas about the kinds of student outcomes that instruction should be designed to produce, but some of them have yet to demonstrate clear relationships between classroom processes and student outcomes. As instructional models are perfected, it will be important to conduct evaluation studies designed to assess the effects on an array of outcome measures of the approaches described here compared to more traditional approaches that feature more breadth but less depth. Studies that spanned an entire school year and included both conventional achievement tests and the kinds of knowledge assessment interviews and other qualitative assessment devices that were used in the research would be ideal.

So would inclusion of affective and dispositional measures (interest in the subject matter, attitudes towards self as a learner of the subject matter, enjoyment of the class, and so forth). The very notion of self-regulated learning (and perhaps the notion of constructing knowledge in an attempt to achieve meaningful understanding as well) implies not only access to relevant knowledge and cognitive strategies, but also dispositions such as motivation to learn the content and the tendency to notice and seek to resolve discrepancies between one's current knowledge and the new input. Several of the authors spoke of the importance of establishing the classroom as a learning community and socializing these dispositional elements in the students, but they tended not to include affective or dispositional measures in assessing student outcomes.

CONCLUSION

Although it is fitting to consider the limitations of the work represented here and sobering to realize that it represents just a small beginning on the much larger task that remains to be done, it is also fitting to conclude this volume on a note of optimism and celebration. Research on teaching has established a knowledge base that continues to grow, theoretical and methodological advances have increased its sophistication, and our understanding of the nature of teaching and what is involved in doing it well continues to develop. Such development includes both increasing differentiation (more and more specific knowledge is being developed about managing classrooms, motivating students, and teaching different subject matter at different grade levels) and increasing integration (we continue to learn more about the commonalities involved in teaching in different situations and about how teachers can play out the different aspects of their role so that they function as mutually supportive elements within a coherent overall approach). The lines of work represented in this volume are among the more important contributors to this progress.

REFERENCES

Bennett, N., & Desforges, C. (1988). Matching classroom tasks to students' attainments. *Elementary School Journal, 88,* 221-234.

Bloom, B., Englehart, M., Furst, E., Hill, W., & Krathwohl, D. (1956). *Taxonomy of educational objectives: The classification of educational goals. Handbook I: Cognitive domain.* New York: Longmans Green.

Brophy, J. (1983). Classroom organization and management. *Elementary School Journal, 83,* 265-285.

Brophy, J. (1987). On motivating students. In D. Berliner & B. Rosenshine (Eds.), *Talks to teachers* (pp. 201-245). New York: Random House.

Brophy, J. (Ed.). (In press). *Advances in research on teaching. Vol. 2: Teachers' knowledge of subject matter as it relates to their teaching practice.* Greenwich, CT: JAI Press.

Doyle, W. (1983). Academic work. *Review of Educational Research, 53,* 159-200.

Doyle, W. (1986). Classroom organization and management. In M. Wittrock (Ed.), *Handbook of research on teaching* (3rd ed., pp. 392-431). New York: Macmillan.

Floden, R., Porter, A., Schmidt, W., Freeman, D., & Schwille, J. (1981). Responses to curriculum pressures: A policy-capturing study of teacher decisions about content. *Journal of Educational Psychology, 73,* 129-141.

Good, T., & Brophy, J. (1987). *Looking in classrooms* (4th ed.). New York: Harper & Row.

Osborn, J. (1984). Workbooks that accompany basal reading programs. In G. Duffy, L. Roehler, & J. Mason (Eds.), *Comprehension instruction: Perspectives and suggestions.* New York: Longman.

Prawat, R. (1988). *Promoting access: The role of organization and awareness factors* (Elementary Subjects Series No. 1). East Lansing, MI: Institute for Research on Teaching, Michigan State University.

Shulman, L. (1986). Those who understand: Knowledge growth in teaching. *Educational Researcher, 15*(2), 4-14.

JAI PRESS

Advances in Reading/Language Research

Edited by **Barbara A. Hutson,** *Division of Curriculum and Instruction, Virginia Polytechnic Institute and State University*

REVIEW: "As should be evident from this review the rebuilding of one's ship at high sea can take many successful forms. In my estimation not all of the truths expounded in this volume are equally productive. Yet, some of the planks, ones I never would have chosen to replace or test for rot, have more potential than my past estimation would have given them.
I found this a good volume for updating my own knowledge and an extremely useful document as I continue to shape me and my graduate students' professional seafaring, ship-rebuilding lives. I believe you and your graduate students will find the volume communicative as well as generative."
— *Journal of Reading Behavior*

Volume 1, 1982, 357 pp. $58.50
ISBN 0-89232-197-0

The first volume of *Advances in Reading/Language Research* reflects a life-span view of the development of oral and written language. Studies range from work with metalinguistic skills in preschoolers to examination of comprehension of propositional structures by older adults. The individual chapters range from critical reviews of research in areas such as ethnographic studies, reading attitudes and writing to theoretical analysis of the affective factors in reading, to syntheses of programs of empirical research in sentence processing, semantic memory and reading, integration of text and illustrations, metacognition and reading, job-related literacy, and on-line cognitive processing in reading.

CONTENTS: List of Contributors. **The Scope of Reading/ Language Research,** *Barbara A. Hutson, V.P.I. and State University.* **Assessing Sentence Processing Skills in Pre-Readers,** *Ellen Bouchard Ryan, University of Notre Dame and George W. Ledger, University of Rhode Island.* **Relations Between Semantic Memory and reading,** *Richard S. Prawat, Michigan State University.* **Cognitive Process and Reading Skills,** *Meredyth Daneman, University of Waterloo, Patricia A. Carpenter and Marcel Adam Just, Carnegie-Mellon University.* **Toward A Paradigm of Children's Writing Classroom Competence,** *Peter Mosenthal, Syracuse University.* **Understanding Discourse A Life-Span Approach,** *Judith O. Harker, David A. Walsh, University of Southern California and Joellen*

T. Hartley, California State University, Long Beach. **Reading: The Affective Domain Reconceptualized,** Irene Athey, Rutgers University. **Literacy at Work,** Thomas G. Sticht, Human Resources and Research Organization, Alexandria, Va. **Children's Impressions of Coherence in Narratives,** Steven R. Yussen, University of Wisconsin, Madison. **Relationships of Illustrations and Text in Reading Technical Material,** David E. Stone, Cornell University and Thomas Leon Crandell, Broome Community College and Cornell University. **The Social Contexts of Reading: A Multidisciplinary Perspective,** David Bloome, University of Michigan and Judith Green, University of Delaware. Author Index, Subject Index.

Volume 2, 1983, 361 pp. $58.50
ISBN 0-89232-200-4

CONTENTS: List of Contributors. Focus and Perspective in Reading/Language Research, Barbara A. Hutson, Virginia Polytechnic Institute. **Text Structure and Its Use in Studying Comprehension Across the Adult Life Span,** Bonnie J. F. Meyer, Arizona State University. **Learning to Represent Meaning,** Joan Tough, The University of Leeds. **Re-Examining Research on Reading Comprehension in Content Areas,** Richard T. Vaca and JoAnne L. Vacca, Kent State University. **Interactive Discourse in the Classroom as Organizational Behavior,** Harold B. Pepinsky and Johanna S. DeStefano, Ohio State University. **If a Text Exists Without a Reader, Is There Meaning? Insights From Literary Theory for Reader-Text Interaction,** Joanne Golden, University of Delaware. **Reading as a Social Process,** David Bloome, University of Michigan. **Reading Stores to Children: A Review-Critique,** Marilyn Cochran-Smith, University of Pennsylvania. **Reading Comprehension and the Assessment and Acquisition of Word Knowledge,** Richard C. Anderson, University of Illinois and Peter Freebody, University of New England. **Building Bridges Between Receptive and Productive Language Processes for Adolescents,** Gladys Knott, Kent State University. **Teaching and Learning as Linguistic Processes: The Emerging Picture,** Judith L. Green and Deborah C. Smith, University of Delaware. Author Index. Subject Index.

Volume 3, 1986, 256 pp. $58.50
ISBN 0-89232-389-2

CONTENTS: List of Contributors. Viewing and Reviewing Reading/Language Research, Barbara A. Hutson, Virginia Polytechnic Institute and State University. **Relationships of Measure of Interest, Prior Knowledge, and Readability to Comprehension of Expository Passages,** Eileen B. Entin, Wentworth Institute of Technology, and George R. Klare, Ohio University. **Spelling as Concept-Governed Problem Solving:**

Volume 4, Cognitive Science and Human Resources Management
1986, 329 pp. $58.50
ISBN 0-89232-631-X

Edited by **Thomas G. Sticht,** *Applied Behavioral & Cognitive Science, Inc.,* **Frederick R. Chang,** *Navy Personnel Research & Development Center* and **Suzanne Wood,** *Naval Postgraduate School.*

Domains, *Sherrie P. Gott, Air Force Human Resources Laboratory.* **Technical Training and Instructional Systems Development: Can A Cognitive Model Help?,** *William E. Montague, Navy Personnel Research and Development Center.* **Cognitive Theory of Technical Training,** *Ray S. Perez and Robert J. Seidel, U.S. Army Research Institute for the Behavioral and Social Sciences.* **Section C. Human Factors Design of Information Display. Modeling Information Processing in the Context of Job Training and Work Performance,** *Richard Kern, U.S. Army Research Institute for the Behavioral and Social Sciences.* **Document and Display Design,** *Wallace H. Wulfeck, Frederick R. Chang, and William E. Montague, Navy Personnel Research and Development Center.* **Artifical Intelligence Applications to Maintenance,** *Brian Dallman, TCHTW/TTGXS.* **Part III. Perspectives on Cognitive Science and Human Resources Management. Introduction,** *Frederick R. Chang.* **Cognitive Science Priniciples and Work Force Education,** *Ann L. Brown and Joseph C. Campione, University of Illinois.* **Applying Cognitive Psychology to Job Training,** *Robert Calfee, Stanford University.* **High Pay-Off Research Areas in the Cognitive Sciences,** *Allan Collins, Bolt, Beranek and Newman, Inc.* **A Cognitive Science Perspective on Selection and Classifi-cation and On Technical Training,** *Robert Glaser, University of Pittsburgh.* **The Cognitive Science Viewpoint in Human Resources Management,** *Earl Hunt, University of Washington.* **Cognitive Science Applications to Human Resources Problems,** *Ernst Z. Rothkopf, Teachers College, Columbia University.* **Cognitive Science in Technical Training and Basic Skills Education,** *Merlin C. Wittrock, University of California, Los Angeles.* **Cognitive Science and Human Resources Management: Outcomes and Perspectives,** *Thomas G. Sticht, Applied Behavioral & Cognitive Sciences, Inc.* Author Index. Subject Index.

Volume 5, In preparation, Spring 1990
ISBN 0-89232-813-4   Approx.: $58.50

International Perspectives on Education and Society

Edited by **Abraham Yogev,** *School of Education and Department of Sociology and Anthropology, Tel Aviv University*

International Perspectives on Education and Society is a new research and policy annual devoted to issues reflecting the mutual relations of education and society. Both the social factors which shape educational processes and structures, and the effect of ecucational systems and their products on society, constitute the scope of interest of this publication.

Each volume will be devoted to a specific theme. This theme will be covered from the angle of various countries, in order to provide a broad comparative understanding of educational issues. The articles to be published are either research-oriented (both qualitative and quantative research methods are welcome), or papers aimed at the evaluation of educational policies throughout the world.

Aviv University. **Education Among Indian Tribes: Implications of Ethnicity,** *Geetha B. Singh, Jawaharlal Nehru University.* **Social Class and Educational and Occupational Attainments of the Scheduled Post-matric Scholars in an Urban Setting,** *Vimal P. Shah and B.S. Vaishnav, Gujarat University.* **Determining Black Student Academic Performance in U.S. Higher Education: Institutional Versus Interpersonal Effects,** *Walter R. Allen, University of Michigan, Ann Arbor and Nesha Z. Haniff, University of the West Indies.* **PART III: PROBLEMS OF LANGUAGE EDUCATION IN MULTIETHNIC CONTEXTS. The Problem of the Language Education of Asian Children in English Primary Schools,** *Ann Rickards, St. Martin's College of Higher Education, Lancaster.* **The Integration of Migrant Children in the Quebec School System: Similarities and Differences Between State Discourse and Views of the Haitian Community,** *Charles Pierre-Jacques, Universite de Montreal.* **PART IV: STUDENTS IN MULTHETHNIC EDUCATION. Feelings of Deprivation and Ethnic Integration: Theoretical Formulation and Preliminary Findings,** *Nura Resh and Yehezkel Dar, The Hebrew University of Jerusalem.* **Multicultural, Anti-Racist and Equal Opportunity Policy in English Tertiary Education: The Consequence of Student Choice in the Face of the Logic of the Labor Market,** *Frank Reeves, Bilston Community College and Mel Chevannes, City of Birmingham Polytechnic.* **Student-Teachers' Images of Ethnic Minorities: A British Case Study,** *Peter M.E. Figueroa, University of Southampton.*

JAI PRESS

Advances in Educational Administration

Edited by **Linda S. Lotto,** *Bureau of Educational Research, University of Illinois* and **Paul W. Thurston,** *Department of Administration, Higher and Continuing Education, University of Illinois*

Prominent scholars from a variety of disciplines have written chapters exploring topics in educational administration which deal with these central themes: leadership, the decline of federal involvement in educational reform, an increase of reform initiative at the state level, and management of schools at the building level. The leadership theme is developed in two chapters which explore the scholarship and changing conceptions of leadership in the school setting. The second theme is developed in four chapters: one documents the decline of judicial activism at the federal level, the second documents educational reform legislation passed in a number of states, the third analyzes state financial support for education and the fourth proposes a framework for analyzing state level policy initiatives. The third theme, management of schools at a building level, is picked up in chapters focusing on teacher evaluation, the inservices development of principals and the role of principles as instructional leaders.

Volume 1, In preparation, Fall 1989
ISBN 0-89232-843-6

Approx. $63.50

J A I P R E S S